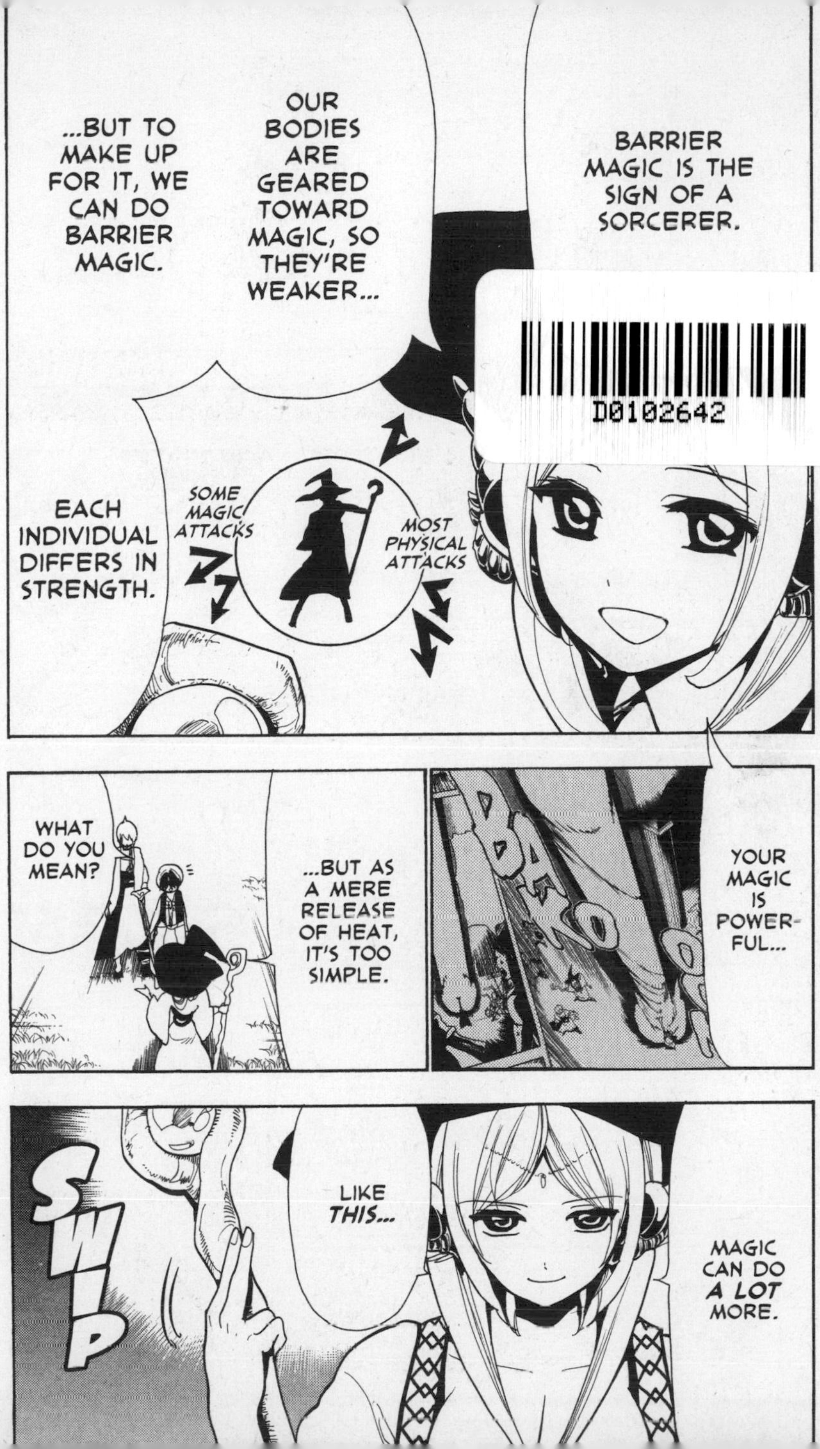
BARRIER MAGIC IS THE SIGN OF A SORCERER.
OUR BODIES ARE GEARED TOWARD MAGIC, SO THEY'RE WEAKER...
...BUT TO MAKE UP FOR IT, WE CAN DO BARRIER MAGIC.
MOST PHYSICAL ATTACKS
SOME MAGIC ATTACKS
EACH INDIVIDUAL DIFFERS IN STRENGTH.
YOUR MAGIC IS POWER-FUL...
...BUT AS A MERE RELEASE OF HEAT, IT'S TOO SIMPLE.
WHAT DO YOU MEAN?
MAGIC CAN DO *A LOT* MORE.
LIKE *THIS...*
SWIP

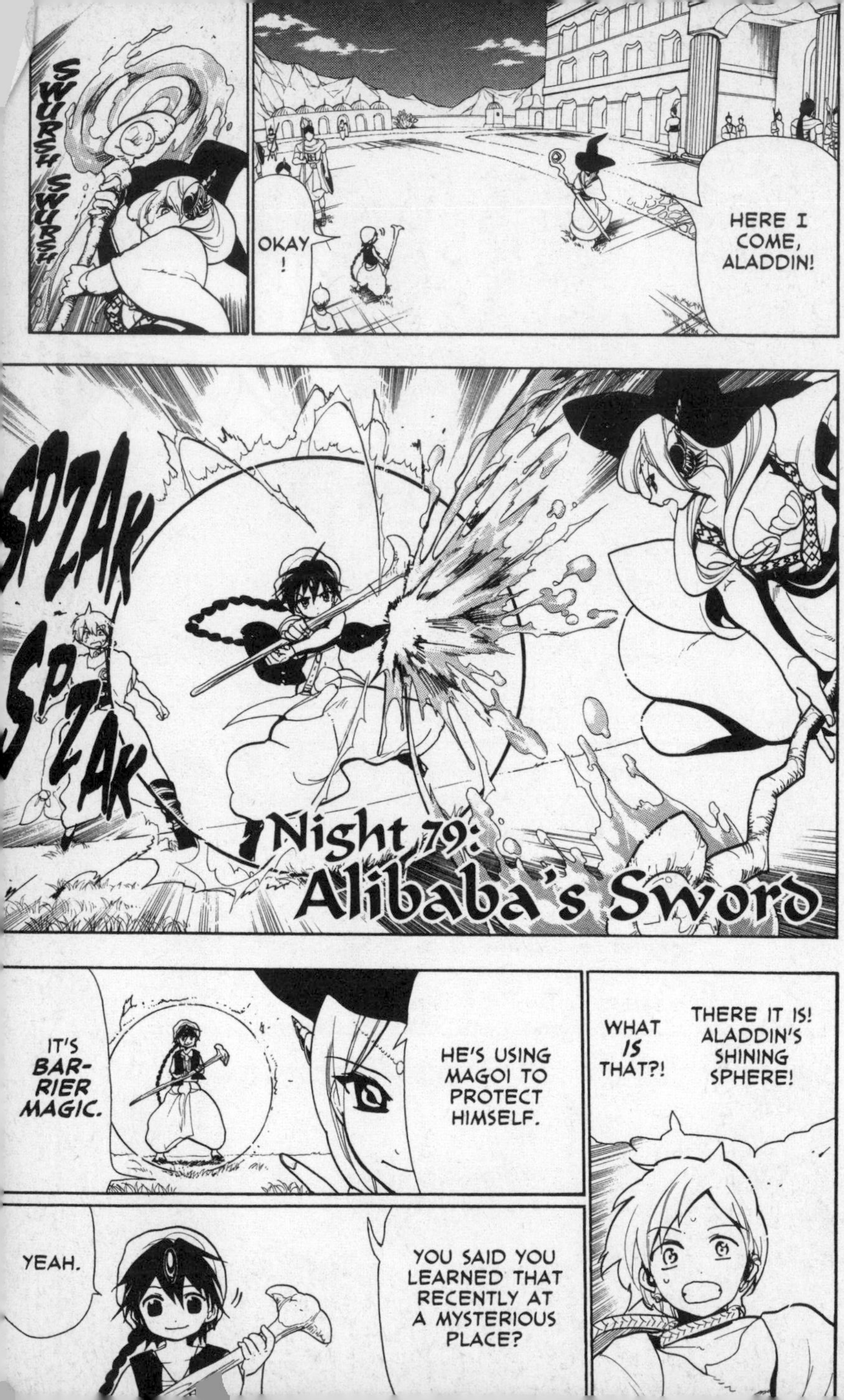
HERE I COME, ALADDIN!
OKAY!
SWURSH SWURSH
SPZAK SPZAK
Night 79: Alibaba's Sword
THERE IT IS! ALADDIN'S SHINING SPHERE!
WHAT IS THAT?!
HE'S USING MAGOI TO PROTECT HIMSELF.
IT'S BARRIER MAGIC.
YOU SAID YOU LEARNED THAT RECENTLY AT A MYSTERIOUS PLACE?
YEAH.

MAGI
The labyrinth of magic

9

CONTENTS

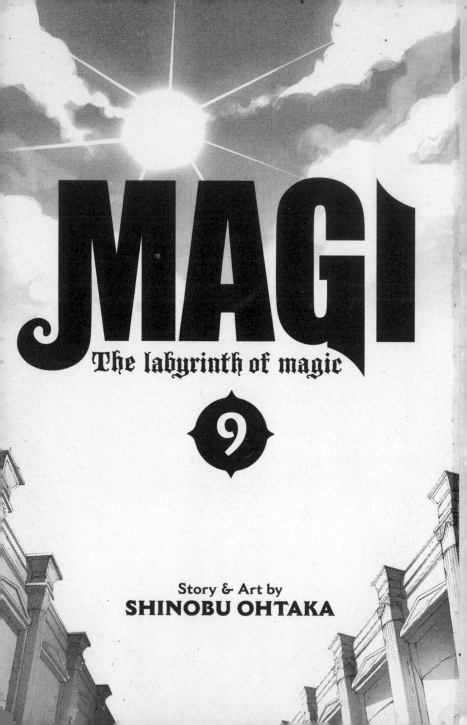

MAGI

The labyrinth of magic

9

Story & Art by
SHINOBU OHTAKA

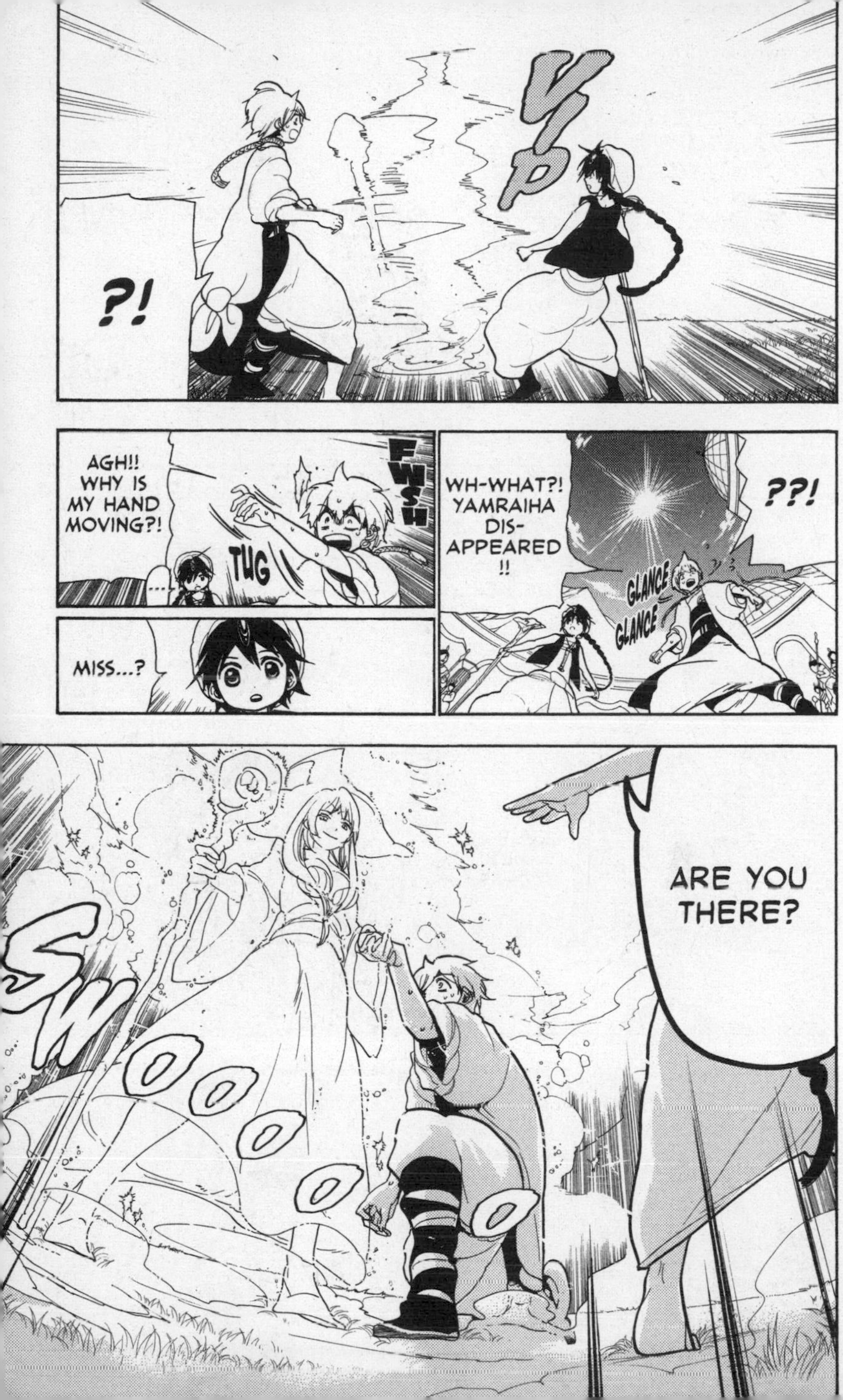
VIP
?!
WH-WHAT?! YAMRAIHA DIS-APPEARED!!
??!
GLANCE
GLANCE
FWSH
AGH!! WHY IS MY HAND MOVING?!
TUG
...
MISS...?
ARE YOU THERE?
SWOOOOOO

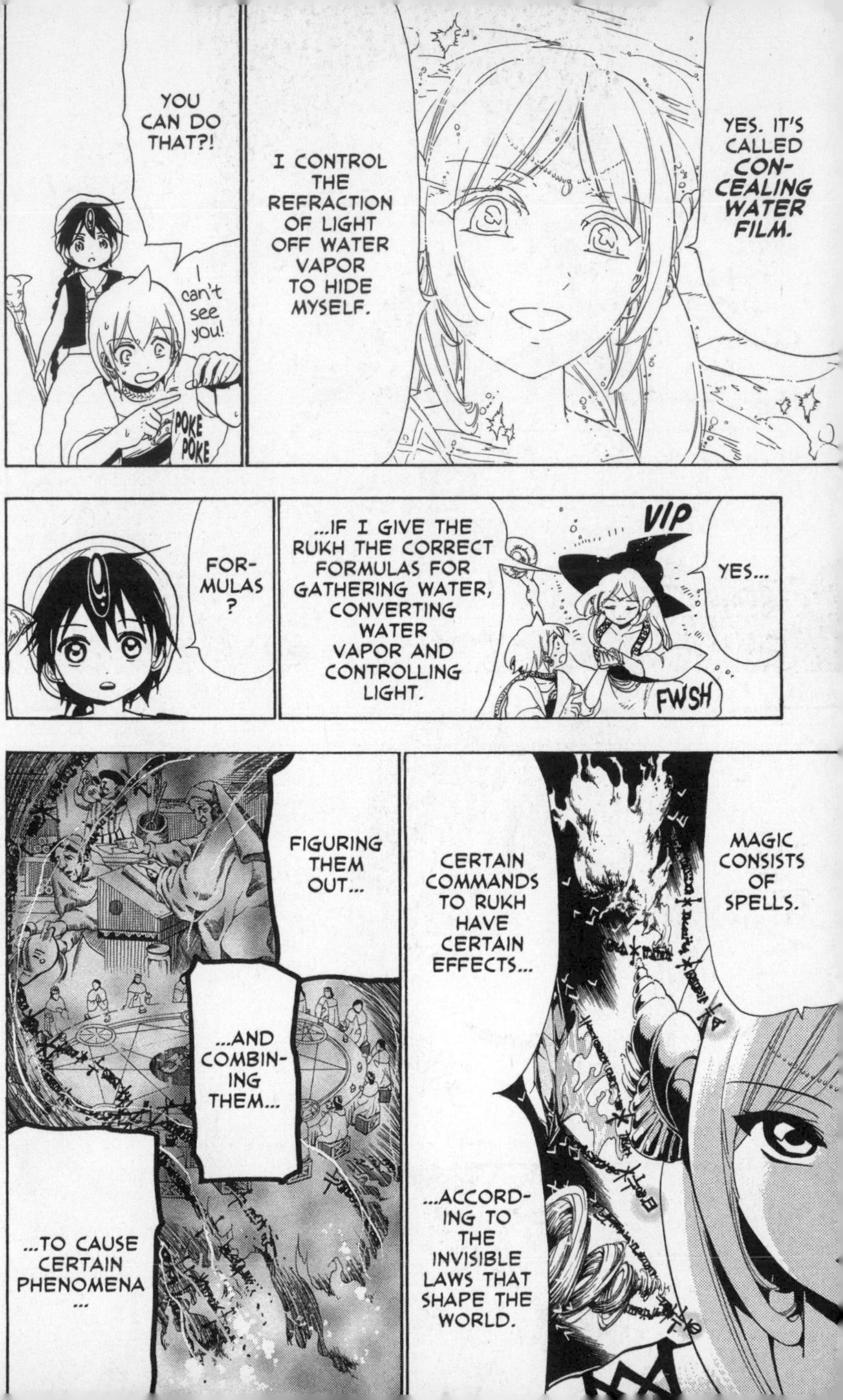
YES. IT'S CALLED CON-CEALING WATER FILM.
I CONTROL THE REFRACTION OF LIGHT OFF WATER VAPOR TO HIDE MYSELF.
YOU CAN DO THAT?!
I can't see you!
POKE POKE
YES...
VIP
...IF I GIVE THE RUKH THE CORRECT FORMULAS FOR GATHERING WATER, CONVERTING WATER VAPOR AND CONTROLLING LIGHT.
FWSH
FOR-MULAS?
MAGIC CONSISTS OF SPELLS.
CERTAIN COMMANDS TO RUKH HAVE CERTAIN EFFECTS...
...ACCORD-ING TO THE INVISIBLE LAWS THAT SHAPE THE WORLD.
FIGURING THEM OUT...
...AND COMBIN-ING THEM...
...TO CAUSE CERTAIN PHENOMENA ...

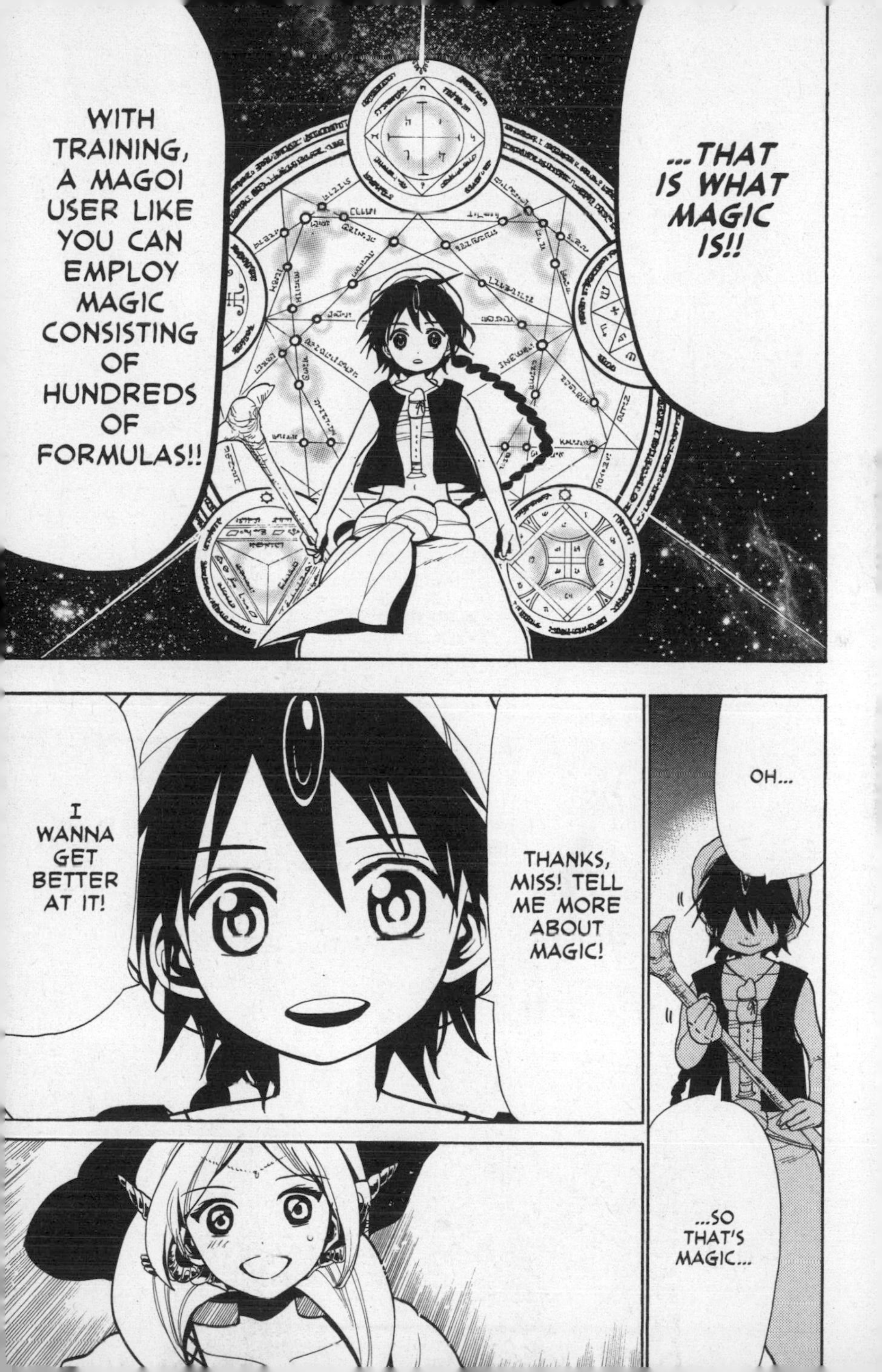
WITH TRAINING, A MAGOI USER LIKE YOU CAN EMPLOY MAGIC CONSISTING OF HUNDREDS OF FORMULAS!!
...THAT IS WHAT MAGIC IS!!
OH...
...SO THAT'S MAGIC...
THANKS, MISS! TELL ME MORE ABOUT MAGIC!
I WANNA GET BETTER AT IT!

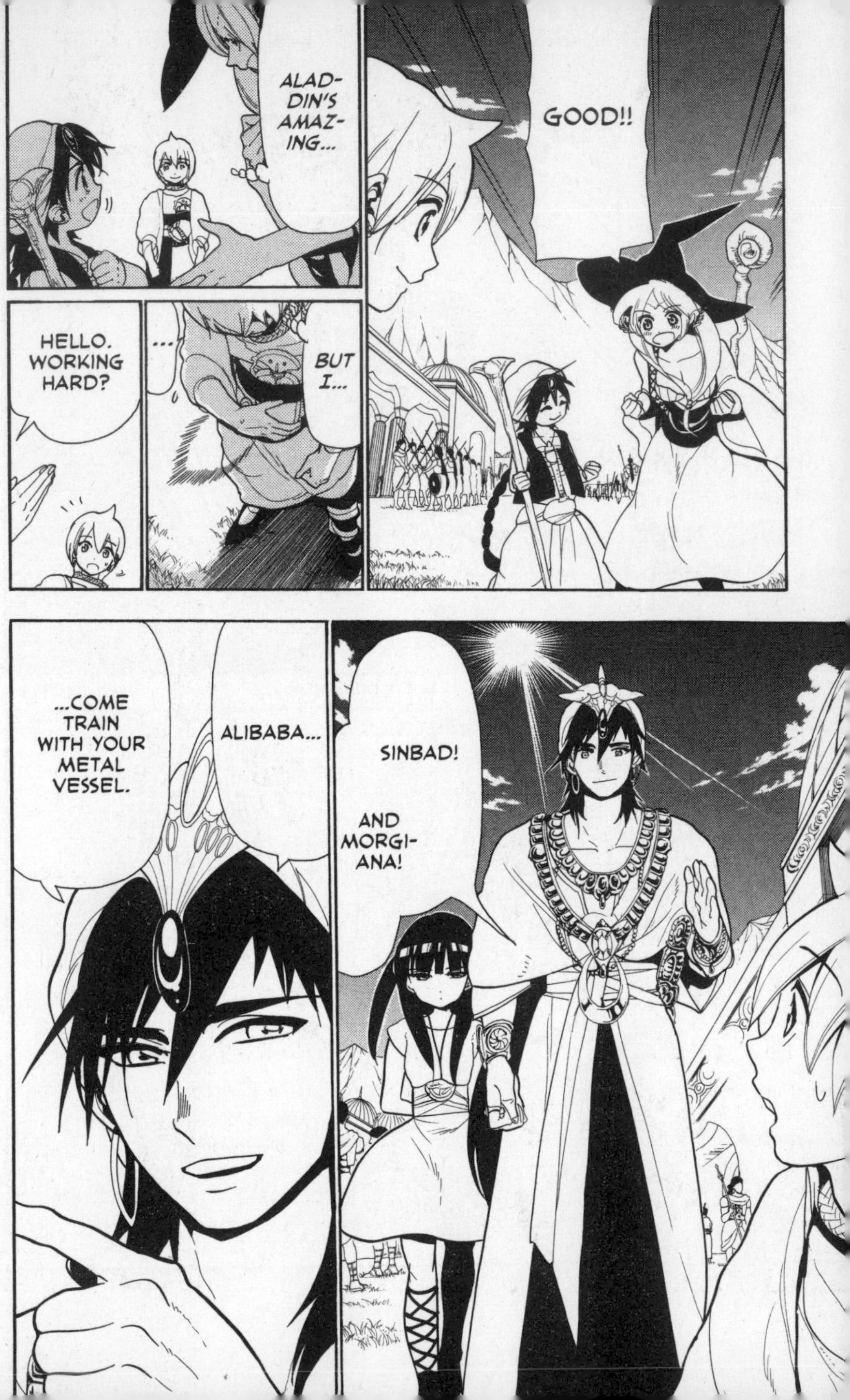
GOOD!!
ALAD-DIN'S AMAZ-ING...
...
BUT I...
HELLO. WORKING HARD?
SINBAD!
AND MORGI-ANA!
ALIBABA...
...COME TRAIN WITH YOUR METAL VESSEL.

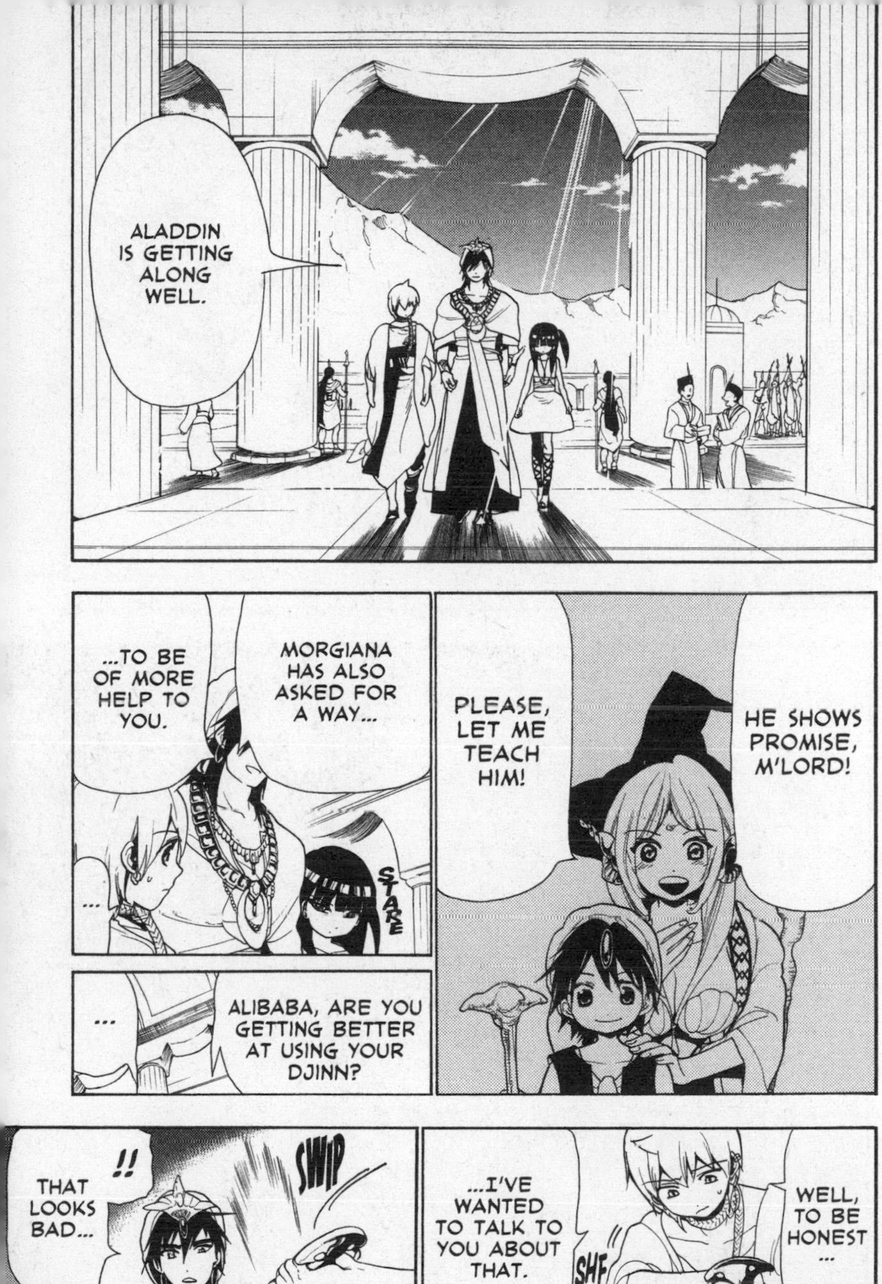
ALADDIN IS GETTING ALONG WELL.
HE SHOWS PROMISE, M'LORD!
PLEASE, LET ME TEACH HIM!
MORGIANA HAS ALSO ASKED FOR A WAY...
...TO BE OF MORE HELP TO YOU.
STARE
...
ALIBABA, ARE YOU GETTING BETTER AT USING YOUR DJINN?
...
WELL, TO BE HONEST...
SHF
...I'VE WANTED TO TALK TO YOU ABOUT THAT.
SWIP
!!
THAT LOOKS BAD...

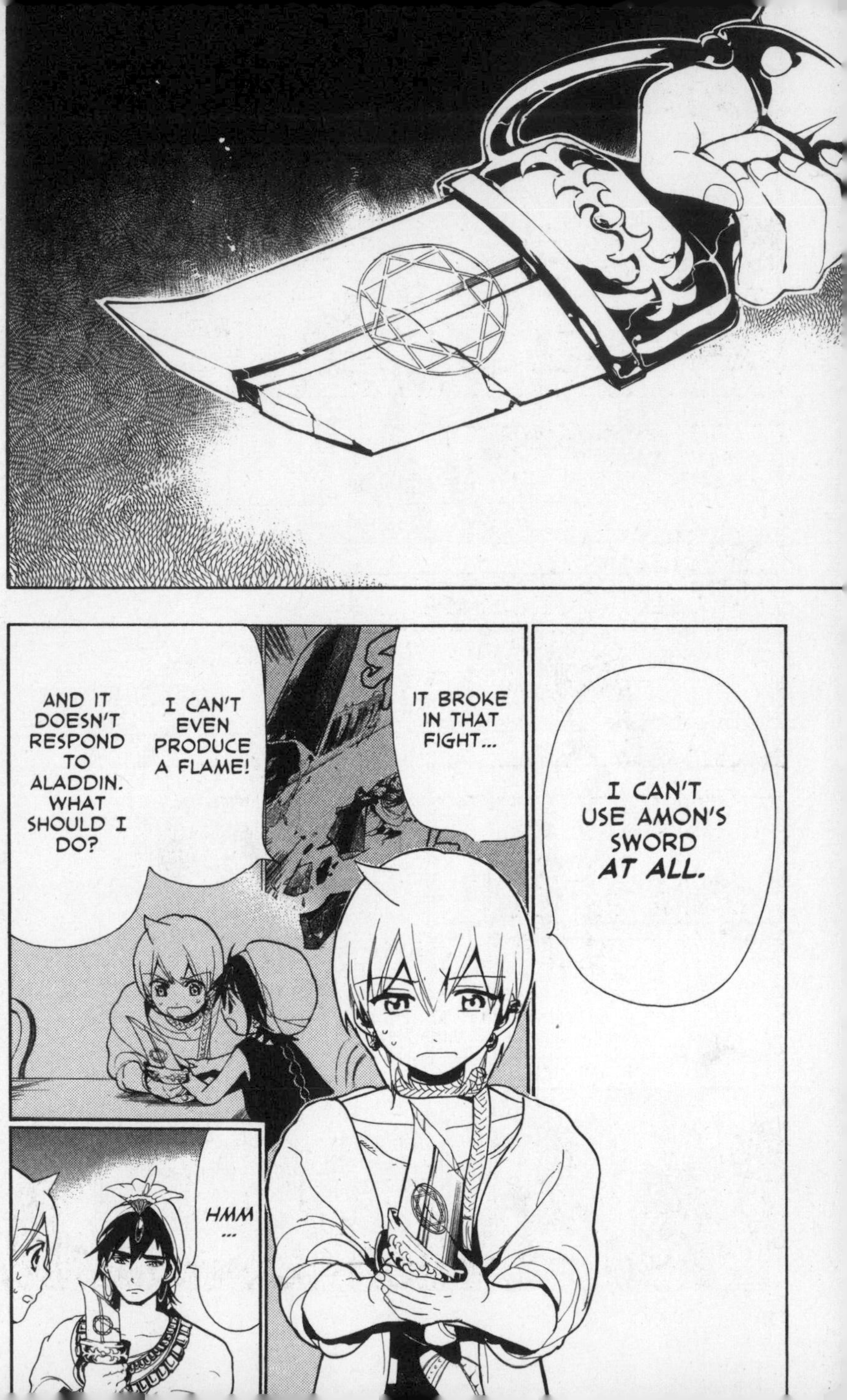
I CAN'T USE AMON'S SWORD *AT ALL.*
IT BROKE IN THAT FIGHT...
I CAN'T EVEN PRODUCE A FLAME!
AND IT DOESN'T RESPOND TO ALADDIN. WHAT SHOULD I DO?
HMM...

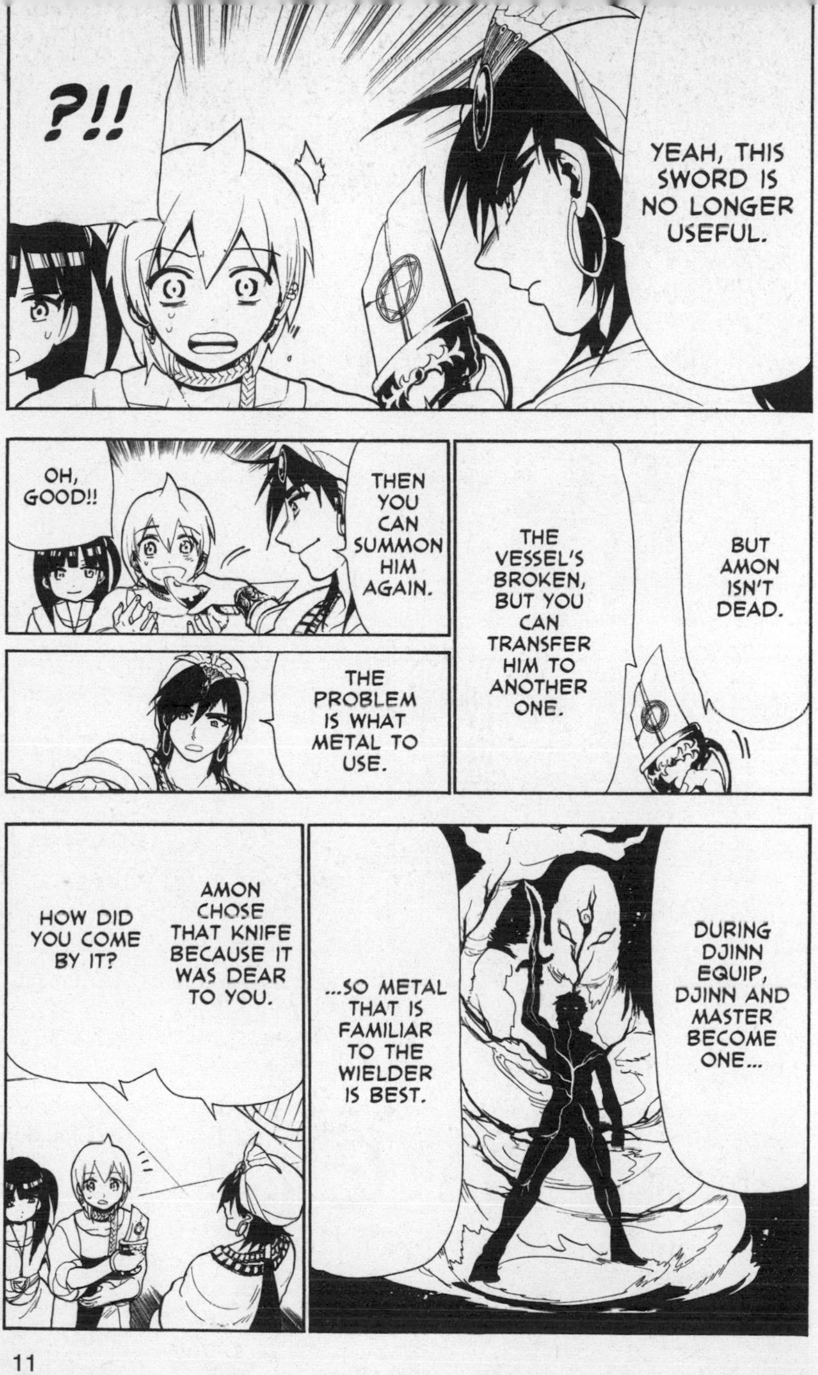
YEAH, THIS SWORD IS NO LONGER USEFUL.
?!!
BUT AMON ISN'T DEAD.
THE VESSEL'S BROKEN, BUT YOU CAN TRANSFER HIM TO ANOTHER ONE.
THEN YOU CAN SUMMON HIM AGAIN.
OH, GOOD!!
THE PROBLEM IS WHAT METAL TO USE.
DURING DJINN EQUIP, DJINN AND MASTER BECOME ONE...
...SO METAL THAT IS FAMILIAR TO THE WIELDER IS BEST.
AMON CHOSE THAT KNIFE BECAUSE IT WAS DEAR TO YOU.
HOW DID YOU COME BY IT?

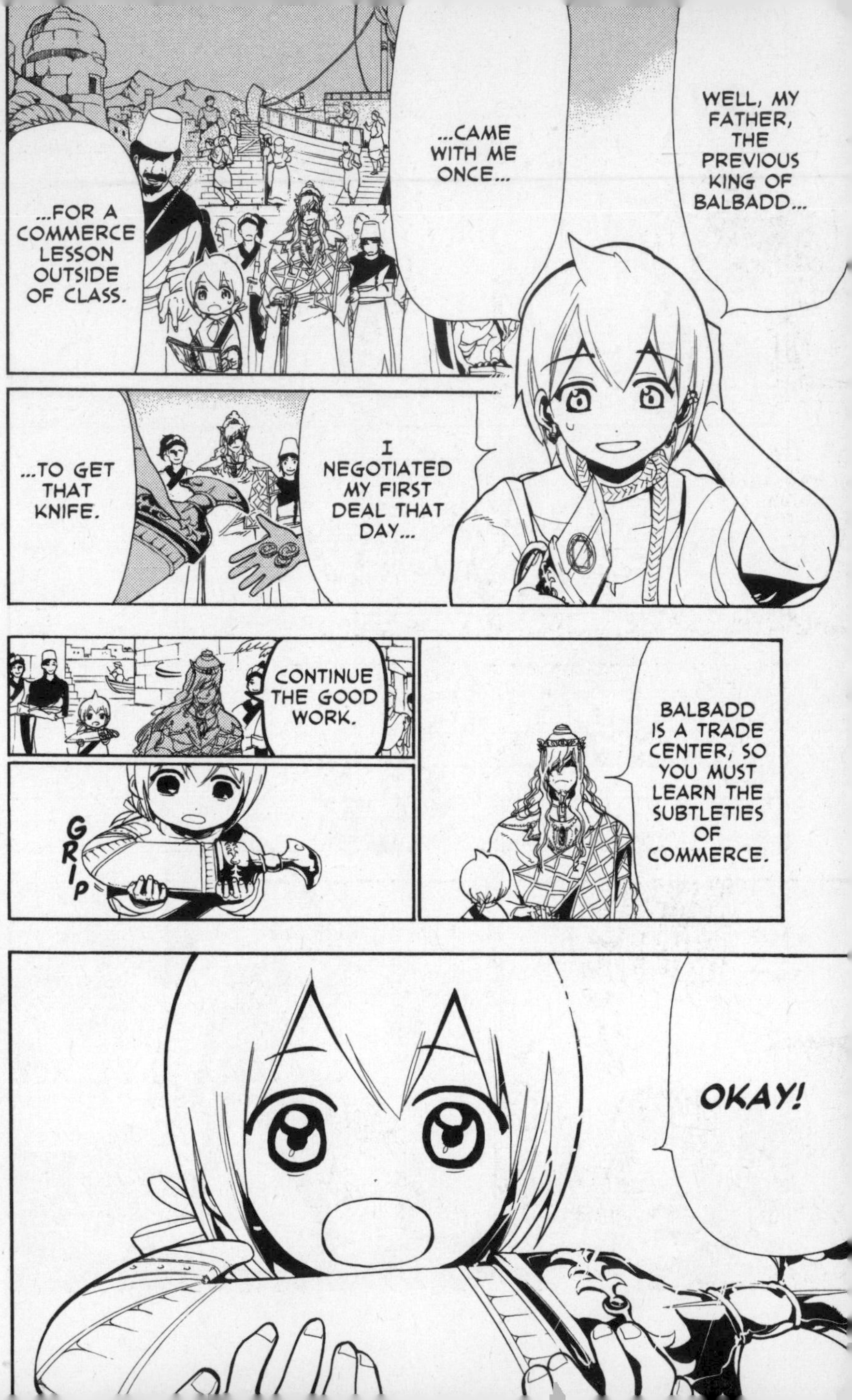
WELL, MY FATHER, THE PREVIOUS KING OF BALBADD...
...CAME WITH ME ONCE...
...FOR A COMMERCE LESSON OUTSIDE OF CLASS.
I NEGOTIATED MY FIRST DEAL THAT DAY...
...TO GET THAT KNIFE.
BALBADD IS A TRADE CENTER, SO YOU MUST LEARN THE SUBTLETIES OF COMMERCE.
CONTINUE THE GOOD WORK.
GRIP
OKAY!

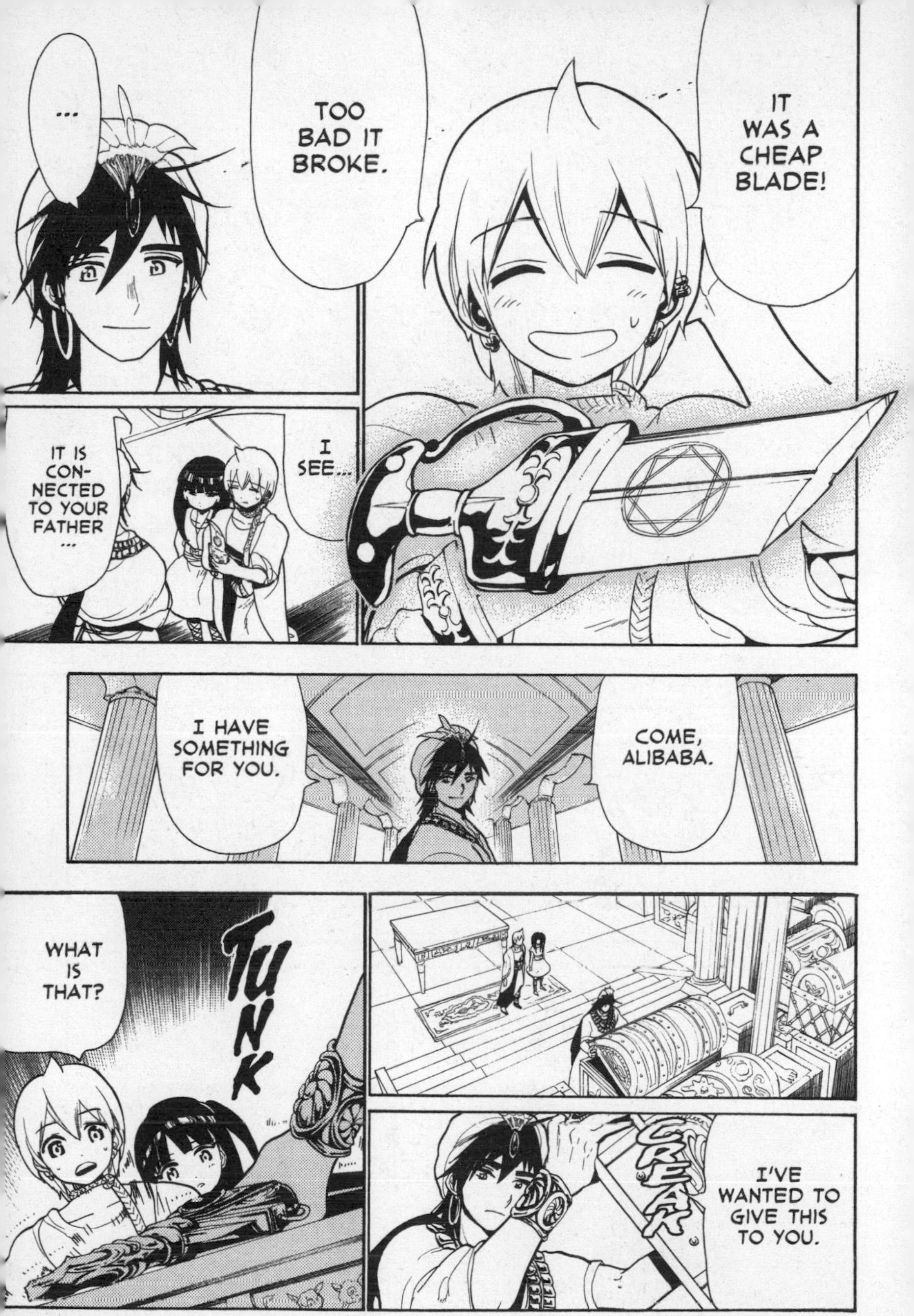

IT WAS A CHEAP BLADE!
TOO BAD IT BROKE.
...
I SEE...
IT IS CON-NECTED TO YOUR FATHER...
COME, ALIBABA.
I HAVE SOMETHING FOR YOU.
CREAK
I'VE WANTED TO GIVE THIS TO YOU.
TUNK
WHAT IS THAT?

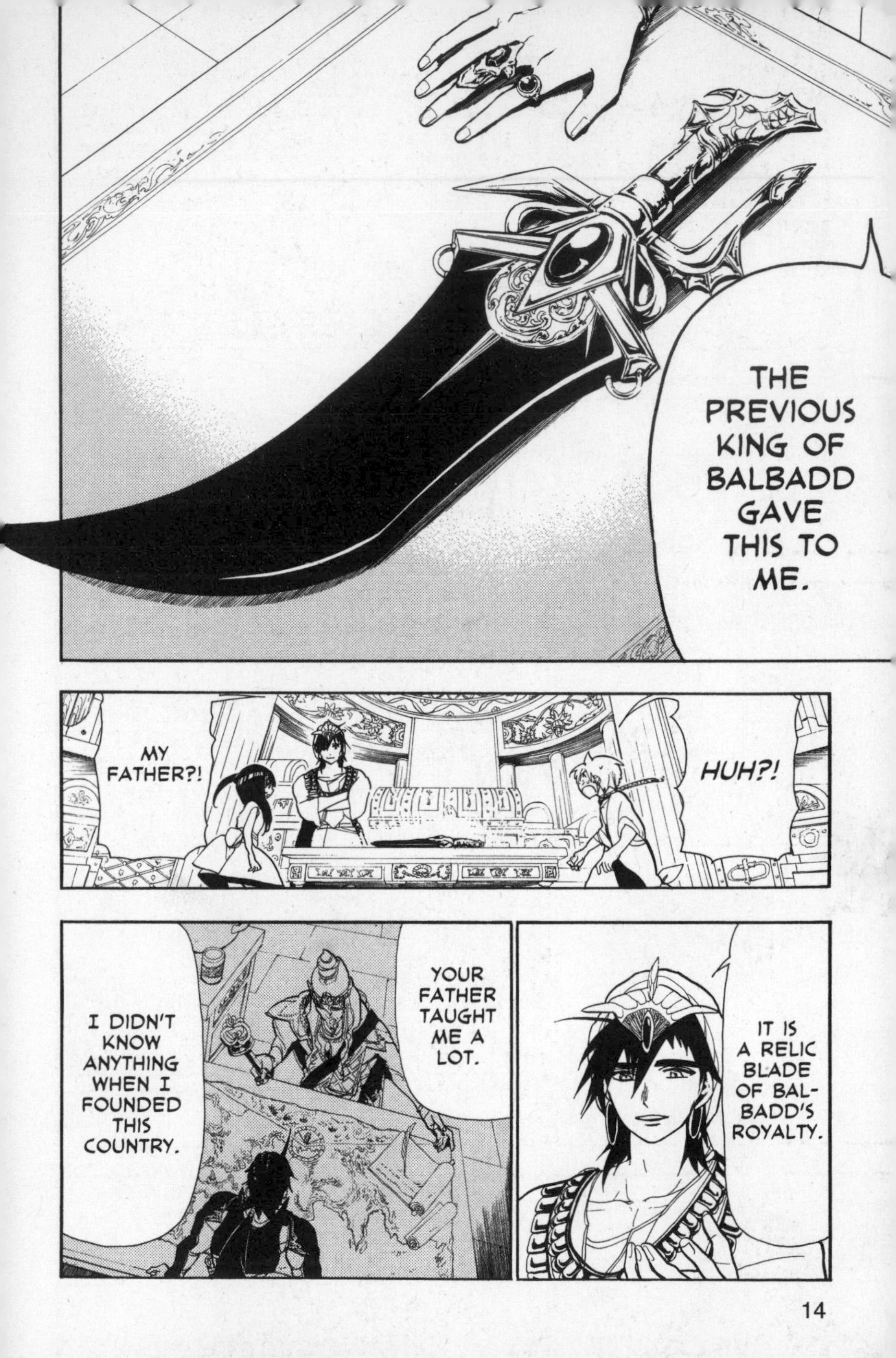
THE PREVIOUS KING OF BALBADD GAVE THIS TO ME.
HUH?!
MY FATHER?!
IT IS A RELIC BLADE OF BAL-BADD'S ROYALTY.
YOUR FATHER TAUGHT ME A LOT.
I DIDN'T KNOW ANYTHING WHEN I FOUNDED THIS COUNTRY.

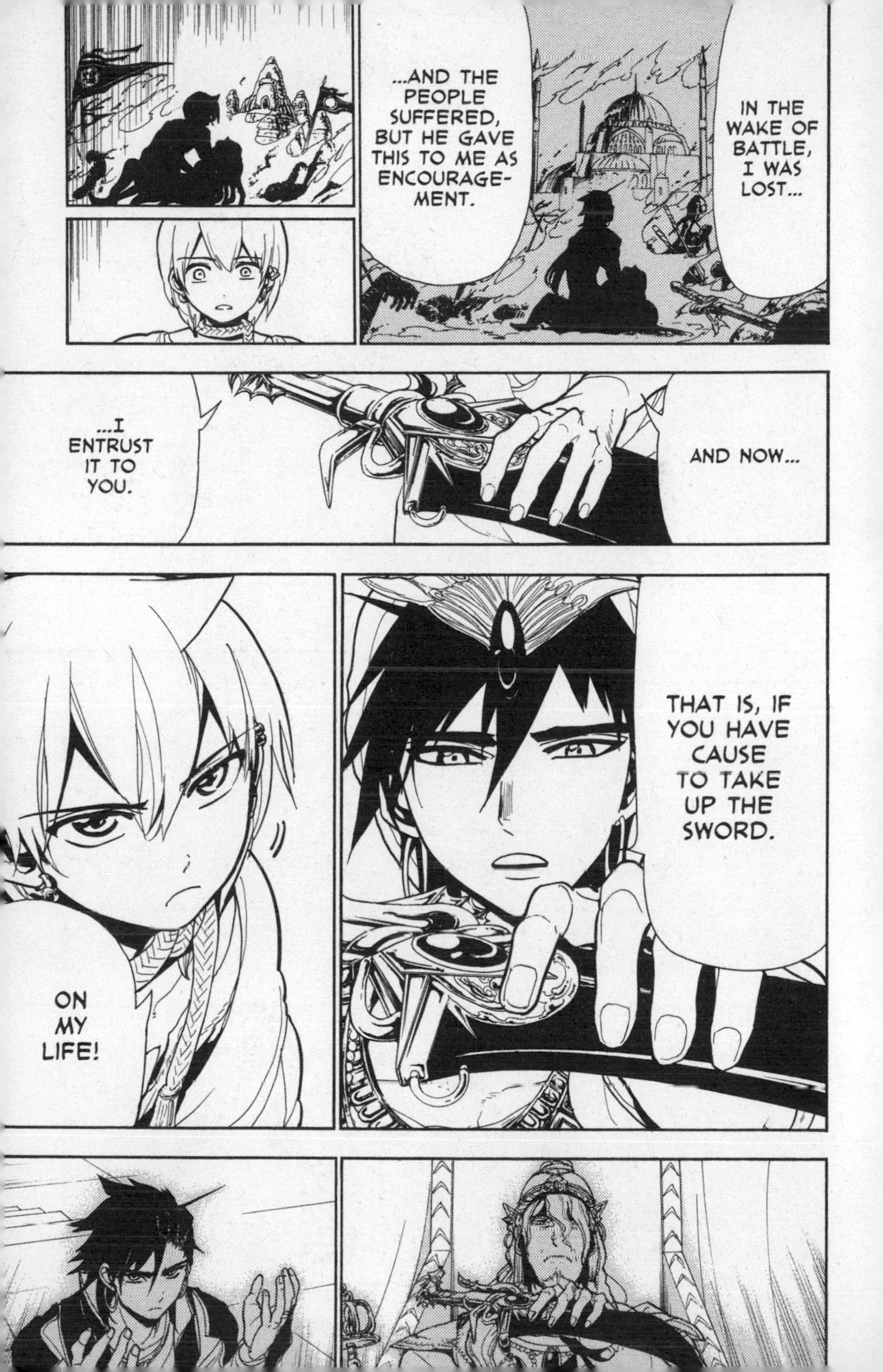
IN THE WAKE OF BATTLE, I WAS LOST...
...AND THE PEOPLE SUFFERED, BUT HE GAVE THIS TO ME AS ENCOURAGE-MENT.
AND NOW...
...I ENTRUST IT TO YOU.
THAT IS, IF YOU HAVE CAUSE TO TAKE UP THE SWORD.
ON MY LIFE!

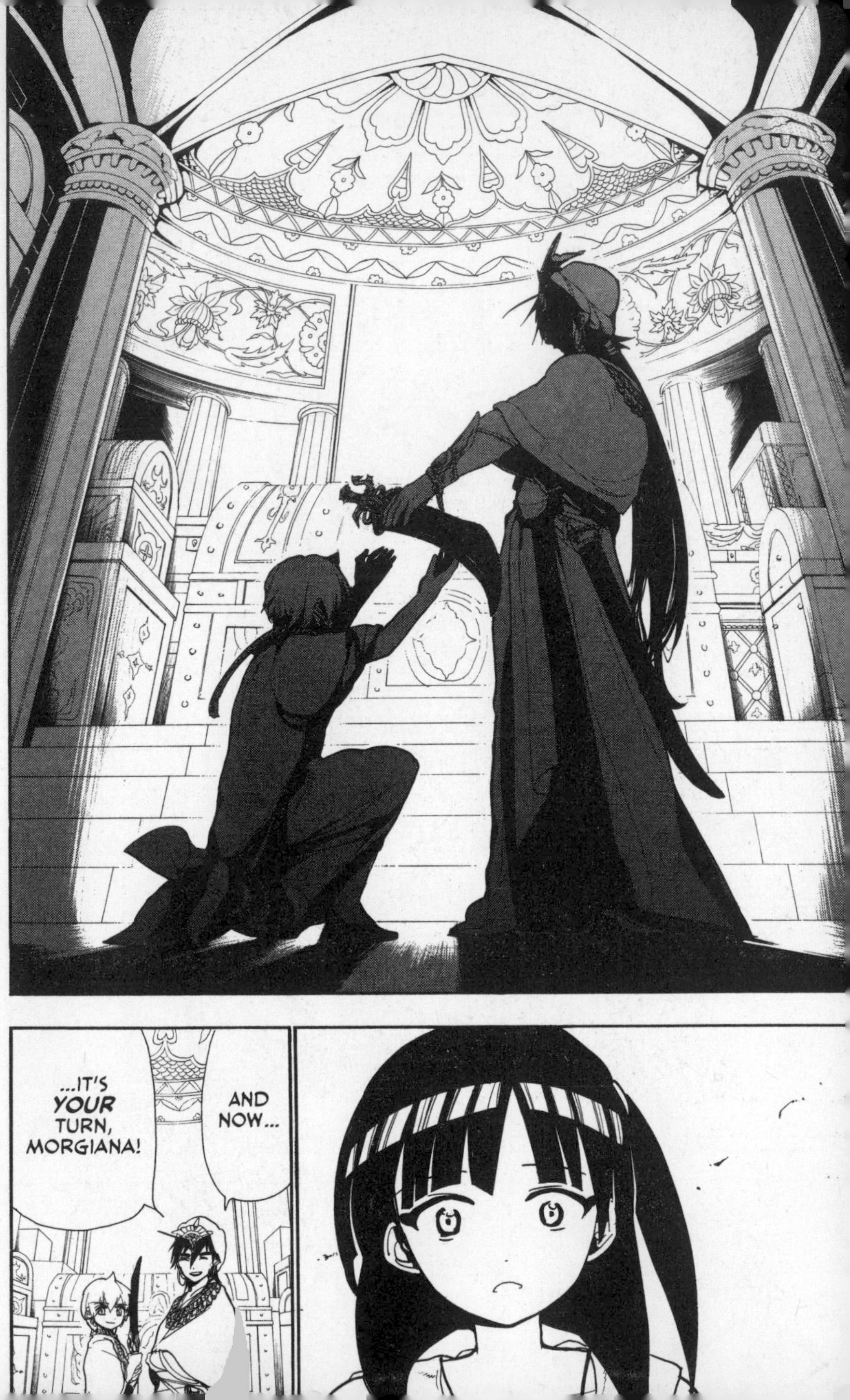
AND NOW...
...IT'S *YOUR* TURN, MORGIANA!

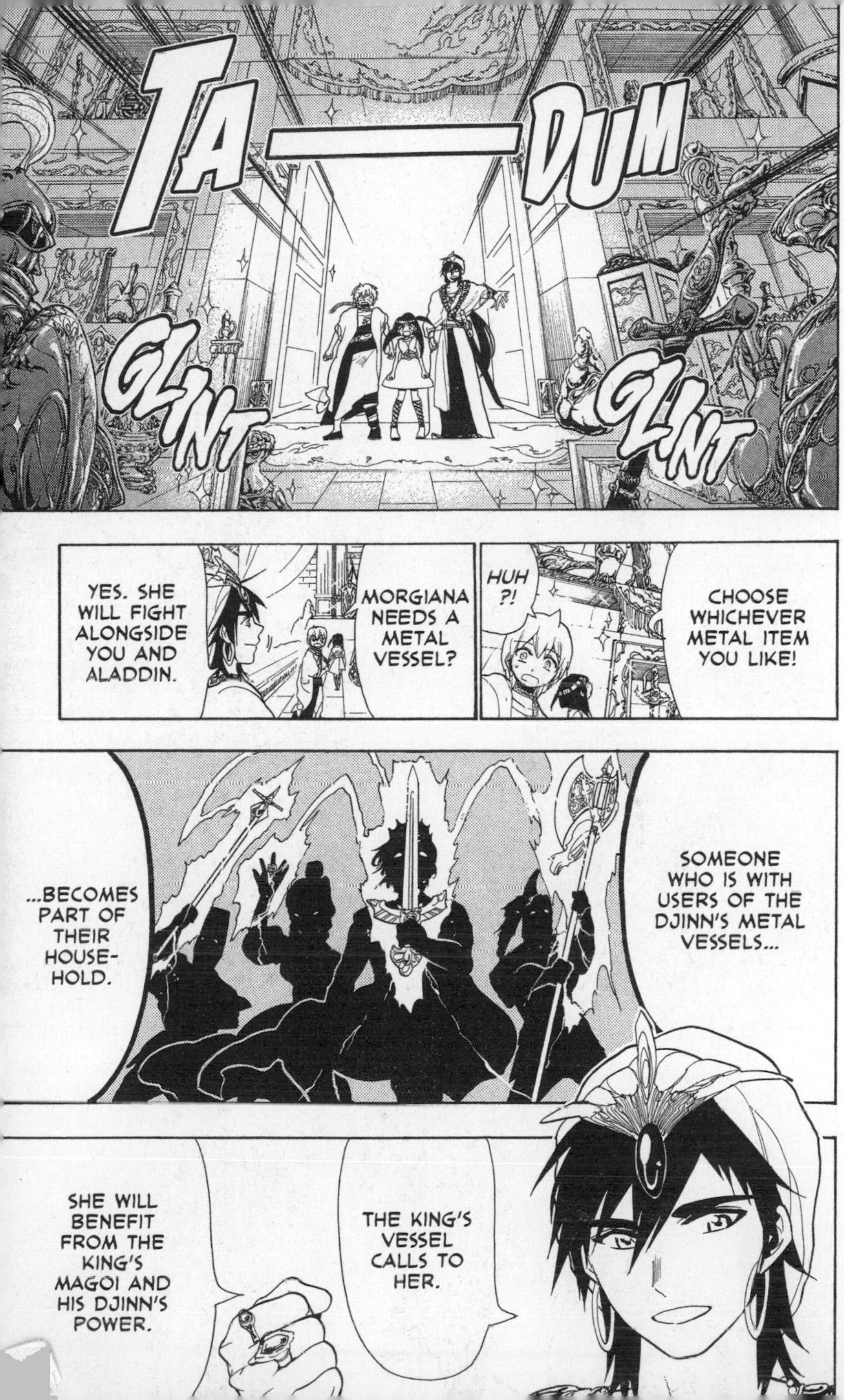
TA——DUM
GLINT
GLINT
CHOOSE WHICHEVER METAL ITEM YOU LIKE!
HUH ?!
MORGIANA NEEDS A METAL VESSEL?
YES. SHE WILL FIGHT ALONGSIDE YOU AND ALADDIN.
SOMEONE WHO IS WITH USERS OF THE DJINN'S METAL VESSELS...
...BECOMES PART OF THEIR HOUSEHOLD.
THE KING'S VESSEL CALLS TO HER.
SHE WILL BENEFIT FROM THE KING'S MAGOI AND HIS DJINN'S POWER.

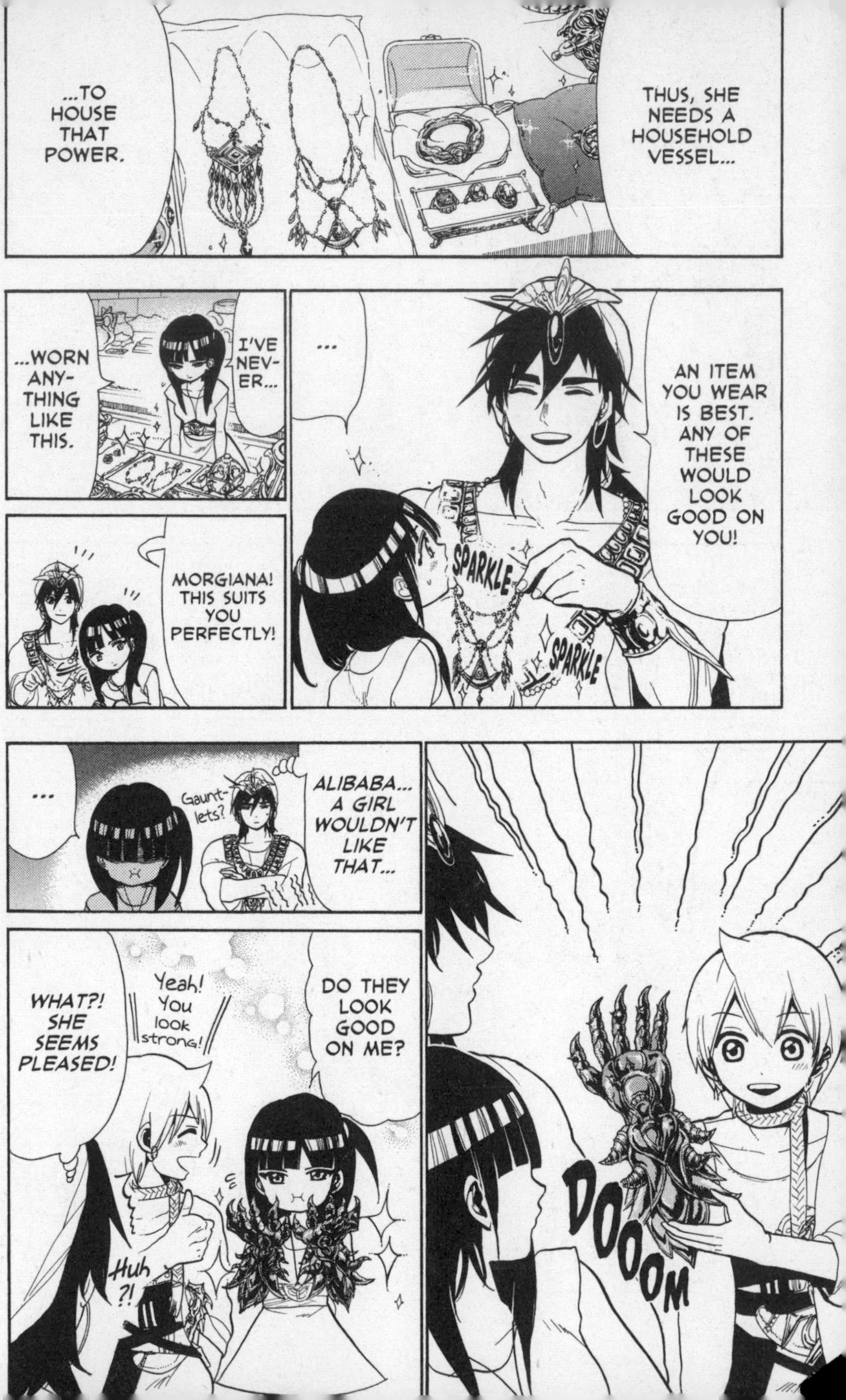
THUS, SHE NEEDS A HOUSEHOLD VESSEL...
...TO HOUSE THAT POWER.
AN ITEM YOU WEAR IS BEST. ANY OF THESE WOULD LOOK GOOD ON YOU!
...
SPARKLE
SPARKLE
I'VE NEVER...
...WORN ANYTHING LIKE THIS.
MORGIANA! THIS SUITS YOU PERFECTLY!
DOOOM
ALIBABA... A GIRL WOULDN'T LIKE THAT...
Gauntlets?
...
DO THEY LOOK GOOD ON ME?
Yeah! You look strong!
WHAT?! SHE SEEMS PLEASED!
Huh?!

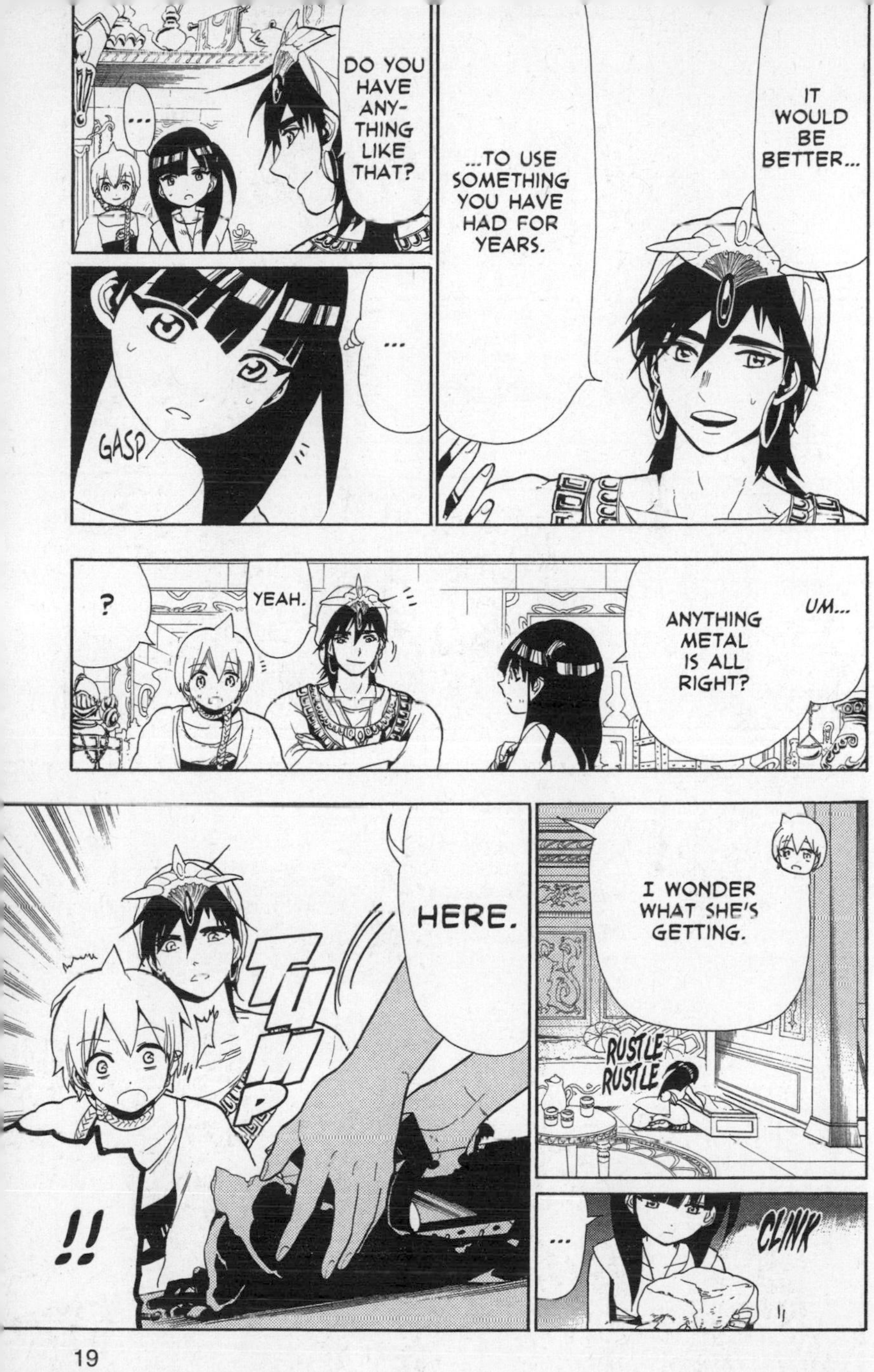
IT WOULD BE BETTER...
...TO USE SOMETHING YOU HAVE HAD FOR YEARS.
DO YOU HAVE ANY-THING LIKE THAT?
...
...
GASP
UM...
ANYTHING METAL IS ALL RIGHT?
YEAH.
?
I WONDER WHAT SHE'S GETTING.
RUSTLE RUSTLE
...
CLINK
HERE.
THUMP
!!

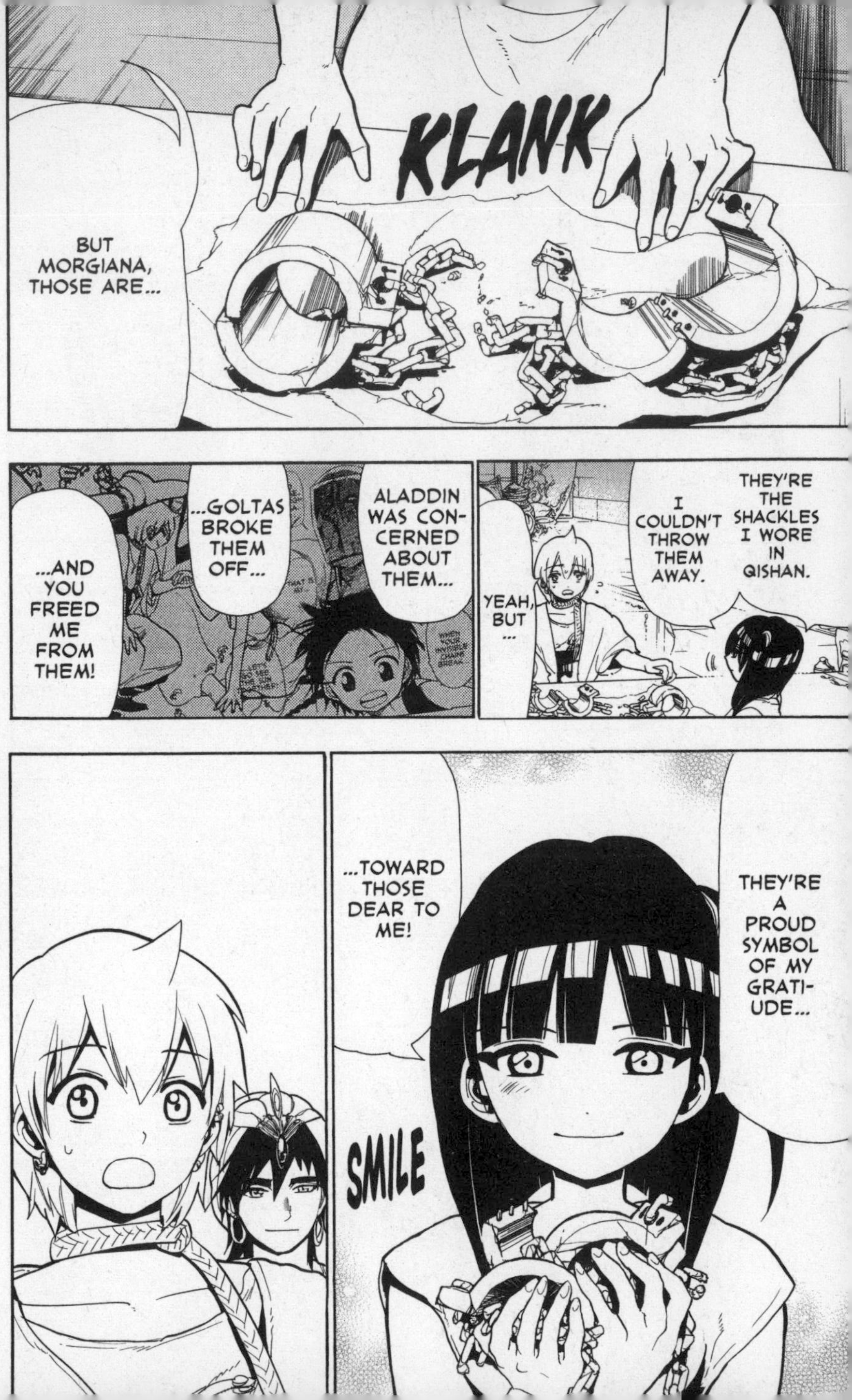
KLANK
BUT MORGIANA, THOSE ARE...
THEY'RE THE SHACKLES I WORE IN QISHAN.
I COULDN'T THROW THEM AWAY.
YEAH, BUT ...
ALADDIN WAS CONCERNED ABOUT THEM...
WHEN YOUR INVISIBLE CHAINS BREAK...
LET'S GO SEE THE SUN TOGETHER!
...GOLTAS BROKE THEM OFF...
...AND YOU FREED ME FROM THEM!
THEY'RE A PROUD SYMBOL OF MY GRATITUDE...
...TOWARD THOSE DEAR TO ME!
SMILE

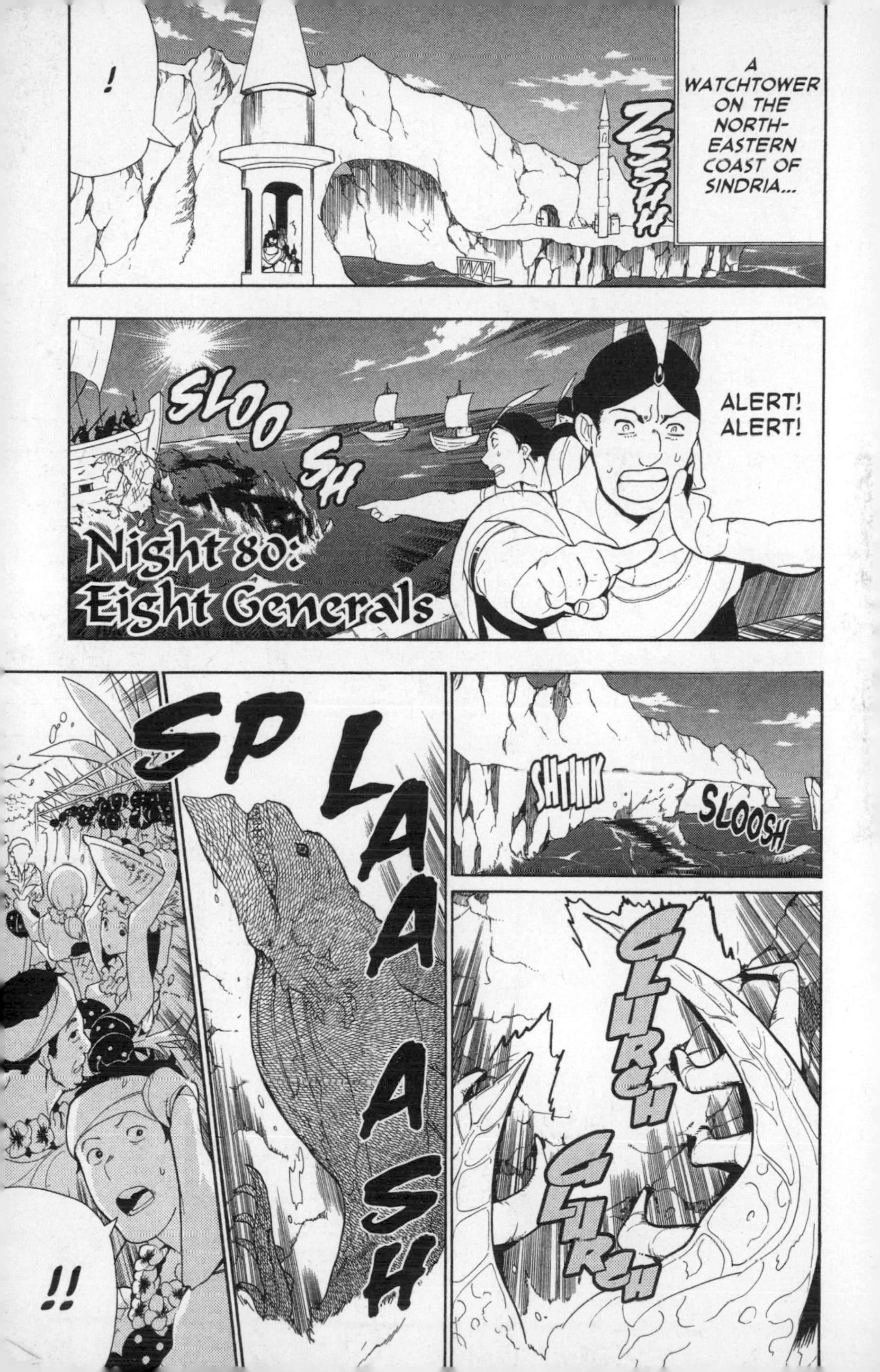
A WATCHTOWER ON THE NORTH-EASTERN COAST OF SINDRIA...
ZWSHH
!
ALERT! ALERT!
SLOOSH
Night 80: Eight Generals
SHTINK
SLOOSH
GLURCH GLURCH
SPLAASH
!!

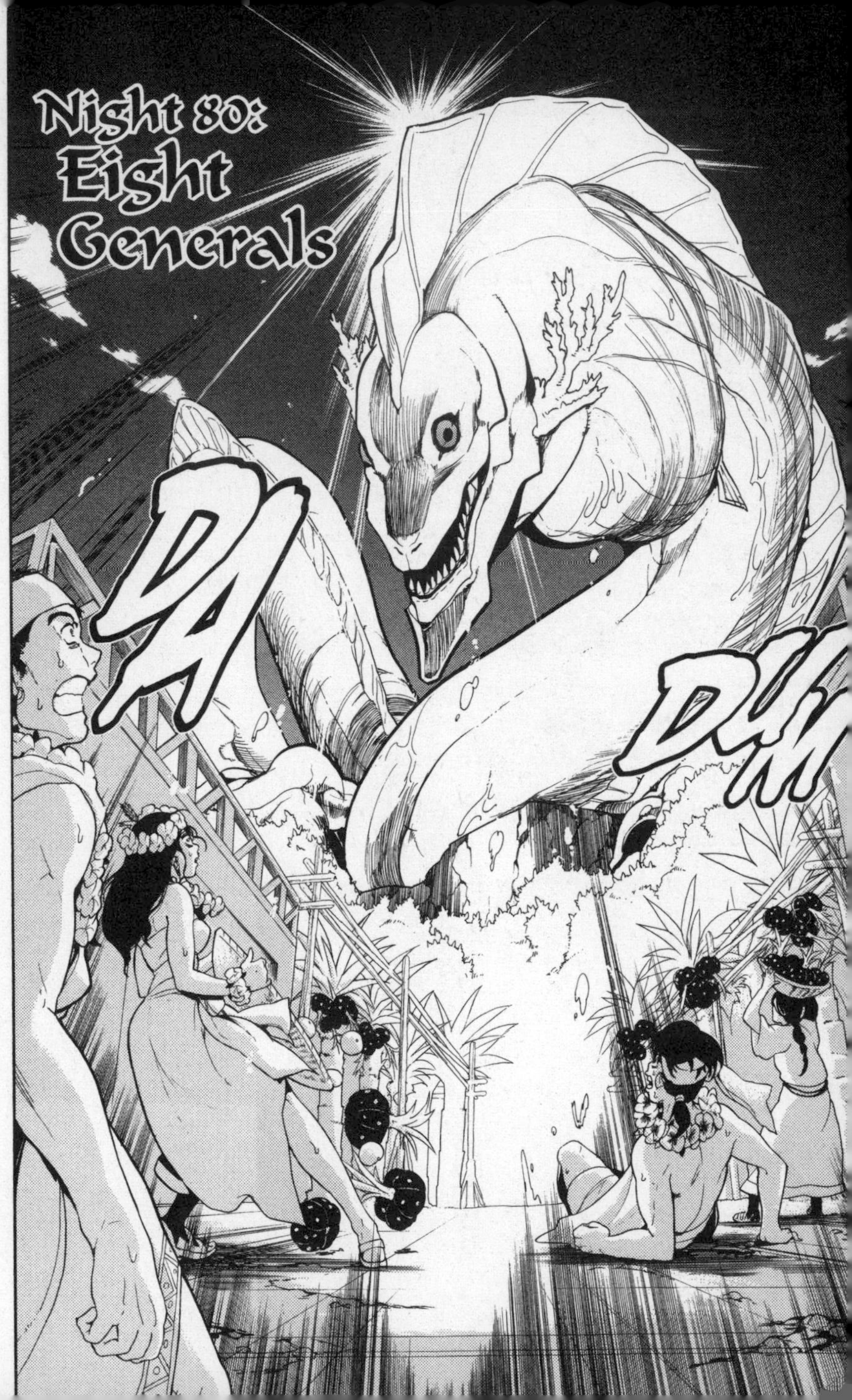
Night 80:
Eight Generals
DA

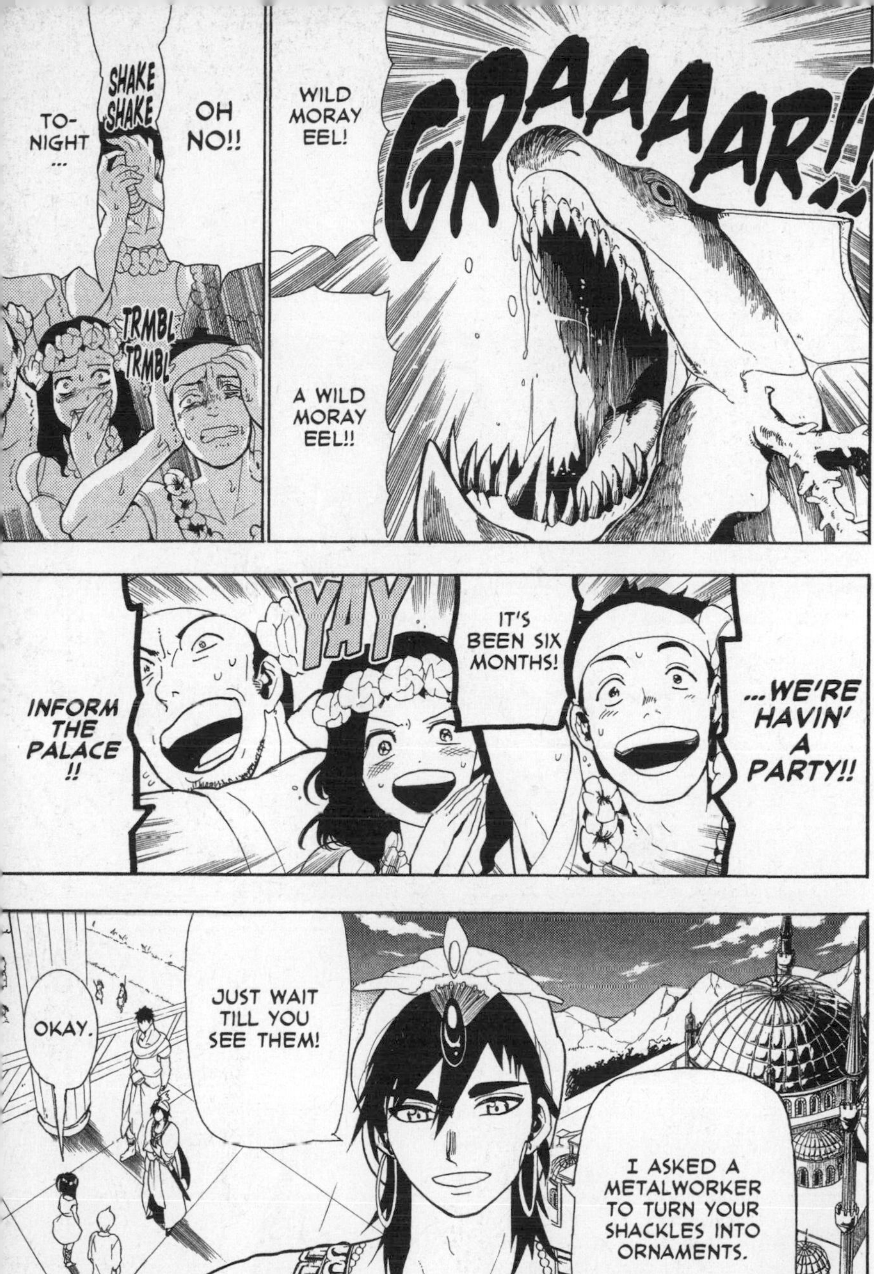
GRAAAAR!!
WILD MORAY EEL!
A WILD MORAY EEL!!
OH NO!!
SHAKE SHAKE
TO-NIGHT ...
TRMBL TRMBL
...WE'RE HAVIN' A PARTY!!
IT'S BEEN SIX MONTHS!
YAY
INFORM THE PALACE !!
I ASKED A METALWORKER TO TURN YOUR SHACKLES INTO ORNAMENTS.
JUST WAIT TILL YOU SEE THEM!
OKAY.

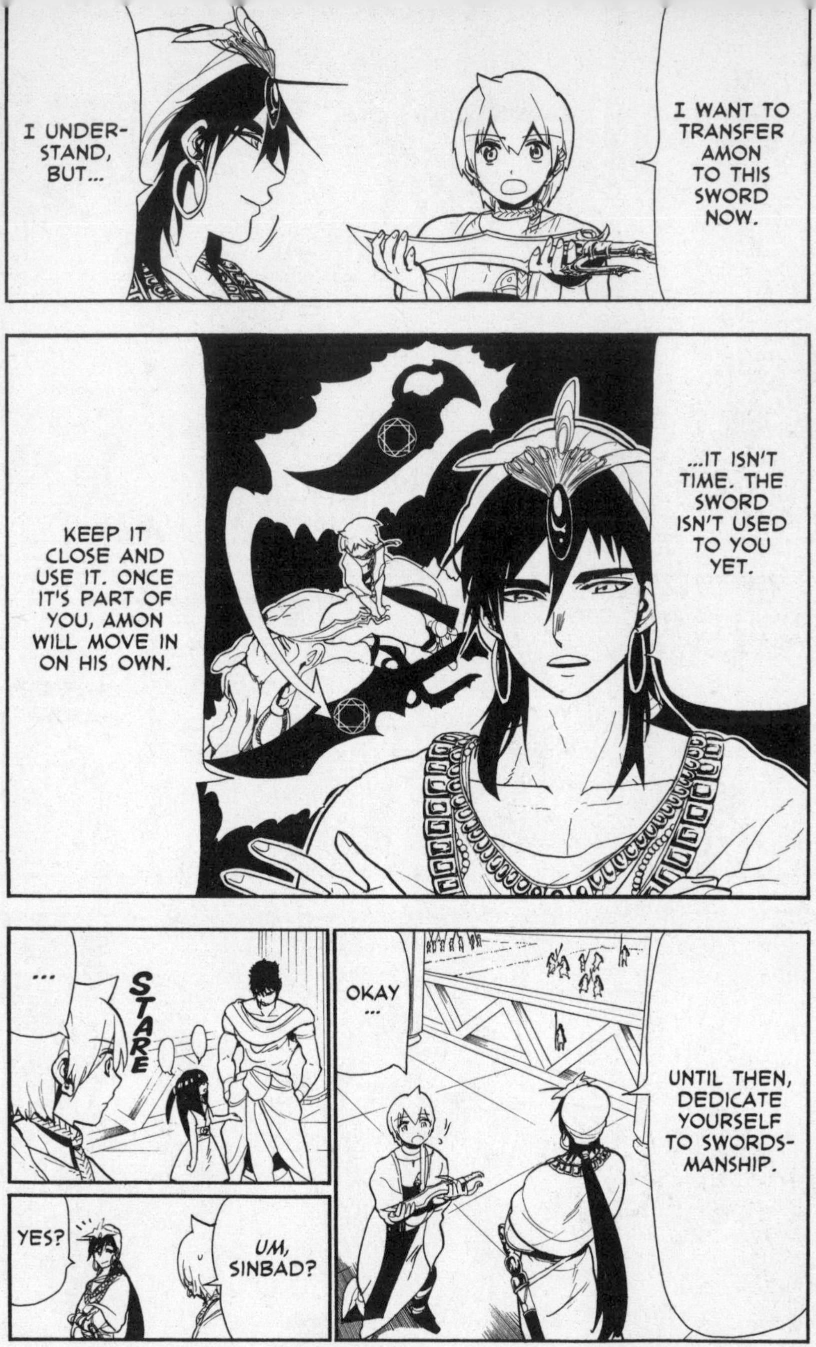
I WANT TO TRANSFER AMON TO THIS SWORD NOW.
I UNDER-STAND, BUT...
...IT ISN'T TIME. THE SWORD ISN'T USED TO YOU YET.
KEEP IT CLOSE AND USE IT. ONCE IT'S PART OF YOU, AMON WILL MOVE IN ON HIS OWN.
UNTIL THEN, DEDICATE YOURSELF TO SWORDS-MANSHIP.
OKAY...
...
STARE
UM, SINBAD?
YES?

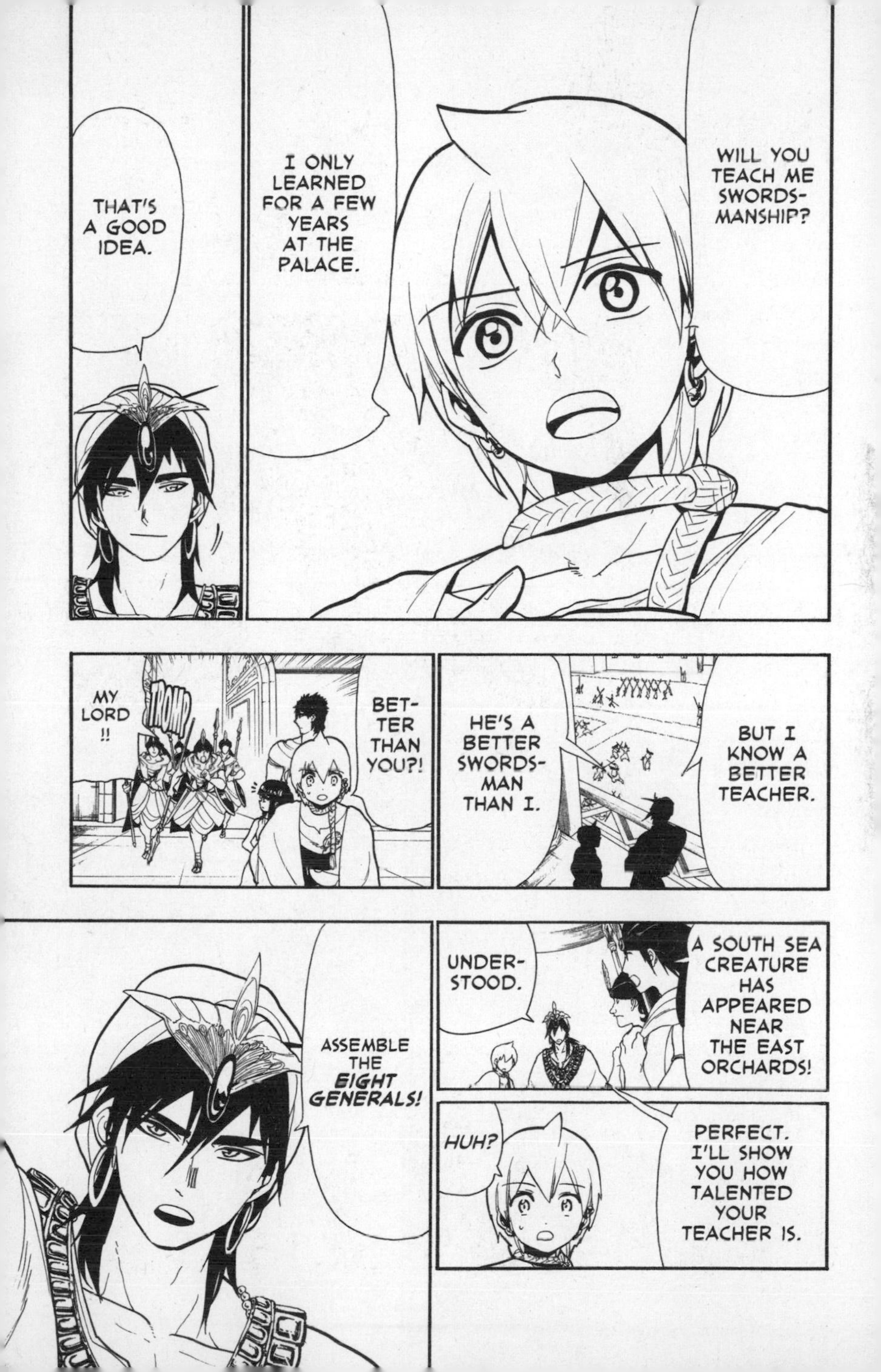
WILL YOU TEACH ME SWORDS-MANSHIP?
I ONLY LEARNED FOR A FEW YEARS AT THE PALACE.
THAT'S A GOOD IDEA.
BUT I KNOW A BETTER TEACHER.
HE'S A BETTER SWORDS-MAN THAN I.
BET-TER THAN YOU?!
THOMP
MY LORD !!
A SOUTH SEA CREATURE HAS APPEARED NEAR THE EAST ORCHARDS!
UNDER-STOOD.
PERFECT. I'LL SHOW YOU HOW TALENTED YOUR TEACHER IS.
HUH?
ASSEMBLE THE *EIGHT GENERALS!*

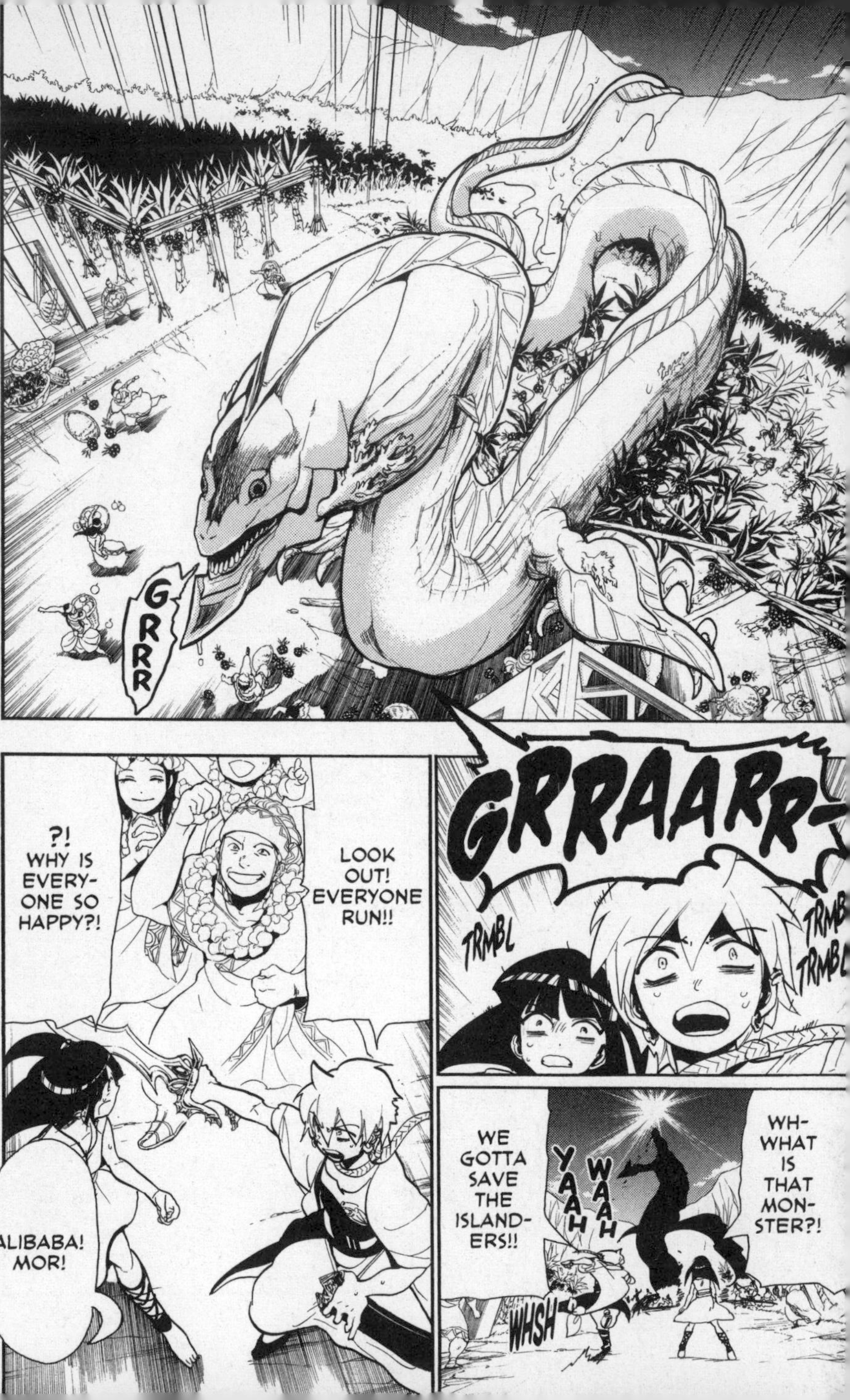
GRRR
GRRAARR-
TRMBL TRMBL
TRMBL
LOOK OUT! EVERYONE RUN!!
?! WHY IS EVERY-ONE SO HAPPY?!
WH-WHAT IS THAT MON-STER?!
WAAH
YAAH
WE GOTTA SAVE THE ISLAND-ERS!!
WHSH
ALIBABA! MOR!

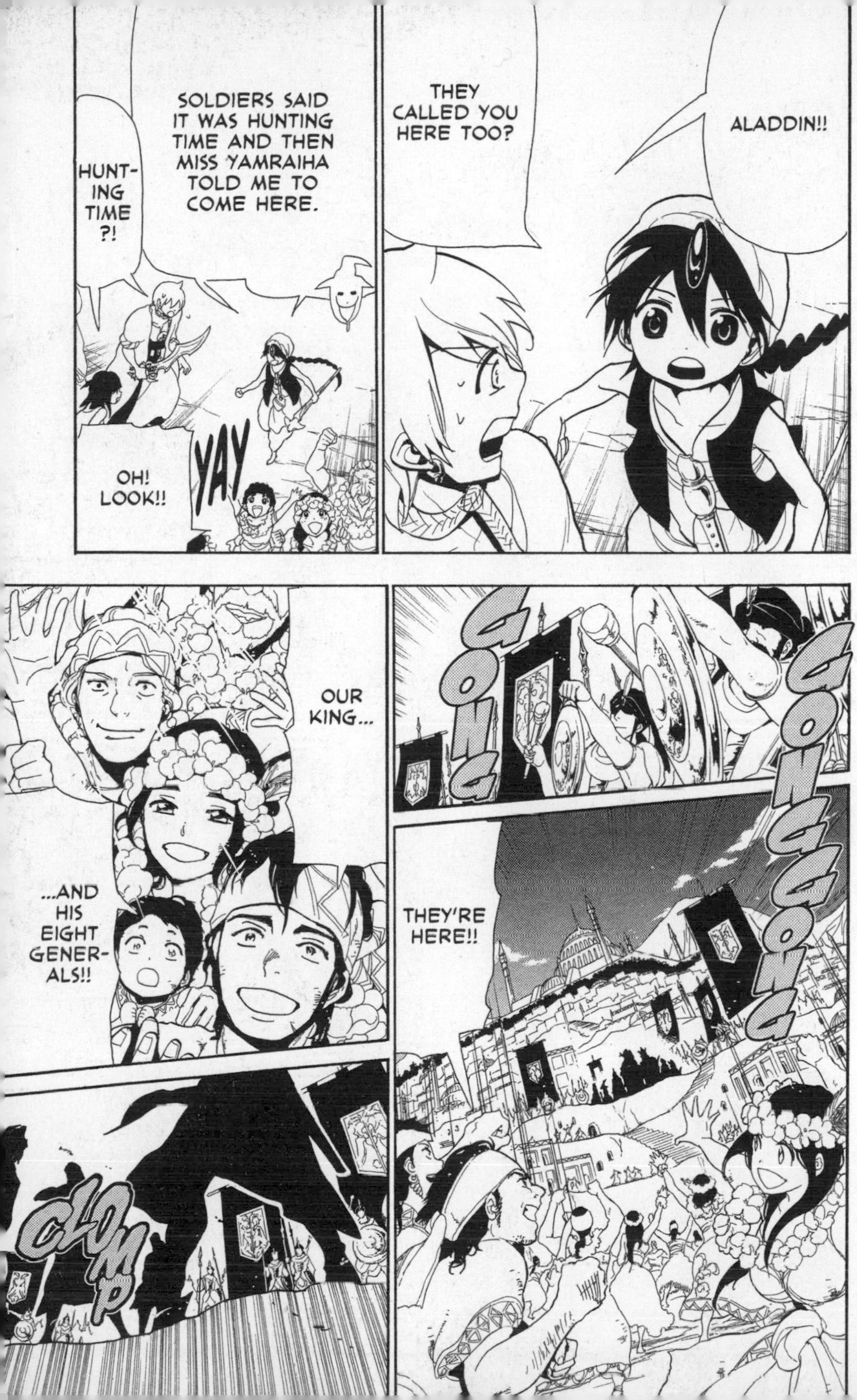
ALADDIN!!
THEY CALLED YOU HERE TOO?
SOLDIERS SAID IT WAS HUNTING TIME AND THEN MISS YAMRAIHA TOLD ME TO COME HERE.
HUNT-ING TIME ?!
YAY
OH! LOOK!!
GONG
GONG
GONG
THEY'RE HERE!!
GONG
OUR KING...
...AND HIS EIGHT GENER-ALS!!
CLOMP

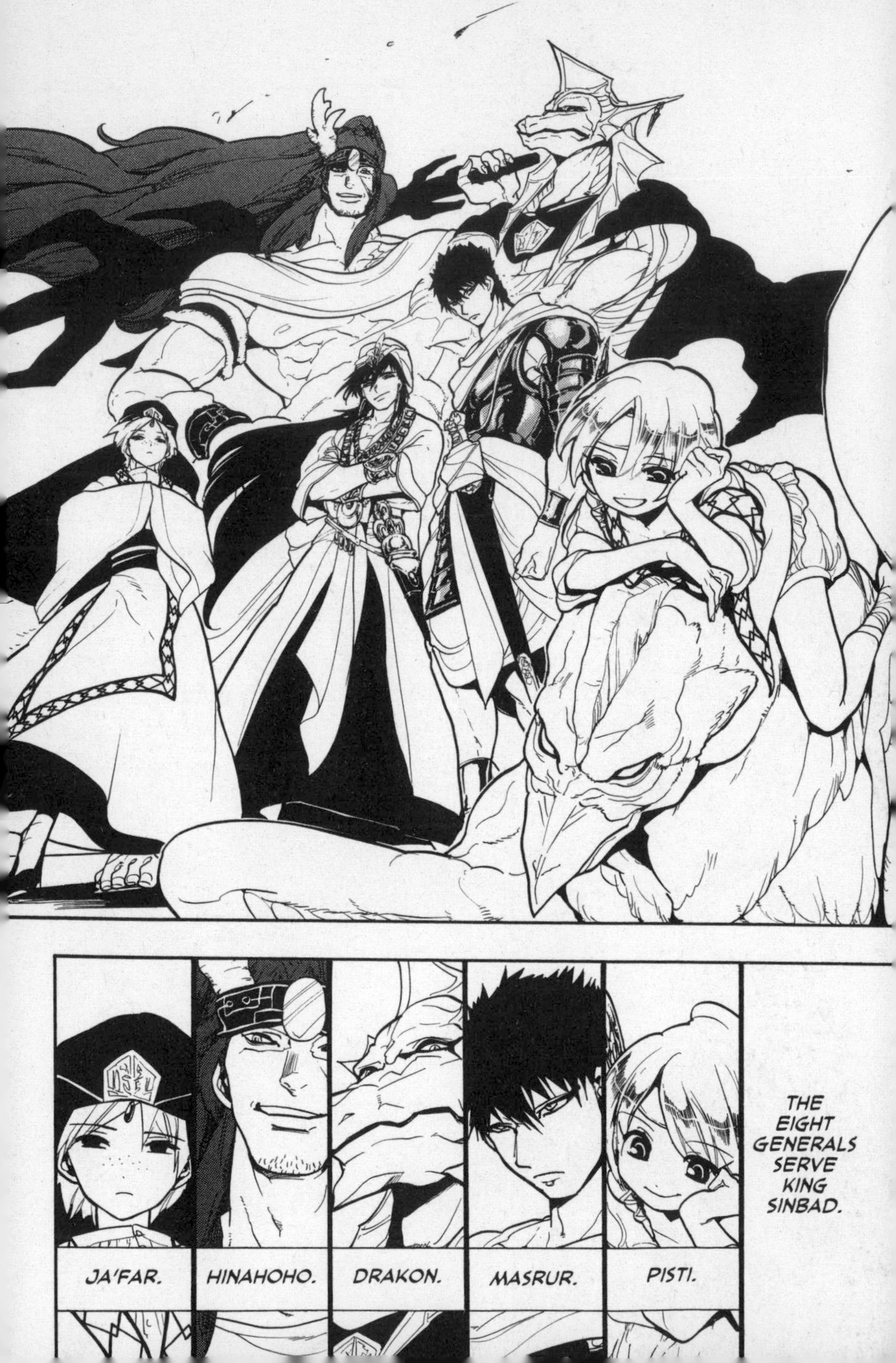
THE EIGHT GENERALS SERVE KING SINBAD.
PISTI.
MASRUR.
DRAKON.
HINAHOHO.
JA'FAR.

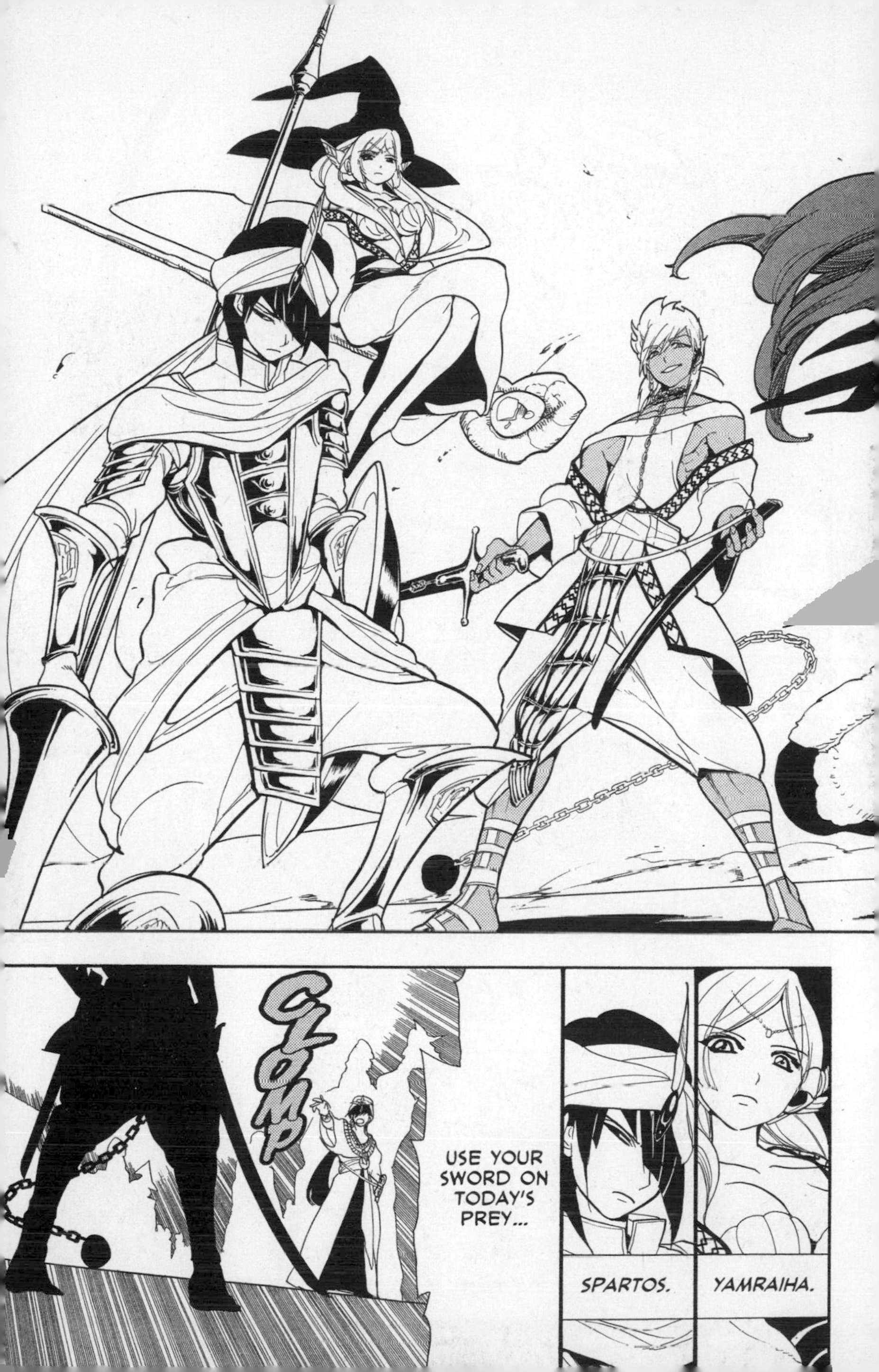
YAMRAIHA.
SPARTOS.
USE YOUR SWORD ON TODAY'S PREY...
CLOMP

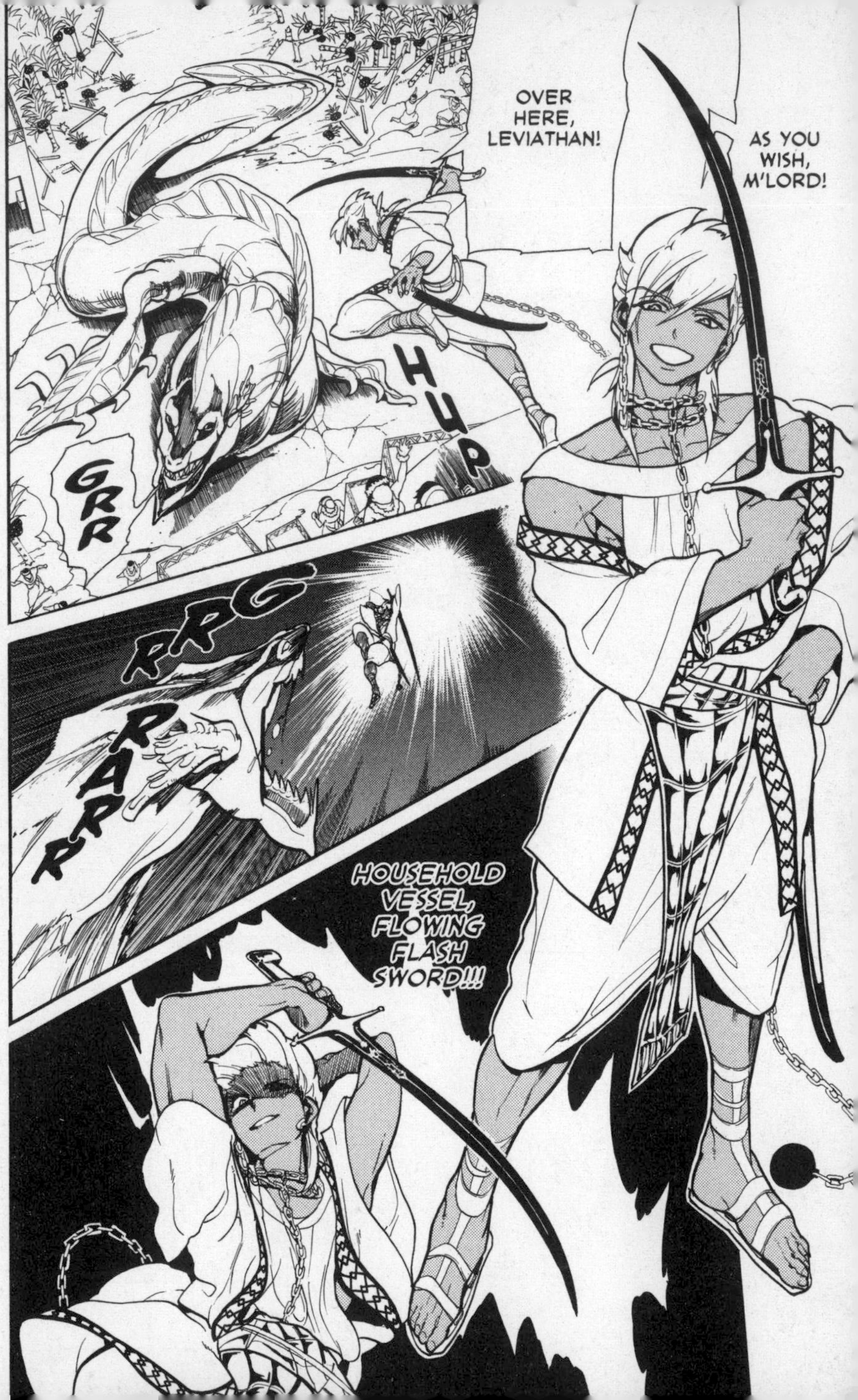
OVER HERE, LEVIATHAN!
AS YOU WISH, M'LORD!
HUP
GRR
RRG
RARR
HOUSEHOLD VESSEL, FLOWING FLASH SWORD!!!

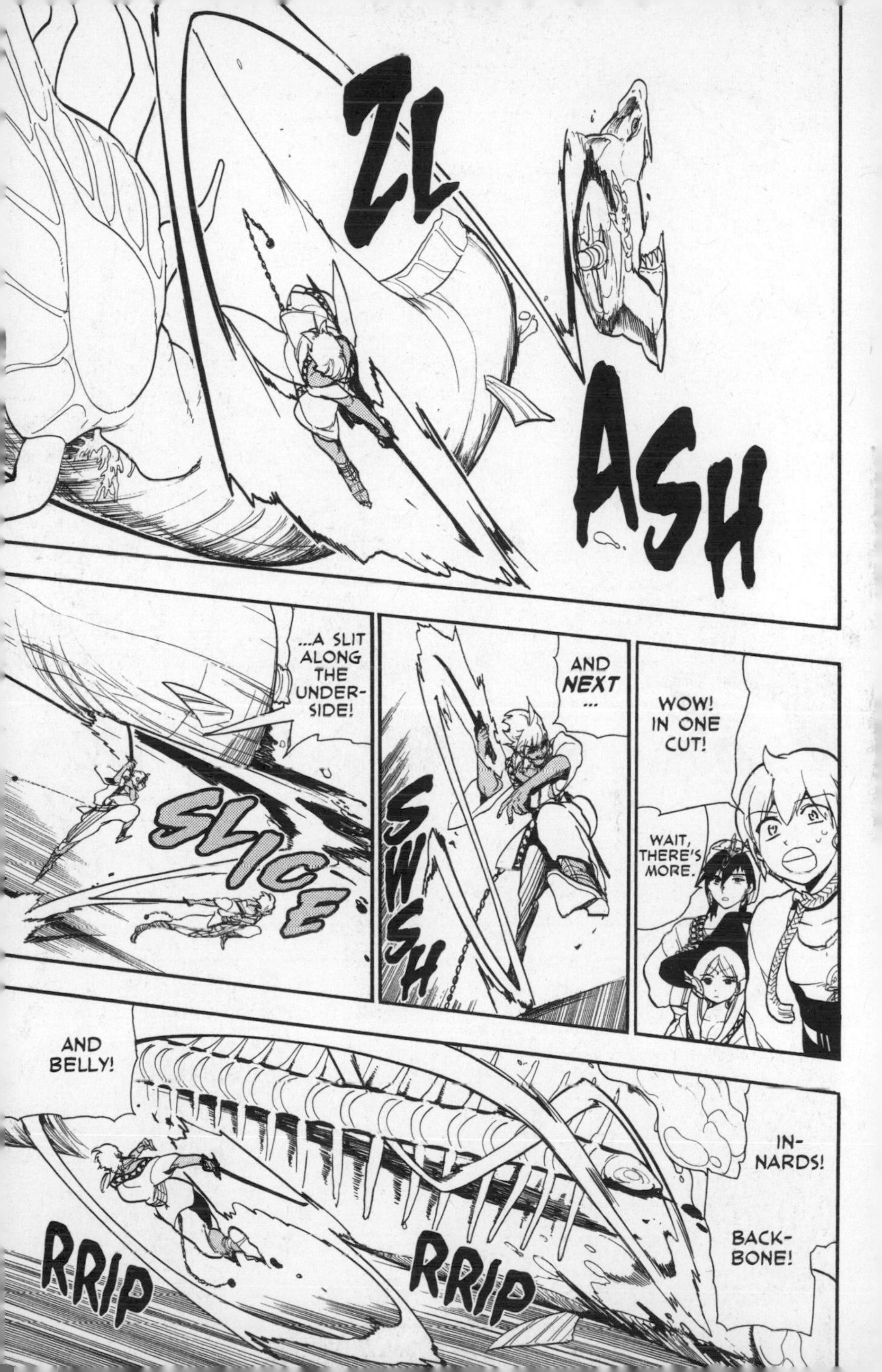
ZZASH
WOW! IN ONE CUT!
WAIT, THERE'S MORE.
AND NEXT ...
SWSH
...A SLIT ALONG THE UNDER-SIDE!
SLICE
IN-NARDS!
BACK-BONE!
RRIP
RRIP
AND BELLY!

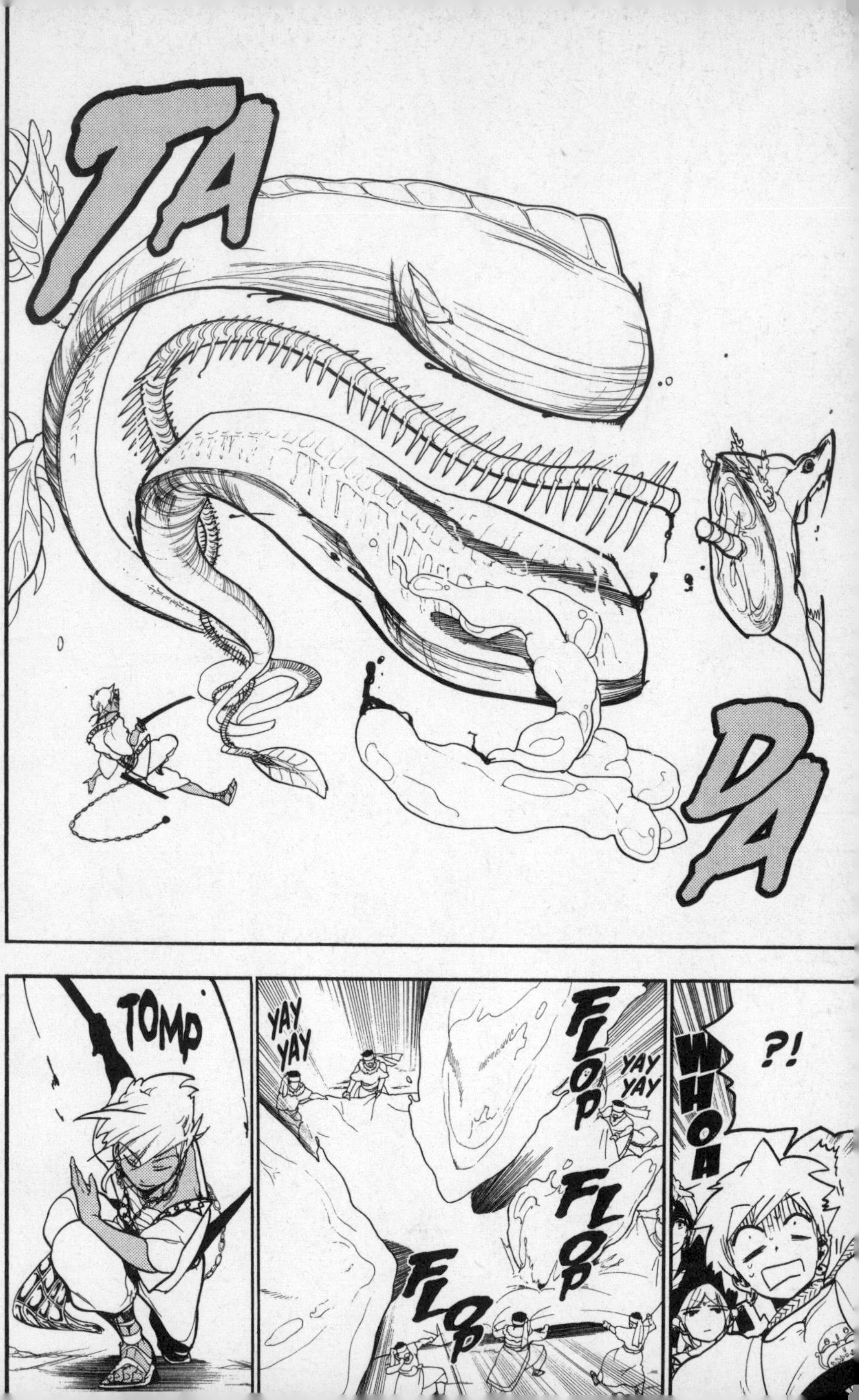
TA
DA
?!
WHOA
YAY YAY
FLOP
FLOP
FLOP
YAY YAY
TOMP

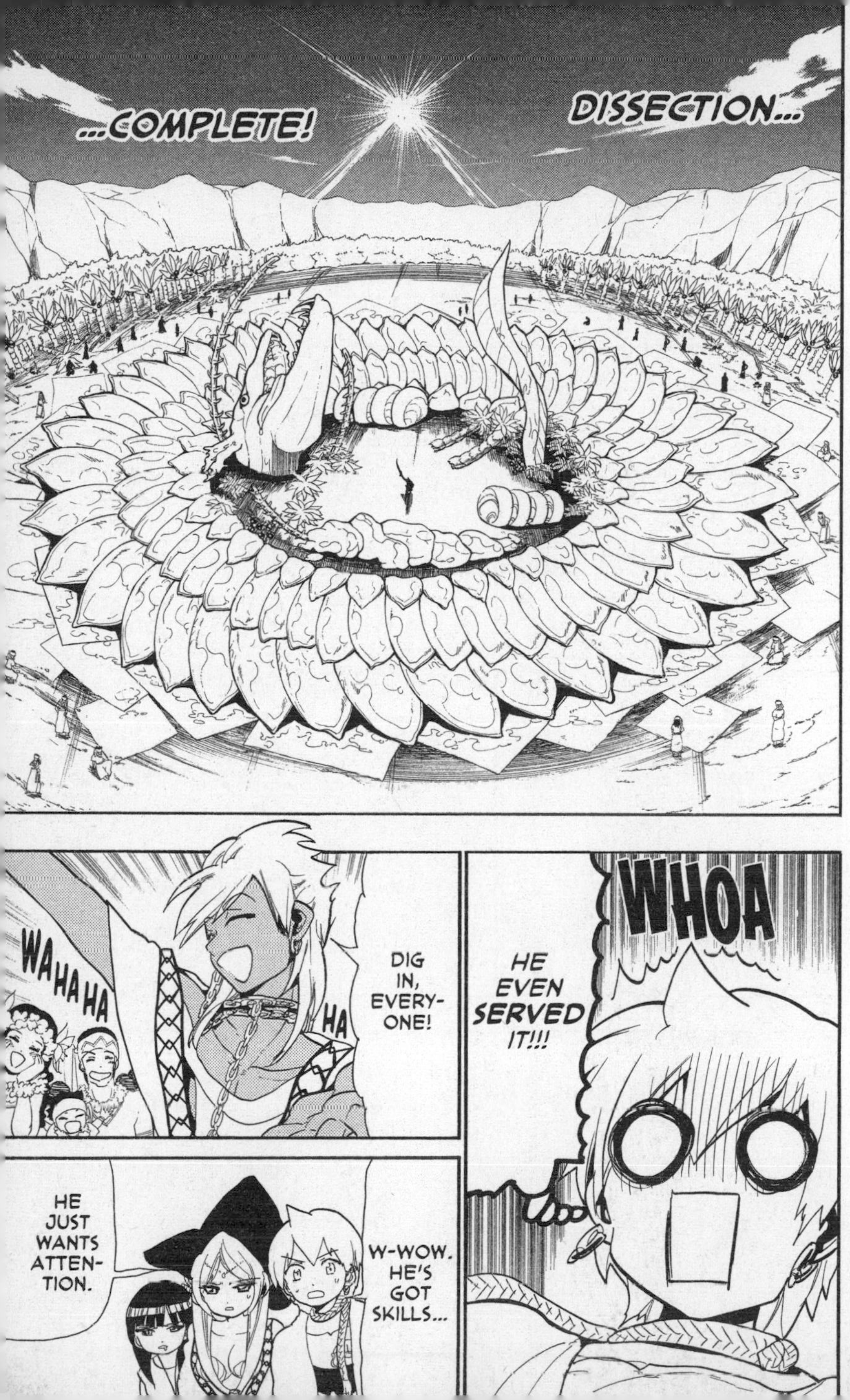
DISSECTION...
...COMPLETE!
WHOA
HE EVEN SERVED IT!!!
DIG IN, EVERY-ONE!
HA
WAHAHA
W-WOW. HE'S GOT SKILLS...
HE JUST WANTS ATTEN-TION.

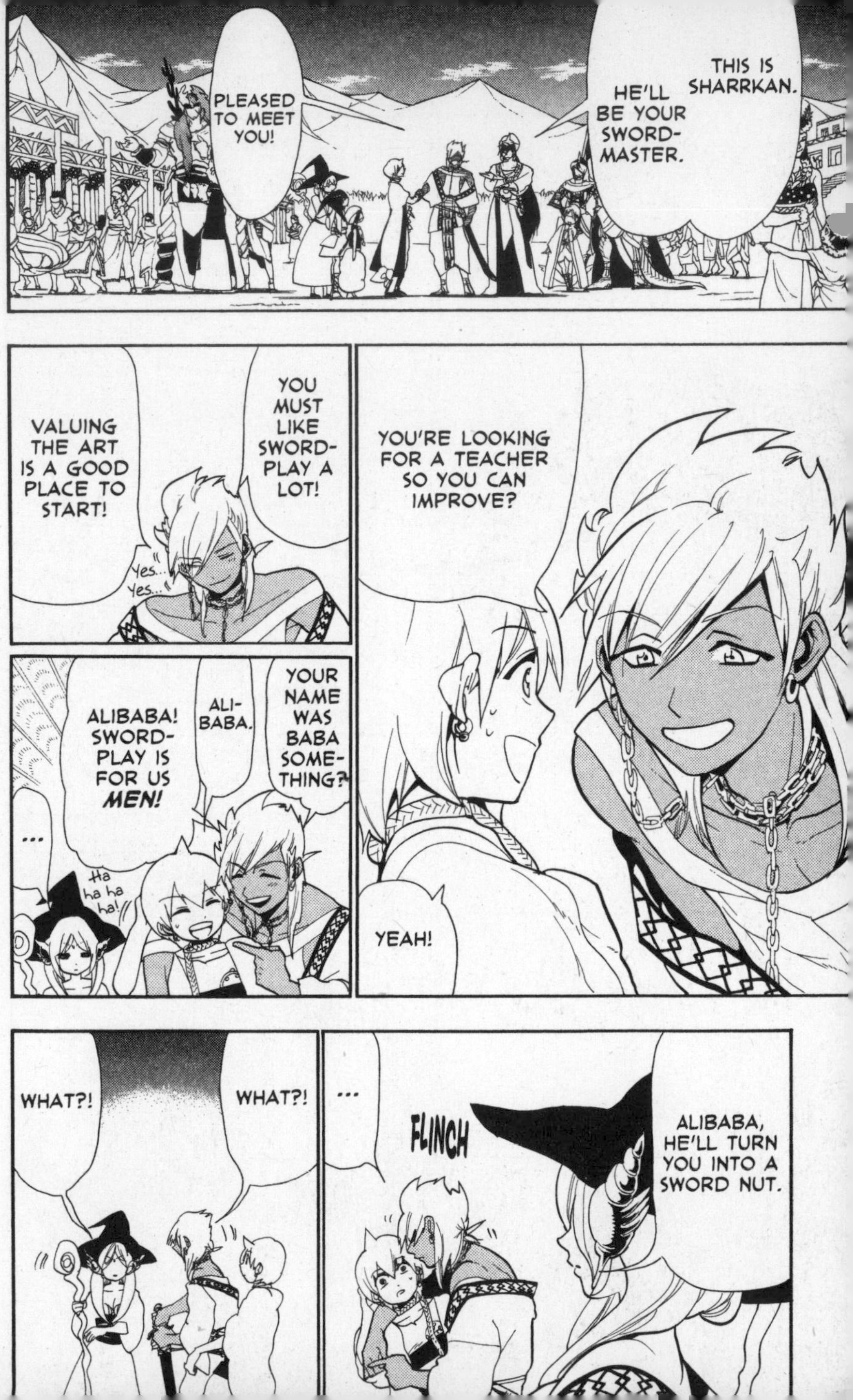
THIS IS SHARRKAN.
HE'LL BE YOUR SWORD-MASTER.
PLEASED TO MEET YOU!
YOU'RE LOOKING FOR A TEACHER SO YOU CAN IMPROVE?
YEAH!
YOU MUST LIKE SWORD-PLAY A LOT!
VALUING THE ART IS A GOOD PLACE TO START!
Yes... Yes...
YOUR NAME WAS BABA SOME-THING?
ALI-BABA.
ALIBABA! SWORD-PLAY IS FOR US *MEN!*
Ha ha ha ha!
...
ALIBABA, HE'LL TURN YOU INTO A SWORD NUT.
FLINCH
...
WHAT?!
WHAT?!

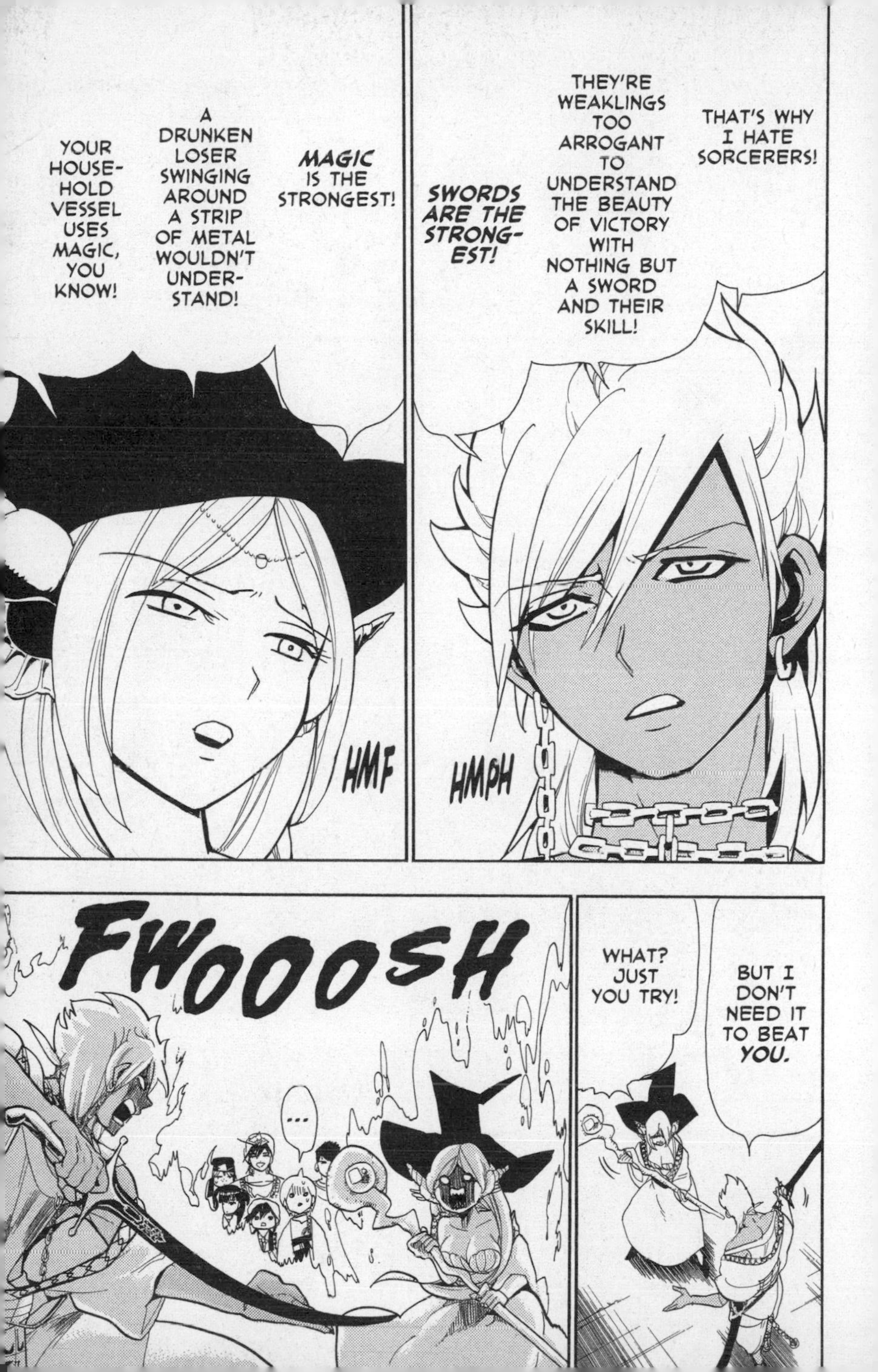
THAT'S WHY I HATE SORCERERS!
THEY'RE WEAKLINGS TOO ARROGANT TO UNDERSTAND THE BEAUTY OF VICTORY WITH NOTHING BUT A SWORD AND THEIR SKILL!
SWORDS ARE THE STRONG-EST!
HMPH
MAGIC IS THE STRONGEST!
A DRUNKEN LOSER SWINGING AROUND A STRIP OF METAL WOULDN'T UNDER-STAND!
YOUR HOUSE-HOLD VESSEL USES MAGIC, YOU KNOW!
HMF
BUT I DON'T NEED IT TO BEAT YOU.
WHAT? JUST YOU TRY!
FWOOOSH
...

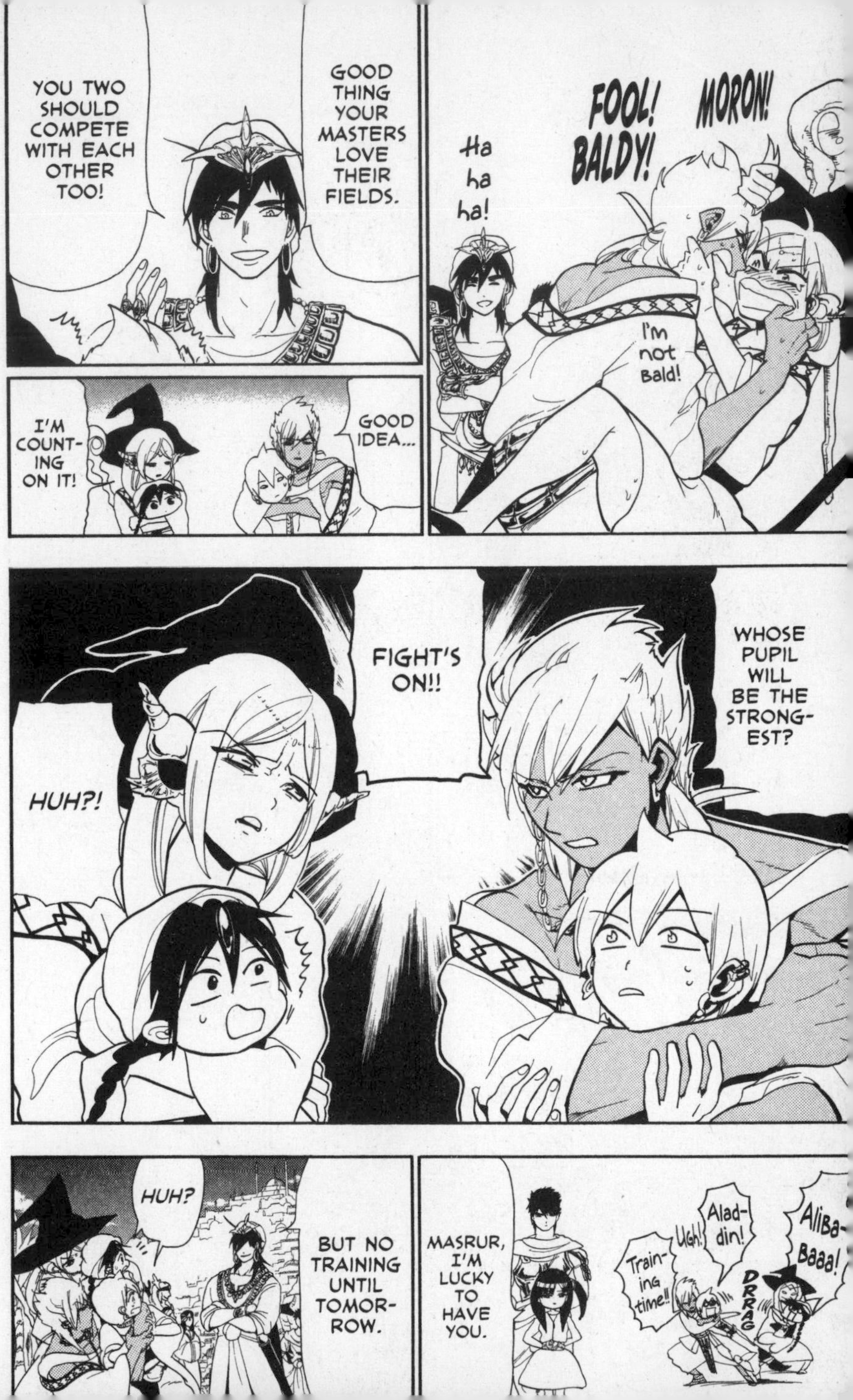
MORON!
FOOL! BALDY!
Ha ha ha!
I'm not Bald!
GOOD THING YOUR MASTERS LOVE THEIR FIELDS.
YOU TWO SHOULD COMPETE WITH EACH OTHER TOO!
GOOD IDEA...
I'M COUNTING ON IT!
WHOSE PUPIL WILL BE THE STRONGEST?
FIGHT'S ON!!
HUH?!
AliBa-Baaa!
Alad-din!
Ugh!
Training time!!
DRRAG
MASRUR, I'M LUCKY TO HAVE YOU.
BUT NO TRAINING UNTIL TOMORROW.
HUH?

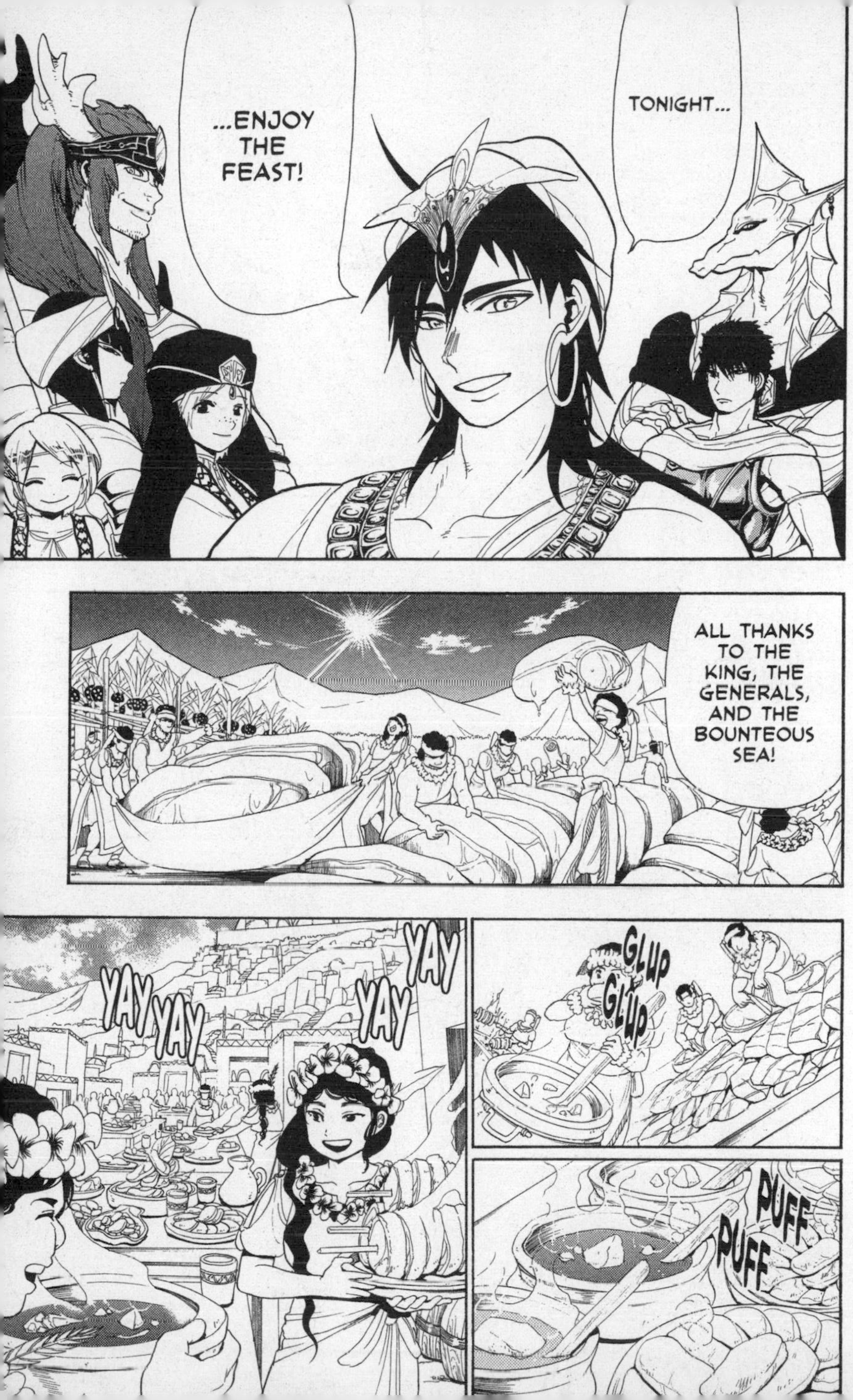
TONIGHT...
...ENJOY THE FEAST!
ALL THANKS TO THE KING, THE GENERALS, AND THE BOUNTEOUS SEA!
GLUP GLUP
PUFF PUFF
YAY
YAY
YAY YAY

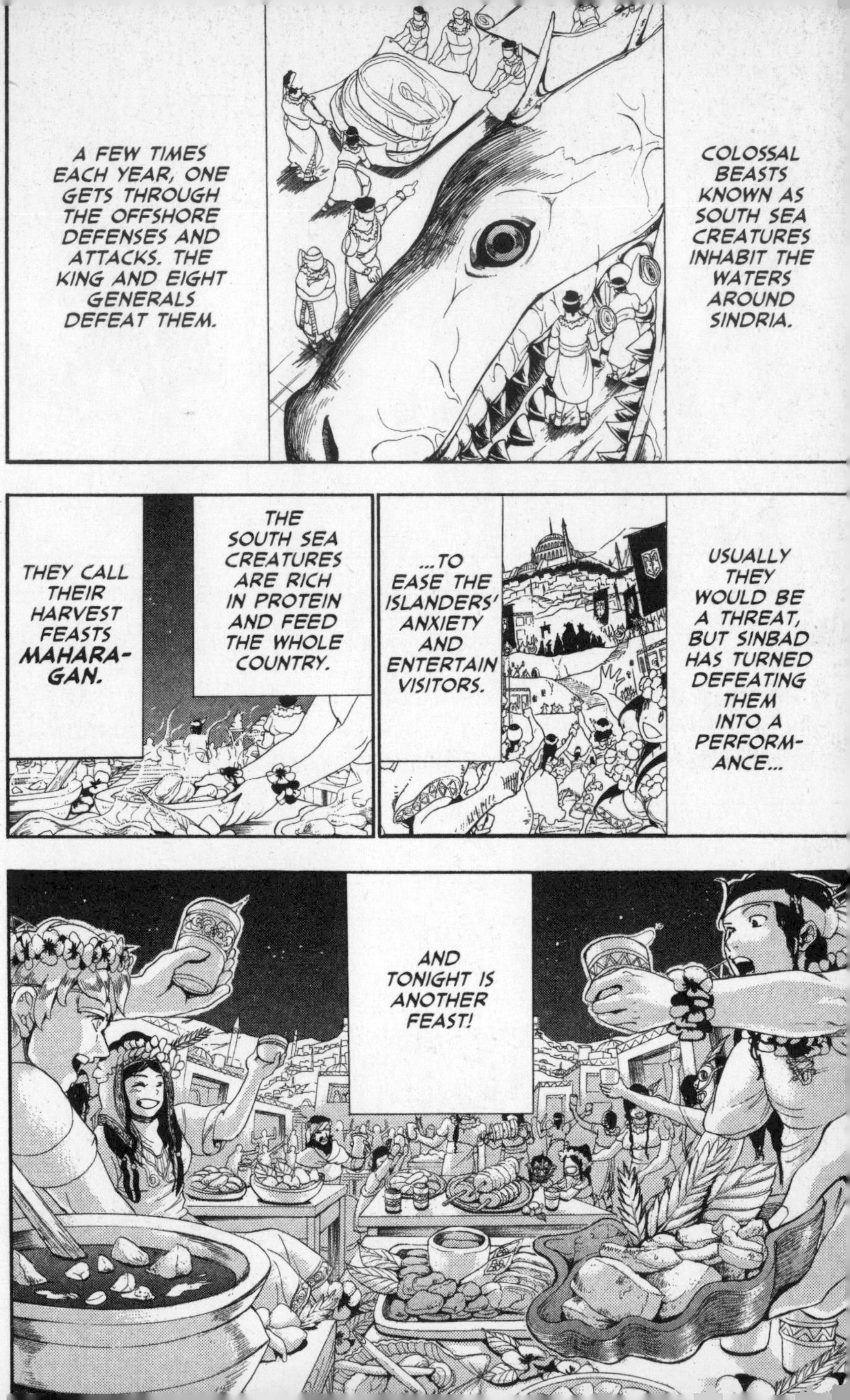
COLOSSAL BEASTS KNOWN AS SOUTH SEA CREATURES INHABIT THE WATERS AROUND SINDRIA.
A FEW TIMES EACH YEAR, ONE GETS THROUGH THE OFFSHORE DEFENSES AND ATTACKS. THE KING AND EIGHT GENERALS DEFEAT THEM.
USUALLY THEY WOULD BE A THREAT, BUT SINBAD HAS TURNED DEFEATING THEM INTO A PERFORMANCE...
...TO EASE THE ISLANDERS' ANXIETY AND ENTERTAIN VISITORS.
THE SOUTH SEA CREATURES ARE RICH IN PROTEIN AND FEED THE WHOLE COUNTRY.
THEY CALL THEIR HARVEST FEASTS **MAHARAGAN.**
AND TONIGHT IS ANOTHER FEAST!

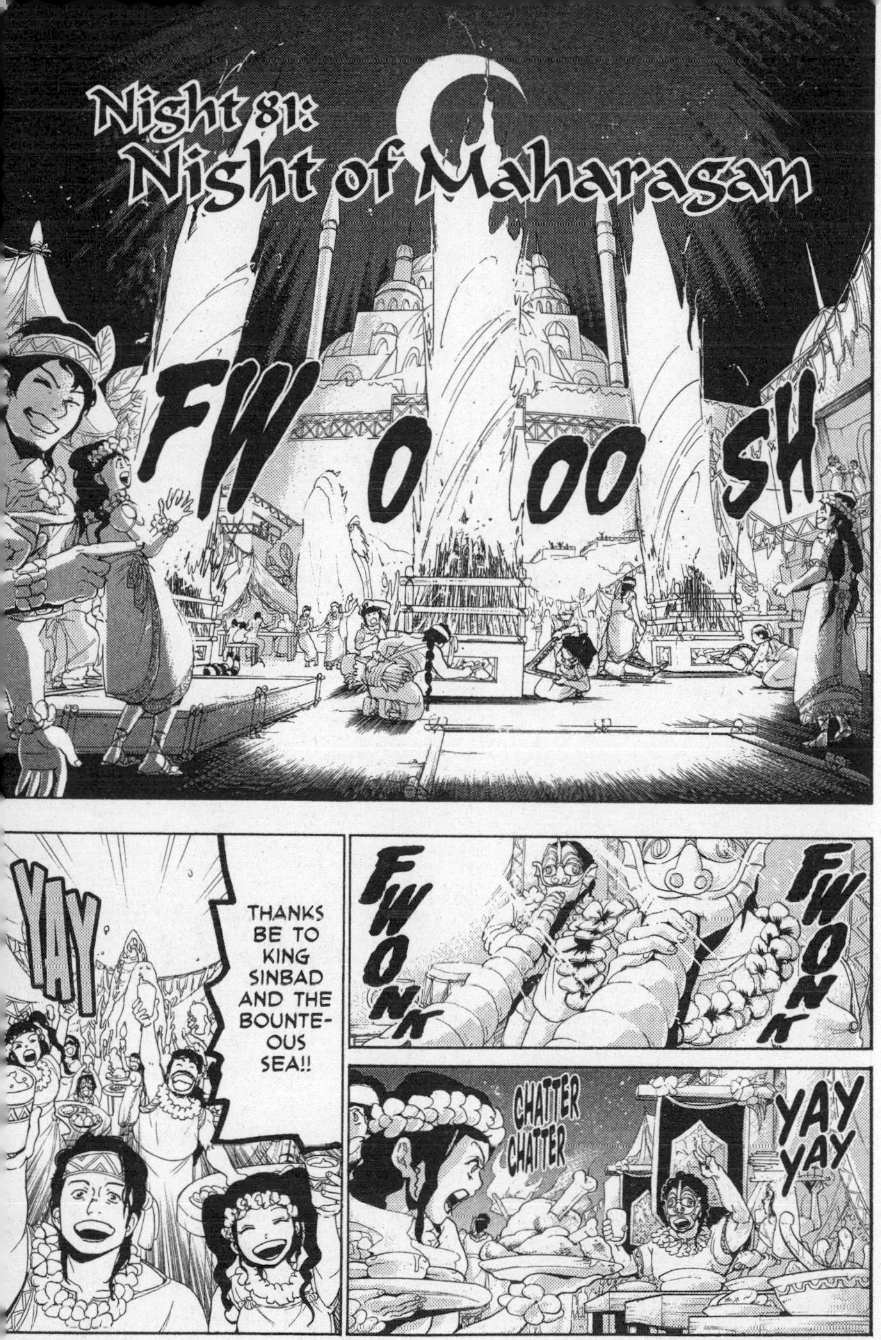
Night 81:
Night of Maharasagan
FWOOOSH
FWONK
FWONK
CHATTER CHATTER
YAY YAY
YAY
THANKS BE TO KING SINBAD AND THE BOUNTEOUS SEA!!

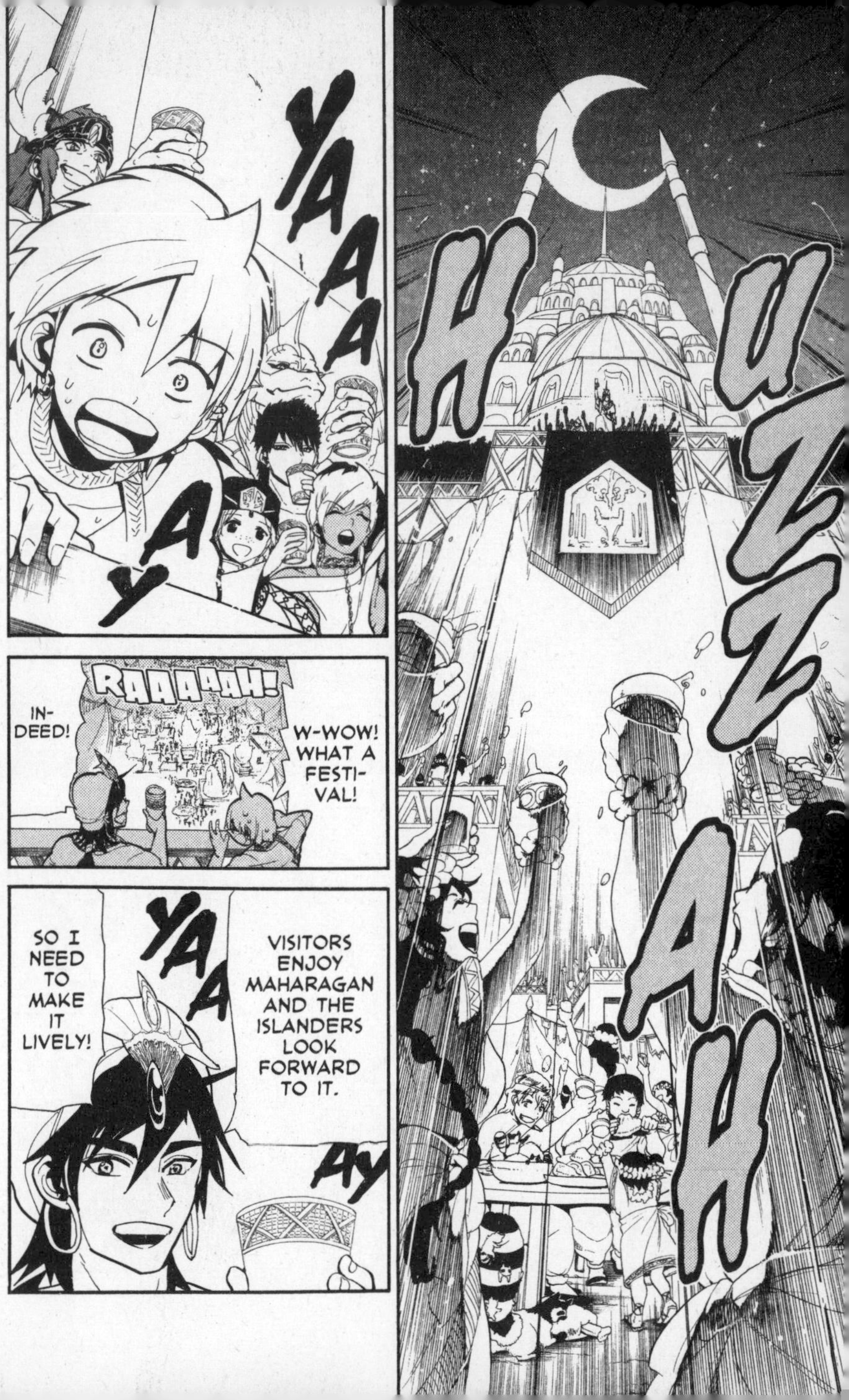
HUZZAAH
YAAAAY
RAAAAAH!
W-WOW! WHAT A FESTIVAL!
INDEED!
VISITORS ENJOY MAHARAGAN AND THE ISLANDERS LOOK FORWARD TO IT.
SO I NEED TO MAKE IT LIVELY!
YAAAY

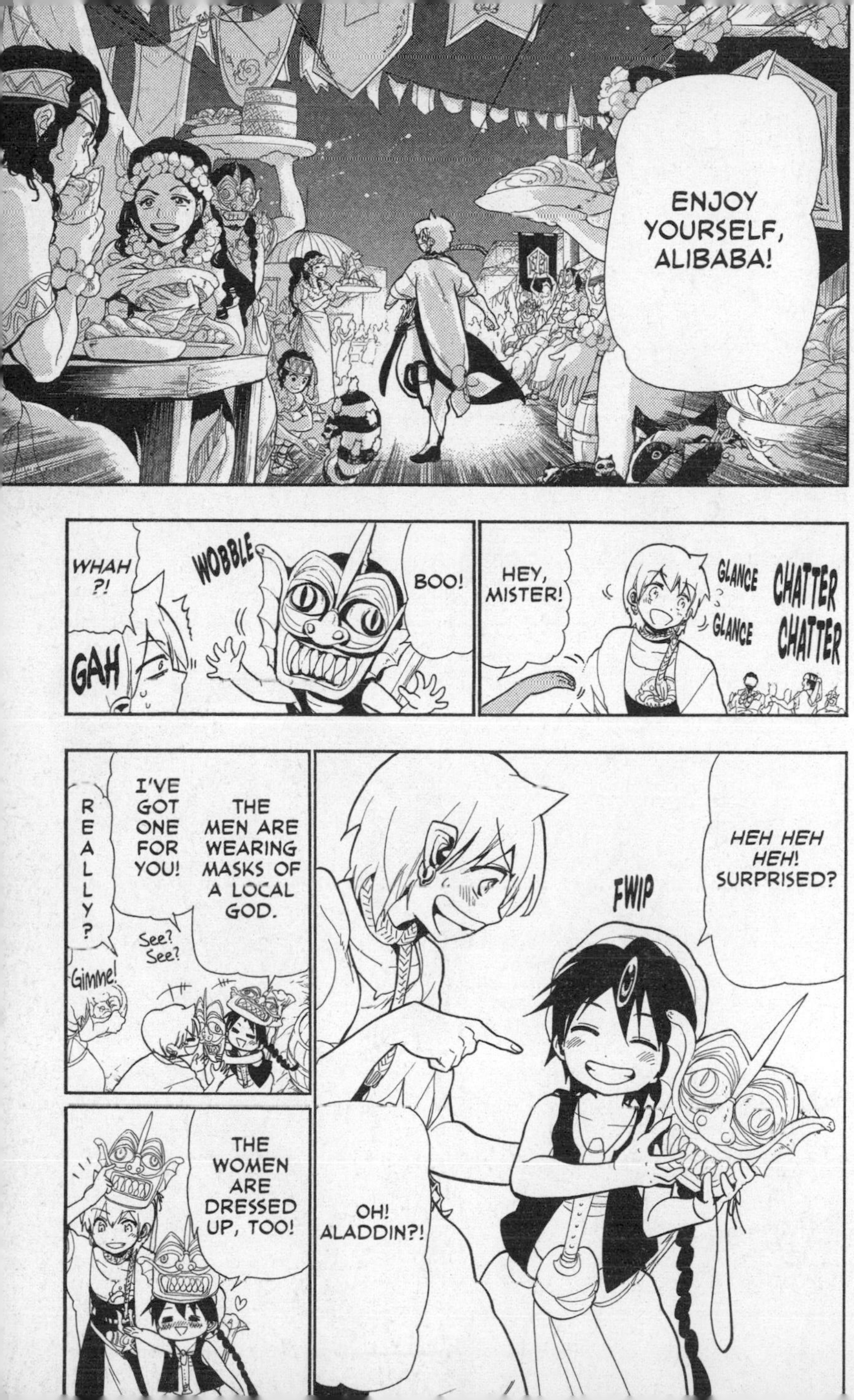
ENJOY YOURSELF, ALIBABA!
CHATTER CHATTER
GLANCE GLANCE
HEY, MISTER!
BOO!
WOBBLE
WHAH?!
GAH
HEH HEH HEH! SURPRISED?
FWIP
OH! ALADDIN?!
THE MEN ARE WEARING MASKS OF A LOCAL GOD.
I'VE GOT ONE FOR YOU!
REALLY?
See? See?
Gimme!
THE WOMEN ARE DRESSED UP, TOO!

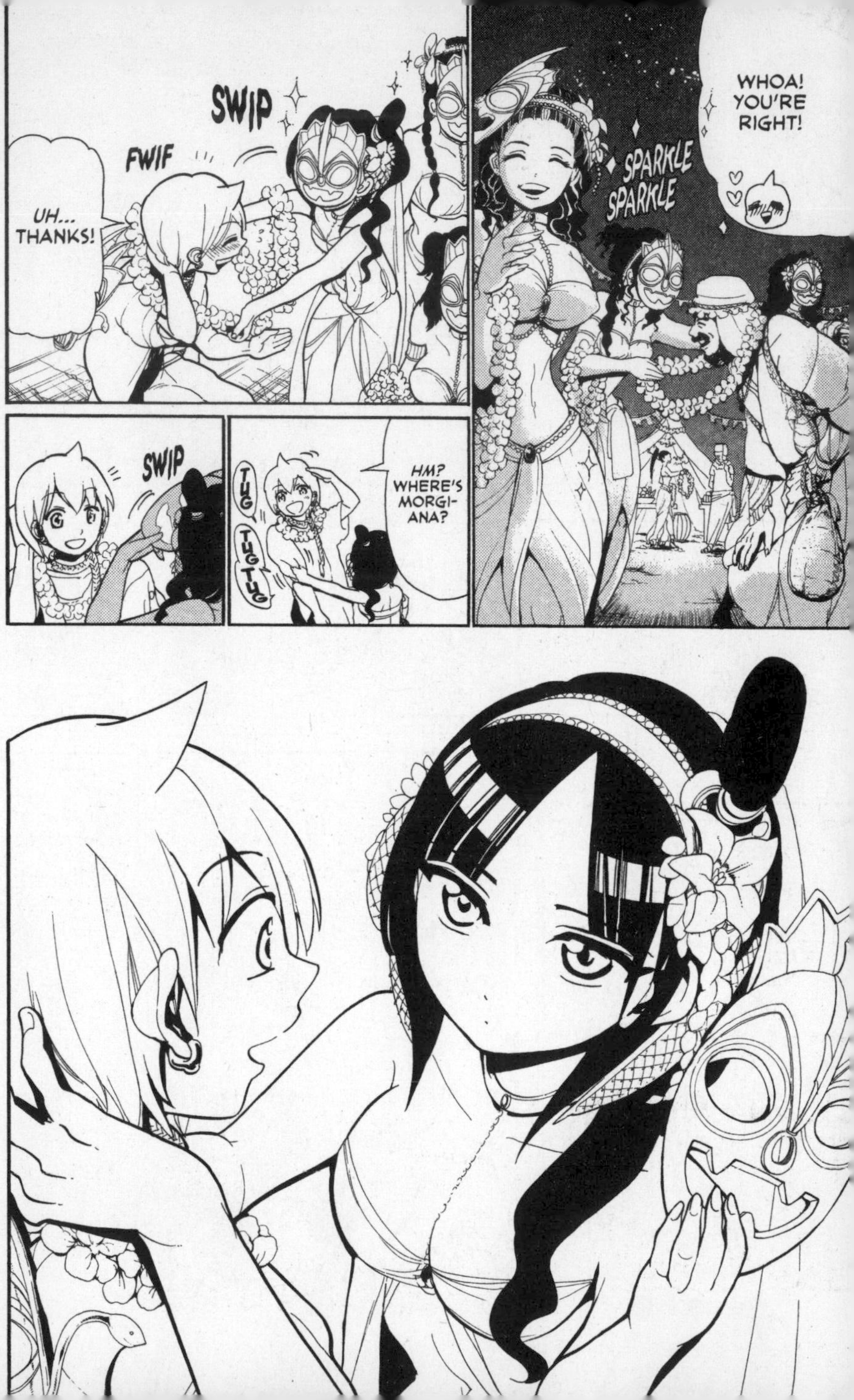
WHOA! YOU'RE RIGHT!
SPARKLE SPARKLE
SWIP
FWIF
UH... THANKS!
HM? WHERE'S MORGIANA?
TUG TUG TUG
SWIP

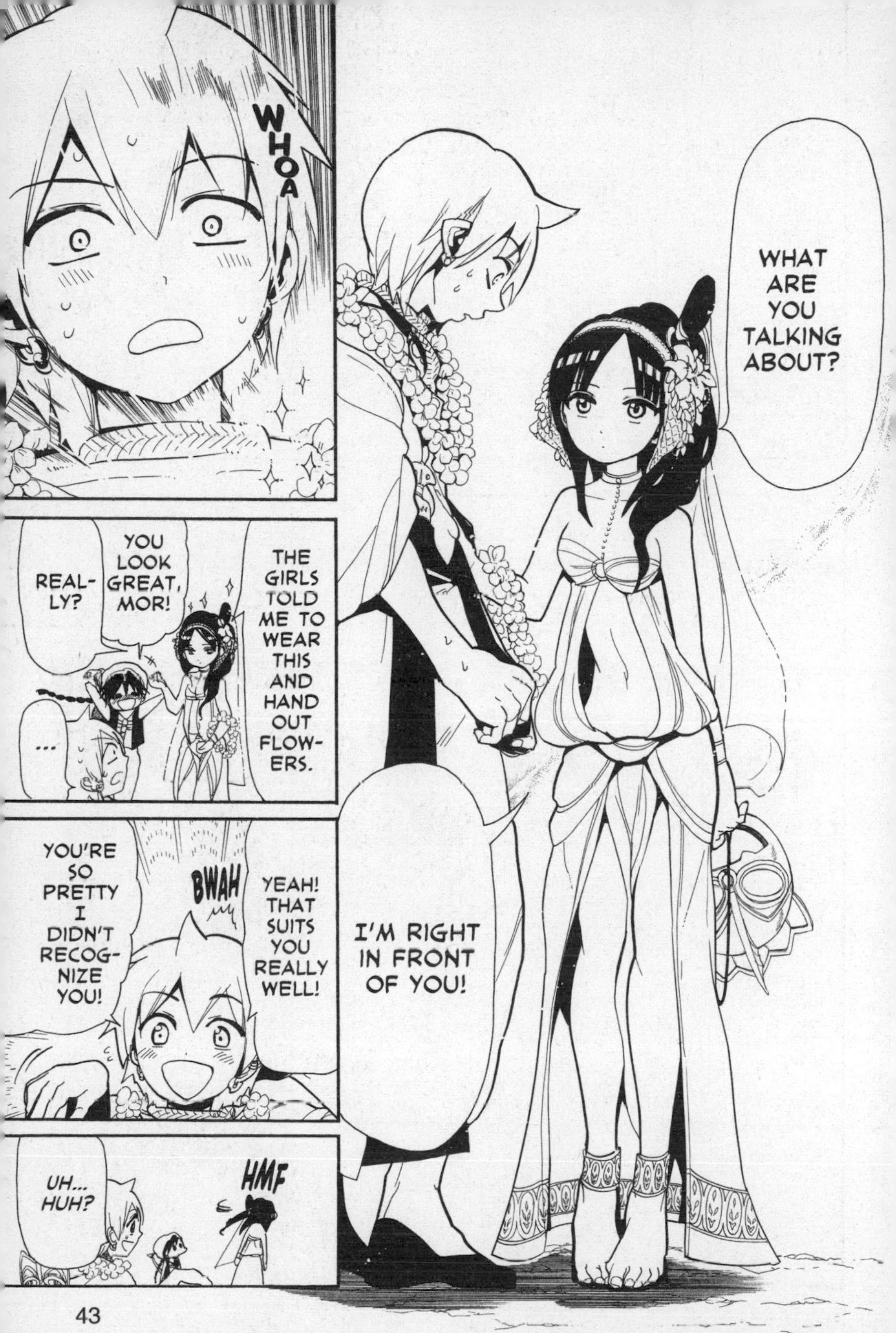
WHAT ARE YOU TALKING ABOUT?
I'M RIGHT IN FRONT OF YOU!
WHOA
THE GIRLS TOLD ME TO WEAR THIS AND HAND OUT FLOWERS.
YOU LOOK GREAT, MOR!
REALLY?
...
YEAH! THAT SUITS YOU REALLY WELL!
BWAH
YOU'RE SO PRETTY I DIDN'T RECOGNIZE YOU!
HMF
UH... HUH?

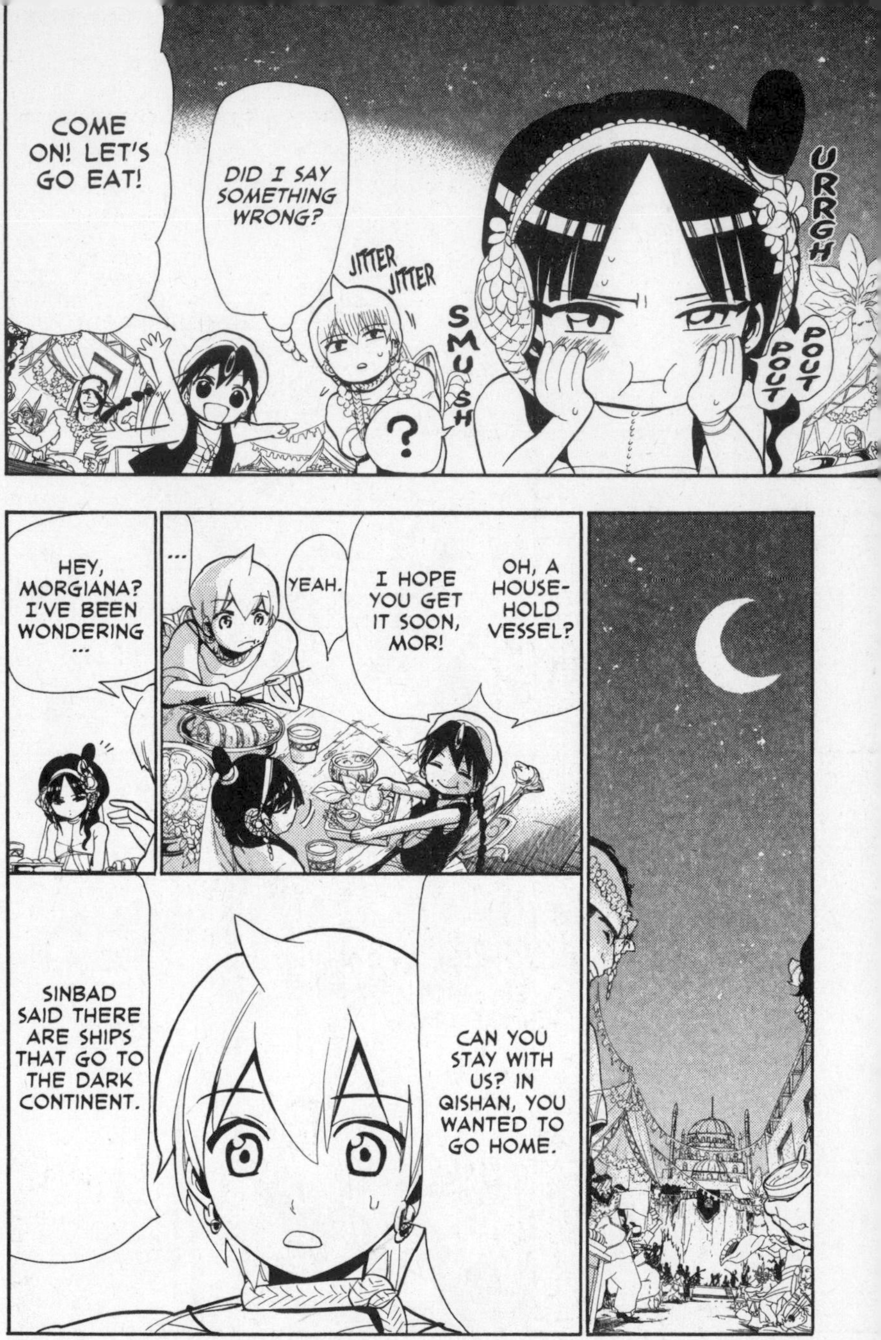
URRGH
POUT POUT
SMUSH
?
JITTER JITTER
DID I SAY SOMETHING WRONG?
COME ON! LET'S GO EAT!
OH, A HOUSE-HOLD VESSEL?
I HOPE YOU GET IT SOON, MOR!
YEAH.
...
HEY, MORGIANA? I'VE BEEN WONDERING ...
CAN YOU STAY WITH US? IN QISHAN, YOU WANTED TO GO HOME.
SINBAD SAID THERE ARE SHIPS THAT GO TO THE DARK CONTINENT.

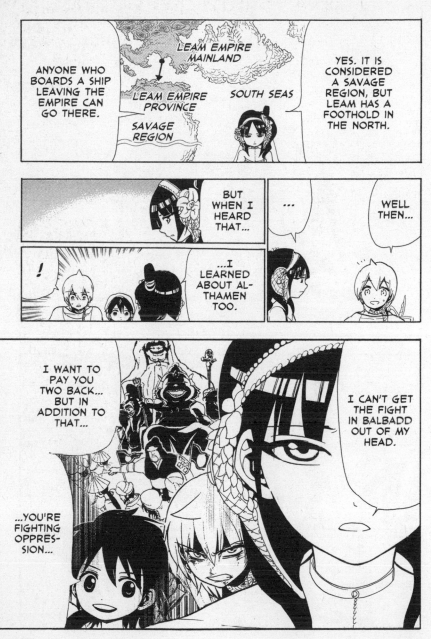

YES. IT IS CONSIDERED A SAVAGE REGION, BUT LEAM HAS A FOOTHOLD IN THE NORTH.
LEAM EMPIRE MAINLAND
SOUTH SEAS
LEAM EMPIRE PROVINCE
SAVAGE REGION
ANYONE WHO BOARDS A SHIP LEAVING THE EMPIRE CAN GO THERE.
WELL THEN...
...
BUT WHEN I HEARD THAT...
...I LEARNED ABOUT AL-THAMEN TOO.
!
I CAN'T GET THE FIGHT IN BALBADD OUT OF MY HEAD.
I WANT TO PAY YOU TWO BACK... BUT IN ADDITION TO THAT...
...YOU'RE FIGHTING OPPRES-SION...

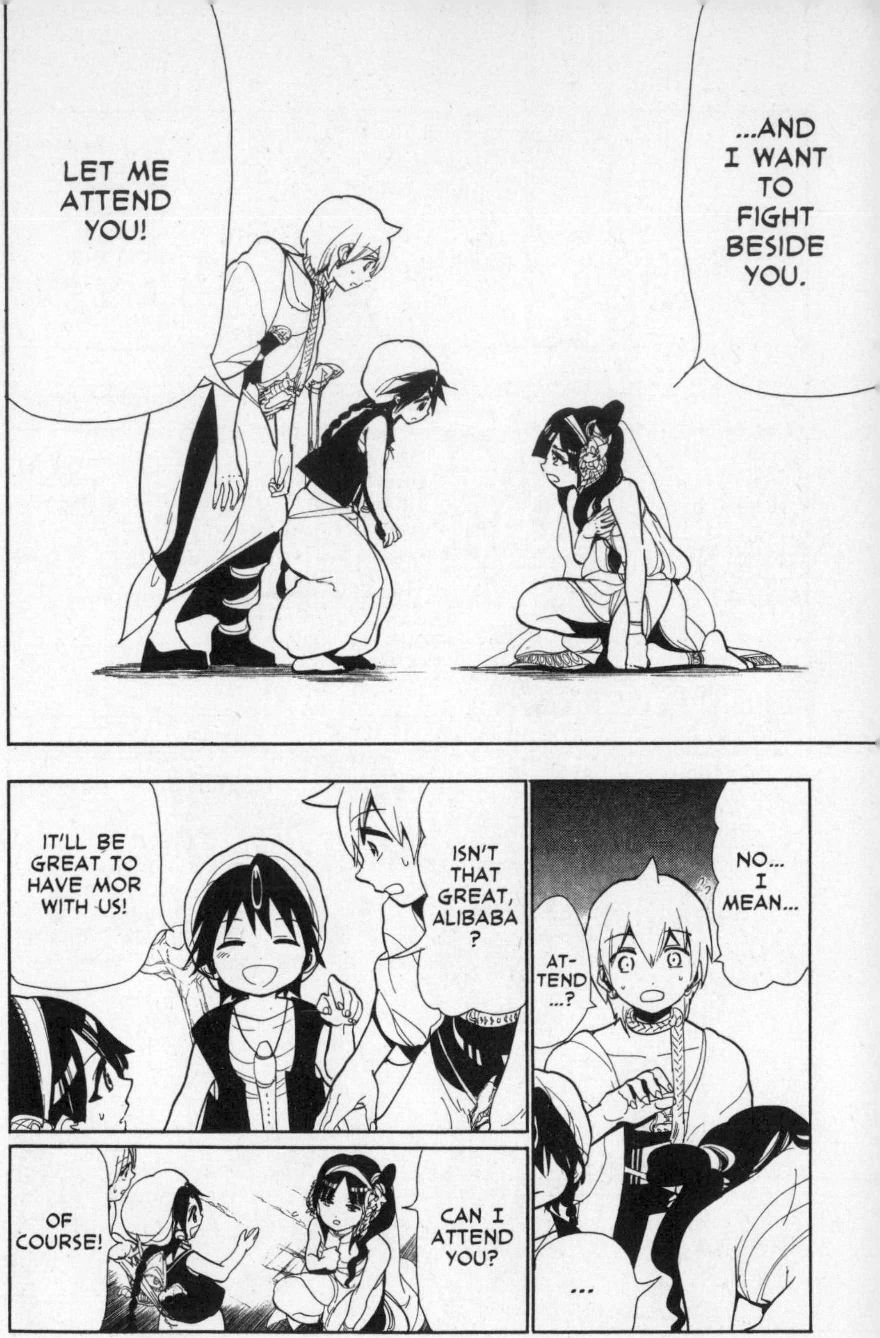
LET ME ATTEND YOU!
...AND I WANT TO FIGHT BESIDE YOU.
NO... I MEAN...
AT-TEND ...?
...
ISN'T THAT GREAT, ALIBABA ?
IT'LL BE GREAT TO HAVE MOR WITH US!
CAN I ATTEND YOU?
OF COURSE!

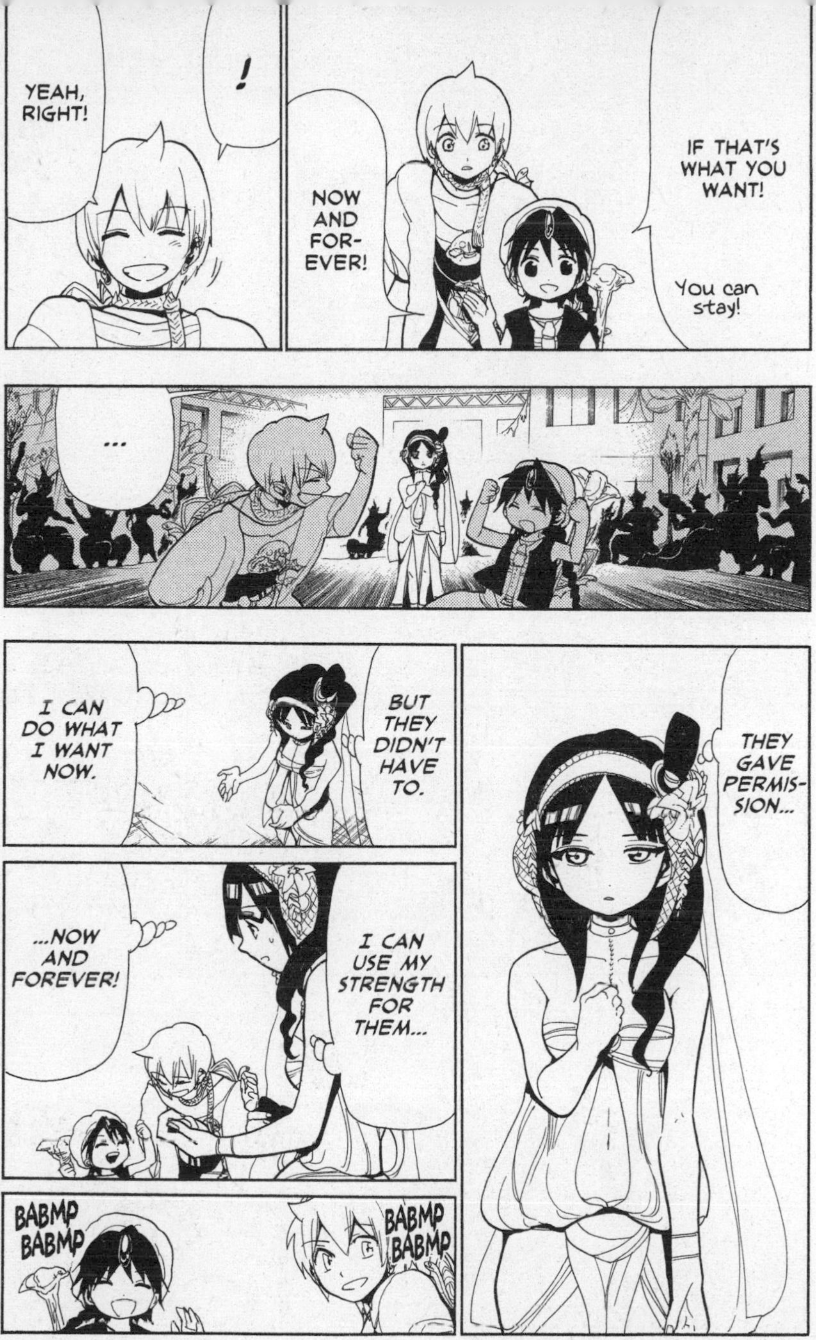
IF THAT'S WHAT YOU WANT!
You can stay!
NOW AND FOR-EVER!
!
YEAH, RIGHT!
...
THEY GAVE PERMIS-SION...
BUT THEY DIDN'T HAVE TO.
I CAN DO WHAT I WANT NOW.
I CAN USE MY STRENGTH FOR THEM...
...NOW AND FOREVER!
BABMP BABMP
BABMP BABMP

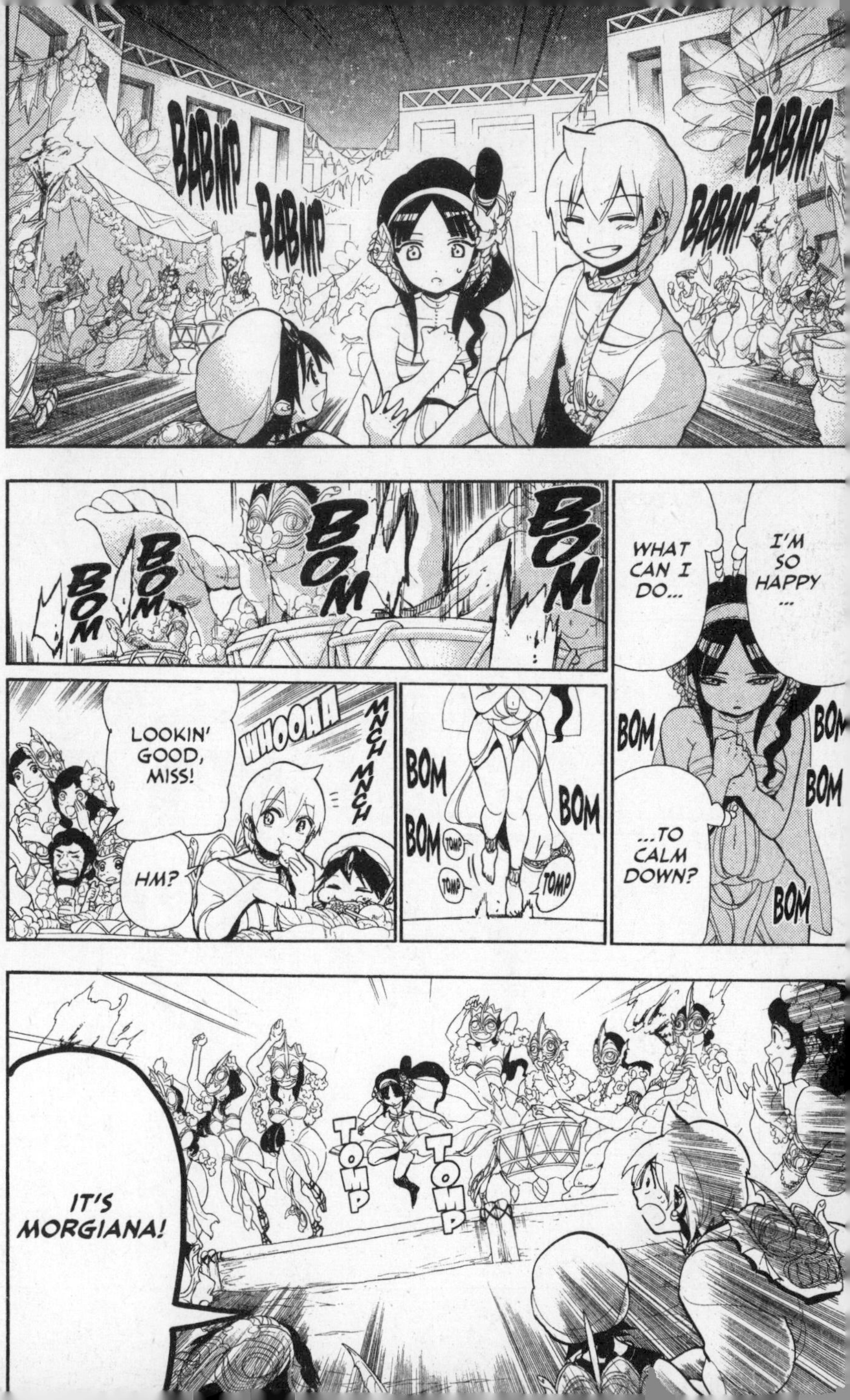
BABMP
BABMP
BABMP
BABMP
I'M SO HAPPY ...
WHAT CAN I DO...
...TO CALM DOWN?
BOM
BOM
BOM
BOM
BOM
BOM
BOM
BOM
BOM
BOM
BOM
TOMP
TOMP
TOMP
WHOOAA
MNCH MNCH
LOOKIN' GOOD, MISS!
HM?
TOMP
TOMP
IT'S MORGIANA!

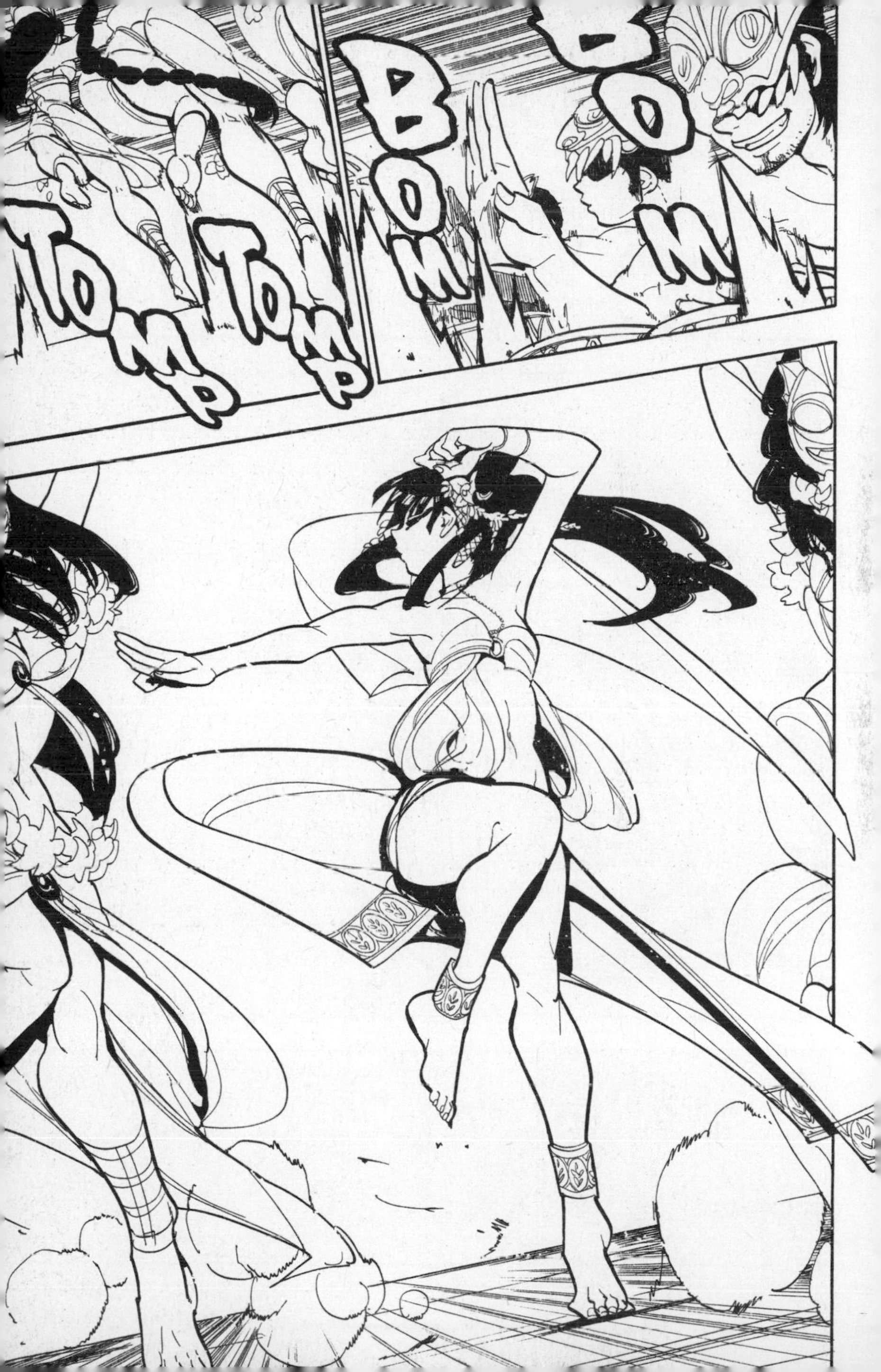
BOOM
BOOM
TOMP TOMP
TOMP

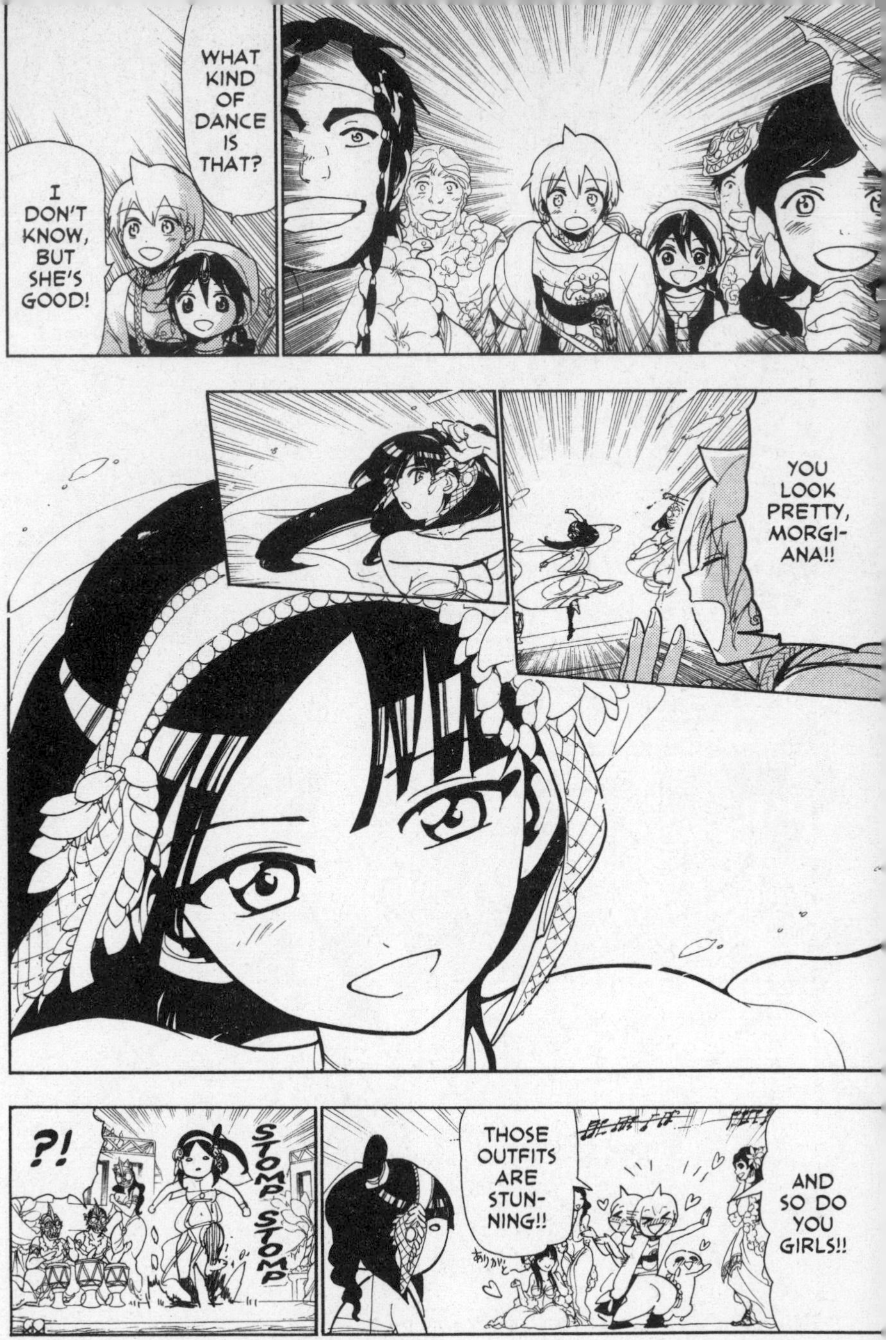
WHAT KIND OF DANCE IS THAT?
I DON'T KNOW, BUT SHE'S GOOD!
YOU LOOK PRETTY, MORGIANA!!
THOSE OUTFITS ARE STUN-NING!!
AND SO DO YOU GIRLS!!
ありがと～
?!
STOMP STOMP STOMP

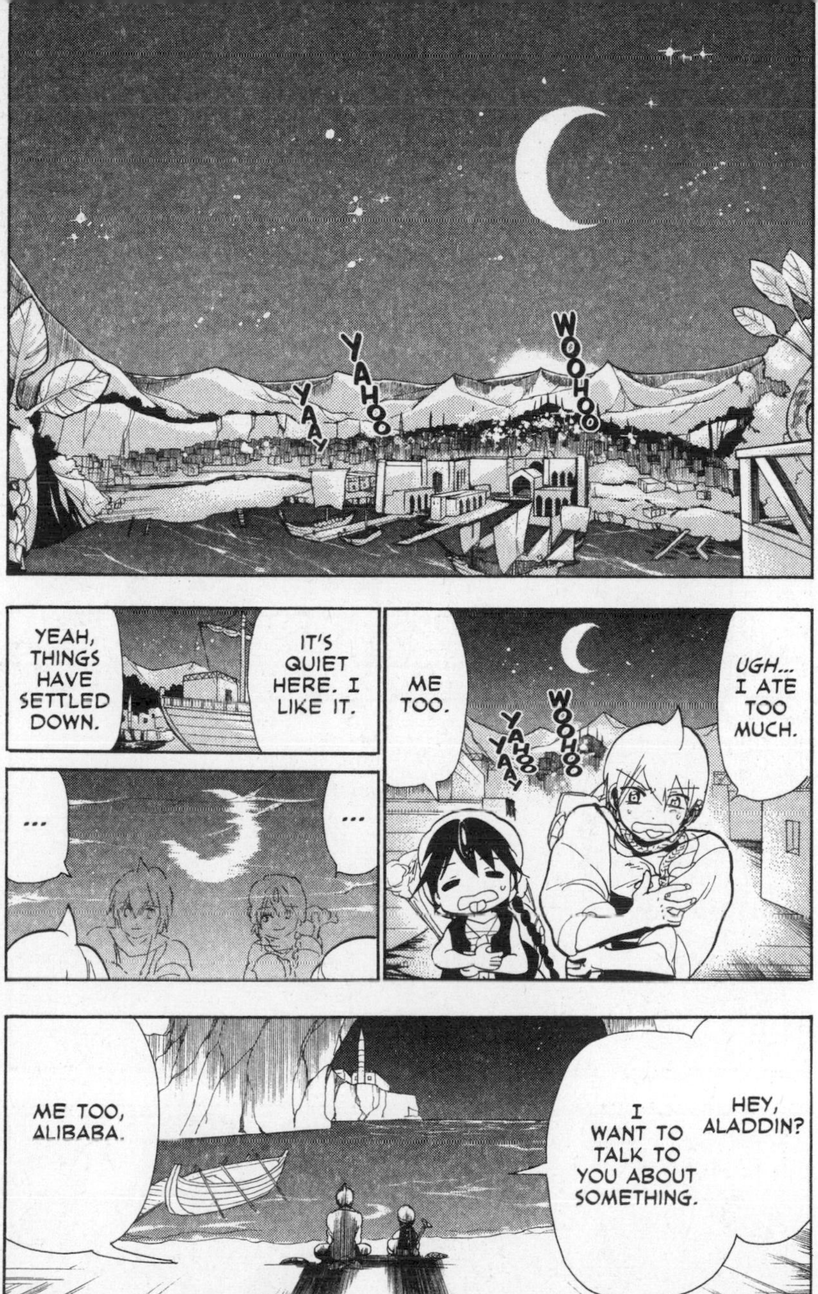
WOOHOO
YAHOO
YAAY
UGH... I ATE TOO MUCH.
WOOHOO
YAHOO
YAAY
ME TOO.
IT'S QUIET HERE. I LIKE IT.
YEAH, THINGS HAVE SETTLED DOWN.
...
...
HEY, ALADDIN?
I WANT TO TALK TO YOU ABOUT SOMETHING.
ME TOO, ALIBABA.

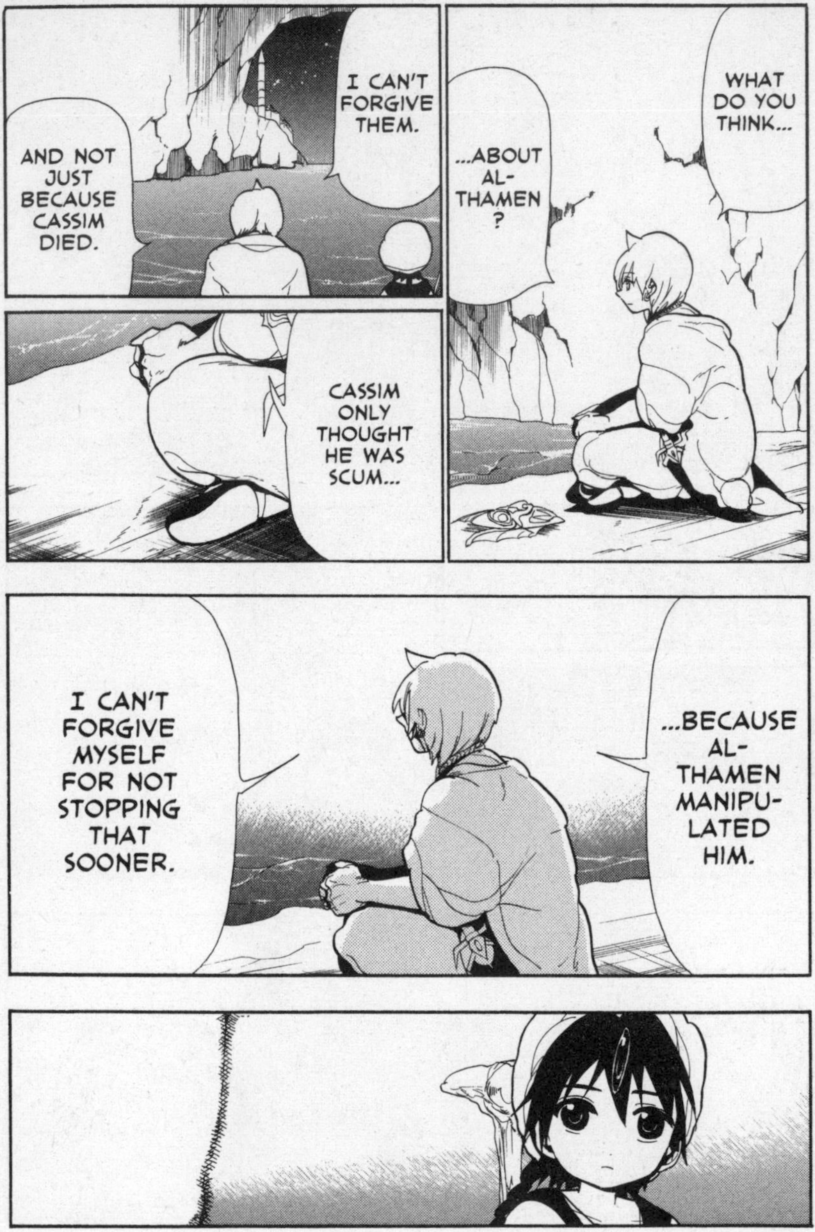
WHAT DO YOU THINK...
...ABOUT AL-THAMEN?
I CAN'T FORGIVE THEM.
AND NOT JUST BECAUSE CASSIM DIED.
CASSIM ONLY THOUGHT HE WAS SCUM...
...BECAUSE AL-THAMEN MANIPULATED HIM.
I CAN'T FORGIVE MYSELF FOR NOT STOPPING THAT SOONER.

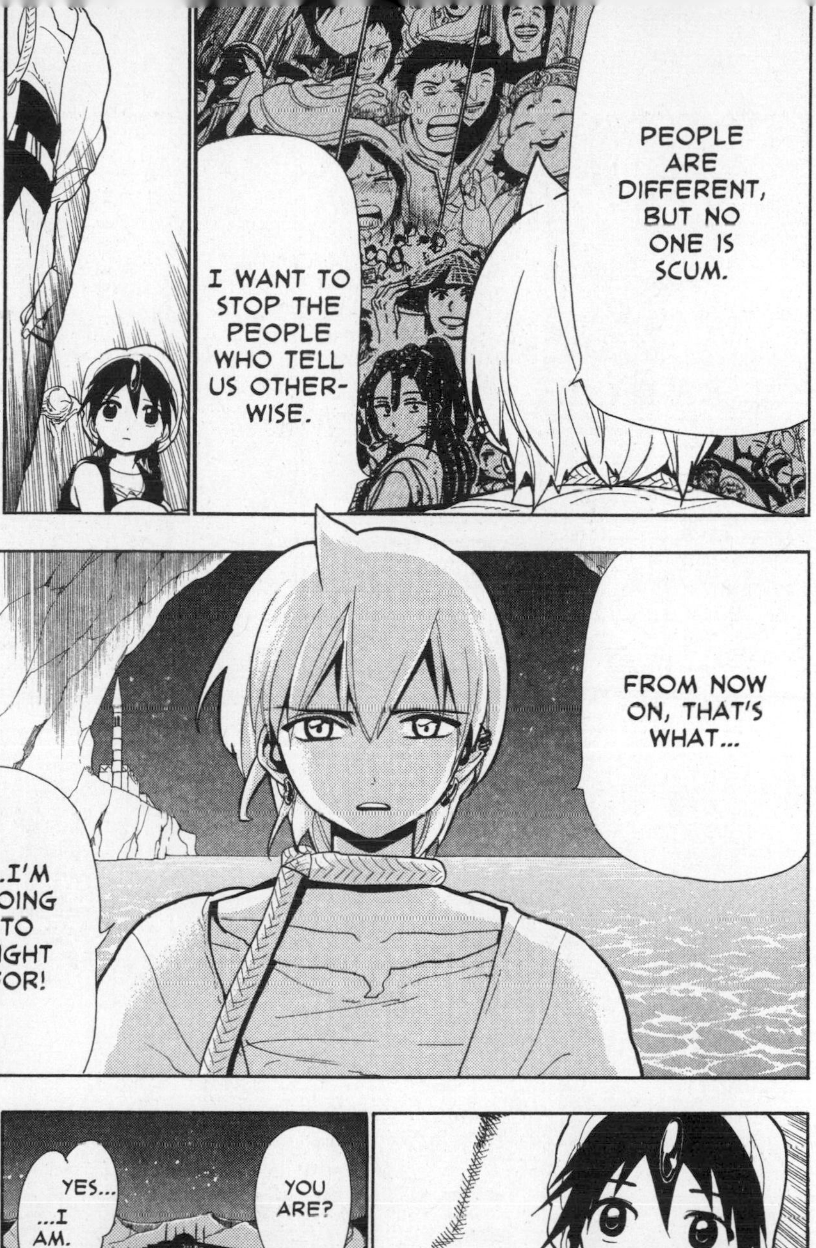
PEOPLE ARE DIFFERENT, BUT NO ONE IS SCUM.
I WANT TO STOP THE PEOPLE WHO TELL US OTHER-WISE.
FROM NOW ON, THAT'S WHAT...
...I'M GOING TO FIGHT FOR!
YOU ARE?
YES... ...I AM.

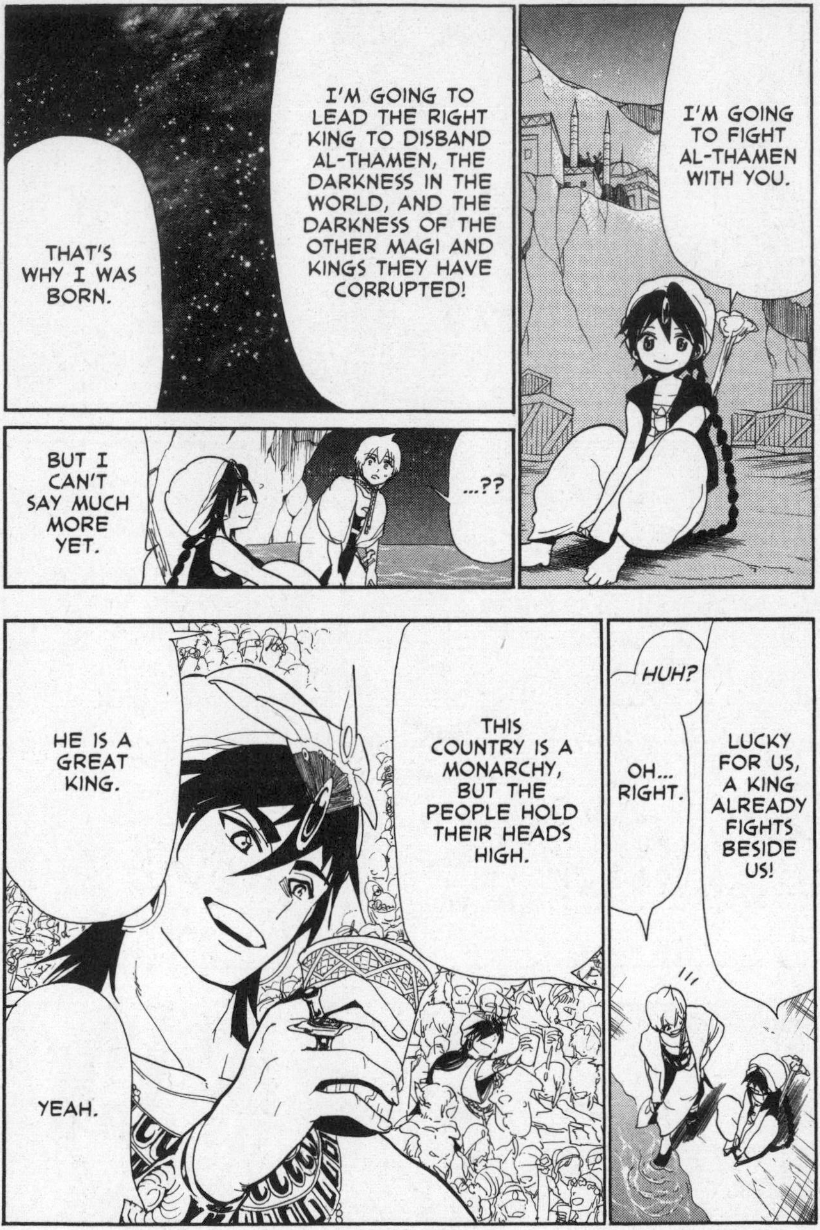

I'M GOING TO FIGHT AL-THAMEN WITH YOU.
I'M GOING TO LEAD THE RIGHT KING TO DISBAND AL-THAMEN, THE DARKNESS IN THE WORLD, AND THE DARKNESS OF THE OTHER MAGI AND KINGS THEY HAVE CORRUPTED!
THAT'S WHY I WAS BORN.
...??
BUT I CAN'T SAY MUCH MORE YET.
HUH?
LUCKY FOR US, A KING ALREADY FIGHTS BESIDE US!
OH... RIGHT.
THIS COUNTRY IS A MONARCHY, BUT THE PEOPLE HOLD THEIR HEADS HIGH.
HE IS A GREAT KING.
YEAH.

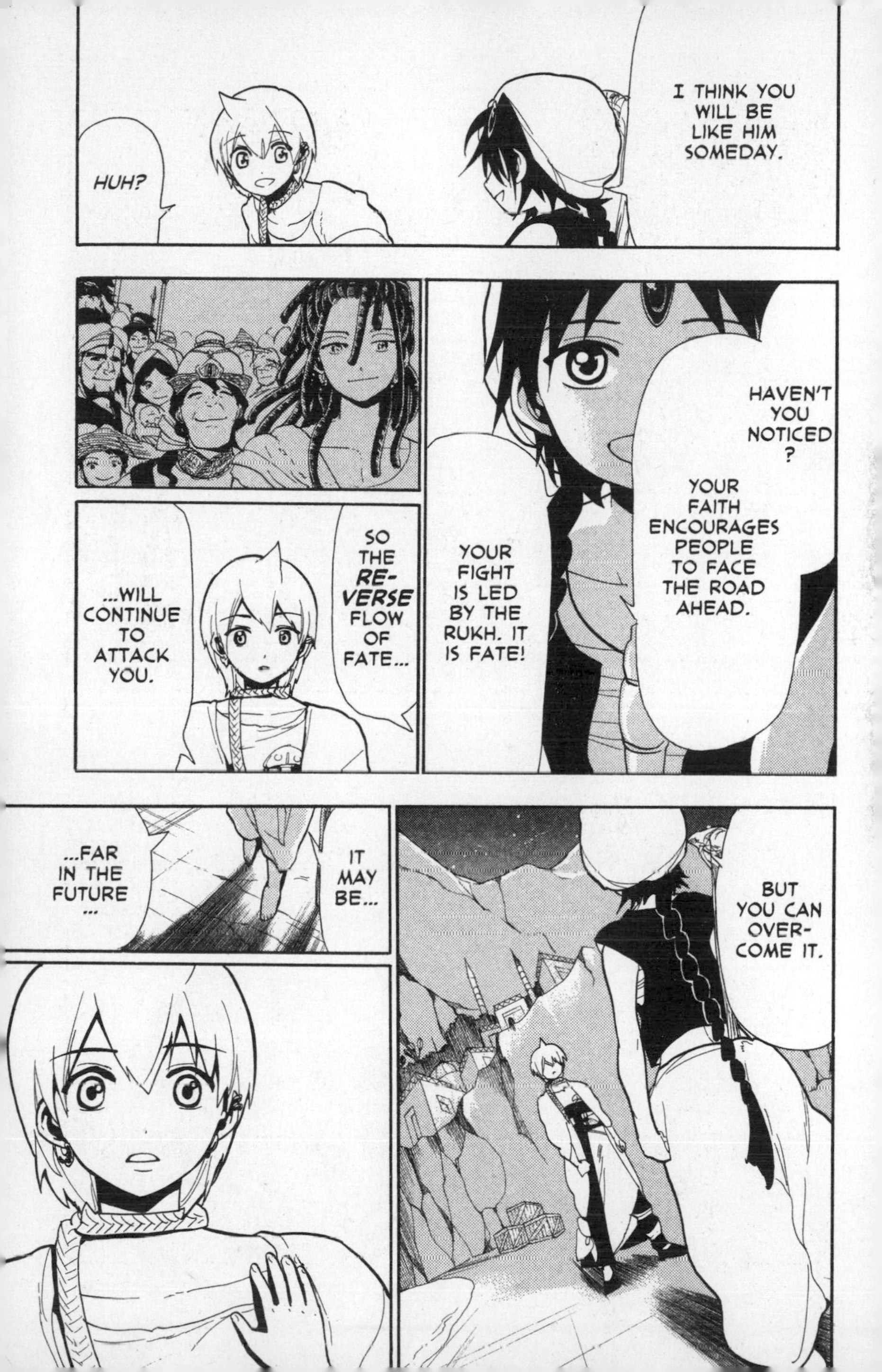
I THINK YOU WILL BE LIKE HIM SOMEDAY.
HUH?
HAVEN'T YOU NOTICED?
YOUR FAITH ENCOURAGES PEOPLE TO FACE THE ROAD AHEAD.
YOUR FIGHT IS LED BY THE RUKH. IT IS FATE!
SO THE *REVERSE* FLOW OF FATE...
...WILL CONTINUE TO ATTACK YOU.
BUT YOU CAN OVERCOME IT.
IT MAY BE...
...FAR IN THE FUTURE ...

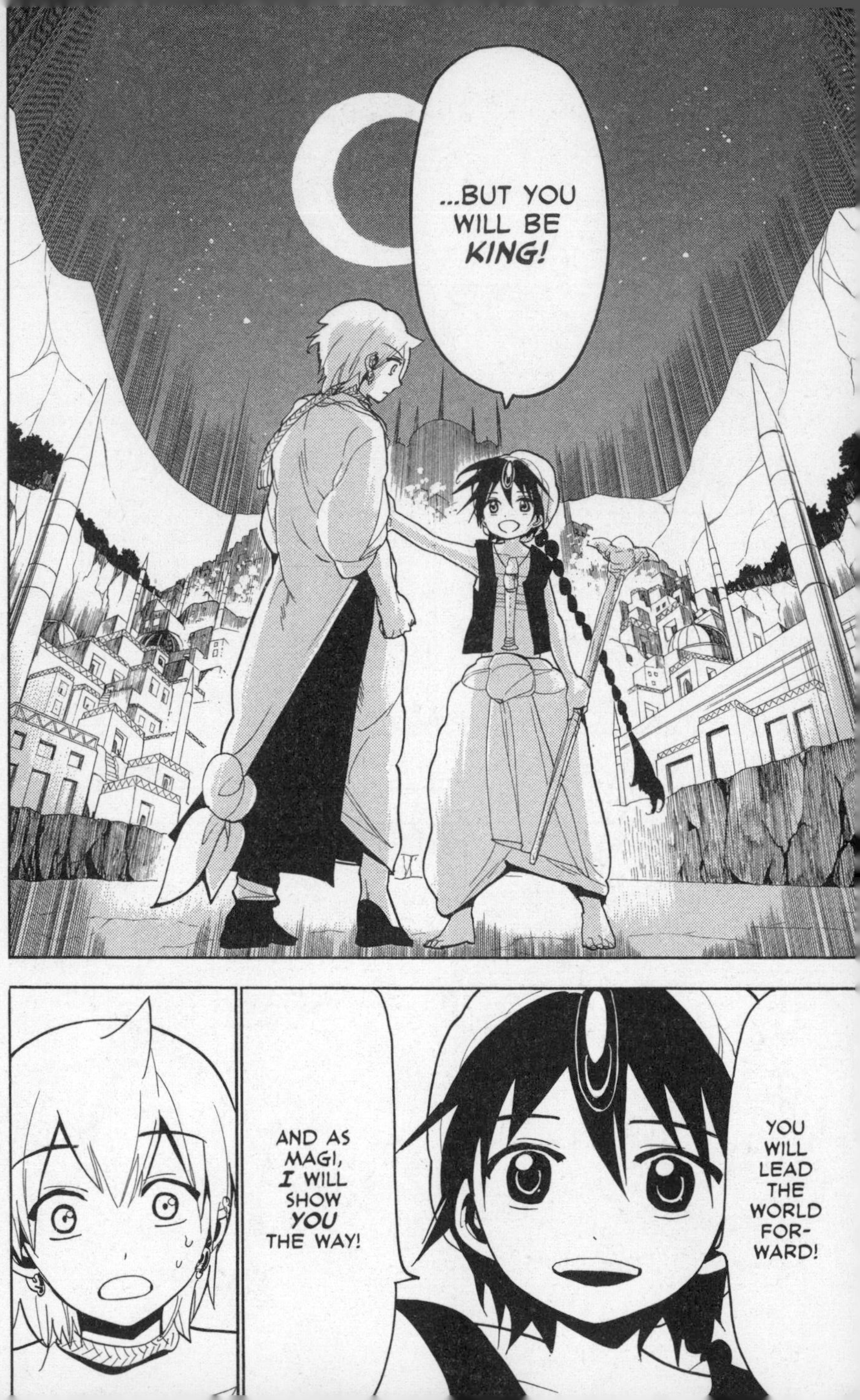
...BUT YOU WILL BE KING!
YOU WILL LEAD THE WORLD FOR-WARD!
AND AS MAGI, I WILL SHOW YOU THE WAY!

Night 82: A Big Country

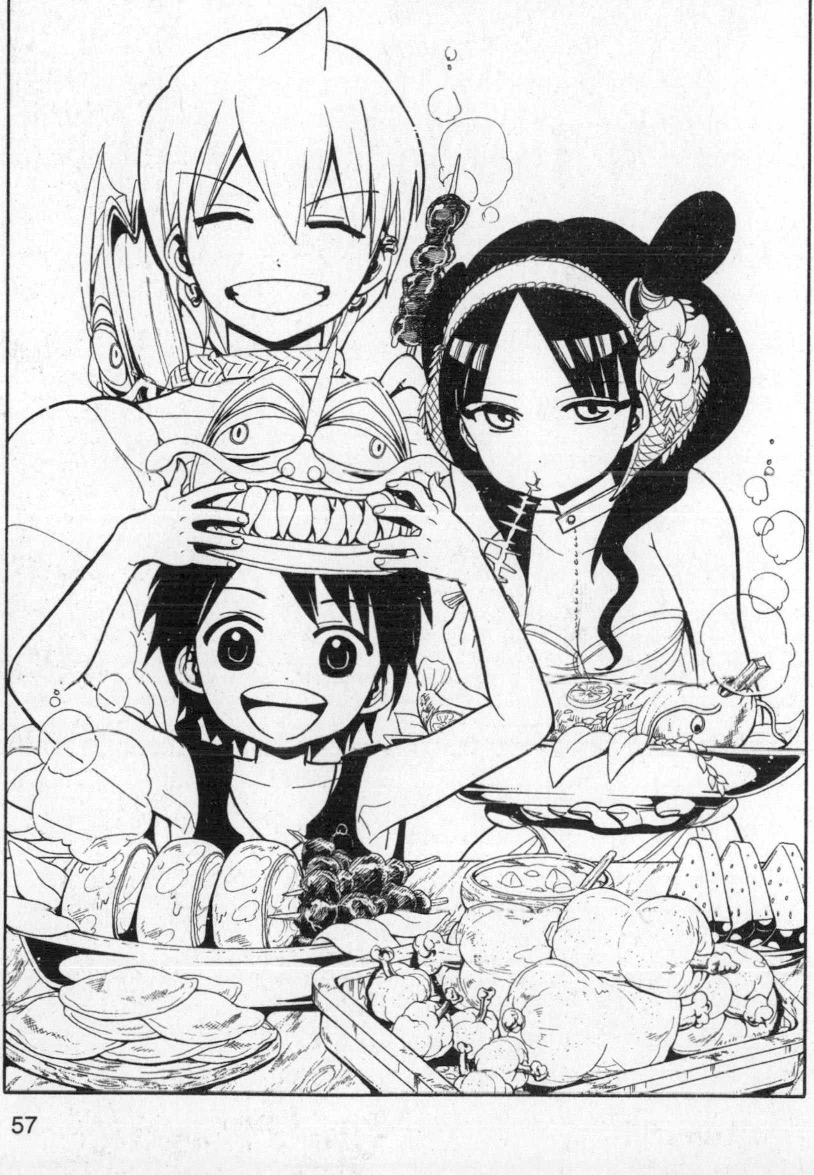

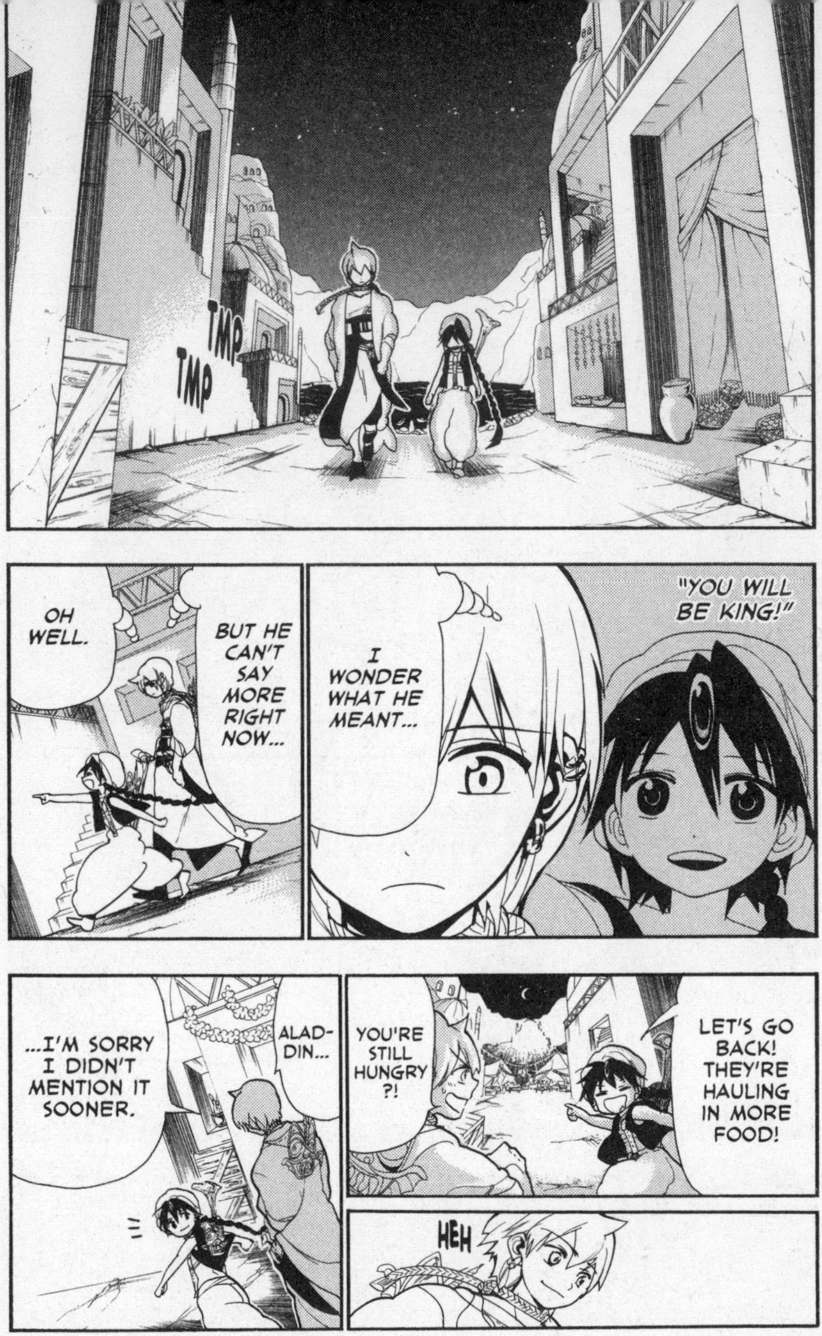
TMP
TMP
"YOU WILL BE KING!"
I WONDER WHAT HE MEANT...
BUT HE CAN'T SAY MORE RIGHT NOW...
OH WELL.
LET'S GO BACK! THEY'RE HAULING IN MORE FOOD!
YOU'RE STILL HUNGRY?!
HEH
ALAD-DIN...
...I'M SORRY I DIDN'T MENTION IT SOONER.

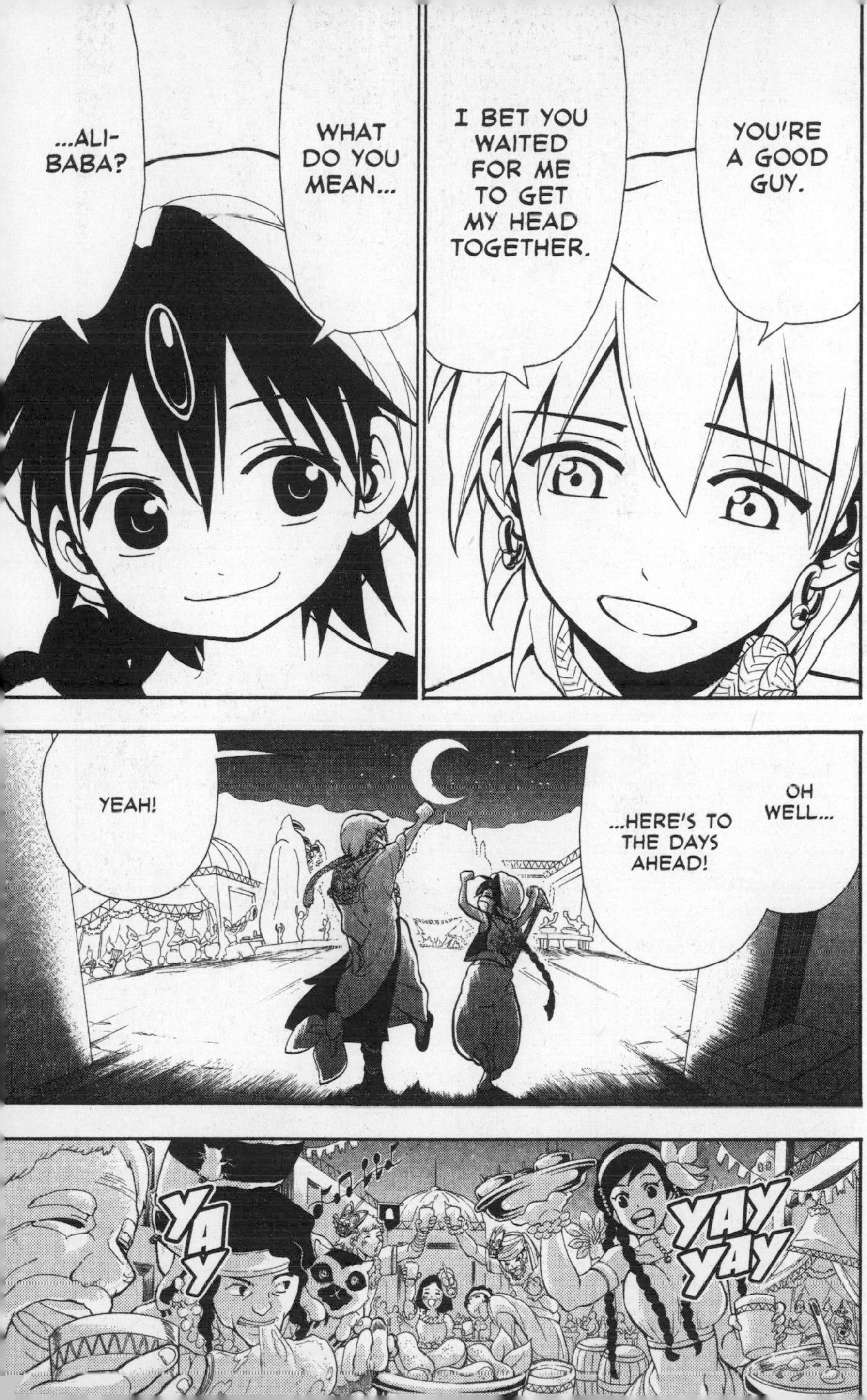
YOU'RE A GOOD GUY.
I BET YOU WAITED FOR ME TO GET MY HEAD TOGETHER.
WHAT DO YOU MEAN...
...ALI-BABA?
OH WELL...
...HERE'S TO THE DAYS AHEAD!
YEAH!
YAY YAY
YAY

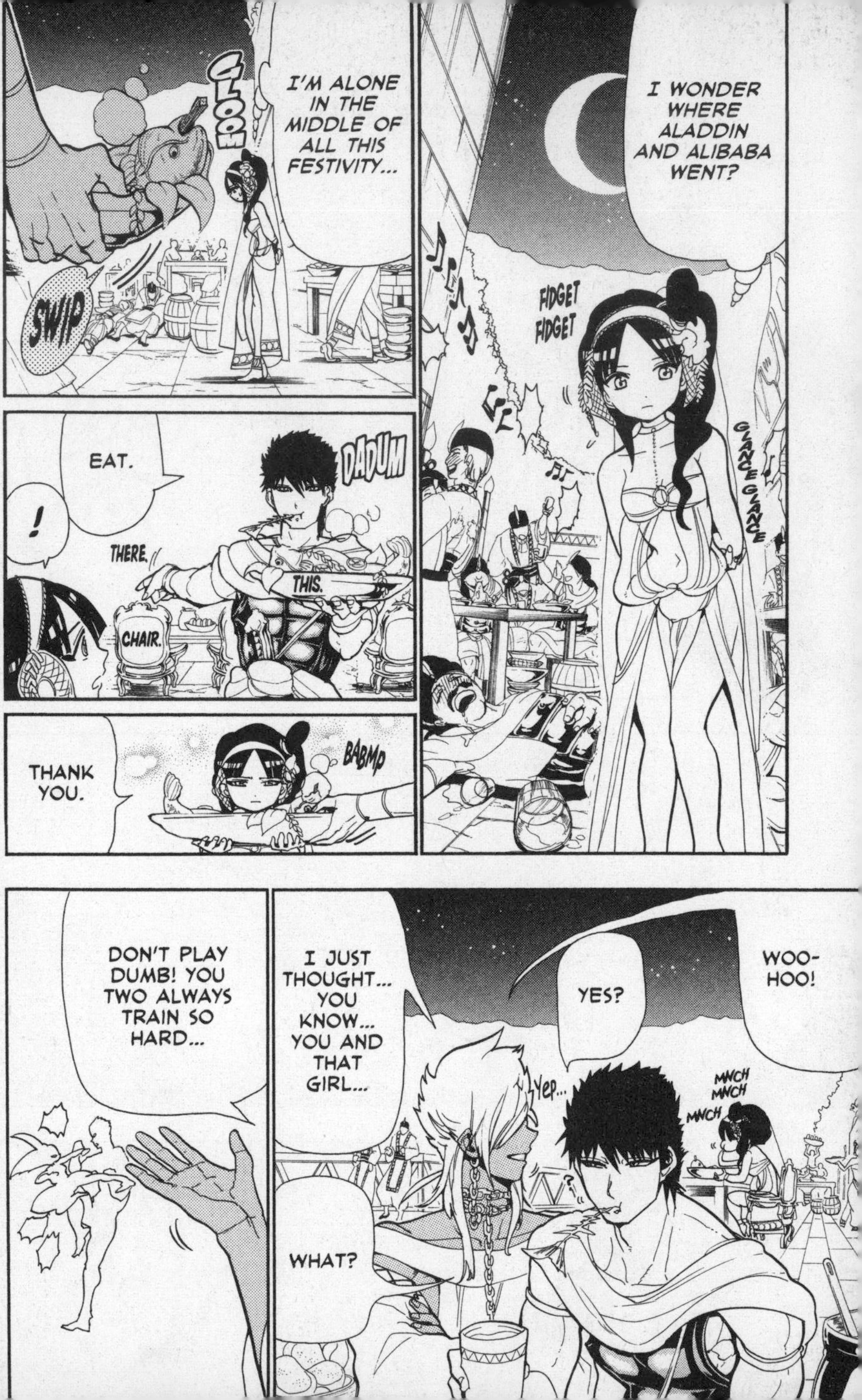
I WONDER WHERE ALADDIN AND ALIBABA WENT?
FIDGET FIDGET
GLANCE GLANCE
GLOOM
I'M ALONE IN THE MIDDLE OF ALL THIS FESTIVITY...
SWIP
DADUM
EAT.
!
THERE.
THIS.
CHAIR.
BABMP
THANK YOU.
WOO-HOO!
YES?
MNCH MNCH MNCH
Yep...
I JUST THOUGHT... YOU KNOW... YOU AND THAT GIRL...
WHAT?
DON'T PLAY DUMB! YOU TWO ALWAYS TRAIN SO HARD...

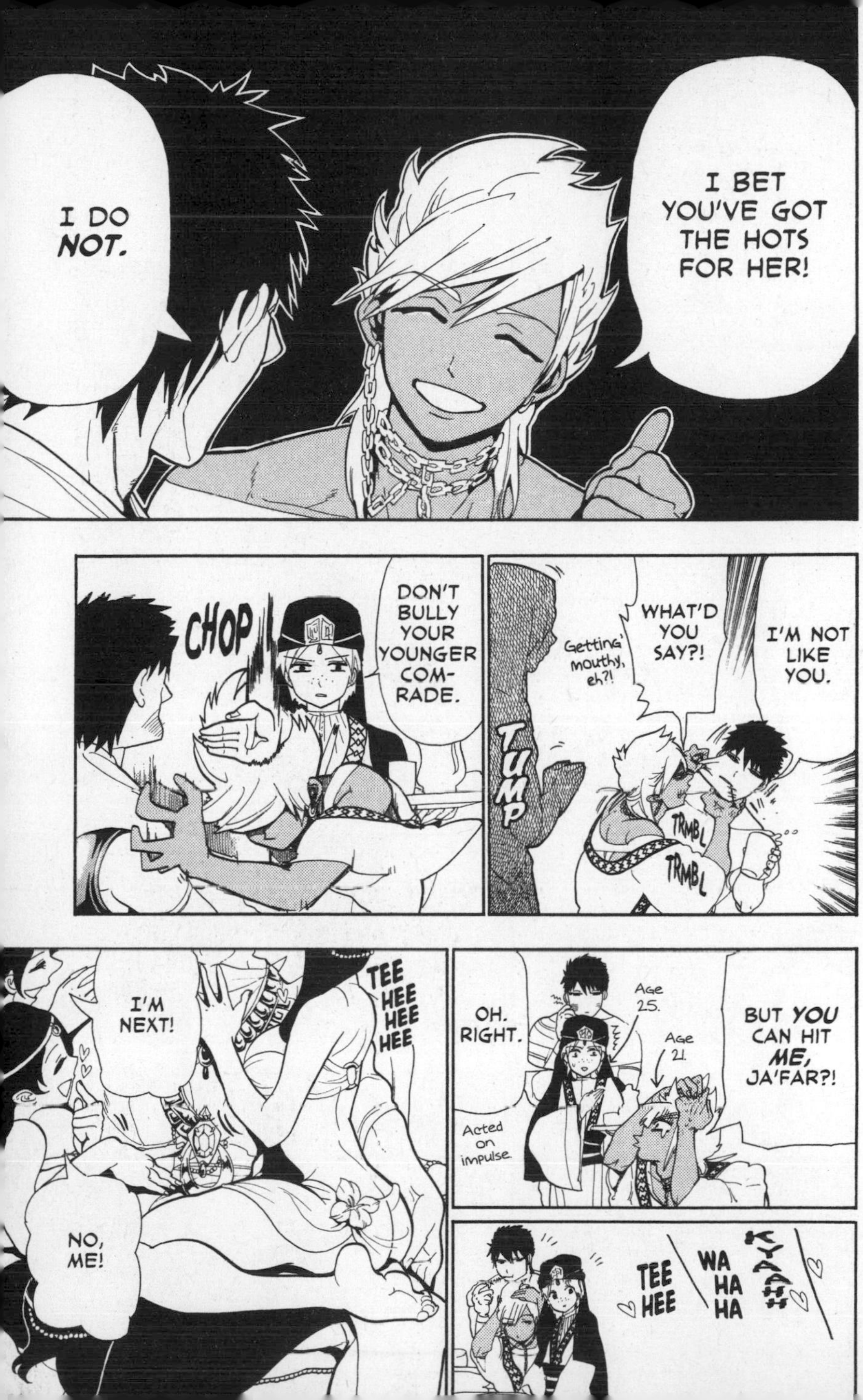

I BET YOU'VE GOT THE HOTS FOR HER!
I DO NOT.
I'M NOT LIKE YOU.
WHAT'D YOU SAY?!
Getting' mouthy, eh?!
TRMBL
TRMBL
TUMP
DON'T BULLY YOUR YOUNGER COM-RADE.
CHOP
BUT YOU CAN HIT ME, JA'FAR?!
Age 21.
Age 25.
OH. RIGHT.
Acted on impulse.
KYAAHH
WA HA HA
TEE HEE
TEE HEE HEE HEE
I'M NEXT!
NO, ME!

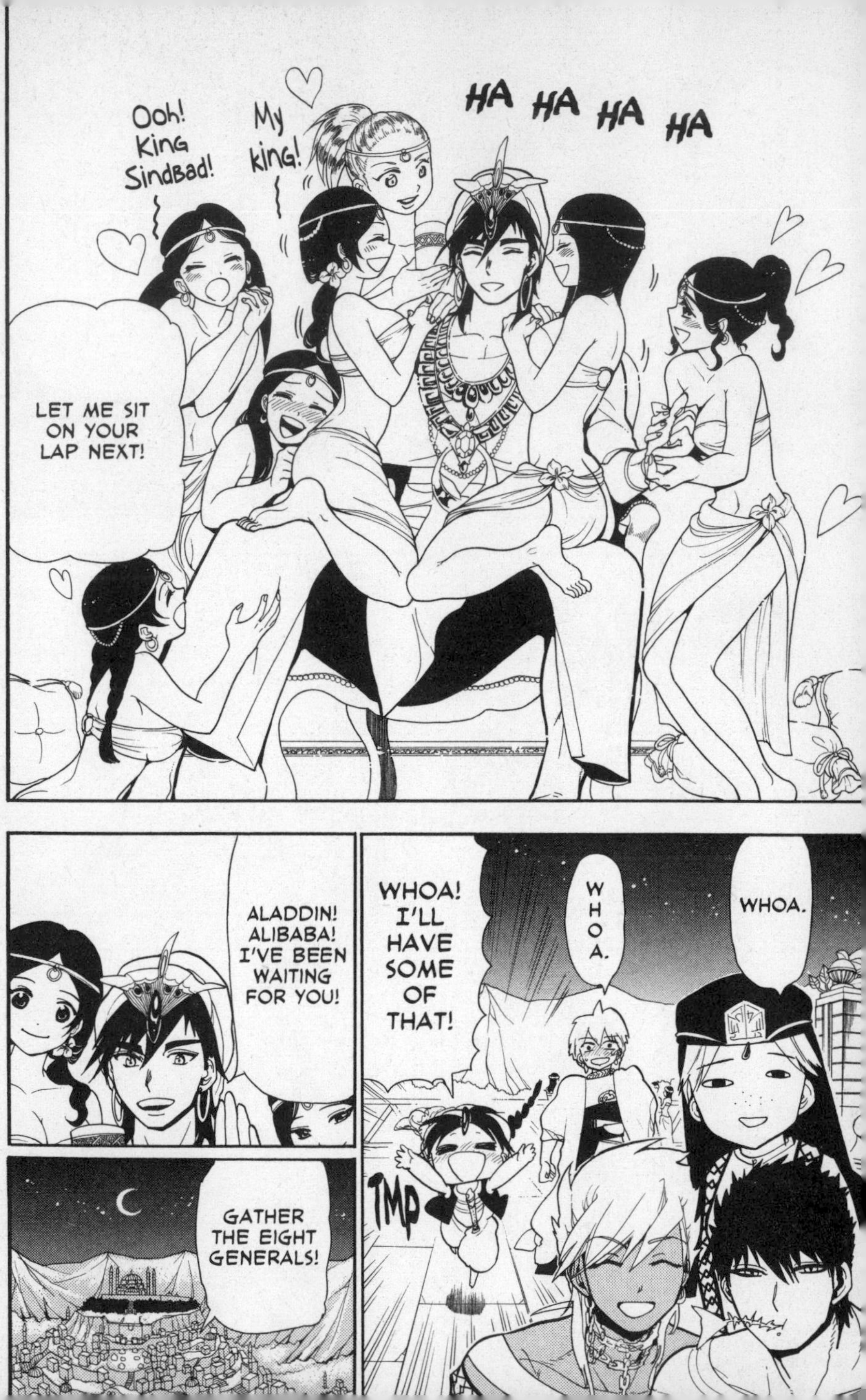
HA HA HA HA
My king!
Ooh! King Sindbad!
LET ME SIT ON YOUR LAP NEXT!
WHOA.
WHOA.
WHOA! I'LL HAVE SOME OF THAT!
TMP
ALADDIN! ALIBABA! I'VE BEEN WAITING FOR YOU!
GATHER THE EIGHT GENERALS!

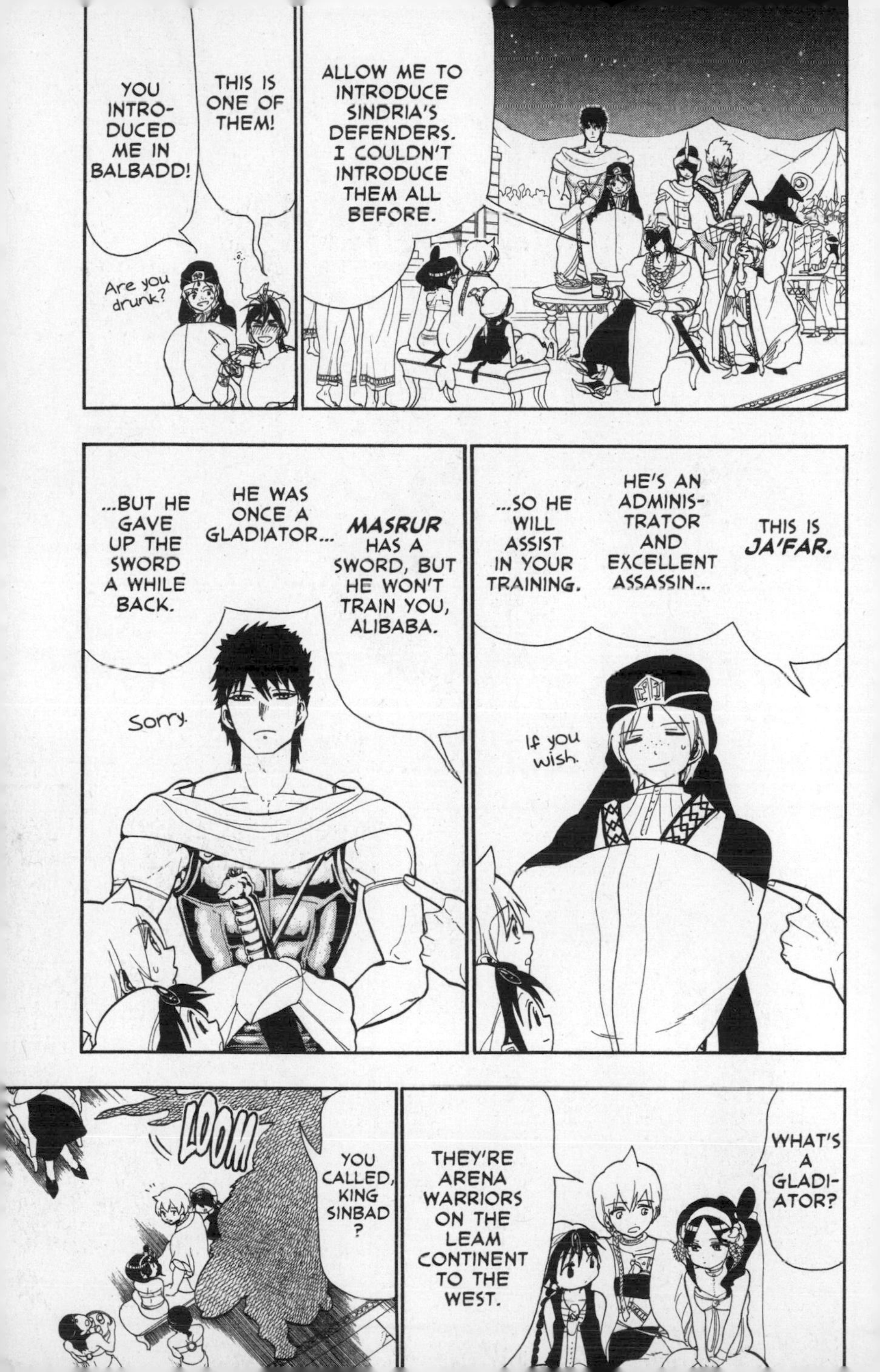
ALLOW ME TO INTRODUCE SINDRIA'S DEFENDERS. I COULDN'T INTRODUCE THEM ALL BEFORE.
THIS IS ONE OF THEM!
YOU INTRO-DUCED ME IN BALBADD!
Are you drunk?
THIS IS JA'FAR.
HE'S AN ADMINIS-TRATOR AND EXCELLENT ASSASSIN...
...SO HE WILL ASSIST IN YOUR TRAINING.
If you wish.
MASRUR HAS A SWORD, BUT HE WON'T TRAIN YOU, ALIBABA.
HE WAS ONCE A GLADIATOR...
...BUT HE GAVE UP THE SWORD A WHILE BACK.
Sorry.
WHAT'S A GLADI-ATOR?
THEY'RE ARENA WARRIORS ON THE LEAM CONTINENT TO THE WEST.
YOU CALLED, KING SINBAD?
LOOM

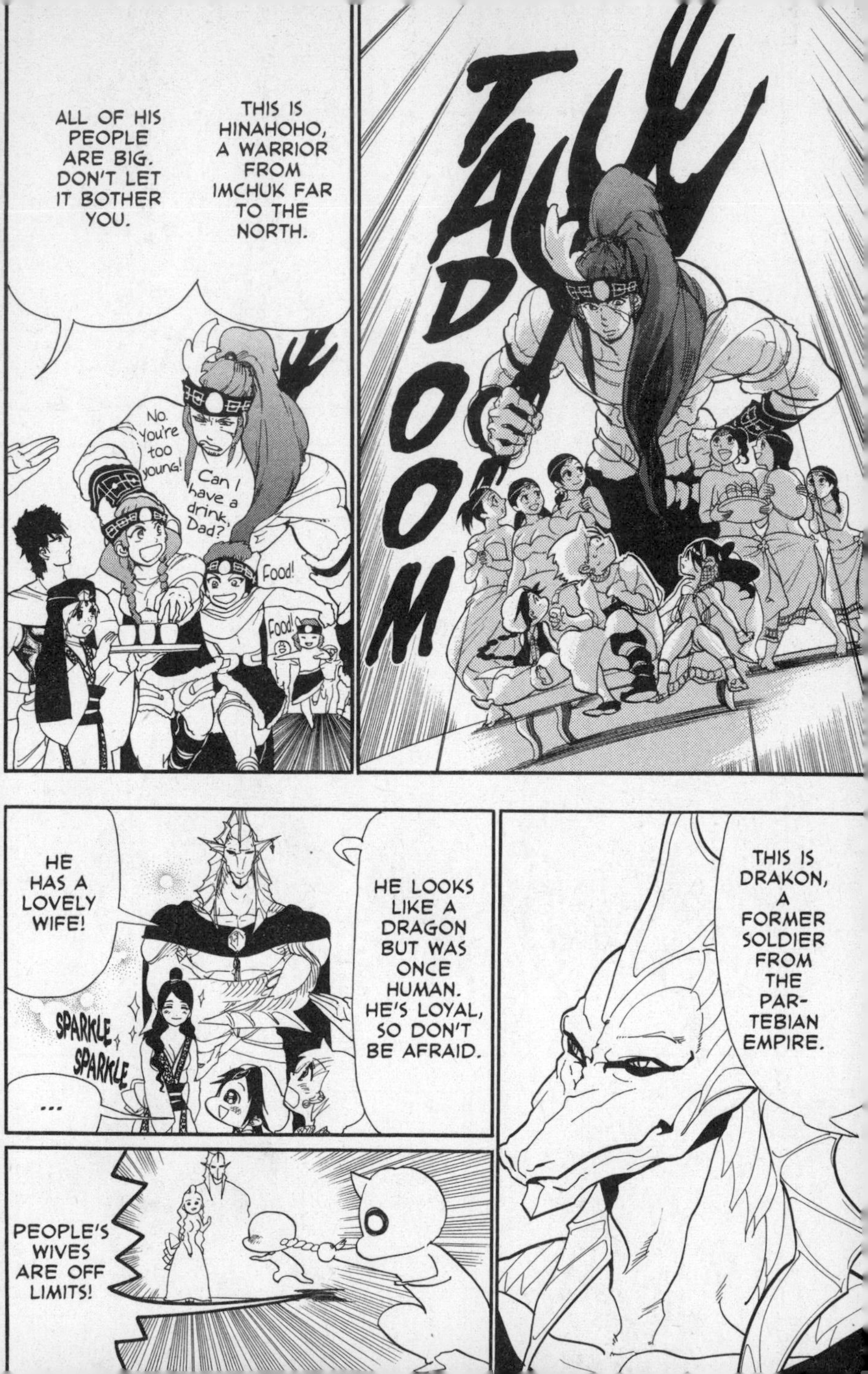
TADOOM
THIS IS HINAHOHO, A WARRIOR FROM IMCHUK FAR TO THE NORTH.
ALL OF HIS PEOPLE ARE BIG. DON'T LET IT BOTHER YOU.
Can I have a drink, Dad?
No. You're too young!
Food!
Food!
THIS IS DRAKON, A FORMER SOLDIER FROM THE PAR-TEBIAN EMPIRE.
HE LOOKS LIKE A DRAGON BUT WAS ONCE HUMAN. HE'S LOYAL, SO DON'T BE AFRAID.
HE HAS A LOVELY WIFE!
SPARKLE SPARKLE
...
PEOPLE'S WIVES ARE OFF LIMITS!

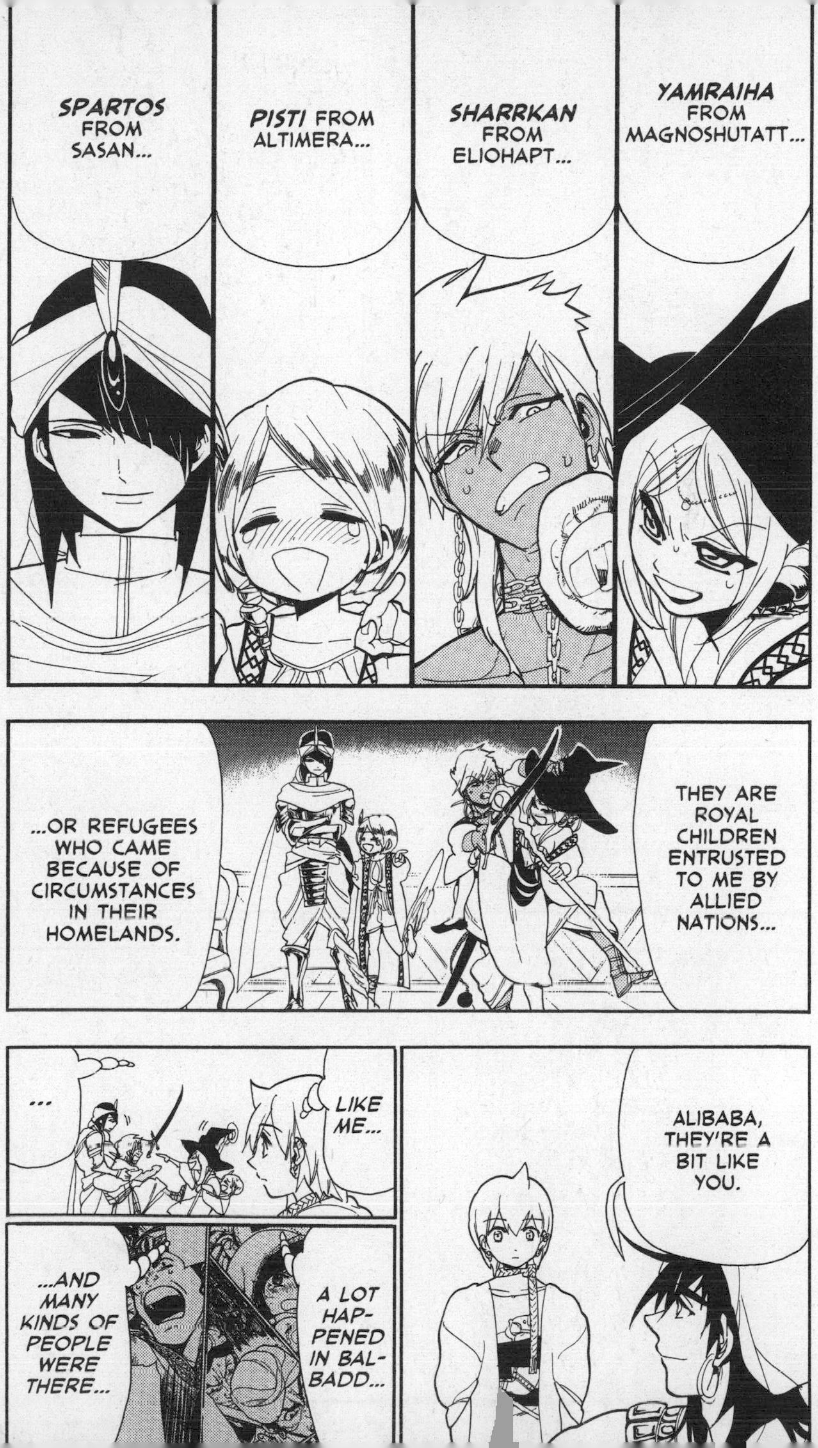
YAMRAIHA FROM MAGNOSHUTATT...
SHARRKAN FROM ELIOHAPT...
PISTI FROM ALTIMERA...
SPARTOS FROM SASAN...
THEY ARE ROYAL CHILDREN ENTRUSTED TO ME BY ALLIED NATIONS...
...OR REFUGEES WHO CAME BECAUSE OF CIRCUMSTANCES IN THEIR HOMELANDS.
ALIBABA, THEY'RE A BIT LIKE YOU.
LIKE ME...
...
A LOT HAP-PENED IN BAL-BADD...
...AND MANY KINDS OF PEOPLE WERE THERE...

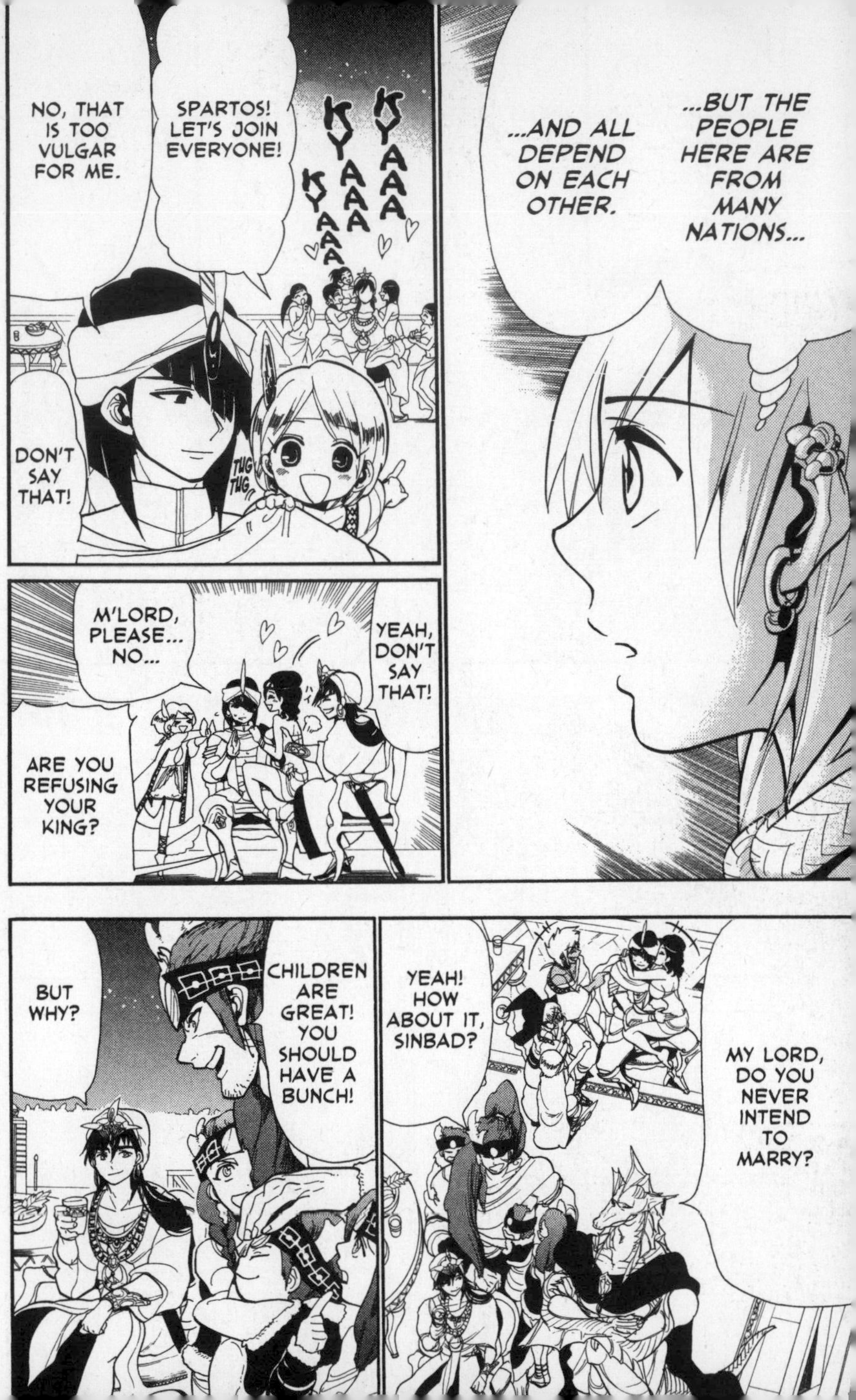
...BUT THE PEOPLE HERE ARE FROM MANY NATIONS...
...AND ALL DEPEND ON EACH OTHER.
KYAAA KYAAA KYAAA
SPARTOS! LET'S JOIN EVERYONE!
NO, THAT IS TOO VULGAR FOR ME.
TUG TUG
DON'T SAY THAT!
YEAH, DON'T SAY THAT!
M'LORD, PLEASE... NO...
ARE YOU REFUSING YOUR KING?
MY LORD, DO YOU NEVER INTEND TO MARRY?
YEAH! HOW ABOUT IT, SINBAD?
CHILDREN ARE GREAT! YOU SHOULD HAVE A BUNCH!
BUT WHY?

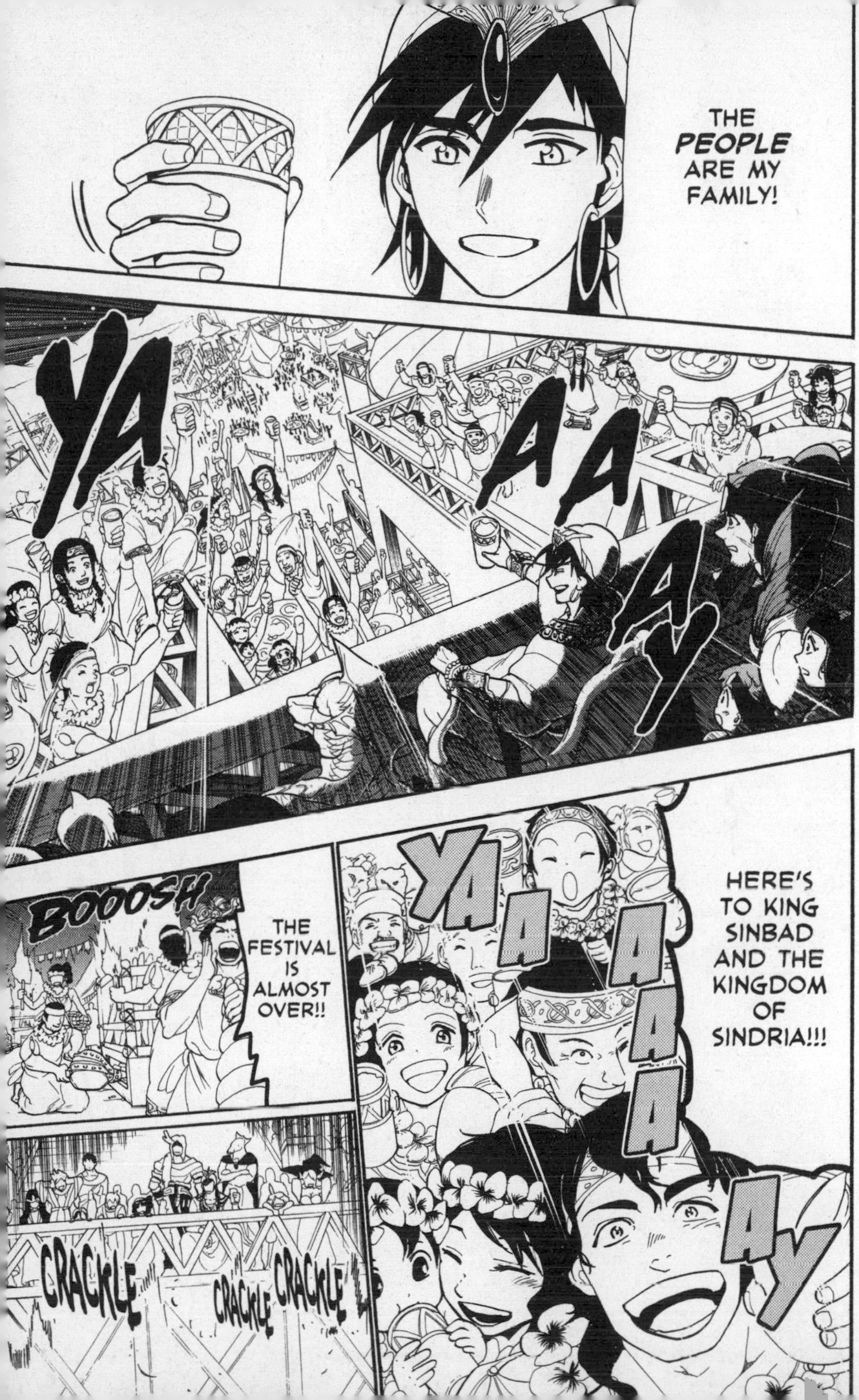
THE PEOPLE ARE MY FAMILY!
YAAAAAY
HERE'S TO KING SINBAD AND THE KINGDOM OF SINDRIA!!!
YAAAAAAAY
BOOOSH
THE FESTIVAL IS ALMOST OVER!!
CRACKLE
CRACKLE CRACKLE

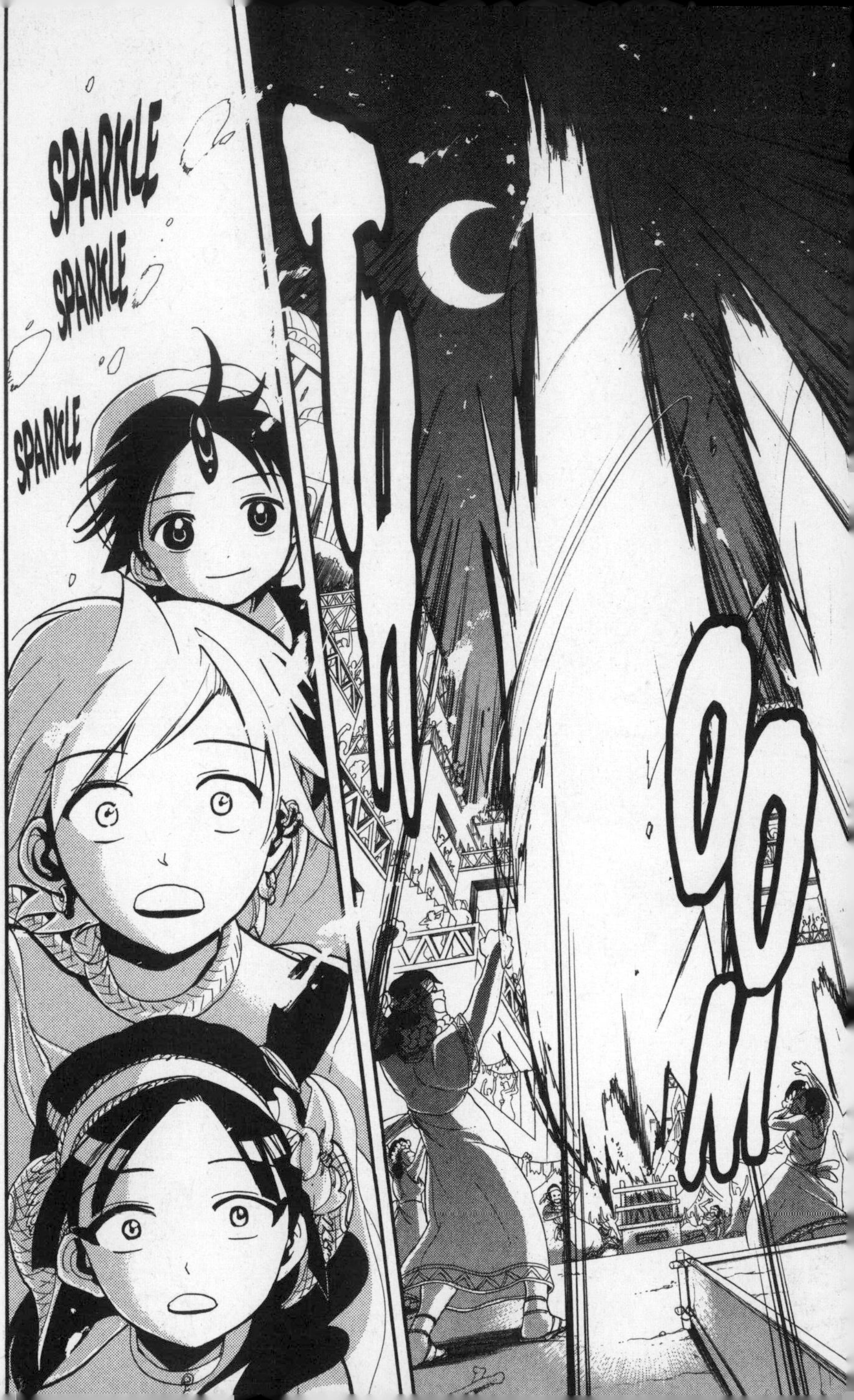
SPARKLE
SPARKLE
SPARKLE

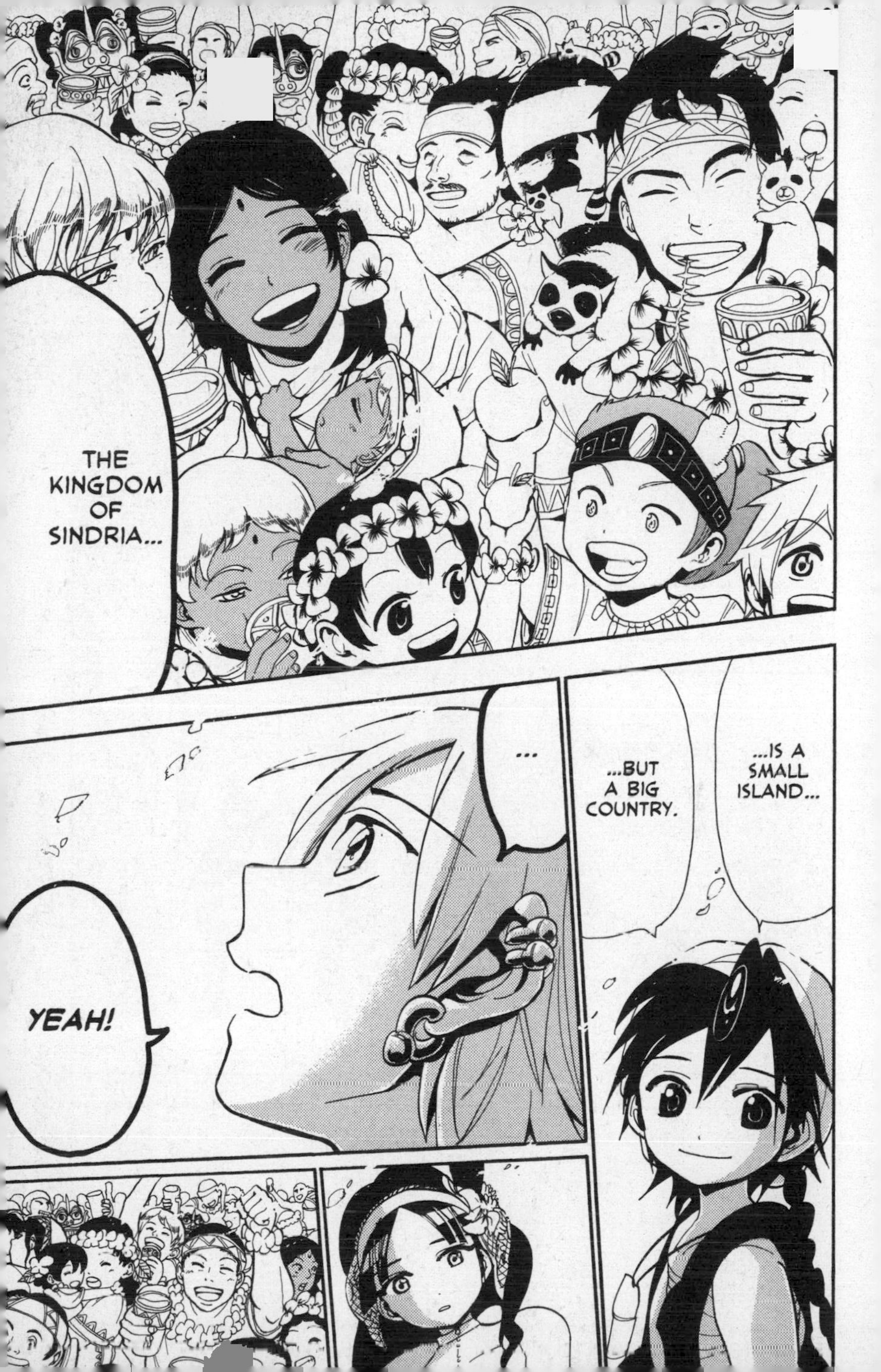
THE KINGDOM OF SINDRIA...
...IS A SMALL ISLAND...
...BUT A BIG COUNTRY.
...
YEAH!

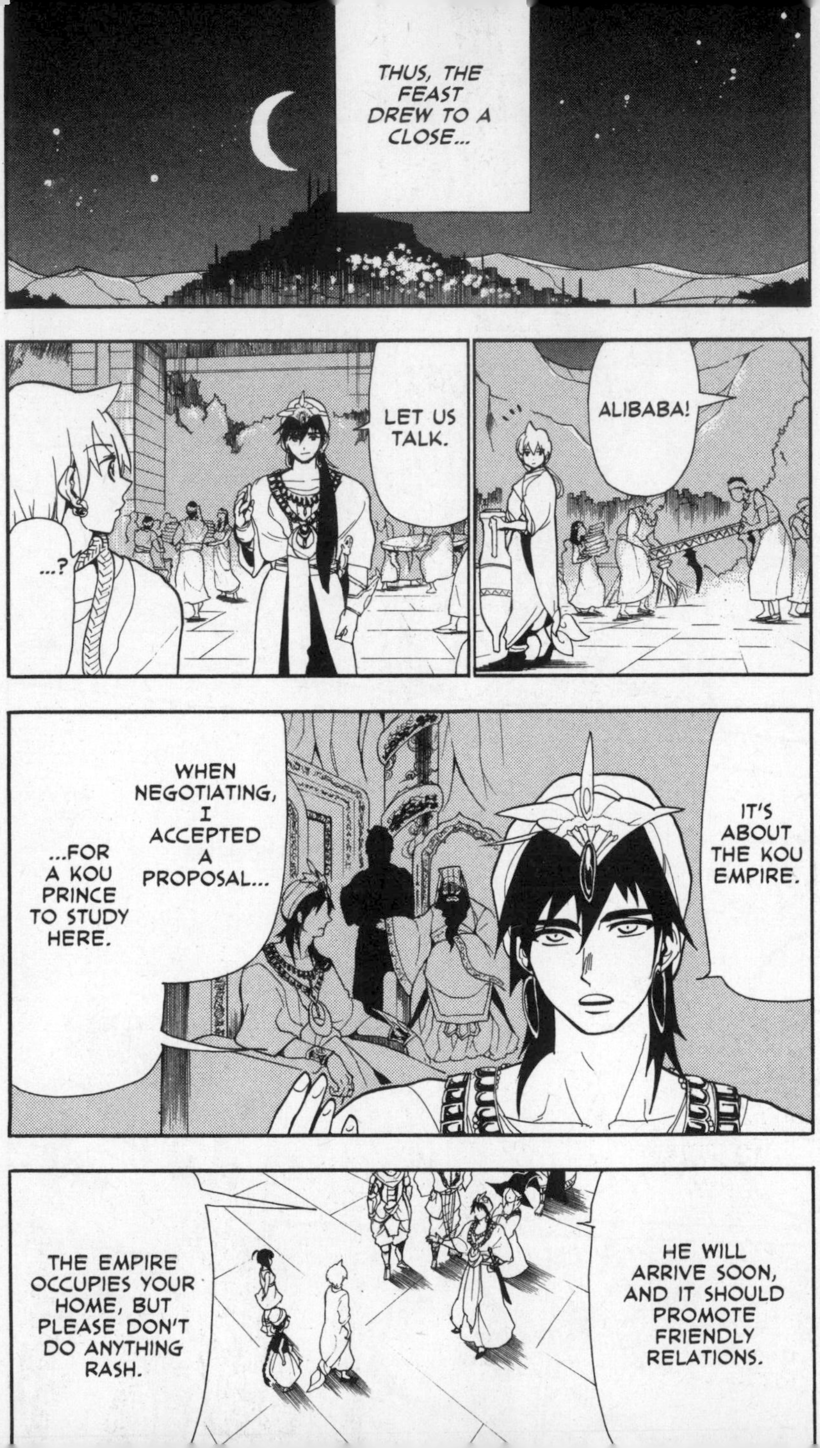
THUS, THE FEAST DREW TO A CLOSE...
ALIBABA!
LET US TALK.
...?
IT'S ABOUT THE KOU EMPIRE.
WHEN NEGOTIATING, I ACCEPTED A PROPOSAL...
...FOR A KOU PRINCE TO STUDY HERE.
HE WILL ARRIVE SOON, AND IT SHOULD PROMOTE FRIENDLY RELATIONS.
THE EMPIRE OCCUPIES YOUR HOME, BUT PLEASE DON'T DO ANYTHING RASH.

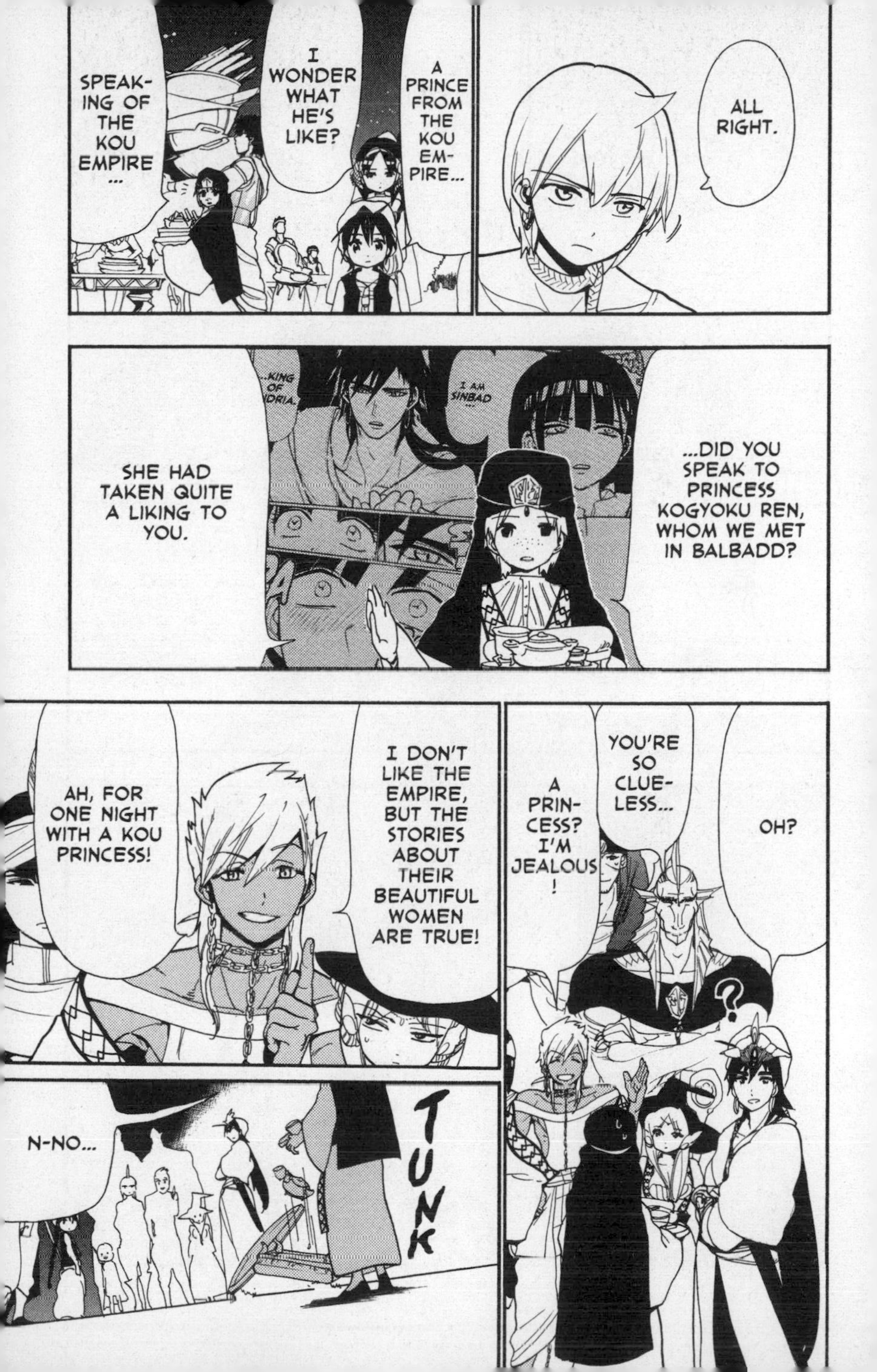
ALL RIGHT.
A PRINCE FROM THE KOU EMPIRE...
I WONDER WHAT HE'S LIKE?
SPEAKING OF THE KOU EMPIRE...
...DID YOU SPEAK TO PRINCESS KOGYOKU REN, WHOM WE MET IN BALBADD?
I AM SINBAD ...
...KING OF DRIA.
SHE HAD TAKEN QUITE A LIKING TO YOU.
OH?
YOU'RE SO CLUELESS...
A PRINCESS? I'M JEALOUS!
I DON'T LIKE THE EMPIRE, BUT THE STORIES ABOUT THEIR BEAUTIFUL WOMEN ARE TRUE!
AH, FOR ONE NIGHT WITH A KOU PRINCESS!
TUNK
N-NO...

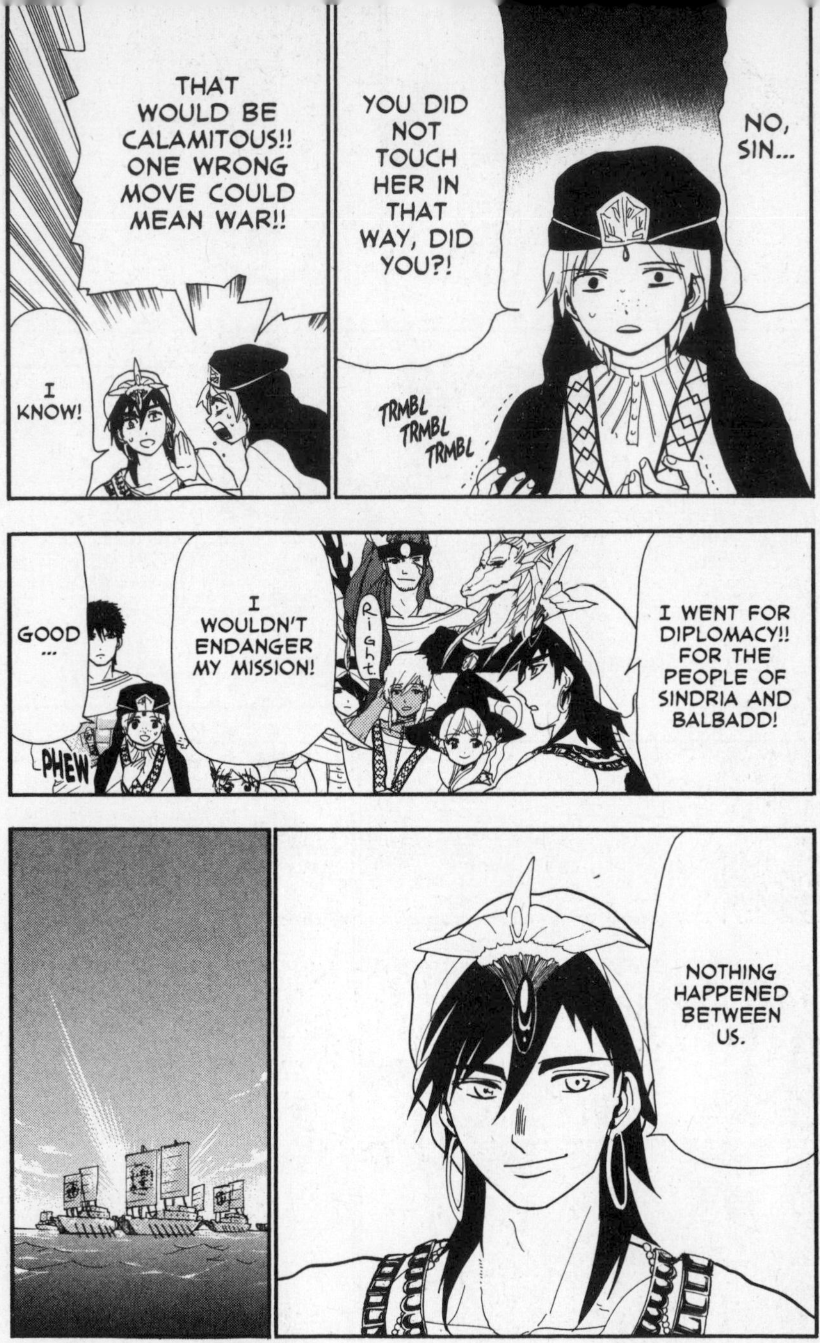
NO, SIN...
YOU DID NOT TOUCH HER IN THAT WAY, DID YOU?!
TRMBL TRMBL TRMBL
THAT WOULD BE CALAMITOUS!! ONE WRONG MOVE COULD MEAN WAR!!
I KNOW!
I WENT FOR DIPLOMACY!! FOR THE PEOPLE OF SINDRIA AND BALBADD!
Right.
I WOULDN'T ENDANGER MY MISSION!
GOOD ...
PHEW
NOTHING HAPPENED BETWEEN US.

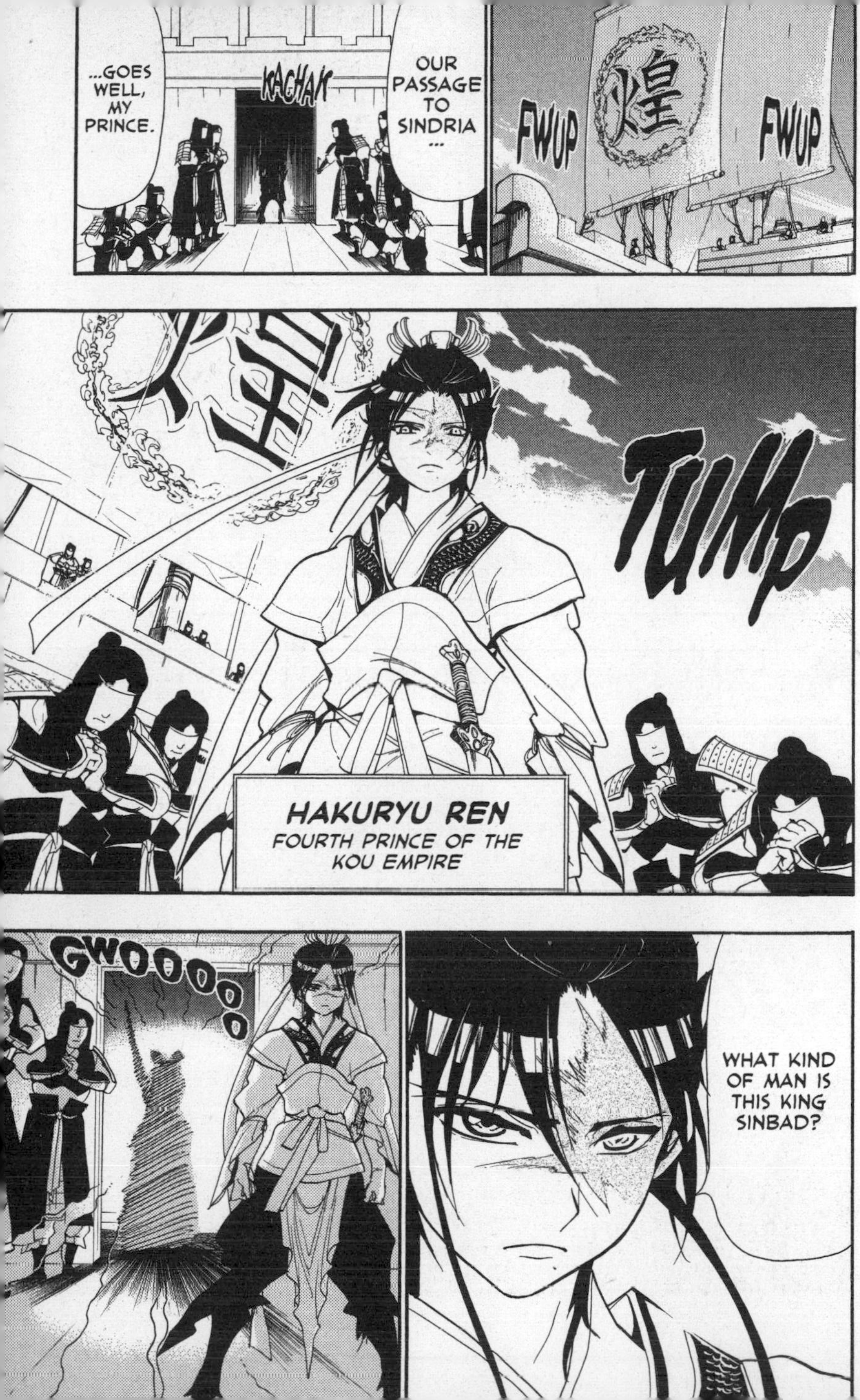
FWUP
煌
FWUP
OUR PASSAGE TO SINDRIA ...
KACHAK
...GOES WELL, MY PRINCE.
TuMp
HAKURYU REN
FOURTH PRINCE OF THE KOU EMPIRE
WHAT KIND OF MAN IS THIS KING SINBAD?
GWOOOOO

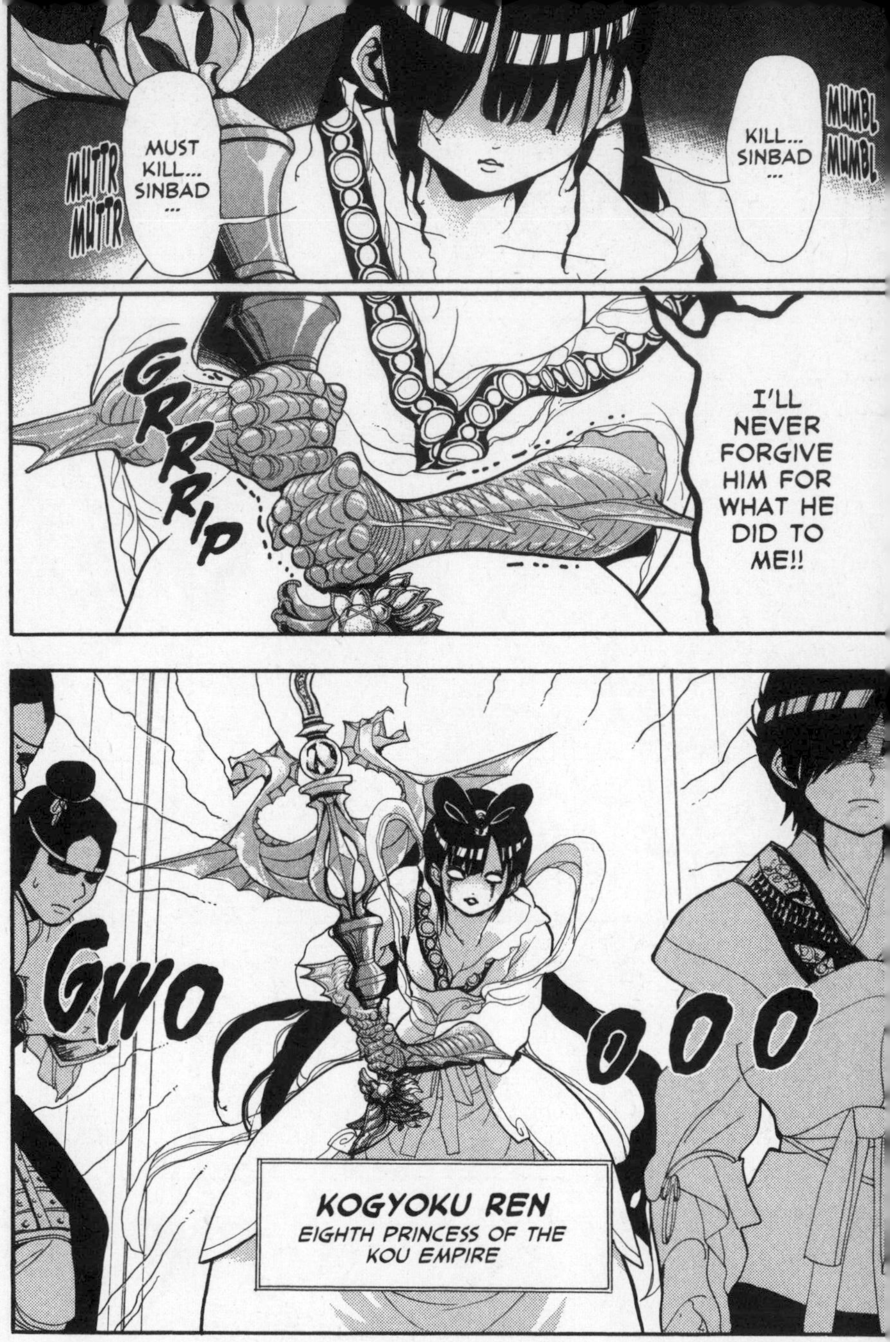
MUMBL MUMBL
KILL... SINBAD ...
MUST KILL... SINBAD ...
MUTTR MUTTR
I'LL NEVER FORGIVE HIM FOR WHAT HE DID TO ME!!
GRRRIP
GWO O O O
KOGYOKU REN
EIGHTH PRINCESS OF THE KOU EMPIRE

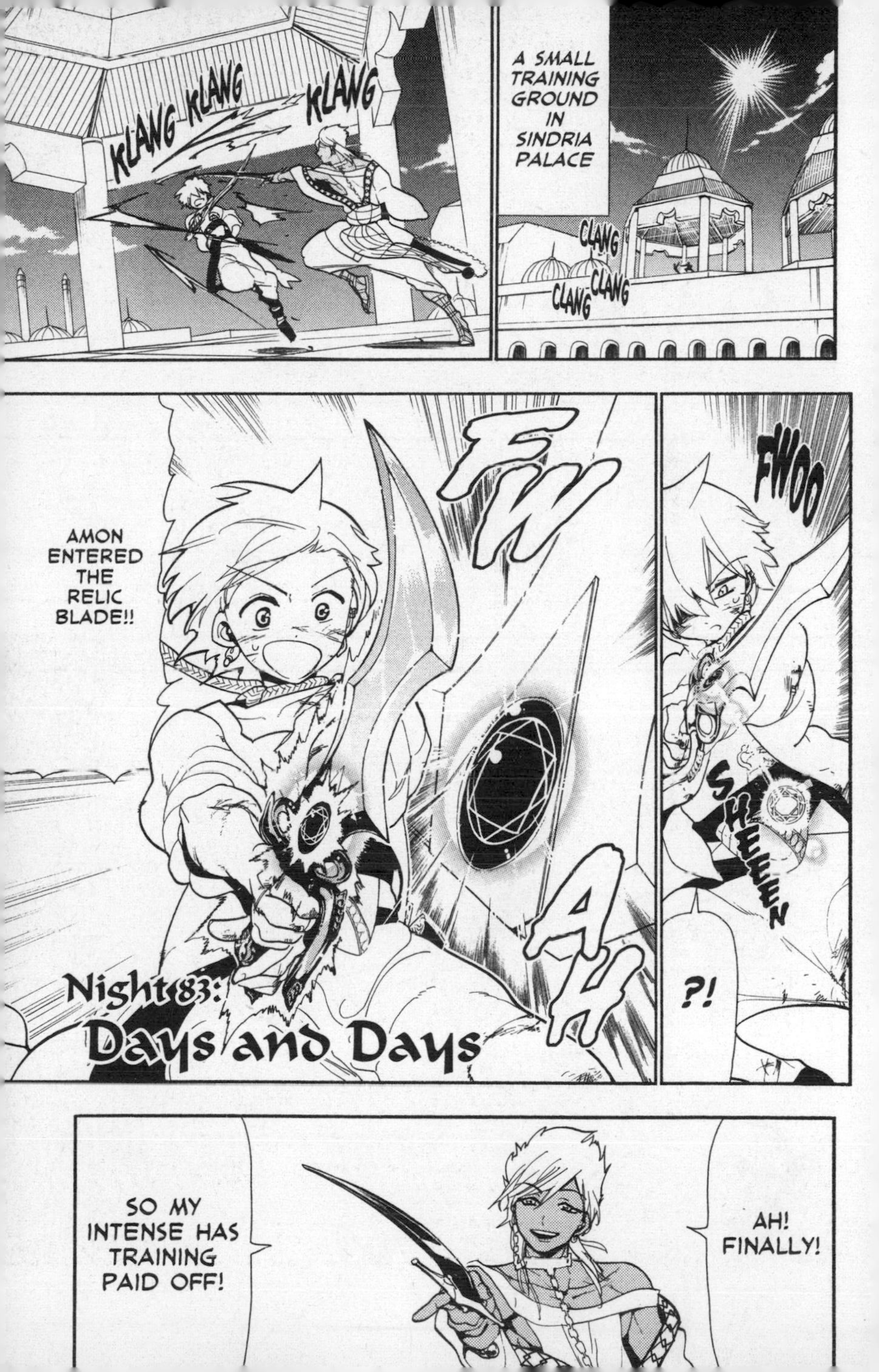
A SMALL TRAINING GROUND IN SINDRIA PALACE
CLANG
CLANG
CLANG
KLANG
KLANG
KLANG
FWOO
SHEEEN
?!
FW
AH
AMON ENTERED THE RELIC BLADE!!
Night 83: Days and Days
AH! FINALLY!
SO MY INTENSE HAS TRAINING PAID OFF!

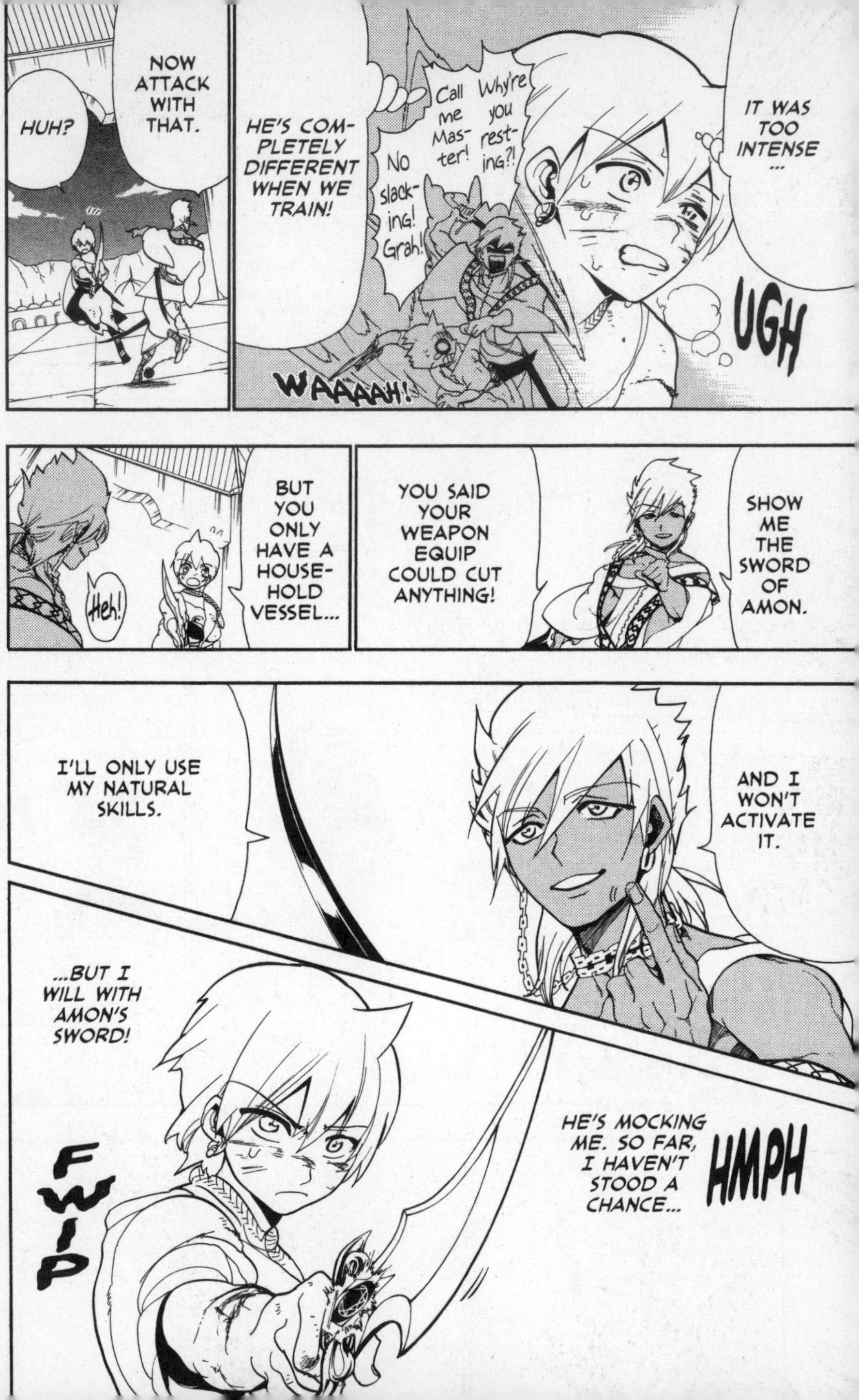
IT WAS TOO INTENSE...
UGH
HE'S COMPLETELY DIFFERENT WHEN WE TRAIN!
Why're you resting?!
Call me Master!
No slacking! Grah!
WAAAAH!
NOW ATTACK WITH THAT.
HUH?
SHOW ME THE SWORD OF AMON.
YOU SAID YOUR WEAPON EQUIP COULD CUT ANYTHING!
BUT YOU ONLY HAVE A HOUSEHOLD VESSEL...
Heh!
AND I WON'T ACTIVATE IT.
I'LL ONLY USE MY NATURAL SKILLS.
HE'S MOCKING ME. SO FAR, I HAVEN'T STOOD A CHANCE...
HMPH
...BUT I WILL WITH AMON'S SWORD!
FWIP

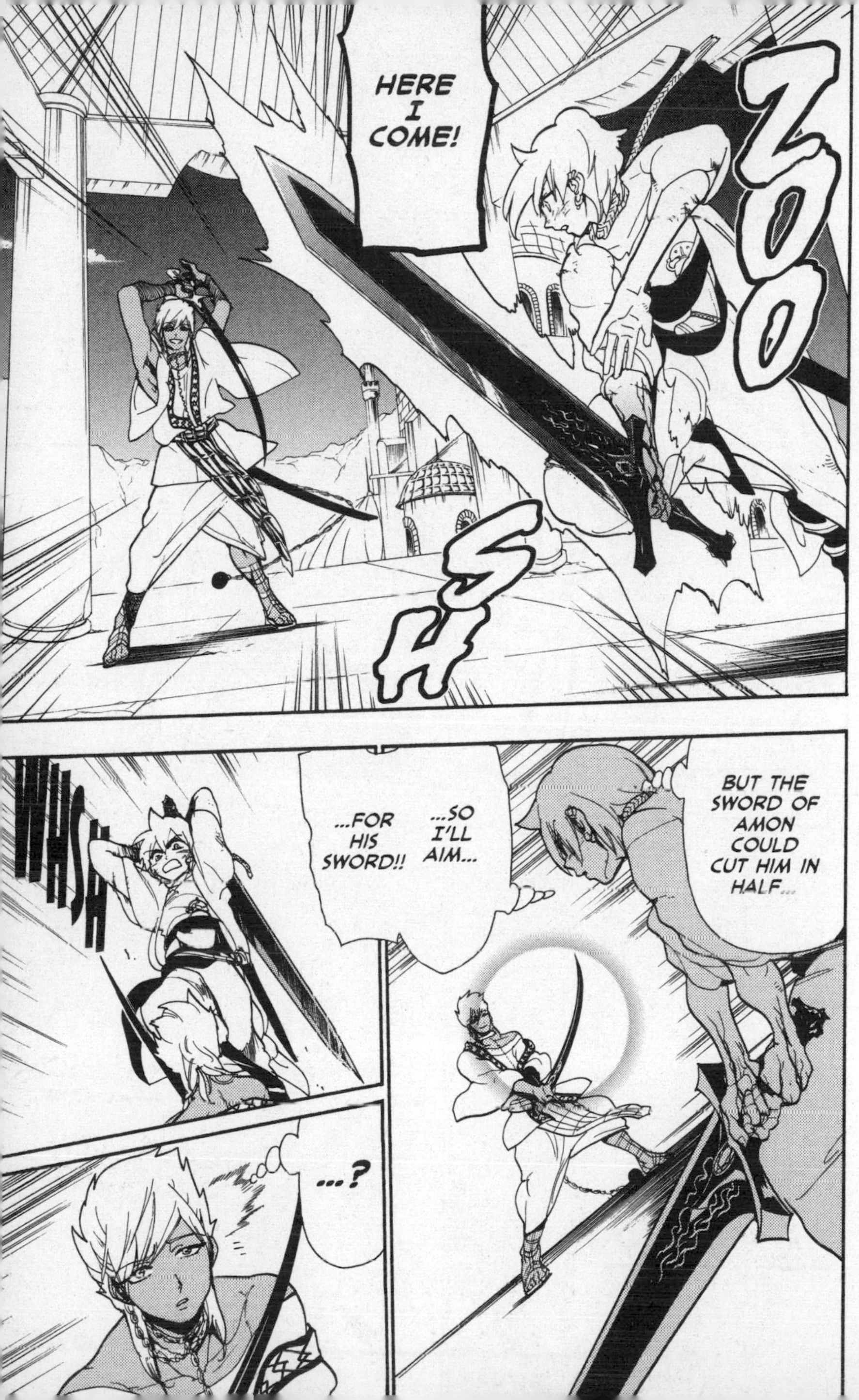
HERE I COME!
ZOOO
SH
BUT THE SWORD OF AMON COULD CUT HIM IN HALF...
...SO I'LL AIM...
...FOR HIS SWORD!!
WHSH
...?

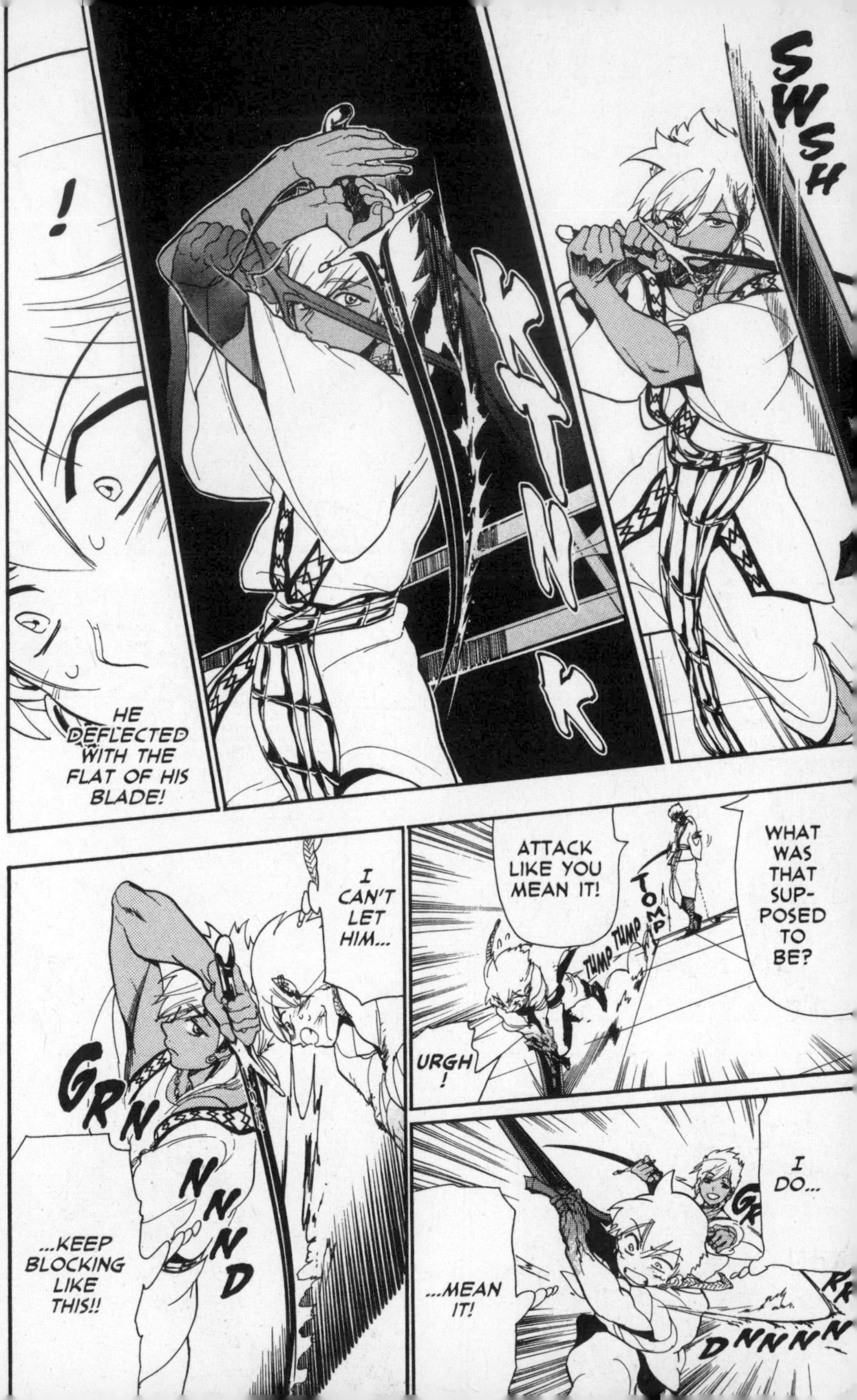
SWSH
!
HE DEFLECTED WITH THE FLAT OF HIS BLADE!
WHAT WAS THAT SUP-POSED TO BE?
ATTACK LIKE YOU MEAN IT!
TOMP
TUMP TUMP
URGH!
I DO...
GR
RR
DNNNN
...MEAN IT!
I CAN'T LET HIM...
GRNNNND
...KEEP BLOCKING LIKE THIS!!

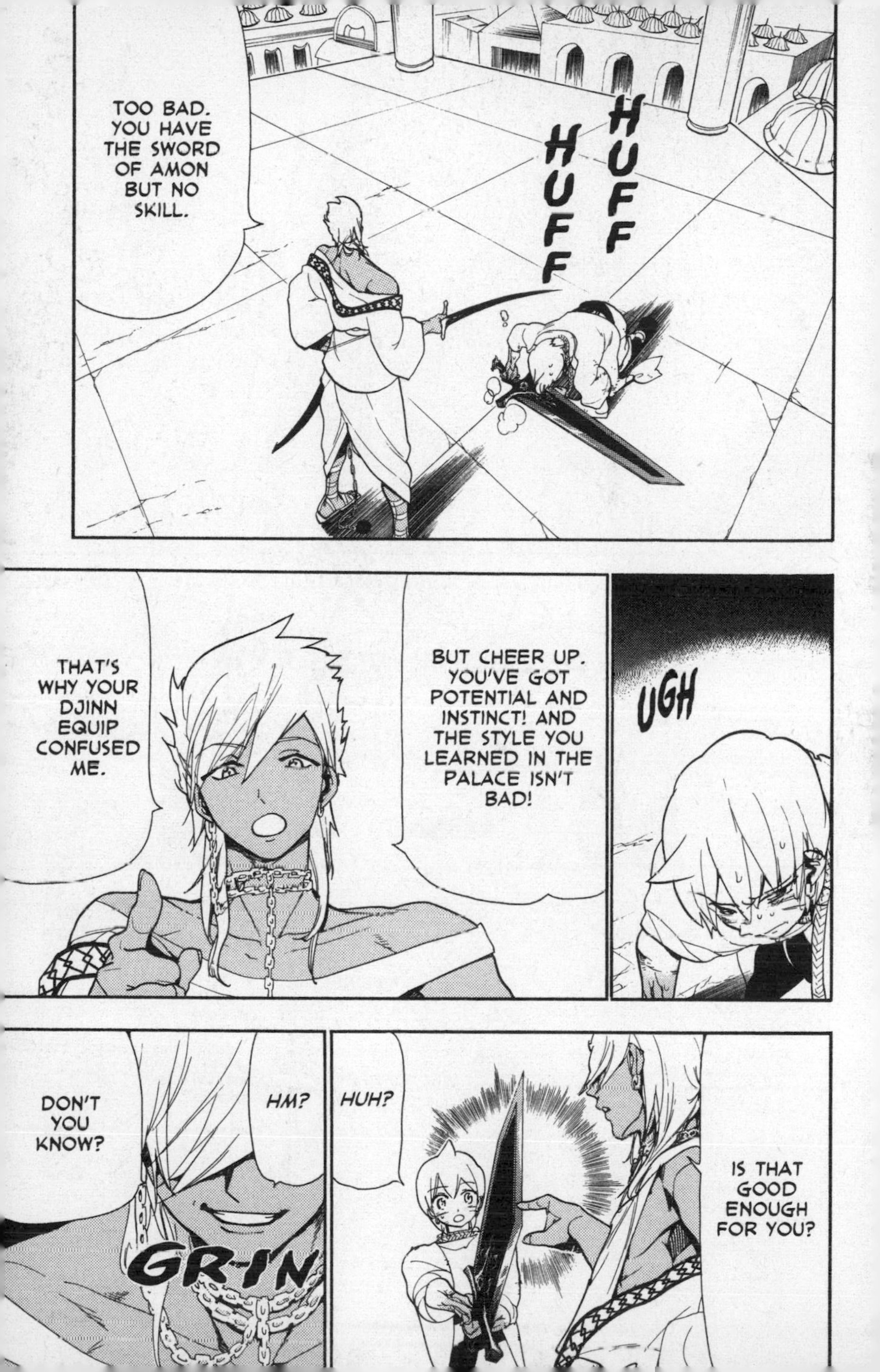
HUFF
HUFF
TOO BAD. YOU HAVE THE SWORD OF AMON BUT NO SKILL.
UGH
BUT CHEER UP. YOU'VE GOT POTENTIAL AND INSTINCT! AND THE STYLE YOU LEARNED IN THE PALACE ISN'T BAD!
THAT'S WHY YOUR DJINN EQUIP CONFUSED ME.
IS THAT GOOD ENOUGH FOR YOU?
HUH?
HM?
DON'T YOU KNOW?
GRIN

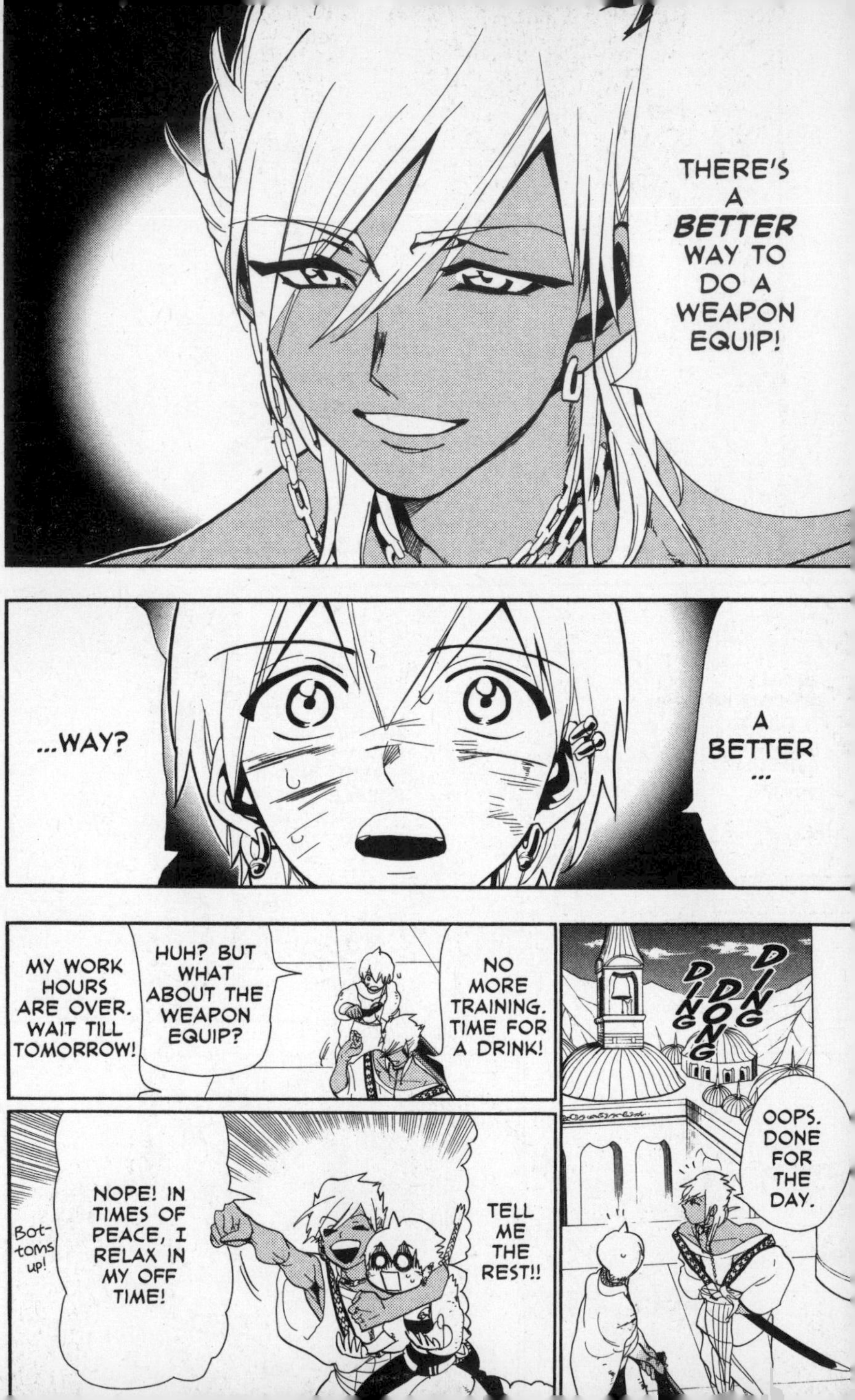
THERE'S A BETTER WAY TO DO A WEAPON EQUIP!
A BETTER ...
...WAY?
DING DONG DING DONG
OOPS. DONE FOR THE DAY.
NO MORE TRAINING. TIME FOR A DRINK!
HUH? BUT WHAT ABOUT THE WEAPON EQUIP?
MY WORK HOURS ARE OVER. WAIT TILL TOMORROW!
TELL ME THE REST!!
NOPE! IN TIMES OF PEACE, I RELAX IN MY OFF TIME!
Bot-toms up!

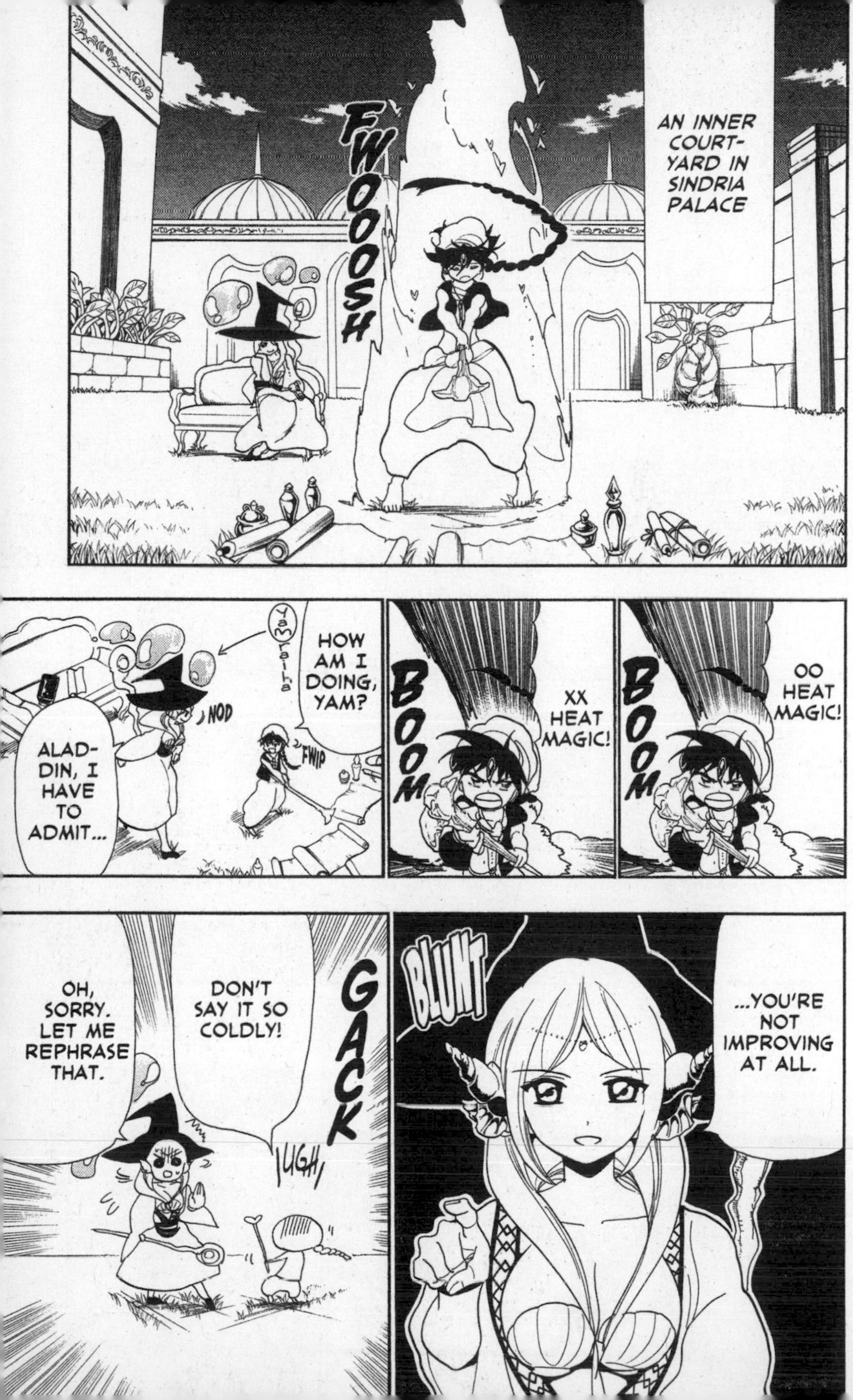
AN INNER COURT-YARD IN SINDRIA PALACE
FWOOOOSH
OO HEAT MAGIC!
BOOOM
XX HEAT MAGIC!
BOOOM
HOW AM I DOING, YAM?
Yamraiha
FWIP
NOD
ALAD-DIN, I HAVE TO ADMIT...
...YOU'RE NOT IMPROVING AT ALL.
BLUNT
GACK
DON'T SAY IT SO COLDLY!
OH, SORRY. LET ME REPHRASE THAT.
UGH

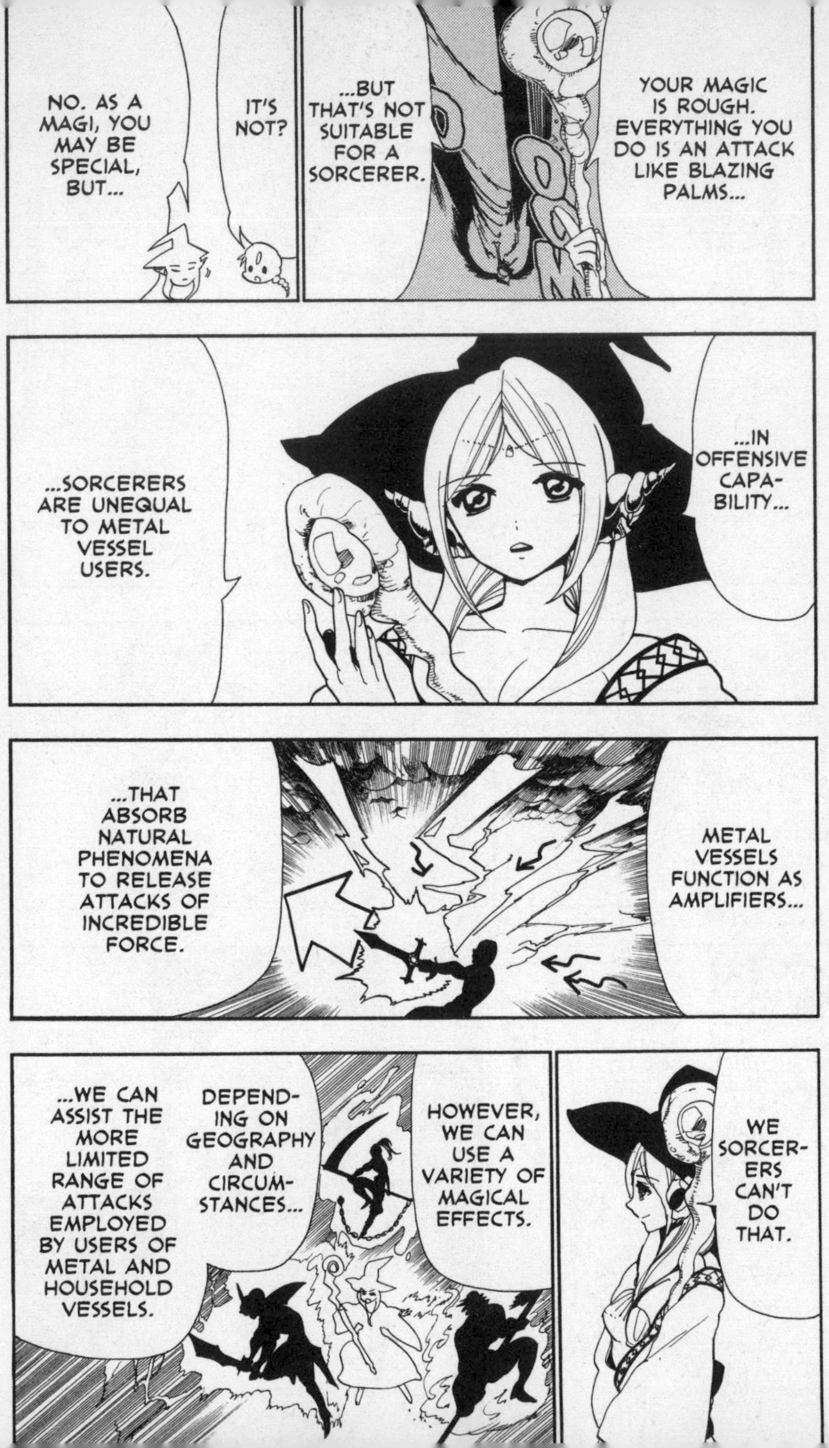
YOUR MAGIC IS ROUGH. EVERYTHING YOU DO IS AN ATTACK LIKE BLAZING PALMS...
...BUT THAT'S NOT SUITABLE FOR A SORCERER.
IT'S NOT?
NO. AS A MAGI, YOU MAY BE SPECIAL, BUT...
...IN OFFENSIVE CAPA-BILITY...
...SORCERERS ARE UNEQUAL TO METAL VESSEL USERS.
METAL VESSELS FUNCTION AS AMPLIFIERS...
...THAT ABSORB NATURAL PHENOMENA TO RELEASE ATTACKS OF INCREDIBLE FORCE.
WE SORCER-ERS CAN'T DO THAT.
HOWEVER, WE CAN USE A VARIETY OF MAGICAL EFFECTS.
DEPEND-ING ON GEOGRAPHY AND CIRCUM-STANCES...
...WE CAN ASSIST THE MORE LIMITED RANGE OF ATTACKS EMPLOYED BY USERS OF METAL AND HOUSEHOLD VESSELS.

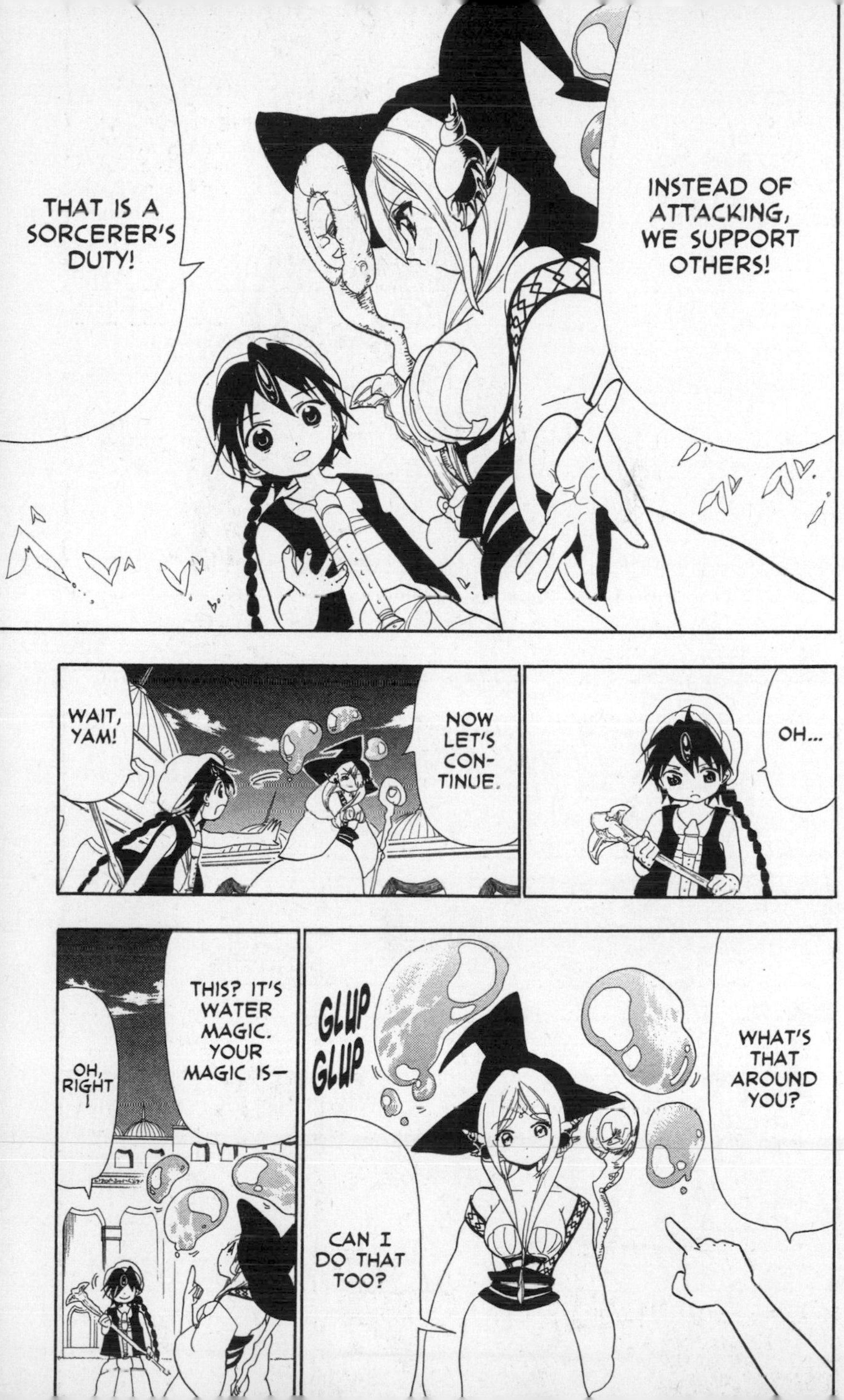
INSTEAD OF ATTACKING, WE SUPPORT OTHERS!
THAT IS A SORCERER'S DUTY!
OH...
NOW LET'S CON-TINUE.
WAIT, YAM!
WHAT'S THAT AROUND YOU?
GLUP GLUP
CAN I DO THAT TOO?
THIS? IT'S WATER MAGIC. YOUR MAGIC IS—
OH, RIGHT!

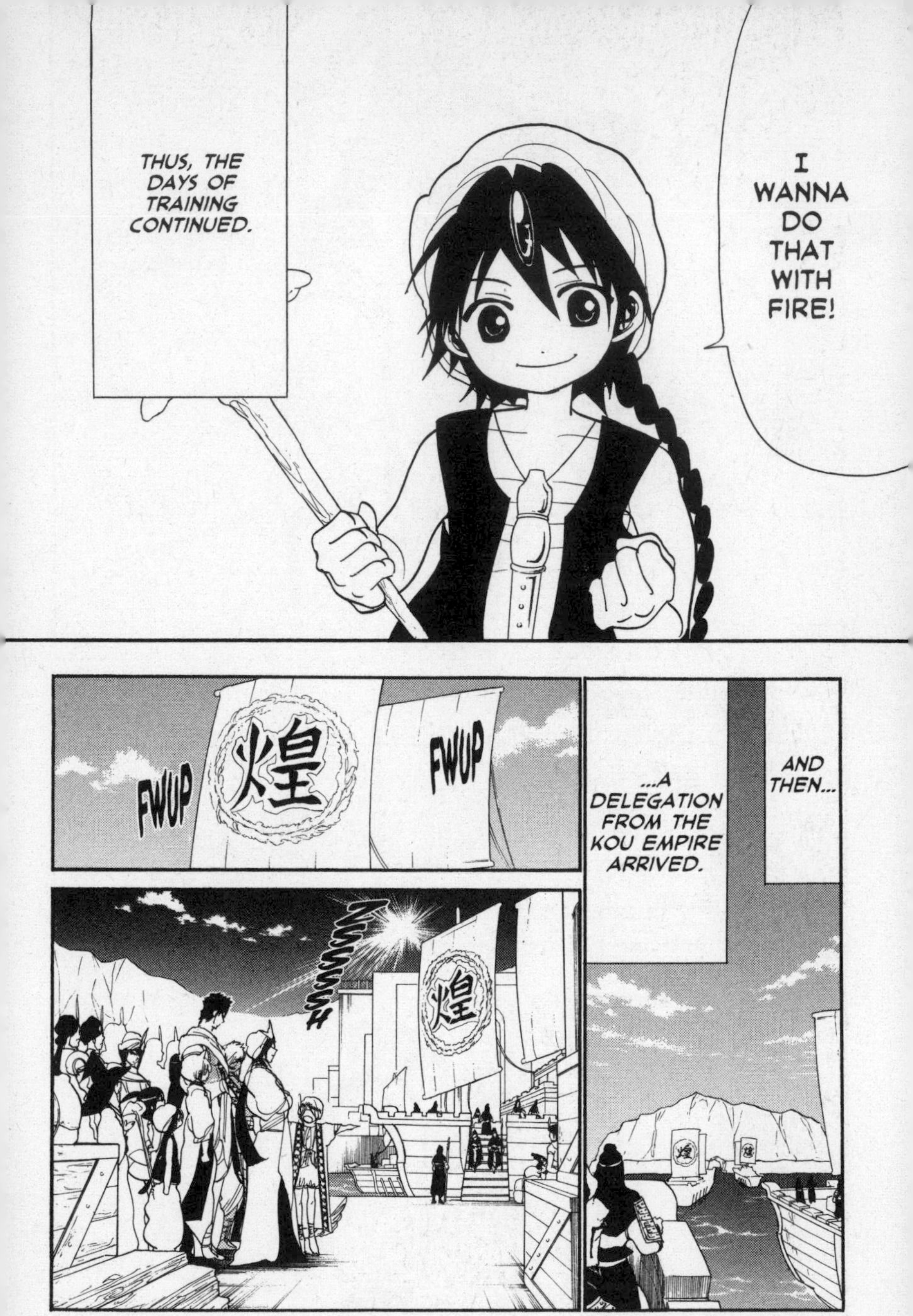
I WANNA DO THAT WITH FIRE!
THUS, THE DAYS OF TRAINING CONTINUED.
AND THEN...
...A DELEGATION FROM THE KOU EMPIRE ARRIVED.
煌
FWUP
FWUP
ZSSSSSH
煌

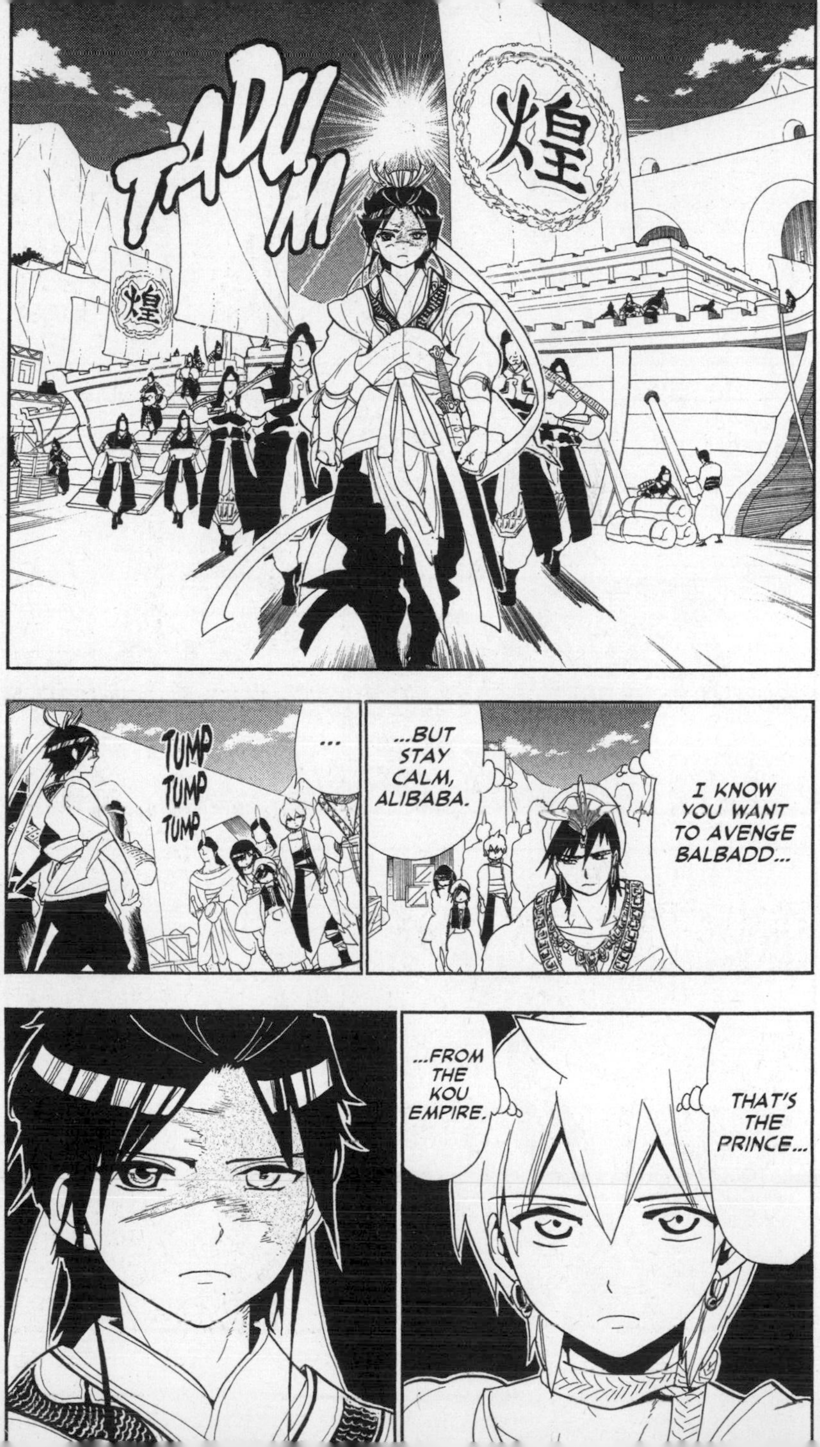
TADUM
煌
煌
I KNOW YOU WANT TO AVENGE BALBADD...
...BUT STAY CALM, ALIBABA.
...
TUMP TUMP TUMP
THAT'S THE PRINCE...
...FROM THE KOU EMPIRE.

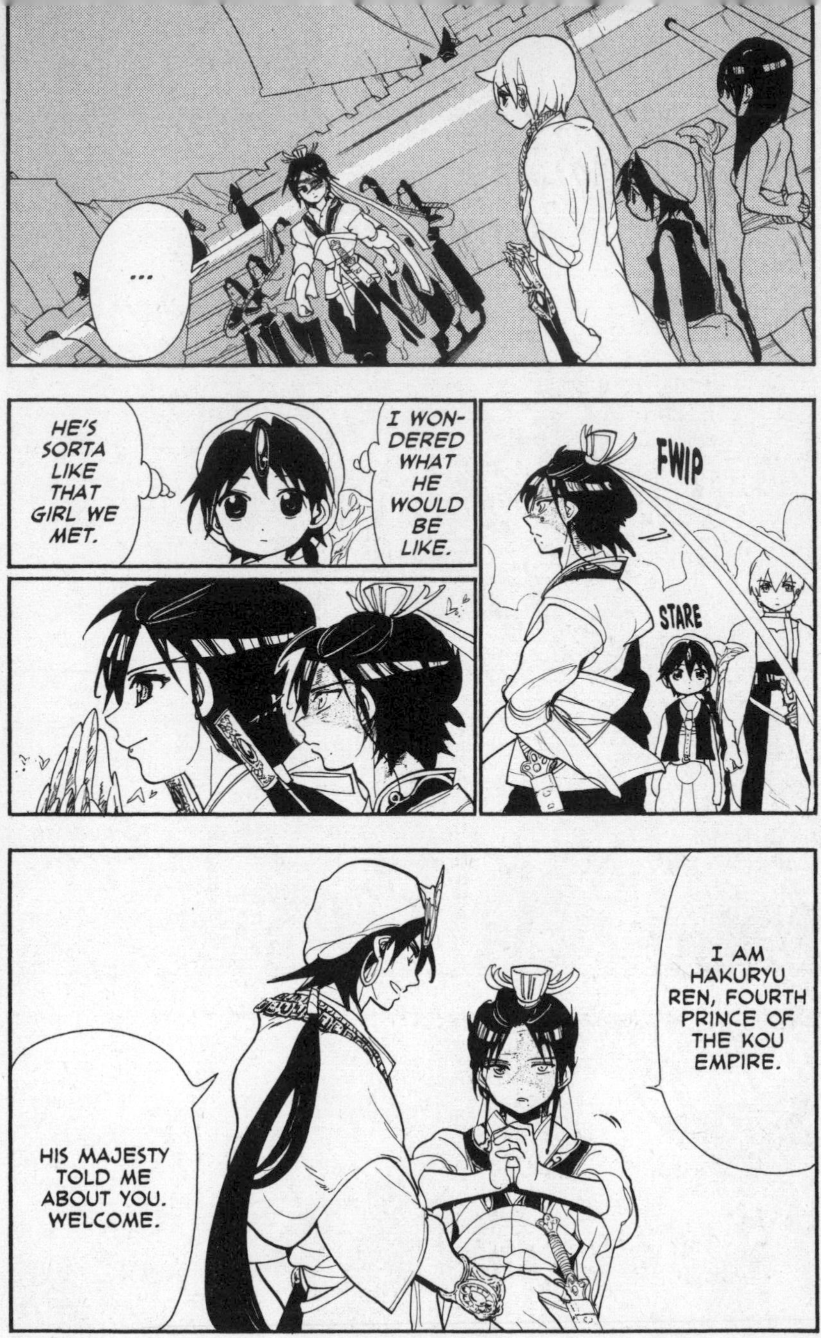
...
FWIP
STARE
I WONDERED WHAT HE WOULD BE LIKE.
HE'S SORTA LIKE THAT GIRL WE MET.
I AM HAKURYU REN, FOURTH PRINCE OF THE KOU EMPIRE.
HIS MAJESTY TOLD ME ABOUT YOU. WELCOME.

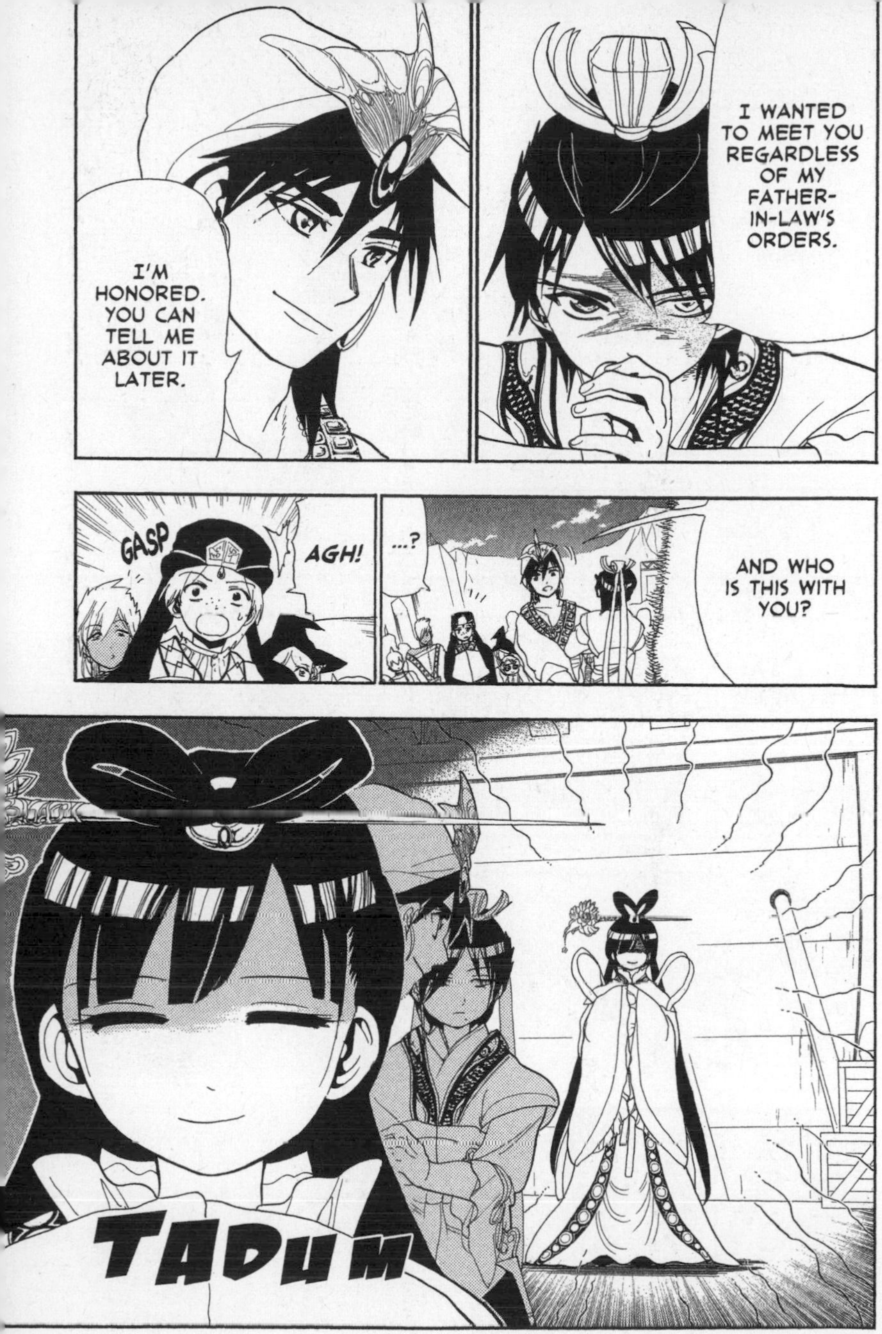
I WANTED TO MEET YOU REGARDLESS OF MY FATHER-IN-LAW'S ORDERS.
I'M HONORED. YOU CAN TELL ME ABOUT IT LATER.
AND WHO IS THIS WITH YOU?
...?
AGH!
GASP
TADUM

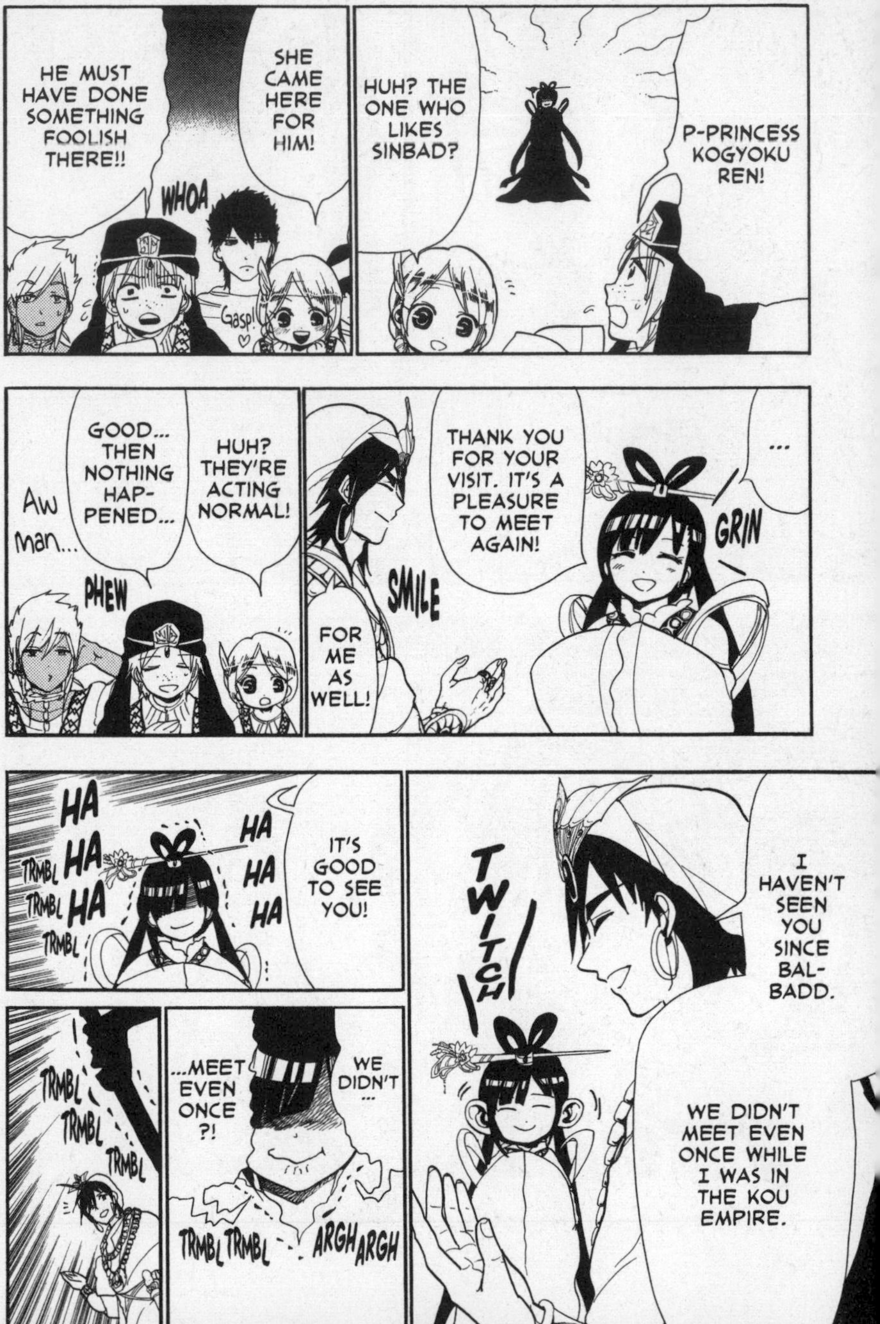
P-PRINCESS KOGYOKU REN!
HUH? THE ONE WHO LIKES SINBAD?
SHE CAME HERE FOR HIM!
HE MUST HAVE DONE SOMETHING FOOLISH THERE!!
WHOA
Gasp!
...
GRIN
THANK YOU FOR YOUR VISIT. IT'S A PLEASURE TO MEET AGAIN!
SMILE
FOR ME AS WELL!
HUH? THEY'RE ACTING NORMAL!
GOOD... THEN NOTHING HAP-PENED...
PHEW
Aw man...
I HAVEN'T SEEN YOU SINCE BAL-BADD.
TWITCH
WE DIDN'T MEET EVEN ONCE WHILE I WAS IN THE KOU EMPIRE.
IT'S GOOD TO SEE YOU!
HA HA HA
HA HA HA
TRMBL TRMBL TRMBL
WE DIDN'T ...
...MEET EVEN ONCE ?!
TRMBL TRMBL
ARGH ARGH
TRMBL TRMBL TRMBL

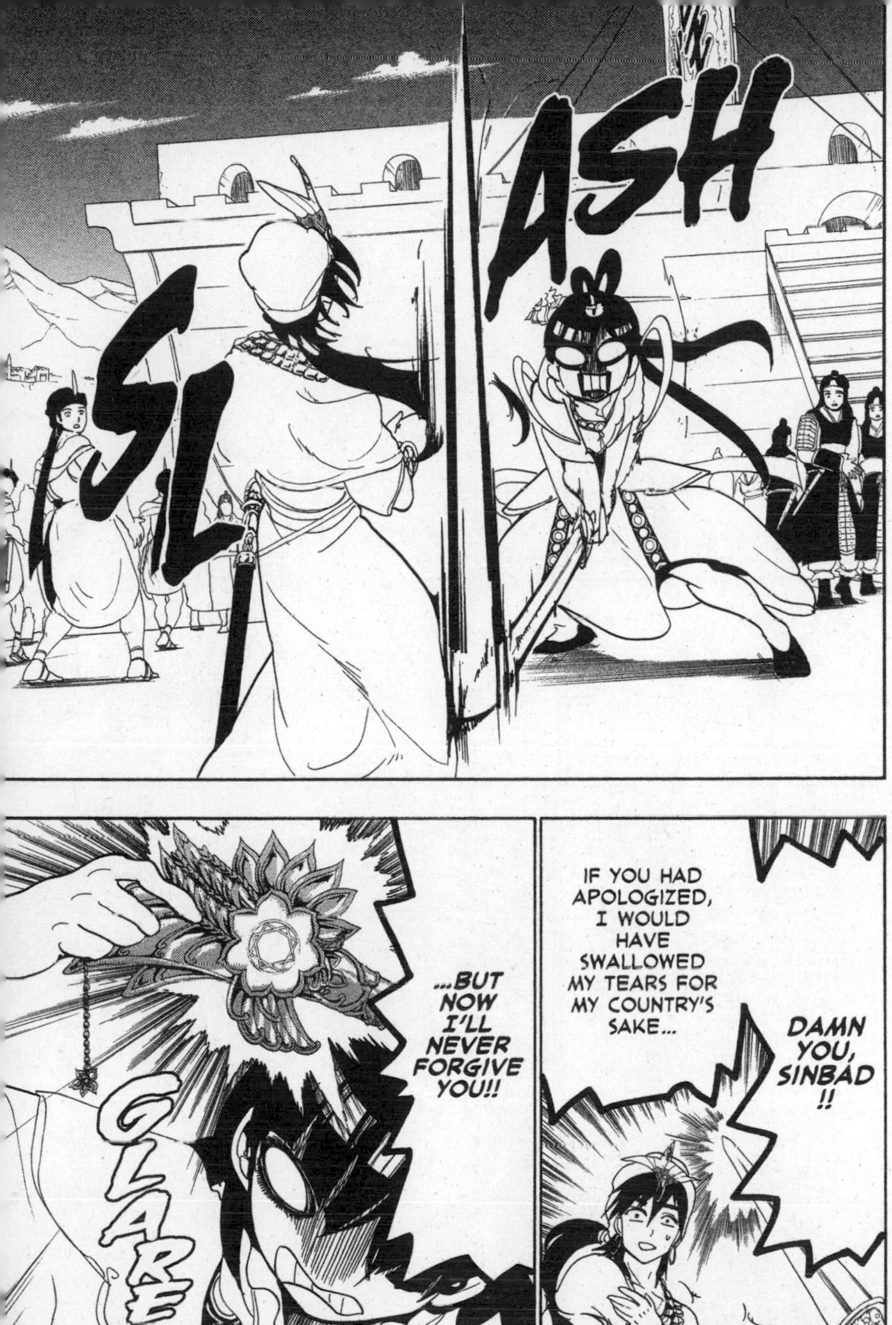
SLASH
IF YOU HAD APOLOGIZED, I WOULD HAVE SWALLOWED MY TEARS FOR MY COUNTRY'S SAKE...
DAMN YOU, SINBAD!!
...BUT NOW I'LL NEVER FORGIVE YOU!!
GLARE

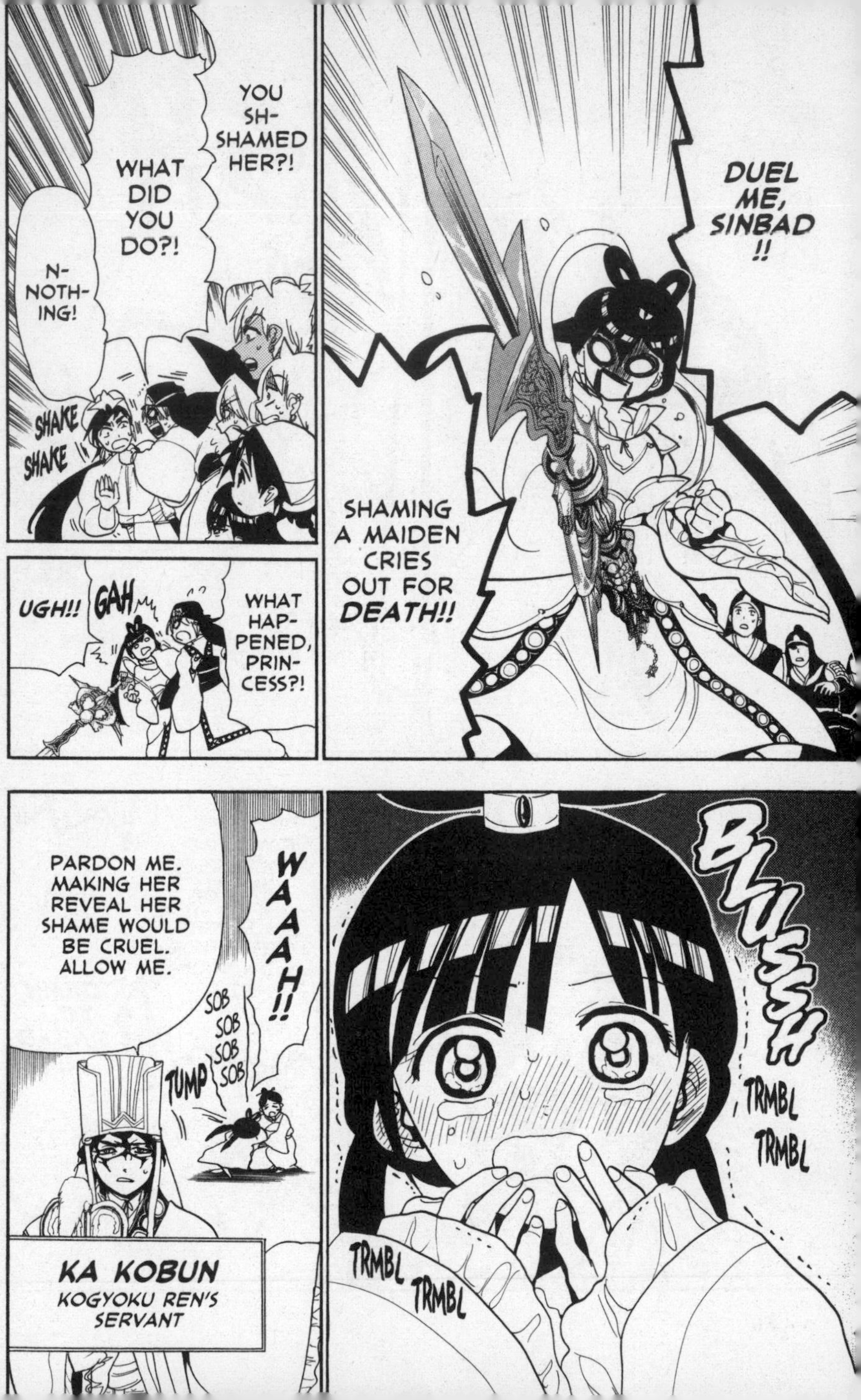
DUEL ME, SINBAD!!
SHAMING A MAIDEN CRIES OUT FOR DEATH!!
YOU SH-SHAMED HER?!
WHAT DID YOU DO?!
N-NOTHING!
SHAKE SHAKE
WHAT HAPPENED, PRINCESS?!
GAH
UGH!!
BLUSSH
TRMBL TRMBL
TRMBL TRMBL
WAAAAH!!
SOB SOB SOB SOB
TUMP
PARDON ME. MAKING HER REVEAL HER SHAME WOULD BE CRUEL. ALLOW ME.
KA KOBUN
KOGYOKU REN'S SERVANT

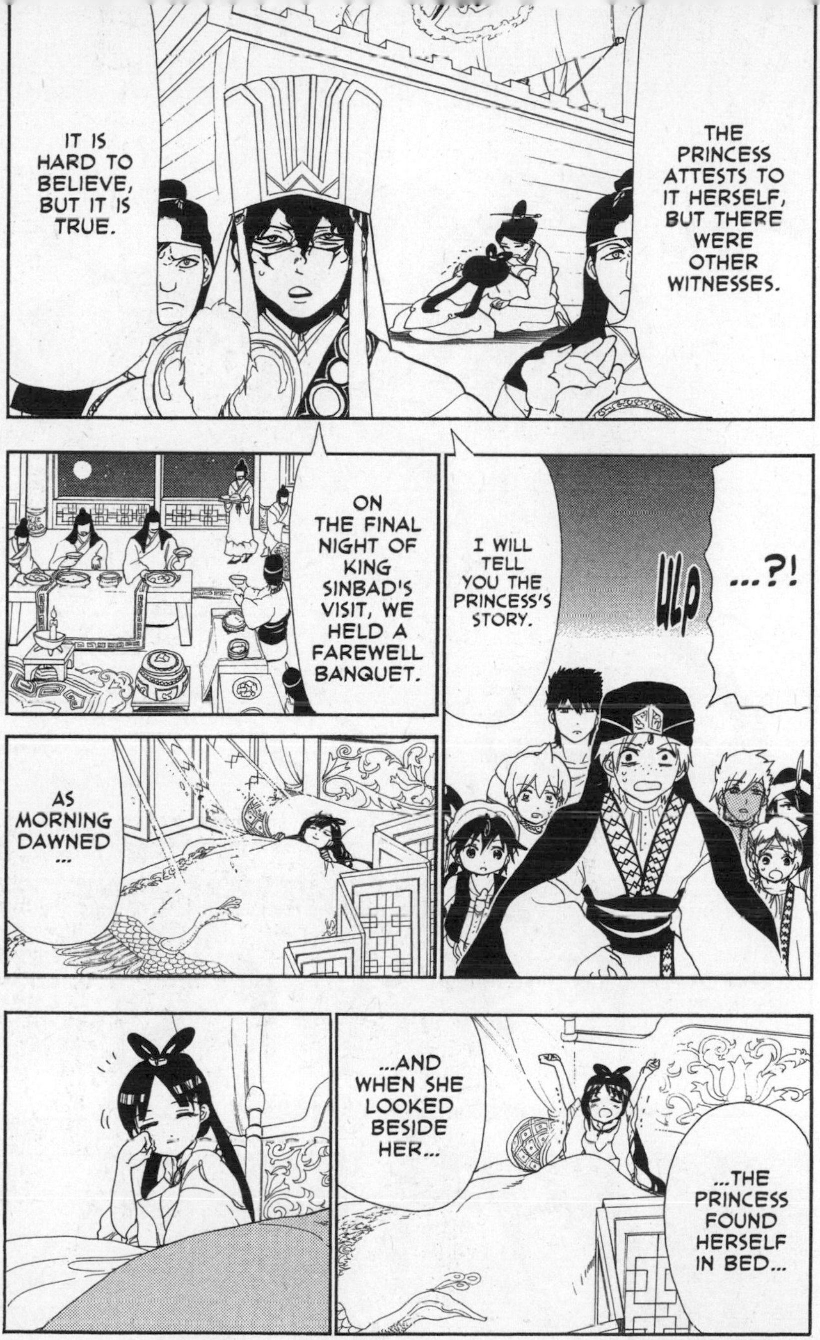
THE PRINCESS ATTESTS TO IT HERSELF, BUT THERE WERE OTHER WITNESSES.
IT IS HARD TO BELIEVE, BUT IT IS TRUE.
I WILL TELL YOU THE PRINCESS'S STORY.
ULP
...?!
ON THE FINAL NIGHT OF KING SINBAD'S VISIT, WE HELD A FAREWELL BANQUET.
AS MORNING DAWNED ...
...THE PRINCESS FOUND HERSELF IN BED...
...AND WHEN SHE LOOKED BESIDE HER...

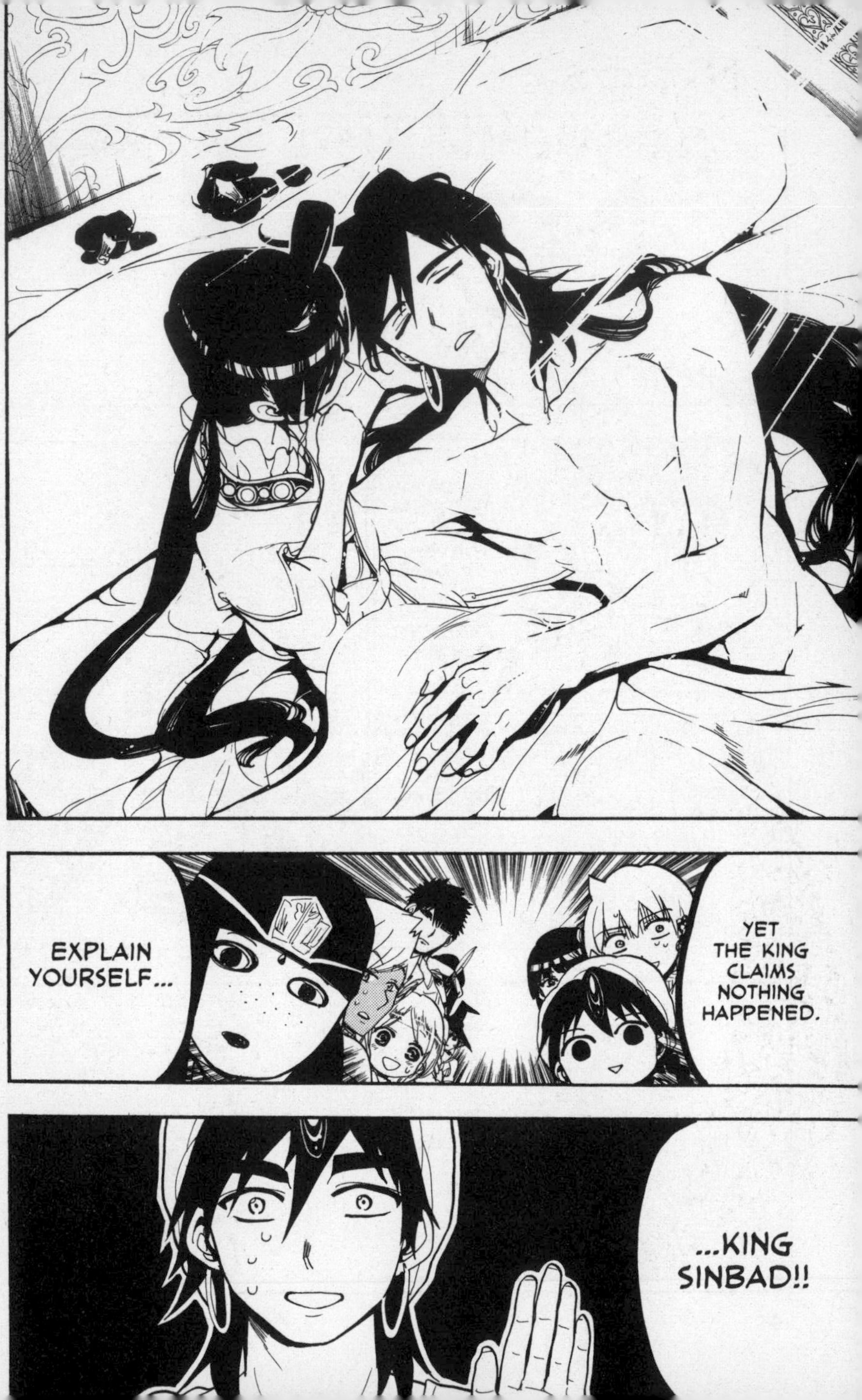
YET THE KING CLAIMS NOTHING HAPPENED.
EXPLAIN YOURSELF...
...KING SINBAD!!

Night 84: Kogyoku and Sinbad

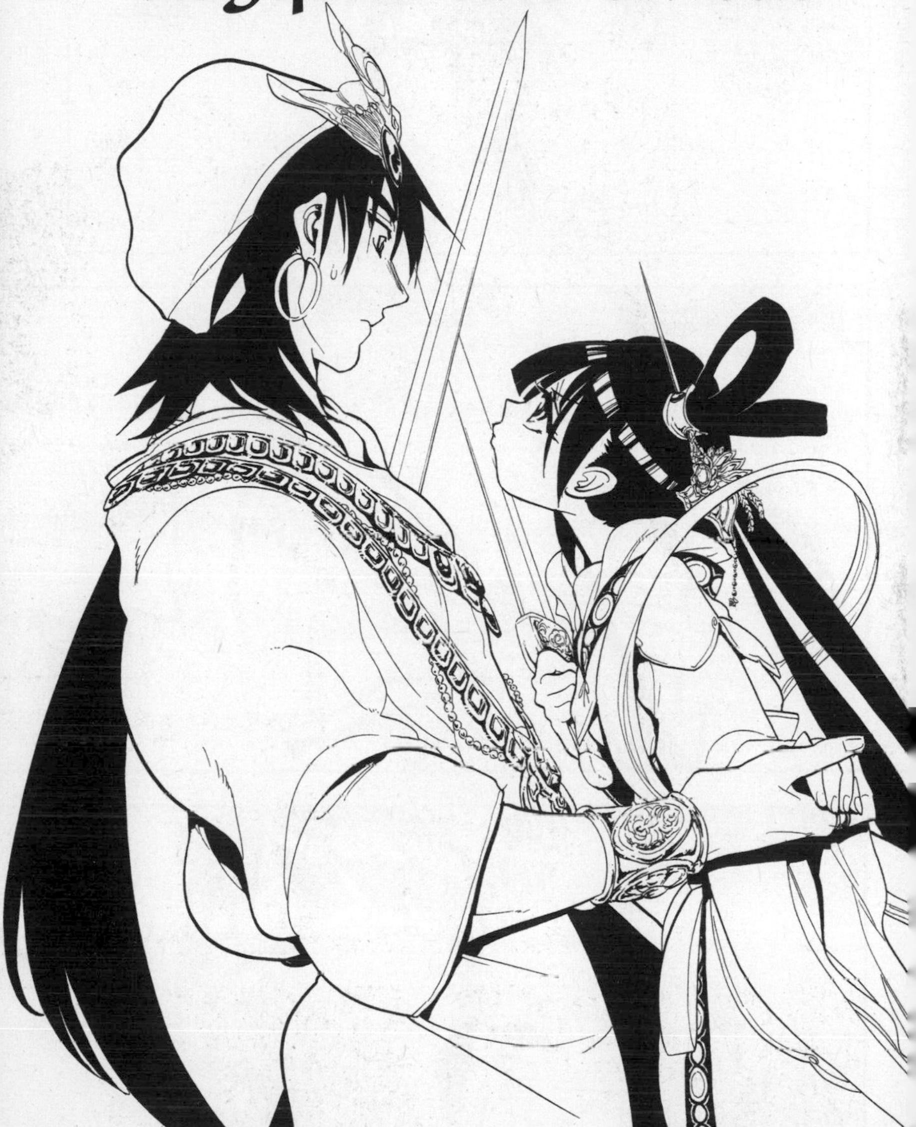

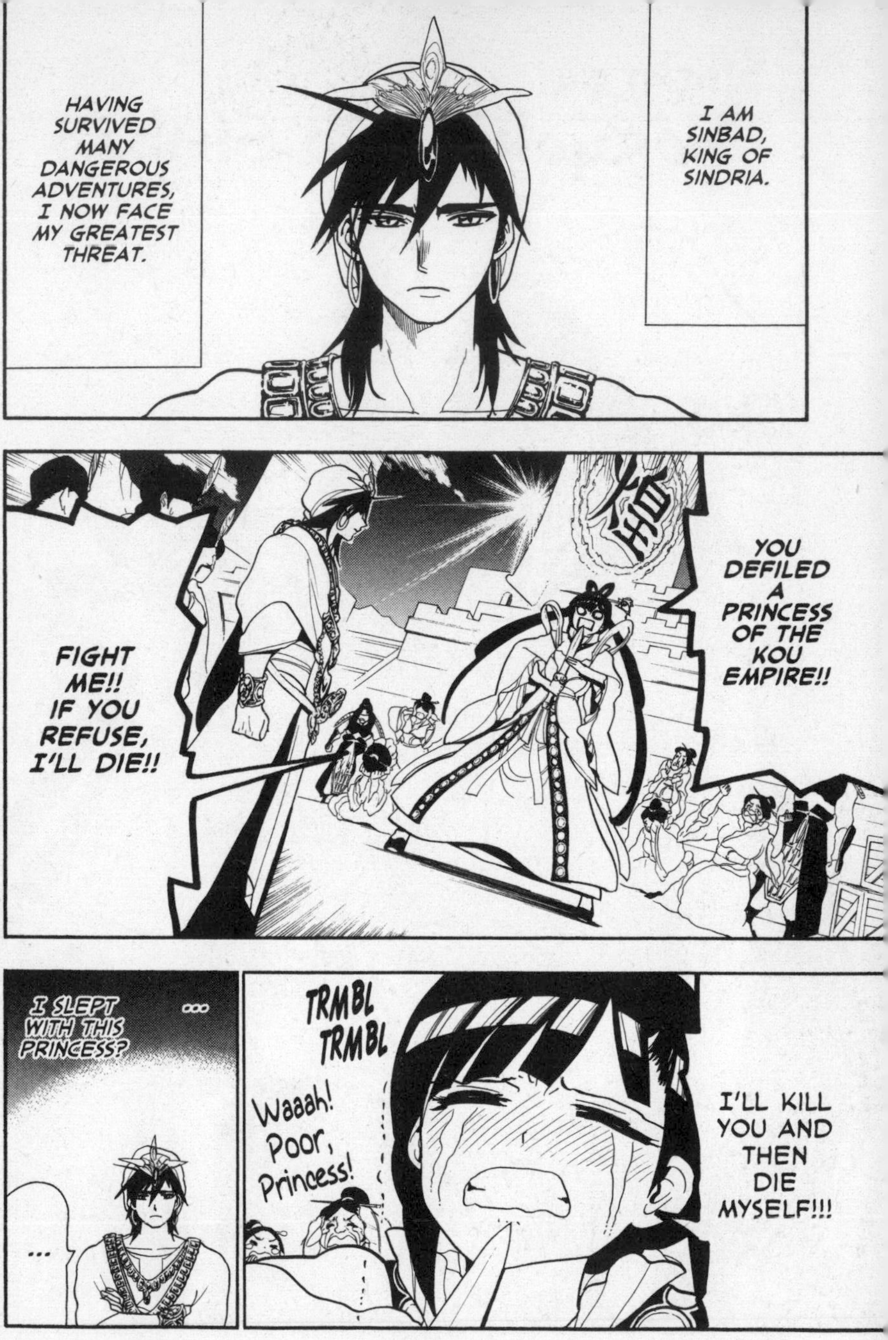

I AM SINBAD, KING OF SINDRIA.
HAVING SURVIVED MANY DANGEROUS ADVENTURES, I NOW FACE MY GREATEST THREAT.
YOU DEFILED A PRINCESS OF THE KOU EMPIRE!!
FIGHT ME!! IF YOU REFUSE, I'LL DIE!!
I'LL KILL YOU AND THEN DIE MYSELF!!!
TRMBL TRMBL
Waaah! Poor, Princess!
...
I SLEPT WITH THIS PRINCESS?
...

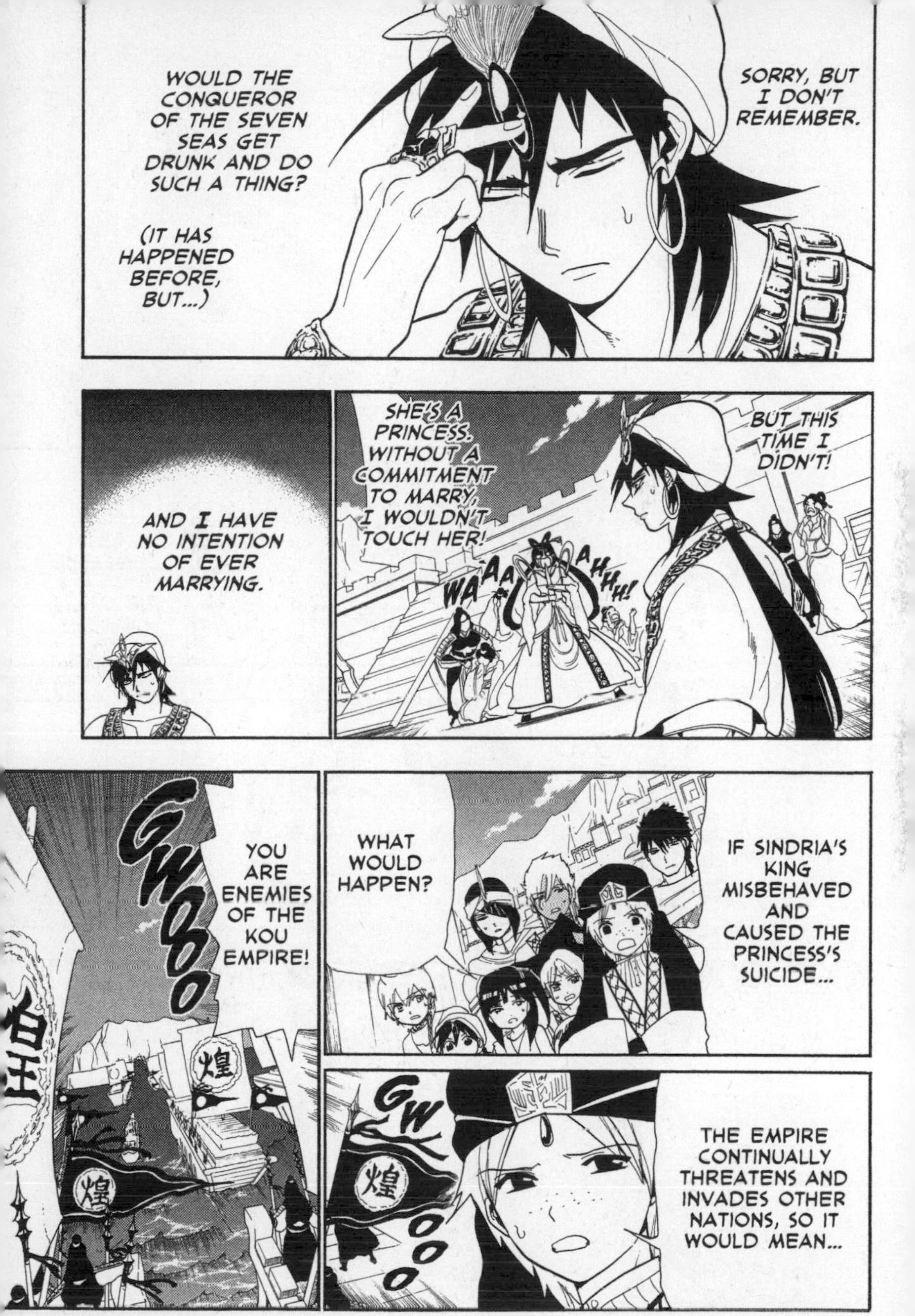
SORRY, BUT I DON'T REMEMBER.
WOULD THE CONQUEROR OF THE SEVEN SEAS GET DRUNK AND DO SUCH A THING?
(IT HAS HAPPENED BEFORE, BUT...)
BUT THIS TIME I DIDN'T!
SHE'S A PRINCESS. WITHOUT A COMMITMENT TO MARRY, I WOULDN'T TOUCH HER!
WAAAAHHH!
AND I HAVE NO INTENTION OF EVER MARRYING.
IF SINDRIA'S KING MISBEHAVED AND CAUSED THE PRINCESS'S SUICIDE...
WHAT WOULD HAPPEN?
THE EMPIRE CONTINUALLY THREATENS AND INVADES OTHER NATIONS, SO IT WOULD MEAN...
GWOOOO
YOU ARE ENEMIES OF THE KOU EMPIRE!
GWOOOO

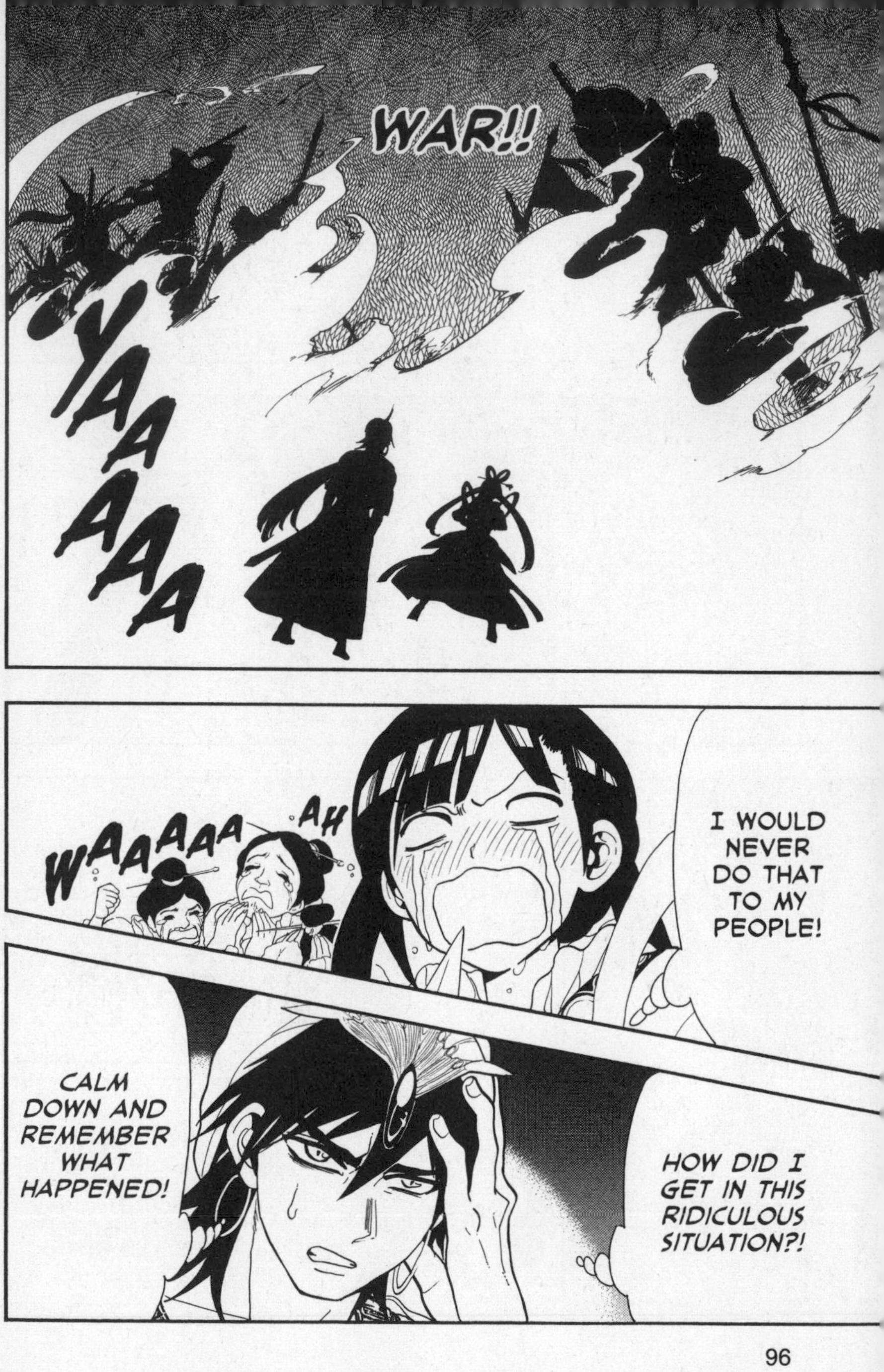
WAR!!
YAAAAAA
I WOULD NEVER DO THAT TO MY PEOPLE!
WAAAAAA
AH
HOW DID I GET IN THIS RIDICULOUS SITUATION?!
CALM DOWN AND REMEMBER WHAT HAPPENED!

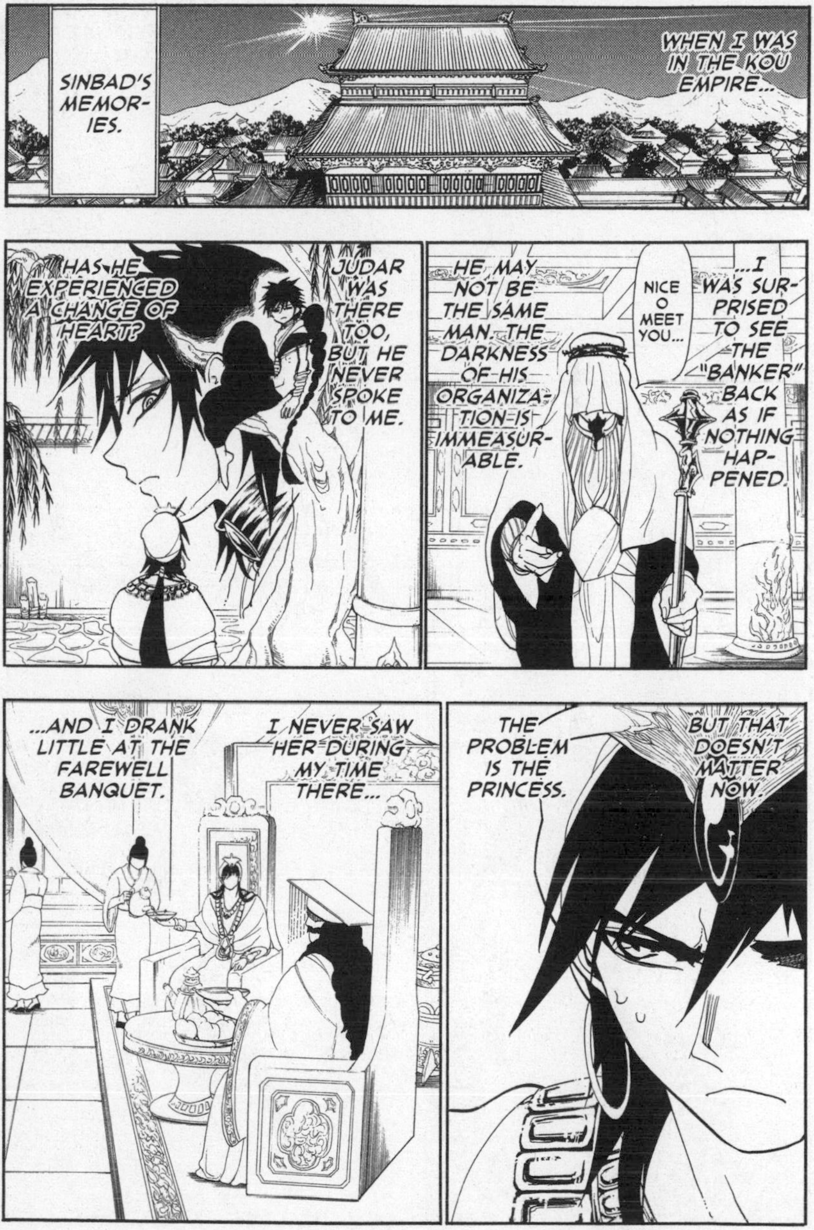
WHEN I WAS IN THE KOU EMPIRE...
SINBAD'S MEMORIES.
...I WAS SURPRISED TO SEE THE "BANKER" BACK AS IF NOTHING HAPPENED.
NICE O MEET YOU...
HE MAY NOT BE THE SAME MAN. THE DARKNESS OF HIS ORGANIZATION IS IMMEASURABLE.
JUDAR WAS THERE TOO, BUT HE NEVER SPOKE TO ME.
HAS HE EXPERIENCED A CHANGE OF HEART?
BUT THAT DOESN'T MATTER NOW.
THE PROBLEM IS THE PRINCESS.
I NEVER SAW HER DURING MY TIME THERE...
...AND I DRANK LITTLE AT THE FAREWELL BANQUET.

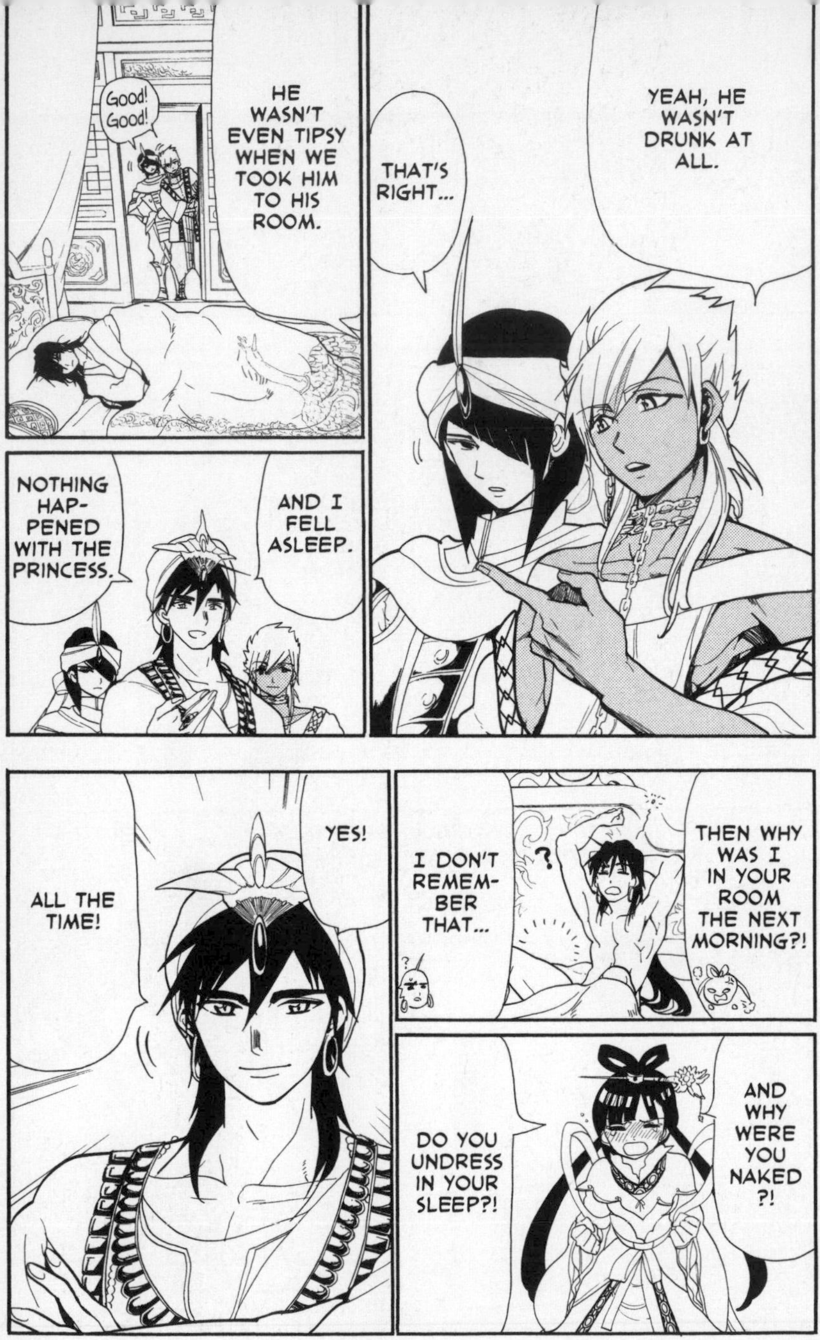
YEAH, HE WASN'T DRUNK AT ALL.
THAT'S RIGHT...
HE WASN'T EVEN TIPSY WHEN WE TOOK HIM TO HIS ROOM.
Good! Good!
AND I FELL ASLEEP.
NOTHING HAP-PENED WITH THE PRINCESS.
THEN WHY WAS I IN YOUR ROOM THE NEXT MORNING?!
I DON'T REMEM-BER THAT...
AND WHY WERE YOU NAKED?!
DO YOU UNDRESS IN YOUR SLEEP?!
YES!
ALL THE TIME!

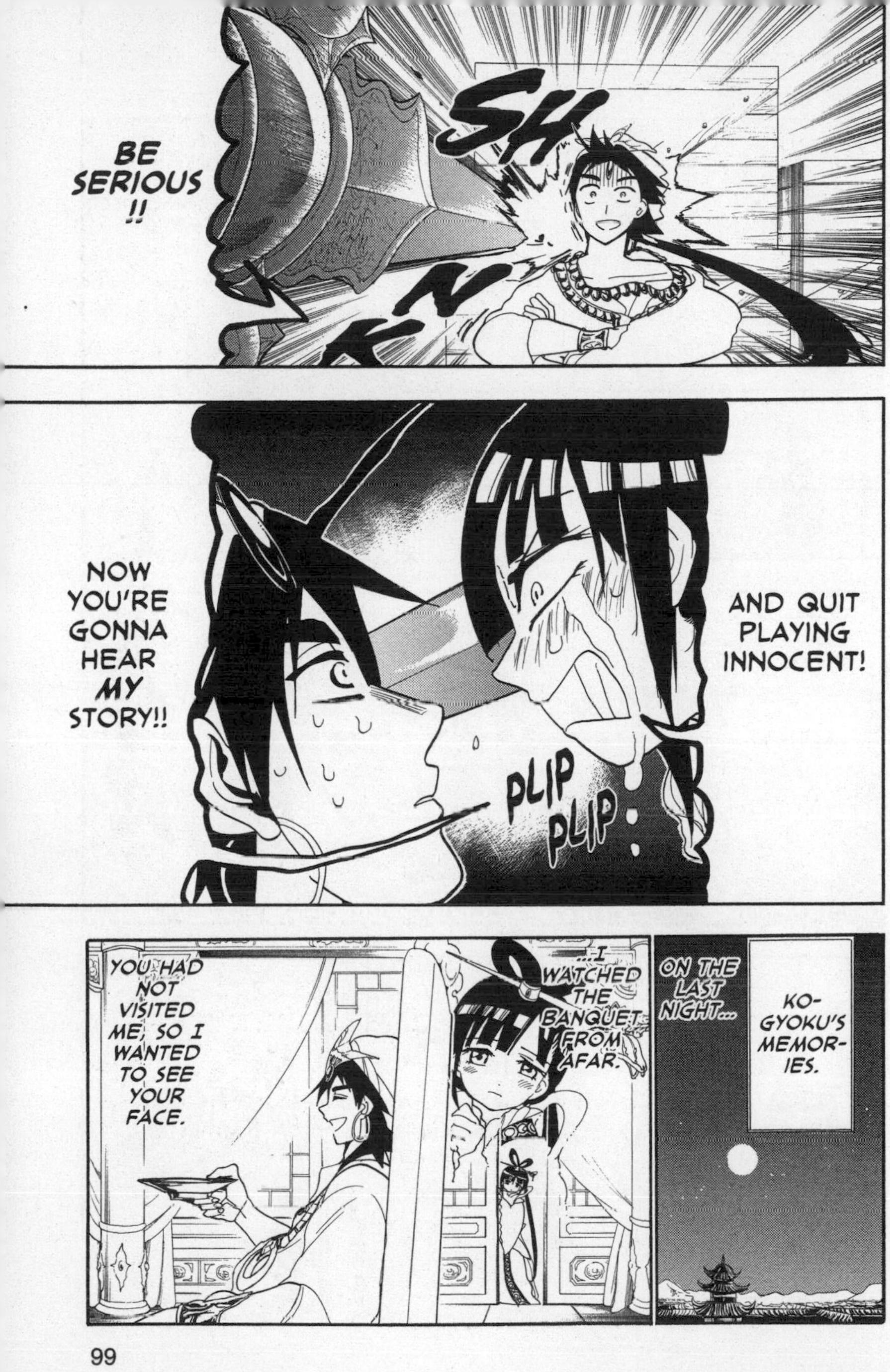
SHNK
BE SERIOUS !!
AND QUIT PLAYING INNOCENT!
PLIP PLIP
NOW YOU'RE GONNA HEAR MY STORY!!
KO-GYOKU'S MEMORIES.
ON THE LAST NIGHT...
...I WATCHED THE BANQUET FROM AFAR.
YOU HAD NOT VISITED ME, SO I WANTED TO SEE YOUR FACE.

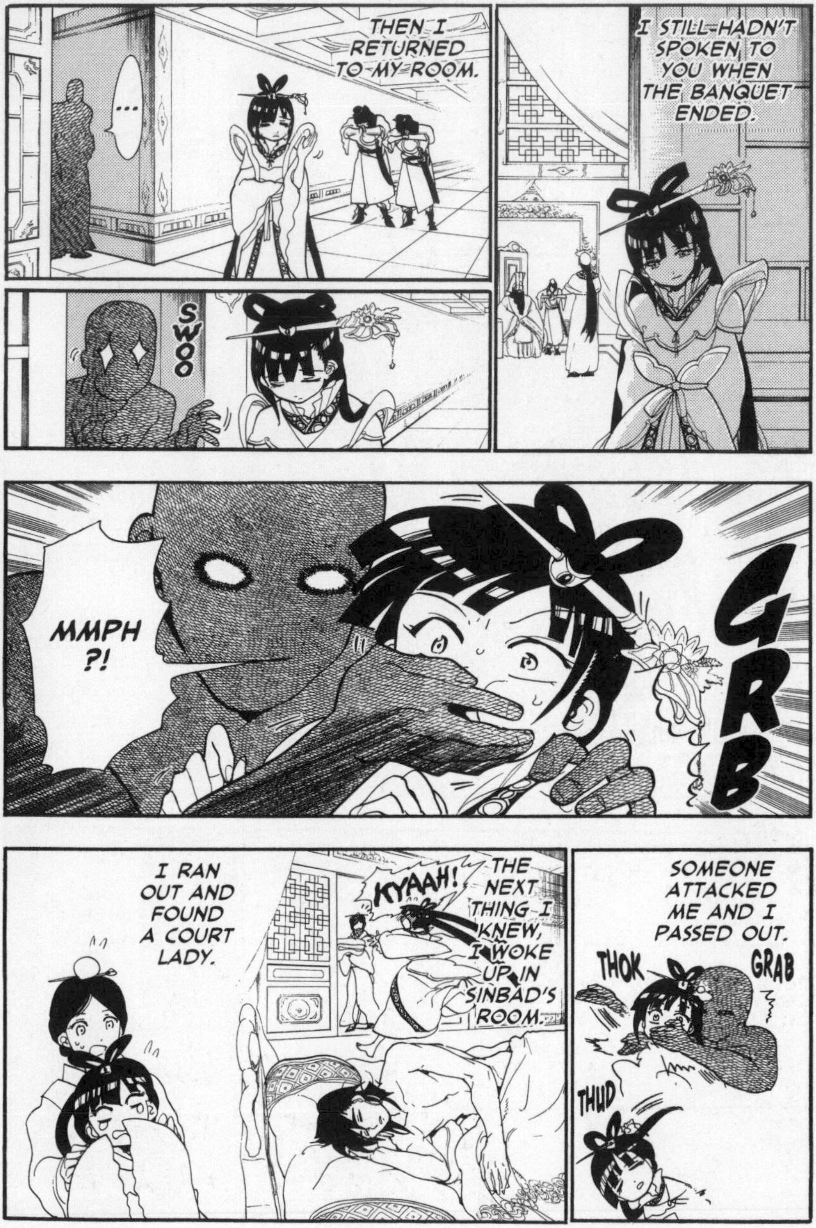
I STILL HADN'T SPOKEN TO YOU WHEN THE BANQUET ENDED.
THEN I RETURNED TO MY ROOM.
...
SWOO
GRB
MMPH ?!
SOMEONE ATTACKED ME AND I PASSED OUT.
GRAB
THOK
THUD
THE NEXT THING I KNEW, I WOKE UP IN SINBAD'S ROOM.
KYAAH!
I RAN OUT AND FOUND A COURT LADY.

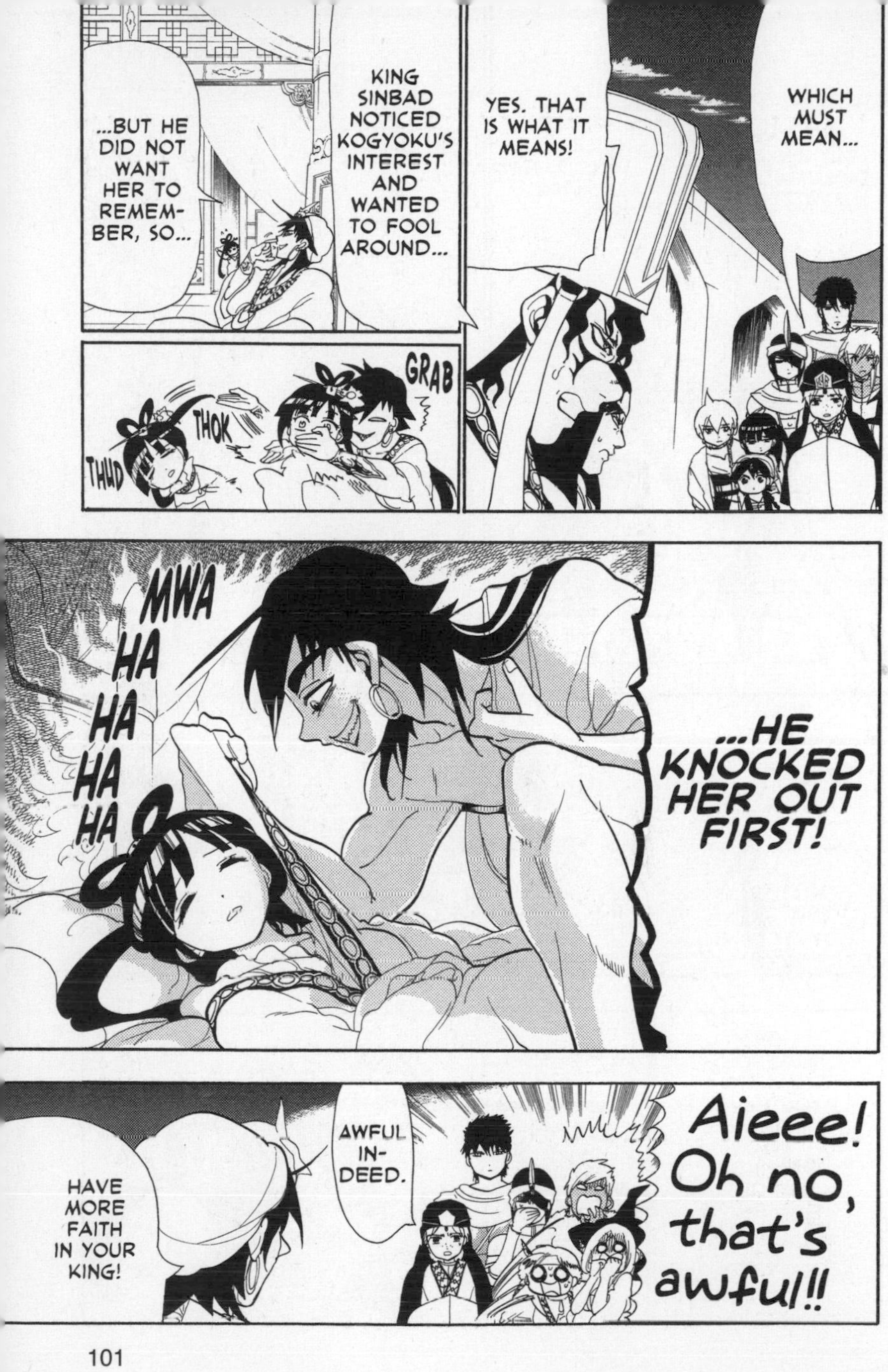
WHICH MUST MEAN...
YES. THAT IS WHAT IT MEANS!
KING SINBAD NOTICED KOGYOKU'S INTEREST AND WANTED TO FOOL AROUND...
...BUT HE DID NOT WANT HER TO REMEMBER, SO...
GRAB
THOK
THUD
...HE KNOCKED HER OUT FIRST!
MWA HA HA HA HA HA
Aieee! Oh no, that's awful!!
AWFUL IN-DEED.
HAVE MORE FAITH IN YOUR KING!

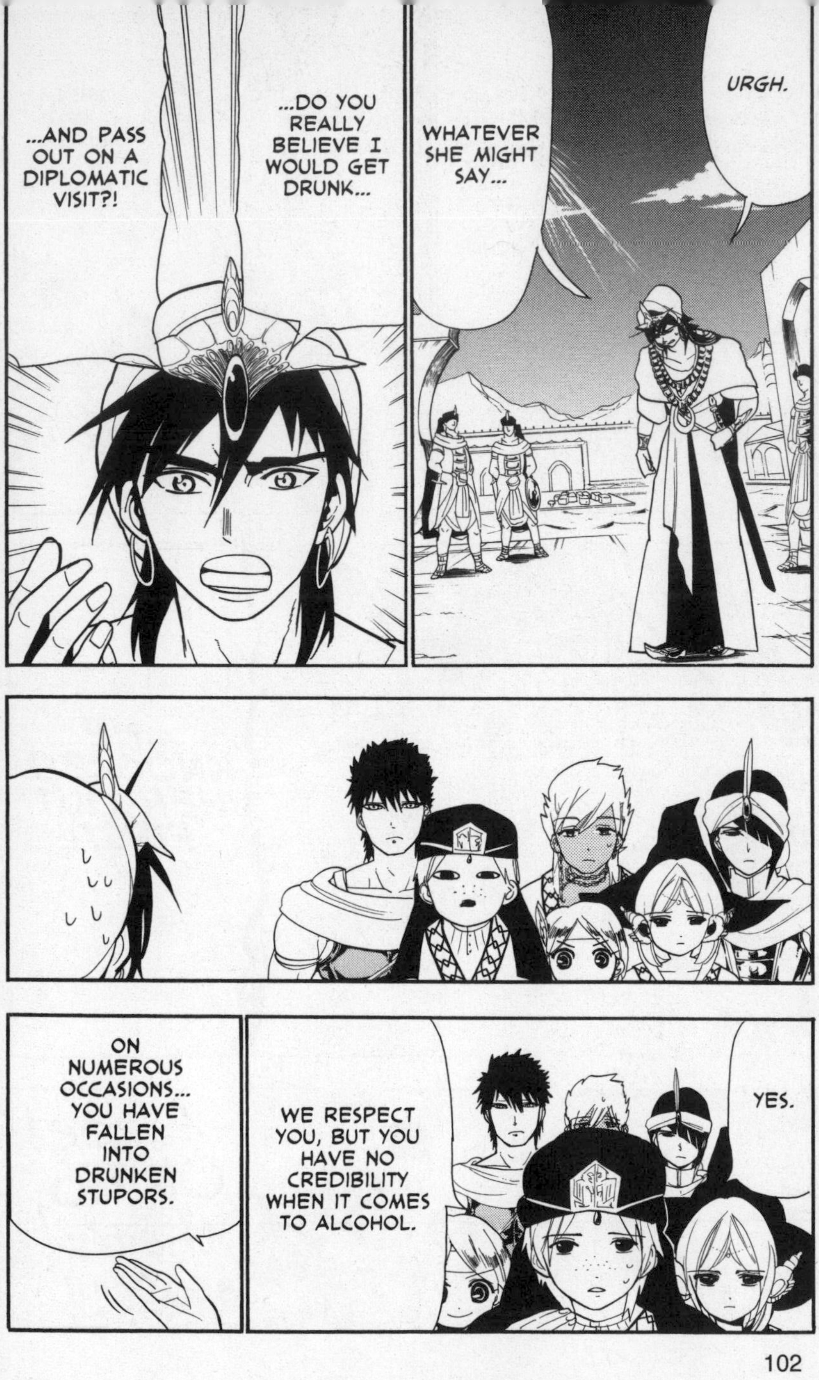
URGH.
WHATEVER SHE MIGHT SAY...
...DO YOU REALLY BELIEVE I WOULD GET DRUNK...
...AND PASS OUT ON A DIPLOMATIC VISIT?!
YES.
WE RESPECT YOU, BUT YOU HAVE NO CREDIBILITY WHEN IT COMES TO ALCOHOL.
ON NUMEROUS OCCASIONS... YOU HAVE FALLEN INTO DRUNKEN STUPORS.

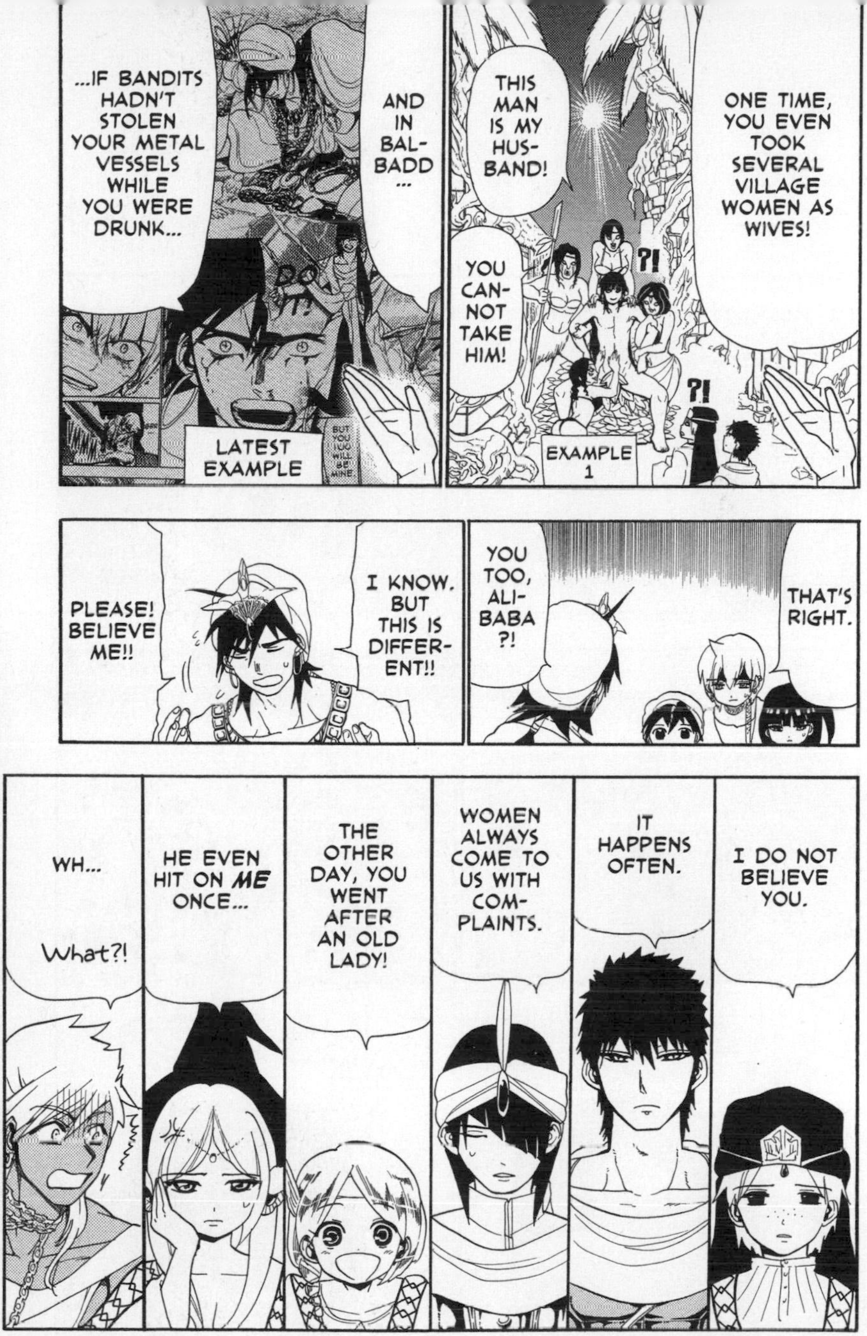
ONE TIME, YOU EVEN TOOK SEVERAL VILLAGE WOMEN AS WIVES!
THIS MAN IS MY HUSBAND!
YOU CANNOT TAKE HIM!
?!
?!
EXAMPLE 1
AND IN BALBADD...
...IF BANDITS HADN'T STOLEN YOUR METAL VESSELS WHILE YOU WERE DRUNK...
DO IT!
BUT YOU TOO WILL BE MINE
LATEST EXAMPLE
THAT'S RIGHT.
YOU TOO, ALIBABA?!
I KNOW. BUT THIS IS DIFFERENT!!
PLEASE! BELIEVE ME!!
I DO NOT BELIEVE YOU.
IT HAPPENS OFTEN.
WOMEN ALWAYS COME TO US WITH COMPLAINTS.
THE OTHER DAY, YOU WENT AFTER AN OLD LADY!
HE EVEN HIT ON *ME* ONCE...
WH...
What?!

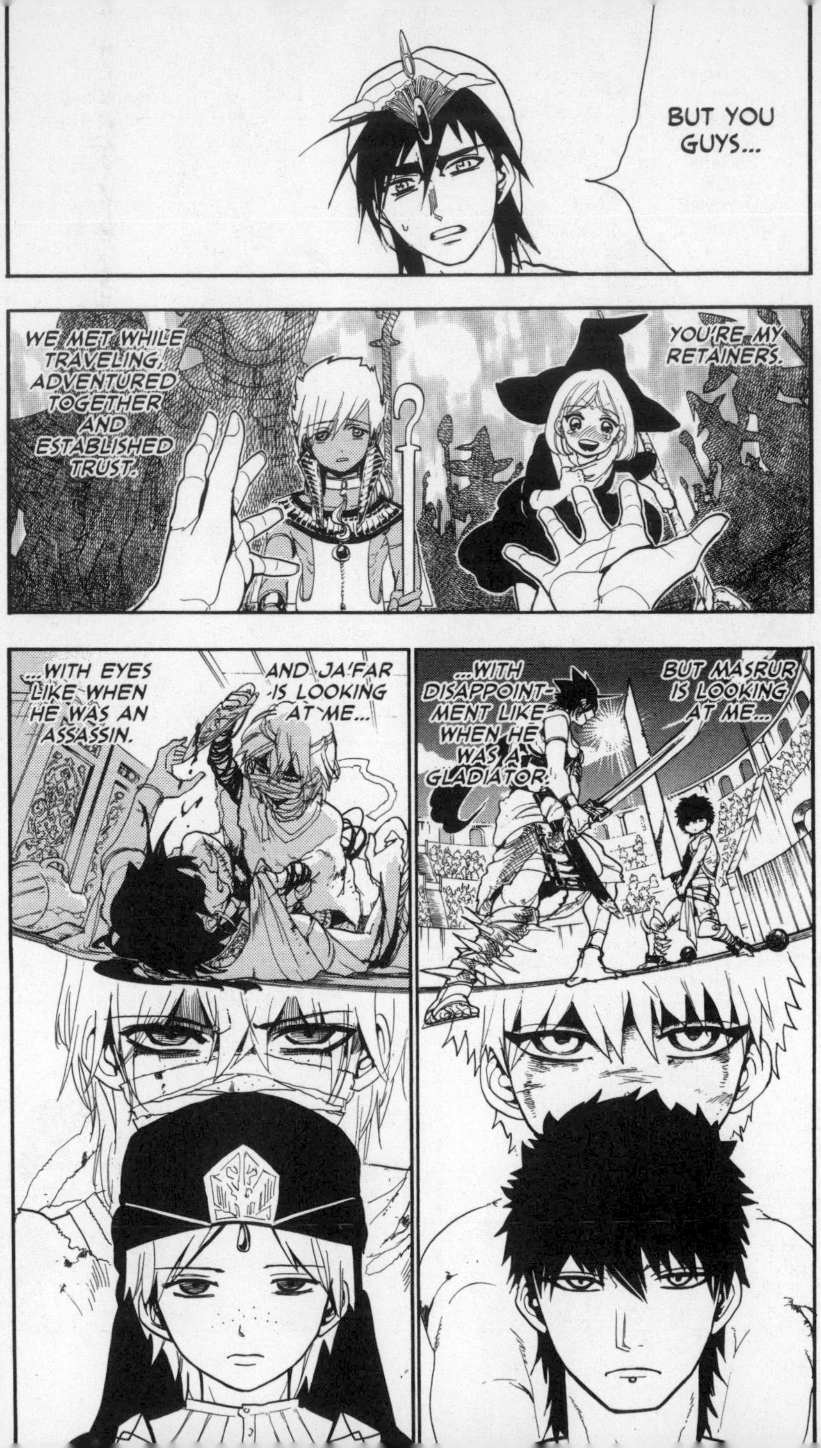
BUT YOU GUYS...
YOU'RE MY RETAINERS.
WE MET WHILE TRAVELING, ADVENTURED TOGETHER AND ESTABLISHED TRUST.
BUT MASRUR IS LOOKING AT ME...
...WITH DISAPPOINT-MENT LIKE WHEN HE WAS A GLADIATOR.
AND JA'FAR IS LOOKING AT ME...
...WITH EYES LIKE WHEN HE WAS AN ASSASSIN.

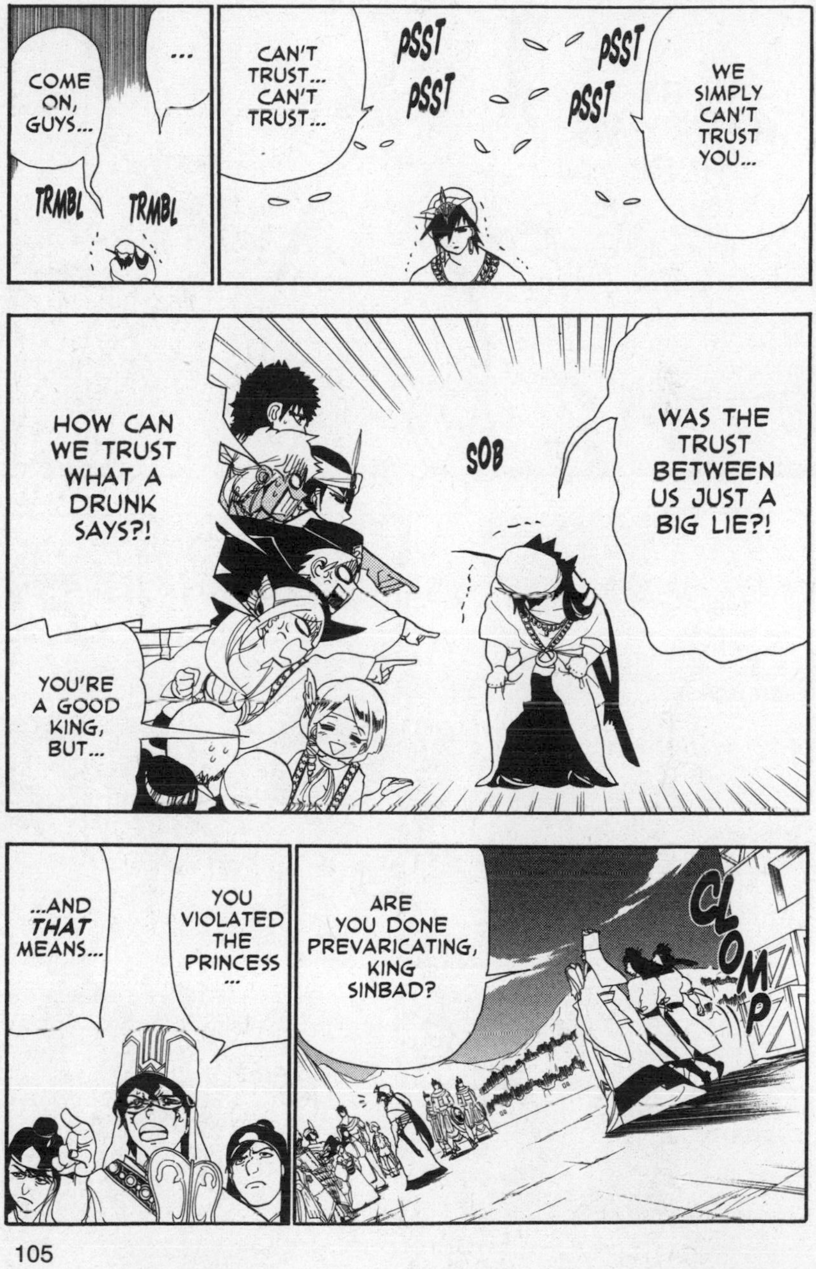

WE SIMPLY CAN'T TRUST YOU...
PSST
PSST
PSST
PSST
CAN'T TRUST... CAN'T TRUST...
...
COME ON, GUYS...
TRMBL
TRMBL
WAS THE TRUST BETWEEN US JUST A BIG LIE?!
SOB
HOW CAN WE TRUST WHAT A DRUNK SAYS?!
YOU'RE A GOOD KING, BUT...
CLOMP
ARE YOU DONE PREVARICATING, KING SINBAD?
YOU VIOLATED THE PRINCESS ...
...AND *THAT* MEANS...

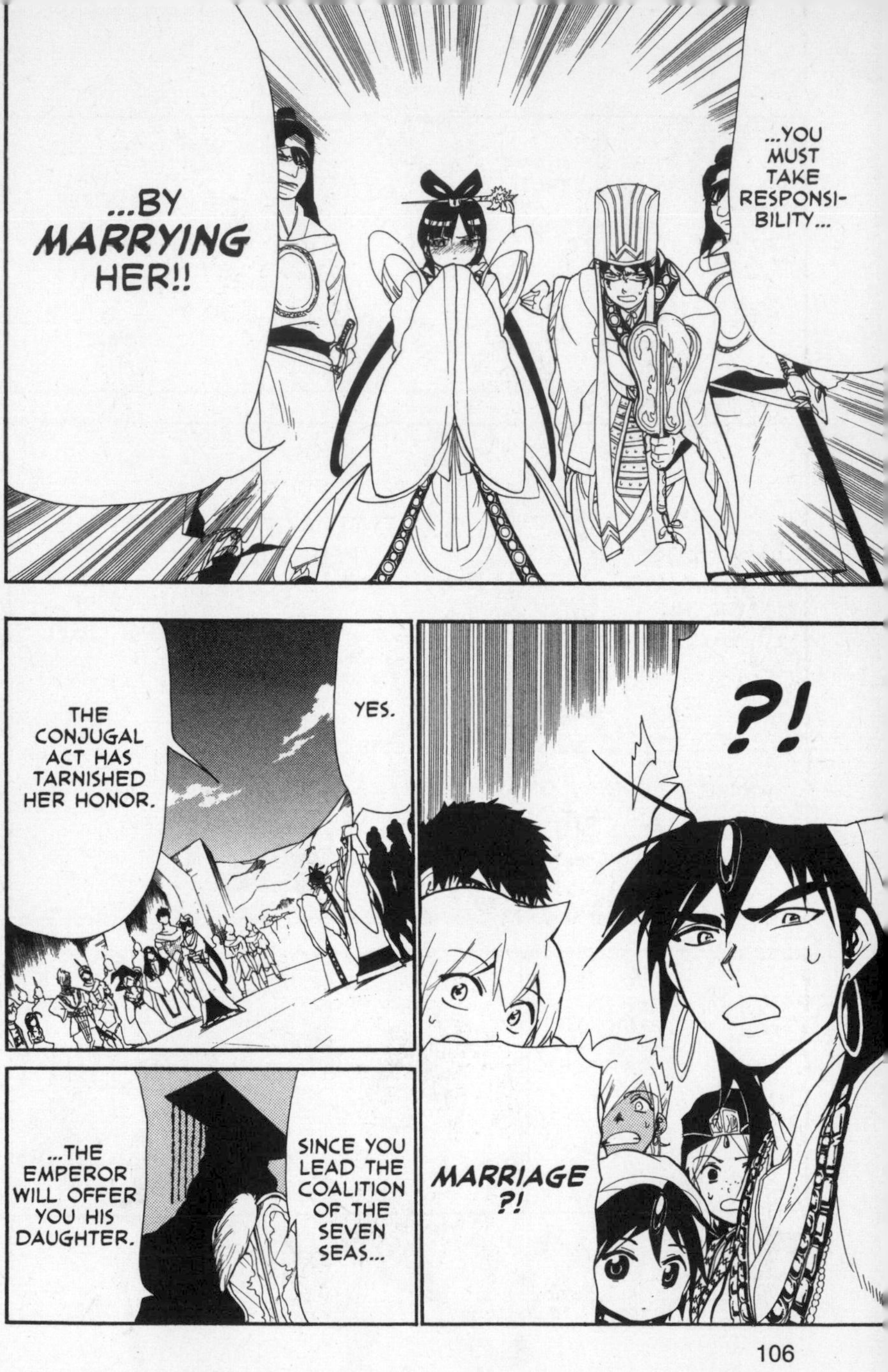
...YOU MUST TAKE RESPONSIBILITY...
...BY *MARRYING* HER!!
?!
MARRIAGE ?!
YES.
THE CONJUGAL ACT HAS TARNISHED HER HONOR.
SINCE YOU LEAD THE COALITION OF THE SEVEN SEAS...
...THE EMPEROR WILL OFFER YOU HIS DAUGHTER.

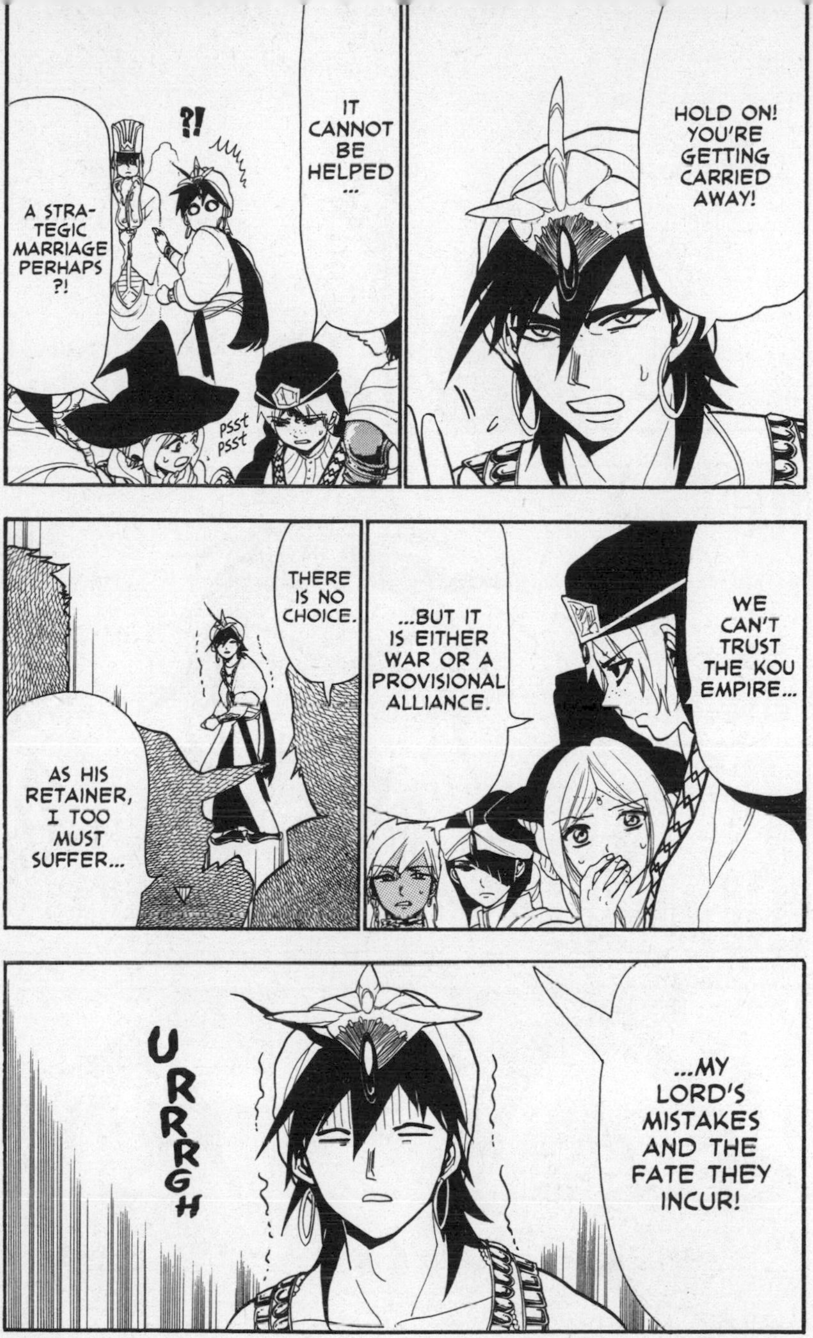
HOLD ON! YOU'RE GETTING CARRIED AWAY!
IT CANNOT BE HELPED ...
?!
A STRATEGIC MARRIAGE PERHAPS ?!
PSST PSST
WE CAN'T TRUST THE KOU EMPIRE...
...BUT IT IS EITHER WAR OR A PROVISIONAL ALLIANCE.
THERE IS NO CHOICE.
AS HIS RETAINER, I TOO MUST SUFFER...
...MY LORD'S MISTAKES AND THE FATE THEY INCUR!
URRRGH

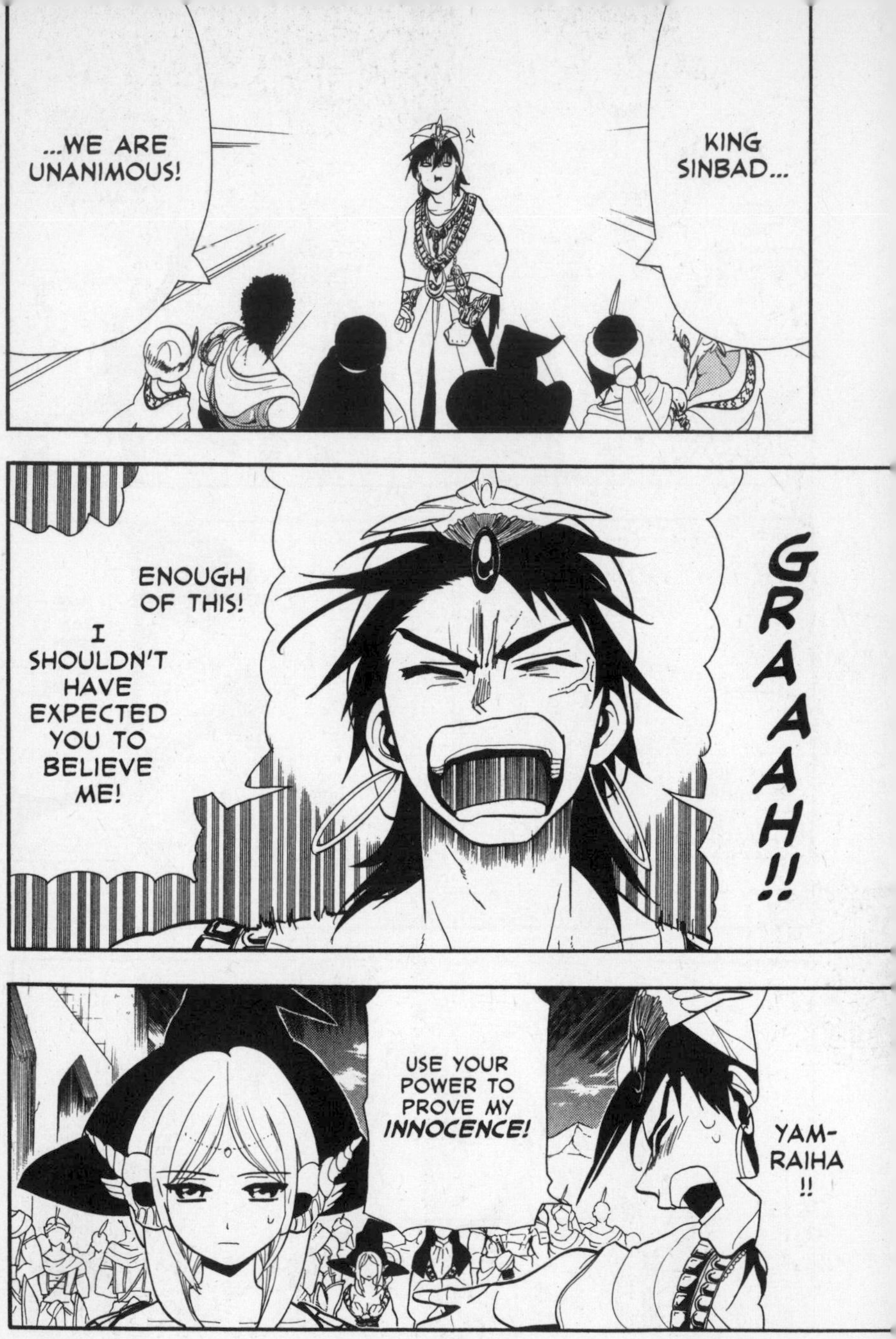
KING SINBAD...
...WE ARE UNANIMOUS!
GRAAAH!!
ENOUGH OF THIS!
I SHOULDN'T HAVE EXPECTED YOU TO BELIEVE ME!
YAM-RAIHA!!
USE YOUR POWER TO PROVE MY *INNOCENCE!*

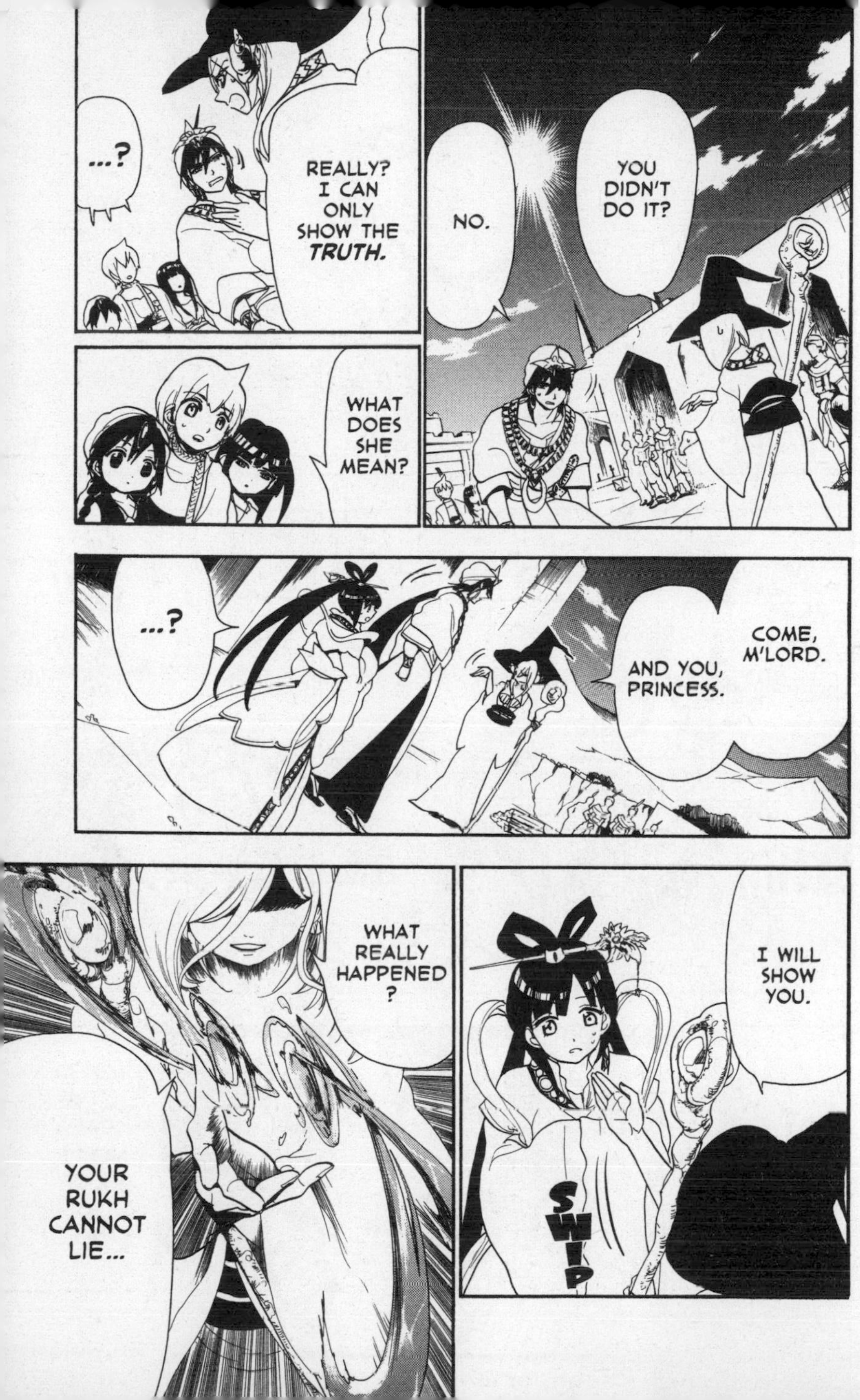
YOU DIDN'T DO IT?
NO.
REALLY? I CAN ONLY SHOW THE *TRUTH.*
...?
WHAT DOES SHE MEAN?
COME, M'LORD.
AND YOU, PRINCESS.
...?
I WILL SHOW YOU.
SWIP
WHAT REALLY HAPPENED?
YOUR RUKH CANNOT LIE...

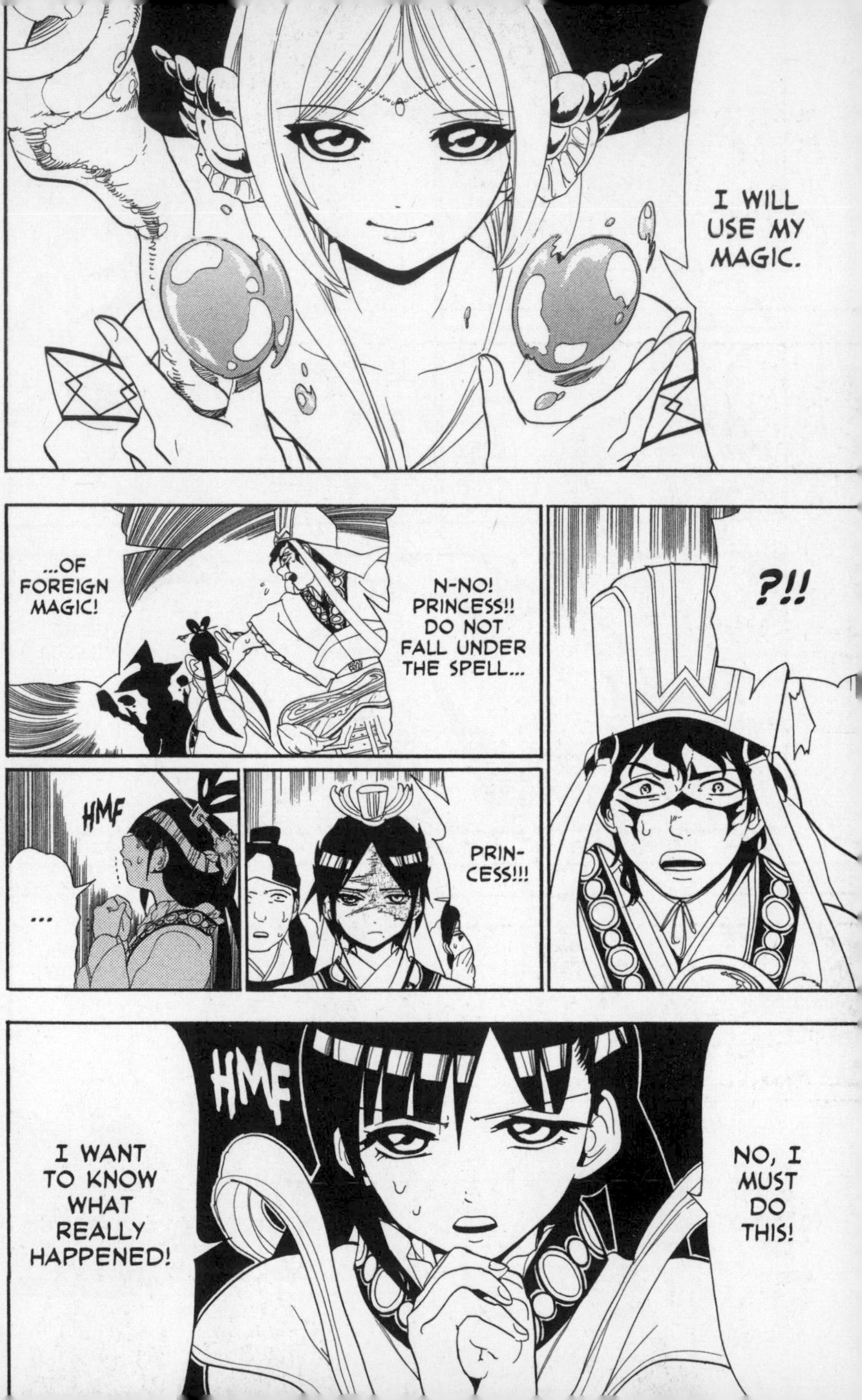
I WILL USE MY MAGIC.
?!!
N-NO! PRINCESS!! DO NOT FALL UNDER THE SPELL...
...OF FOREIGN MAGIC!
PRIN-CESS!!!
HMF
...
HMF
NO, I MUST DO THIS!
I WANT TO KNOW WHAT REALLY HAPPENED!

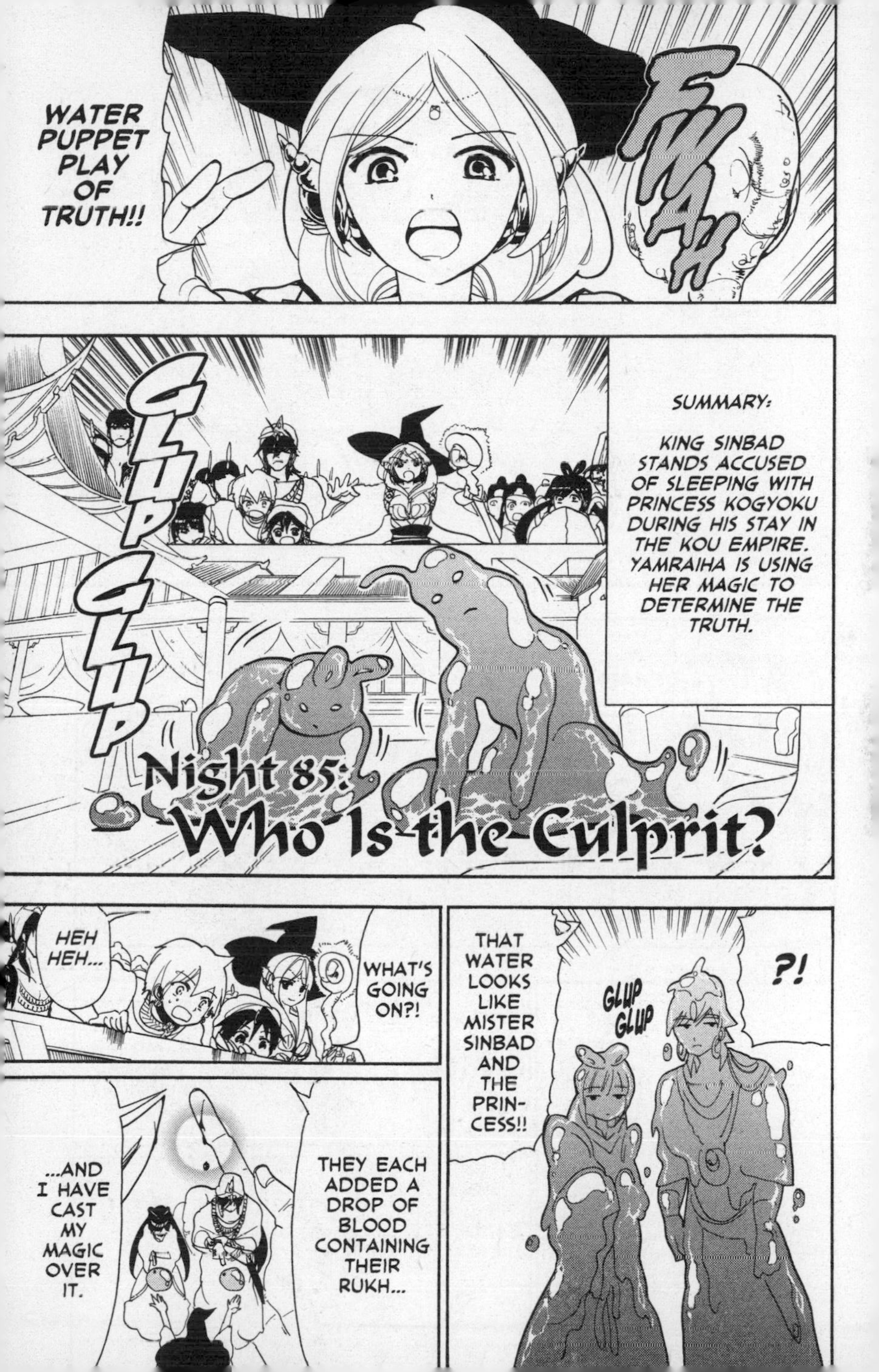

FWAH
WATER PUPPET PLAY OF TRUTH!!
SUMMARY:
KING SINBAD STANDS ACCUSED OF SLEEPING WITH PRINCESS KOGYOKU DURING HIS STAY IN THE KOU EMPIRE. YAMRAIHA IS USING HER MAGIC TO DETERMINE THE TRUTH.
GLUP GLUP GLUP
Night 85: Who Is the Culprit?
?!
GLUP GLUP
THAT WATER LOOKS LIKE MISTER SINBAD AND THE PRIN-CESS!!
WHAT'S GOING ON?!
HEH HEH...
THEY EACH ADDED A DROP OF BLOOD CONTAINING THEIR RUKH...
...AND I HAVE CAST MY MAGIC OVER IT.

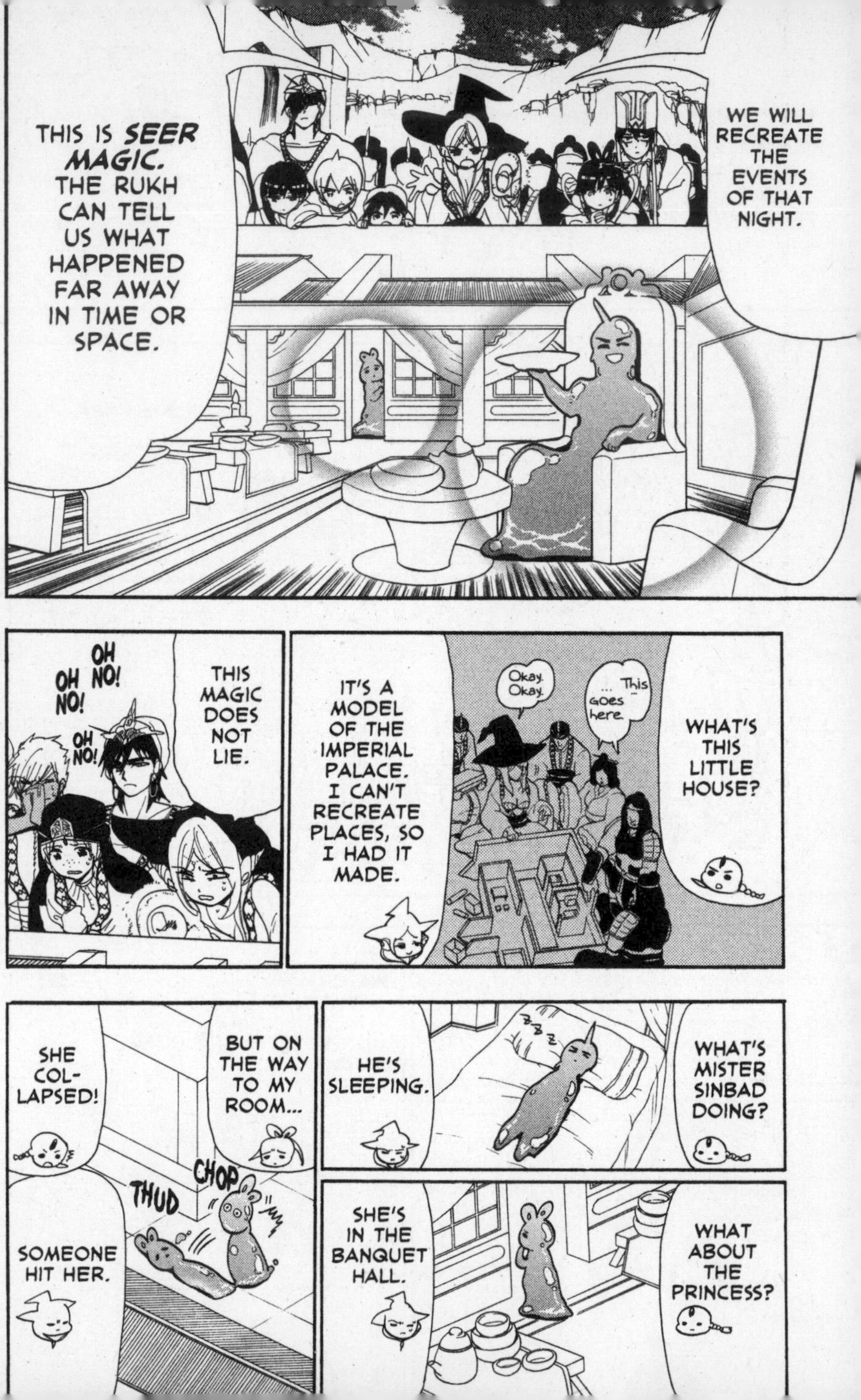
WE WILL RECREATE THE EVENTS OF THAT NIGHT.
THIS IS SEER MAGIC. THE RUKH CAN TELL US WHAT HAPPENED FAR AWAY IN TIME OR SPACE.
WHAT'S THIS LITTLE HOUSE?
... This goes here.
Okay. Okay.
IT'S A MODEL OF THE IMPERIAL PALACE. I CAN'T RECREATE PLACES, SO I HAD IT MADE.
THIS MAGIC DOES NOT LIE.
OH NO! OH NO!
OH NO!
WHAT'S MISTER SINBAD DOING?
HE'S SLEEPING.
WHAT ABOUT THE PRINCESS?
SHE'S IN THE BANQUET HALL.
BUT ON THE WAY TO MY ROOM...
SHE COL-LAPSED!
CHOP
THUD
SOMEONE HIT HER.

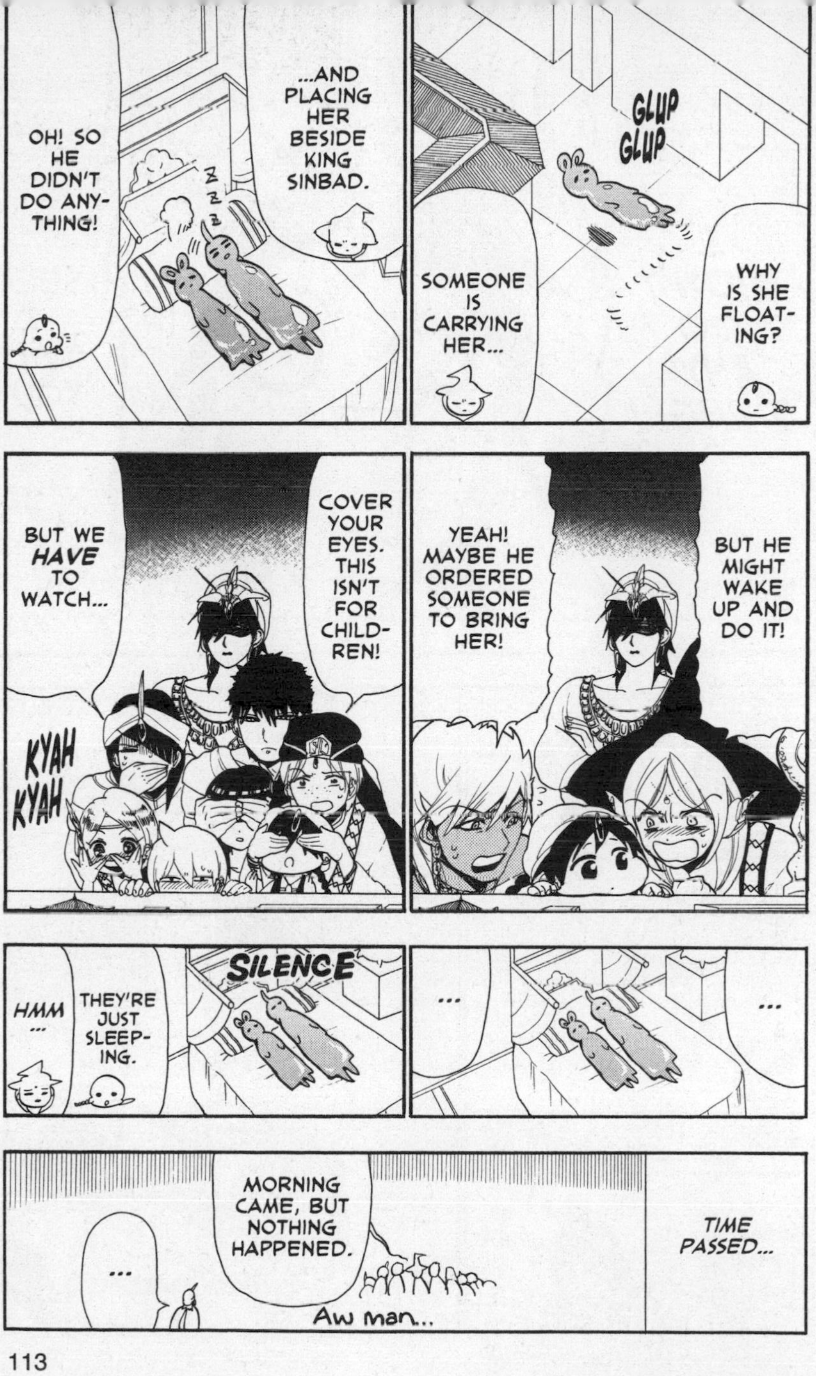
WHY IS SHE FLOATING?
GLUP GLUP
SOMEONE IS CARRYING HER...
...AND PLACING HER BESIDE KING SINBAD.
OH! SO HE DIDN'T DO ANYTHING!
BUT HE MIGHT WAKE UP AND DO IT!
YEAH! MAYBE HE ORDERED SOMEONE TO BRING HER!
COVER YOUR EYES. THIS ISN'T FOR CHILDREN!
BUT WE *HAVE* TO WATCH...
KYAH KYAH
...
...
SILENCE
THEY'RE JUST SLEEPING.
HMM...
TIME PASSED...
MORNING CAME, BUT NOTHING HAPPENED.
...
Aw man...

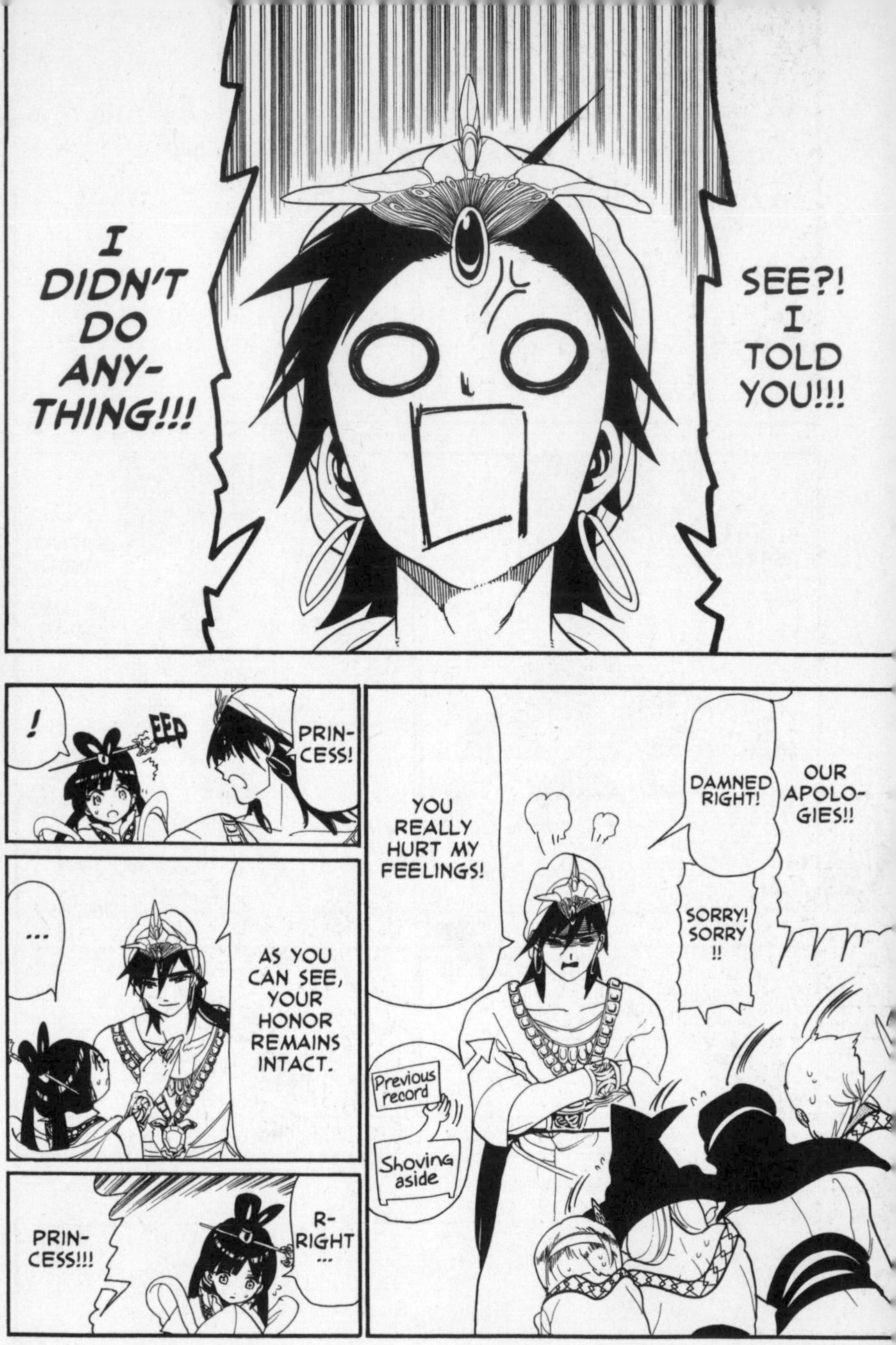
SEE?! I TOLD YOU!!!
I DIDN'T DO ANY-THING!!!
OUR APOLO-GIES!!
DAMNED RIGHT!
SORRY! SORRY !!
YOU REALLY HURT MY FEELINGS!
Previous record
Shoving aside
PRIN-CESS!
EEP
!
AS YOU CAN SEE, YOUR HONOR REMAINS INTACT.
...
R-RIGHT ...
PRIN-CESS!!!

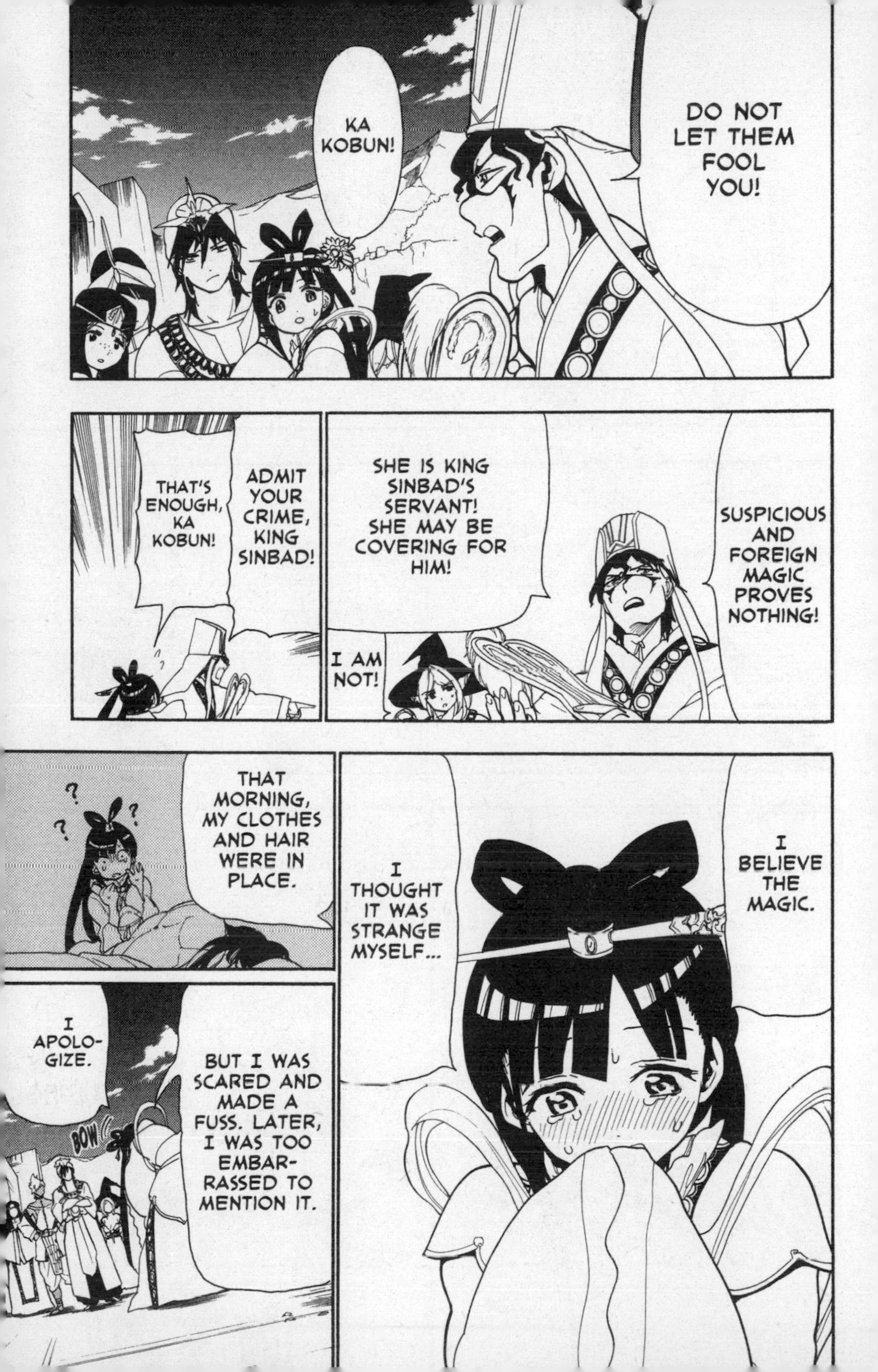
DO NOT LET THEM FOOL YOU!
KA KOBUN!
SUSPICIOUS AND FOREIGN MAGIC PROVES NOTHING!
SHE IS KING SINBAD'S SERVANT! SHE MAY BE COVERING FOR HIM!
I AM NOT!
ADMIT YOUR CRIME, KING SINBAD!
THAT'S ENOUGH, KA KOBUN!
I BELIEVE THE MAGIC.
I THOUGHT IT WAS STRANGE MYSELF...
THAT MORNING, MY CLOTHES AND HAIR WERE IN PLACE.
BUT I WAS SCARED AND MADE A FUSS. LATER, I WAS TOO EMBAR-RASSED TO MENTION IT.
I APOLO-GIZE.
BOW

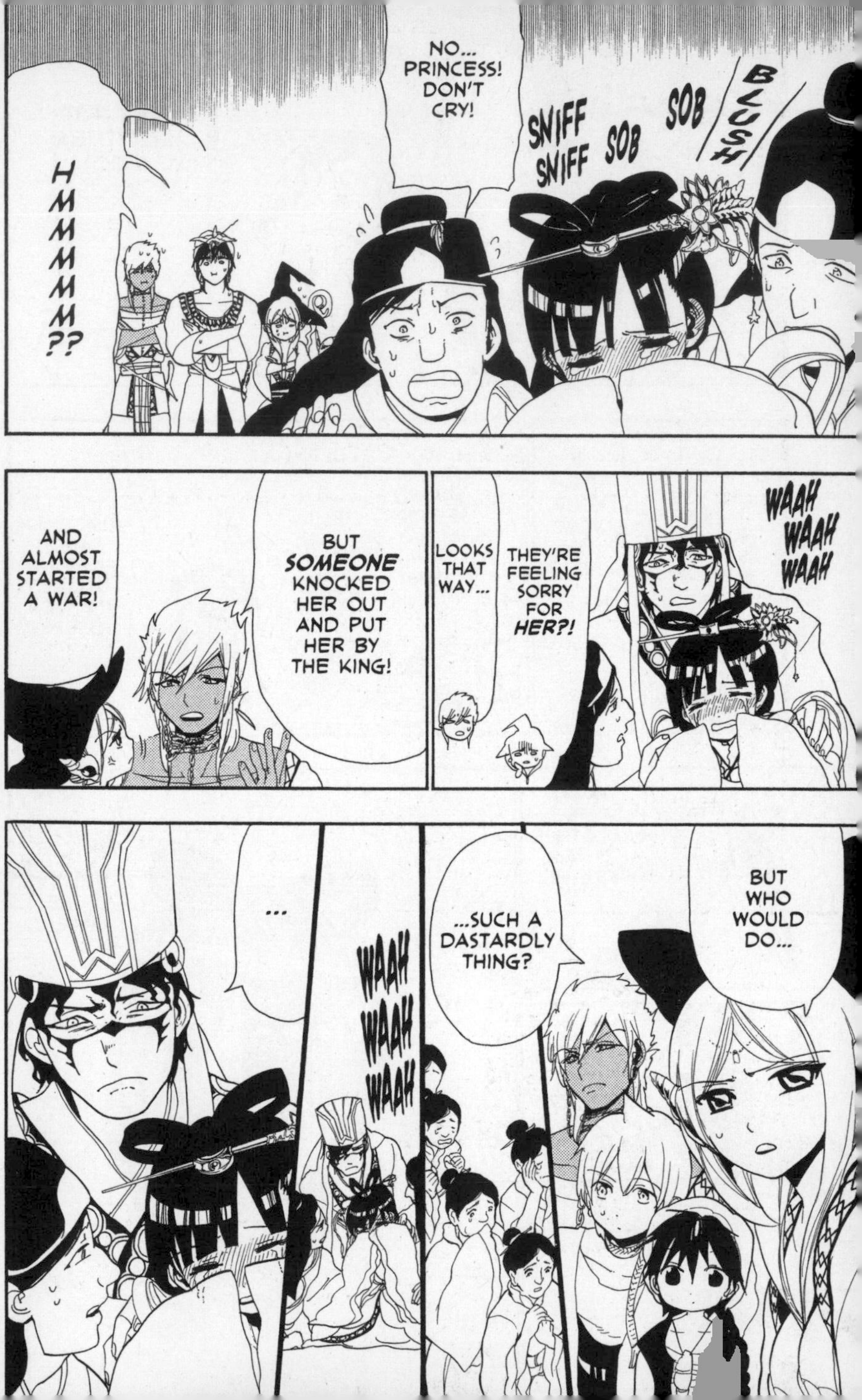
BLUSH
SOB
SOB
SNIFF SNIFF
NO... PRINCESS! DON'T CRY!
HMMMMMMM??
WAAH WAAH WAAH
THEY'RE FEELING SORRY FOR *HER?!*
LOOKS THAT WAY...
BUT *SOMEONE* KNOCKED HER OUT AND PUT HER BY THE KING!
AND ALMOST STARTED A WAR!
BUT WHO WOULD DO...
...SUCH A DASTARDLY THING?
WAAH WAAH WAAH
...

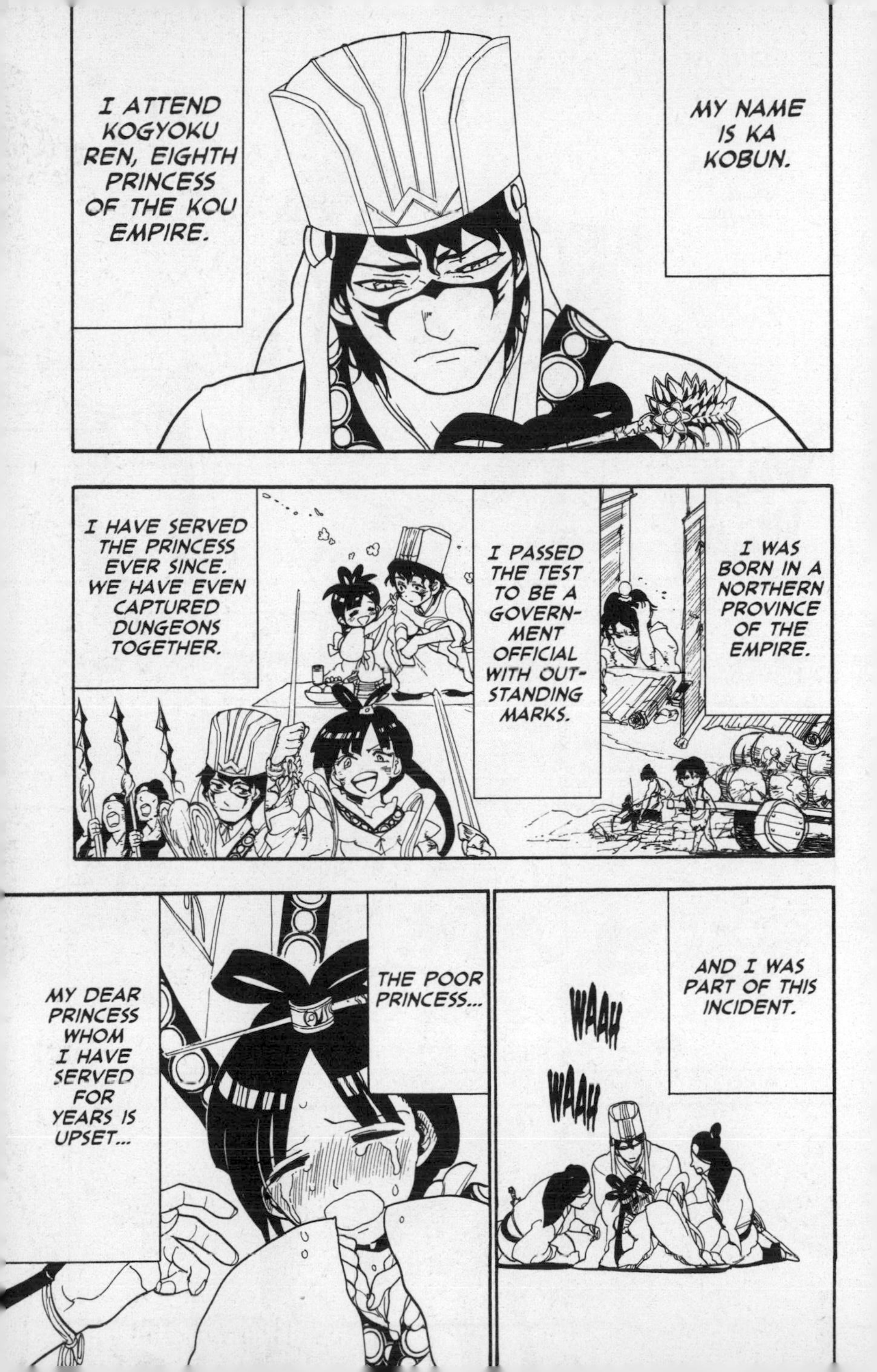
MY NAME IS KA KOBUN.
I ATTEND KOGYOKU REN, EIGHTH PRINCESS OF THE KOU EMPIRE.
I WAS BORN IN A NORTHERN PROVINCE OF THE EMPIRE.
I PASSED THE TEST TO BE A GOVERNMENT OFFICIAL WITH OUTSTANDING MARKS.
I HAVE SERVED THE PRINCESS EVER SINCE. WE HAVE EVEN CAPTURED DUNGEONS TOGETHER.
AND I WAS PART OF THIS INCIDENT.
WAAH
WAAH
THE POOR PRINCESS...
MY DEAR PRINCESS WHOM I HAVE SERVED FOR YEARS IS UPSET...

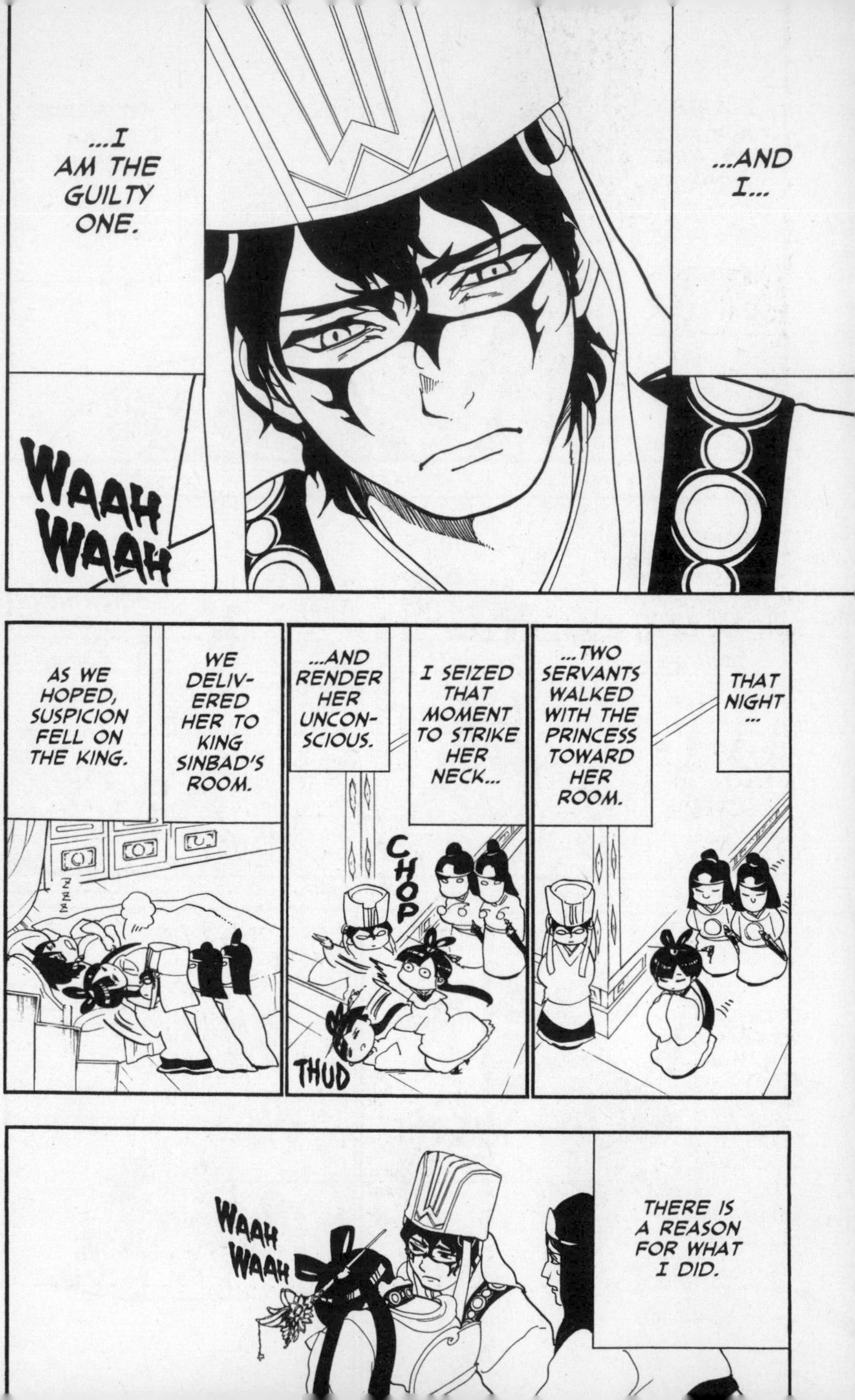
...AND I...
...I AM THE GUILTY ONE.
WAAH WAAH
THAT NIGHT ...
...TWO SERVANTS WALKED WITH THE PRINCESS TOWARD HER ROOM.
I SEIZED THAT MOMENT TO STRIKE HER NECK...
...AND RENDER HER UNCONSCIOUS.
CHOP
THUD
WE DELIV-ERED HER TO KING SINBAD'S ROOM.
AS WE HOPED, SUSPICION FELL ON THE KING.
THERE IS A REASON FOR WHAT I DID.
WAAH WAAH

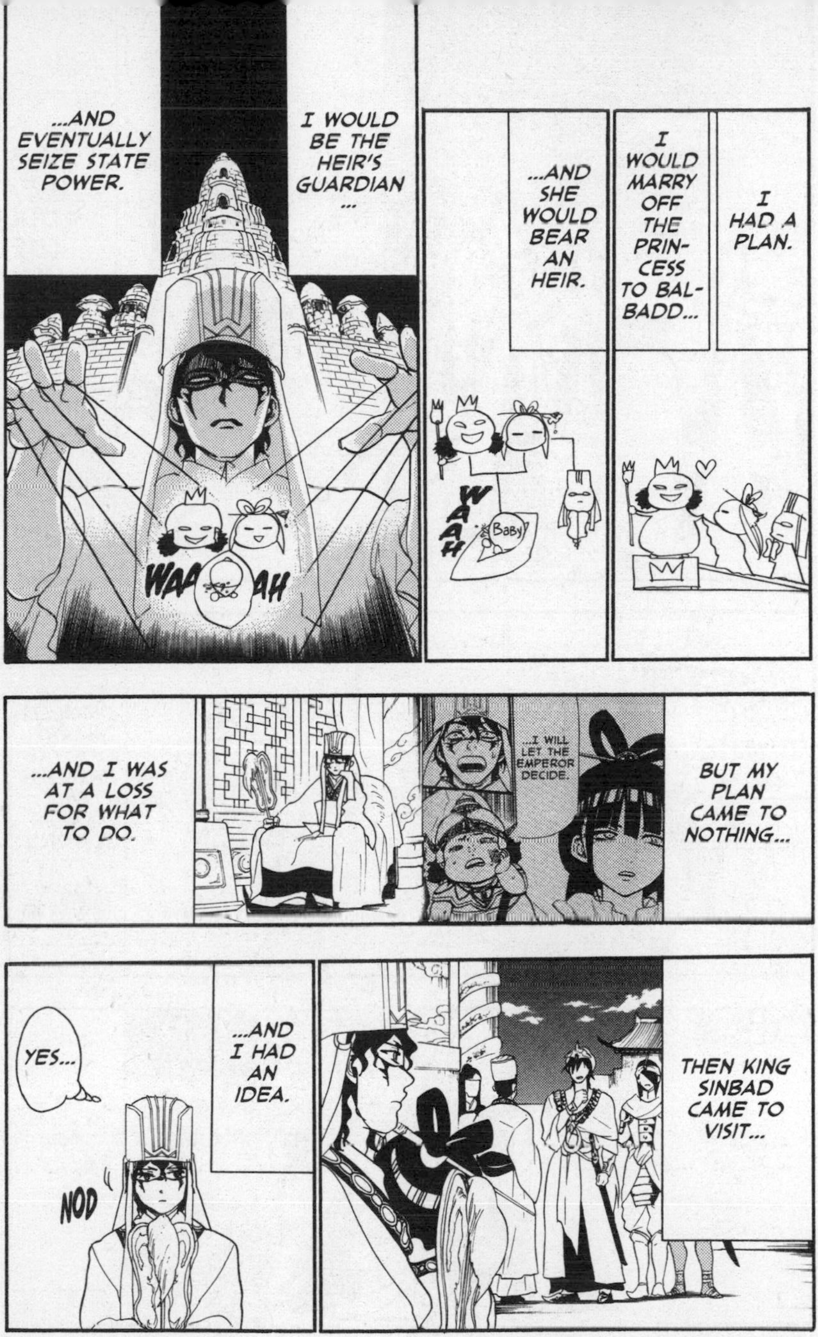
I HAD A PLAN.
I WOULD MARRY OFF THE PRIN-CESS TO BAL-BADD...
...AND SHE WOULD BEAR AN HEIR.
WAAH
Baby
I WOULD BE THE HEIR'S GUARDIAN...
...AND EVENTUALLY SEIZE STATE POWER.
WAAAH
BUT MY PLAN CAME TO NOTHING...
...I WILL LET THE EMPEROR DECIDE.
...AND I WAS AT A LOSS FOR WHAT TO DO.
THEN KING SINBAD CAME TO VISIT...
...AND I HAD AN IDEA.
YES...
NOD

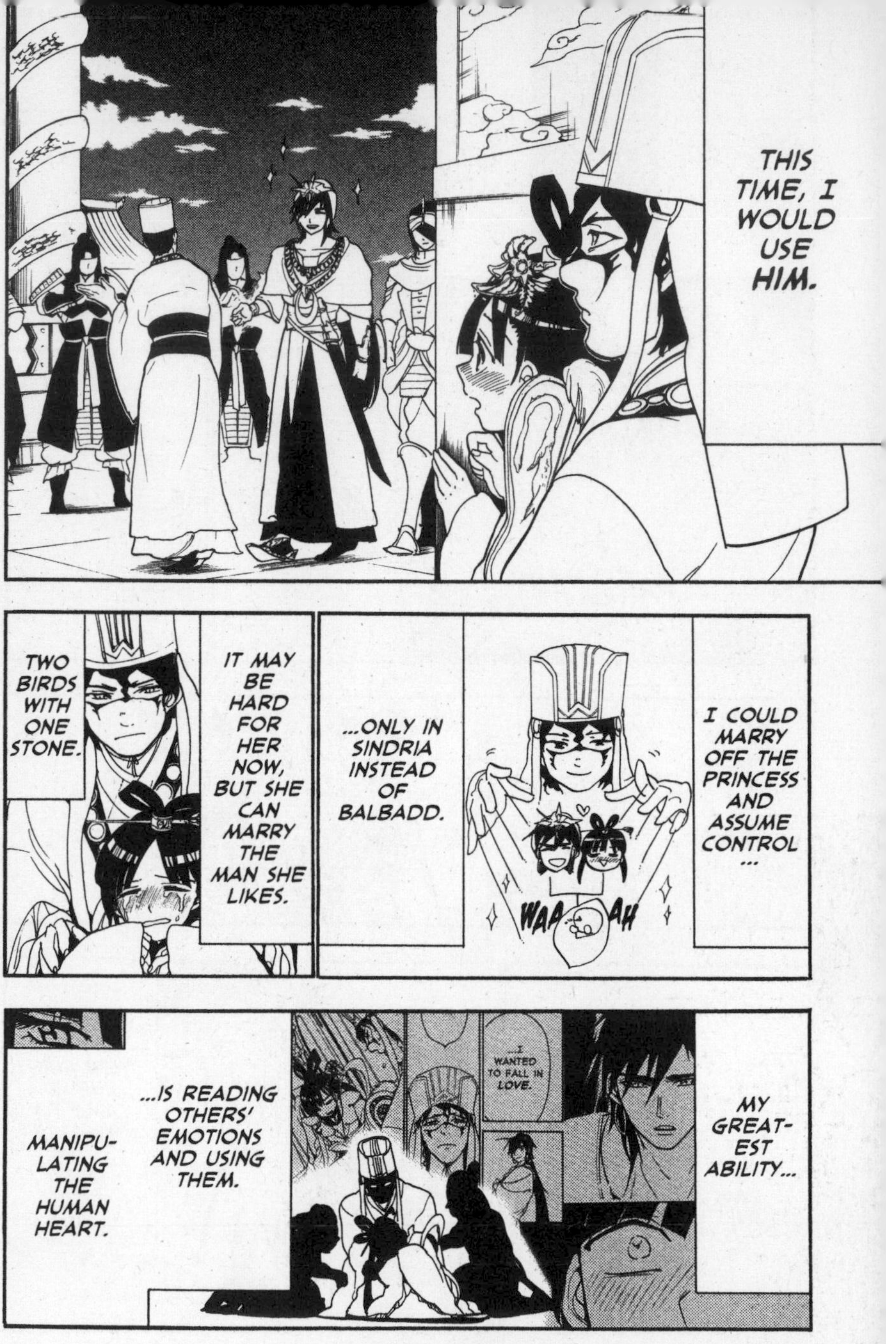
THIS TIME, I WOULD USE HIM.
I COULD MARRY OFF THE PRINCESS AND ASSUME CONTROL...
WAA AH
...ONLY IN SINDRIA INSTEAD OF BALBADD.
IT MAY BE HARD FOR HER NOW, BUT SHE CAN MARRY THE MAN SHE LIKES.
TWO BIRDS WITH ONE STONE.
MY GREAT-EST ABILITY...
...I WANTED TO FALL IN LOVE.
...IS READING OTHERS' EMOTIONS AND USING THEM.
MANIPU-LATING THE HUMAN HEART.

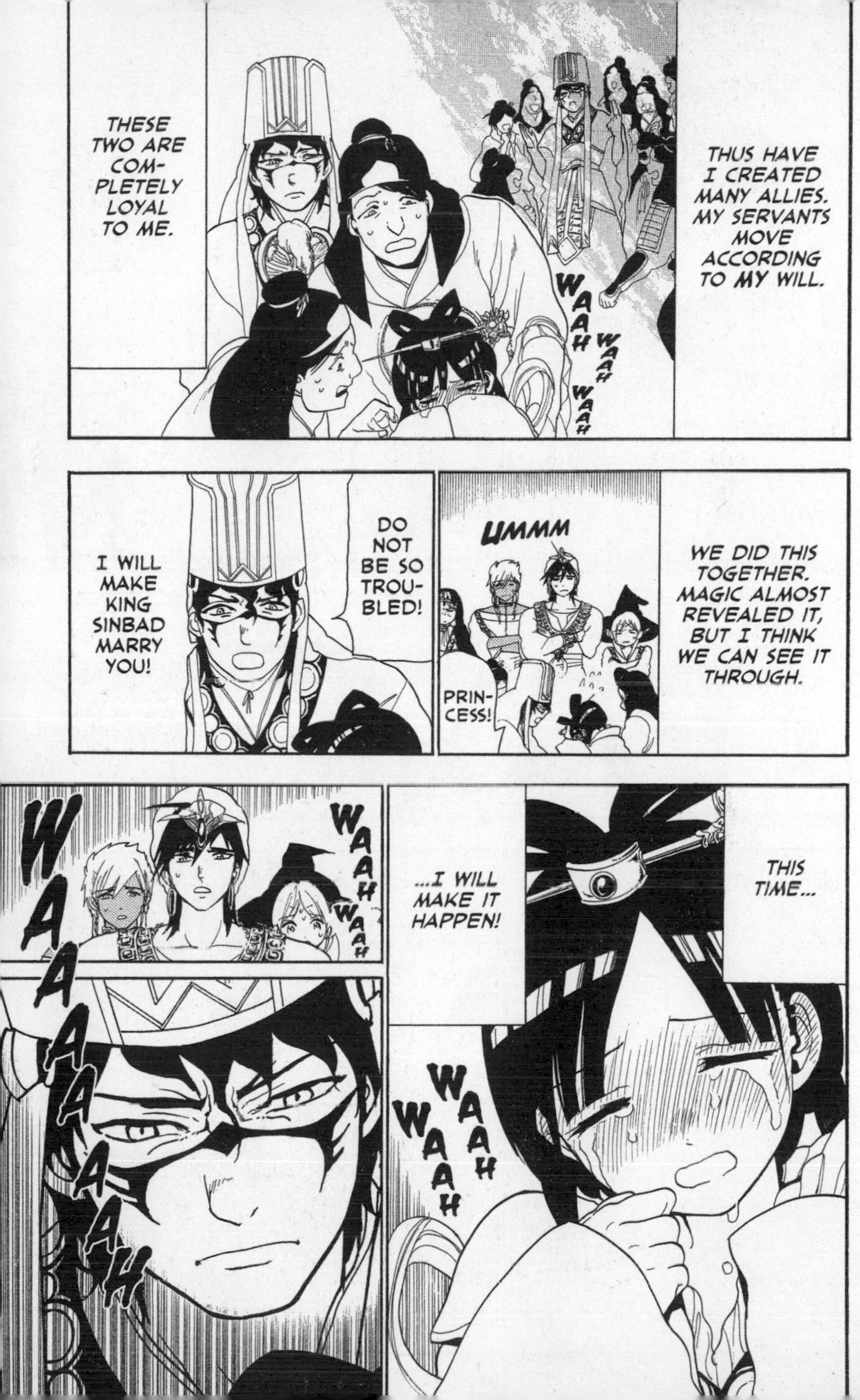
THUS HAVE I CREATED MANY ALLIES. MY SERVANTS MOVE ACCORDING TO MY WILL.
WAAH WAAH WAAH
THESE TWO ARE COM-PLETELY LOYAL TO ME.
WE DID THIS TOGETHER. MAGIC ALMOST REVEALED IT, BUT I THINK WE CAN SEE IT THROUGH.
UMMM
PRINCESS!
DO NOT BE SO TROUBLED!
I WILL MAKE KING SINBAD MARRY YOU!
THIS TIME...
...I WILL MAKE IT HAPPEN!
WAAH WAAH
WAAH WAAH
WAAAAAAH

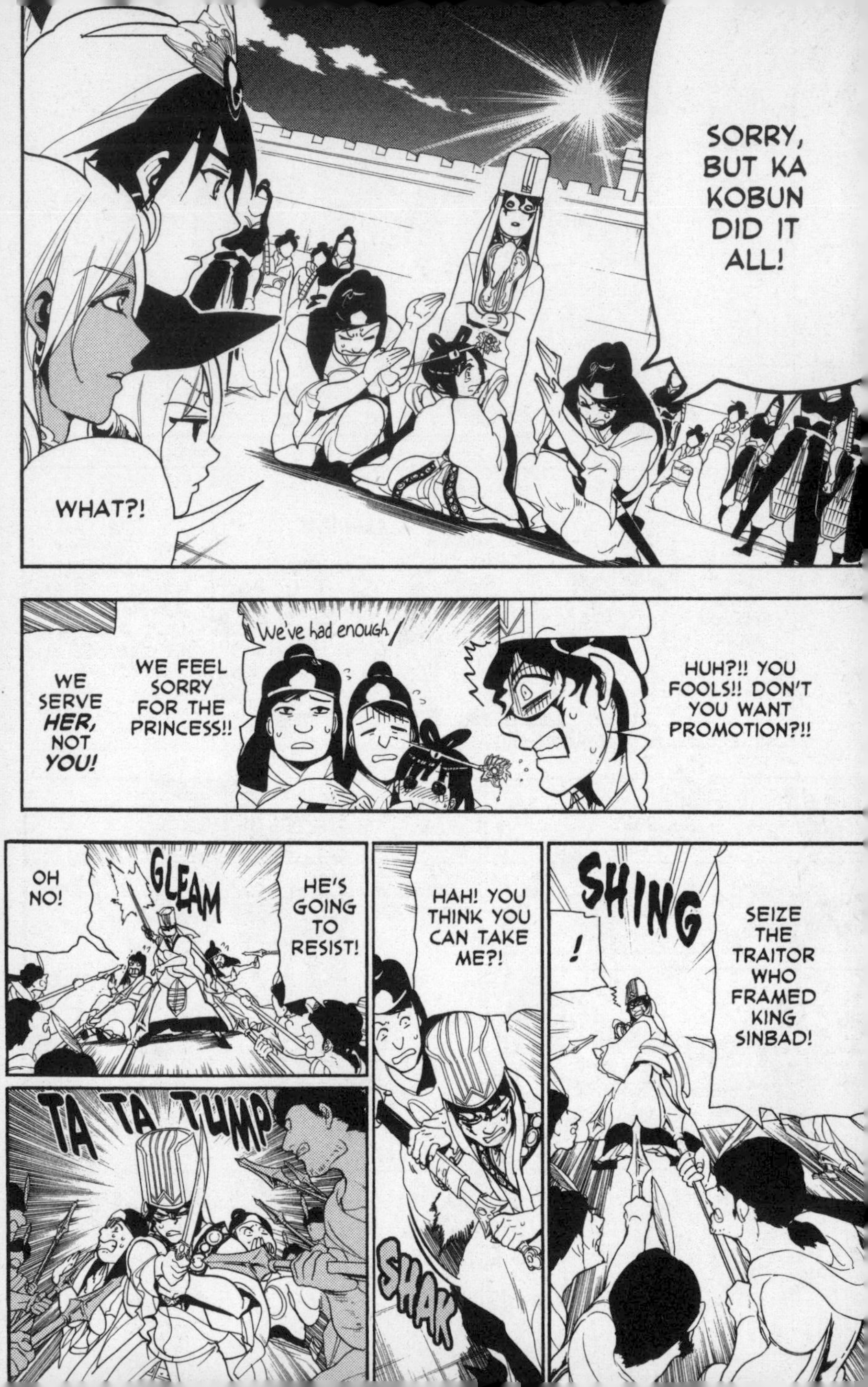
SORRY, BUT KA KOBUN DID IT ALL!
WHAT?!
HUH?!! YOU FOOLS!! DON'T YOU WANT PROMOTION?!!
We've had enough!
WE FEEL SORRY FOR THE PRINCESS!!
WE SERVE *HER,* NOT *YOU!*
SHING
!
SEIZE THE TRAITOR WHO FRAMED KING SINBAD!
HAH! YOU THINK YOU CAN TAKE ME?!
SHAK
GLEAM
HE'S GOING TO RESIST!
OH NO!
TA TA TUMP

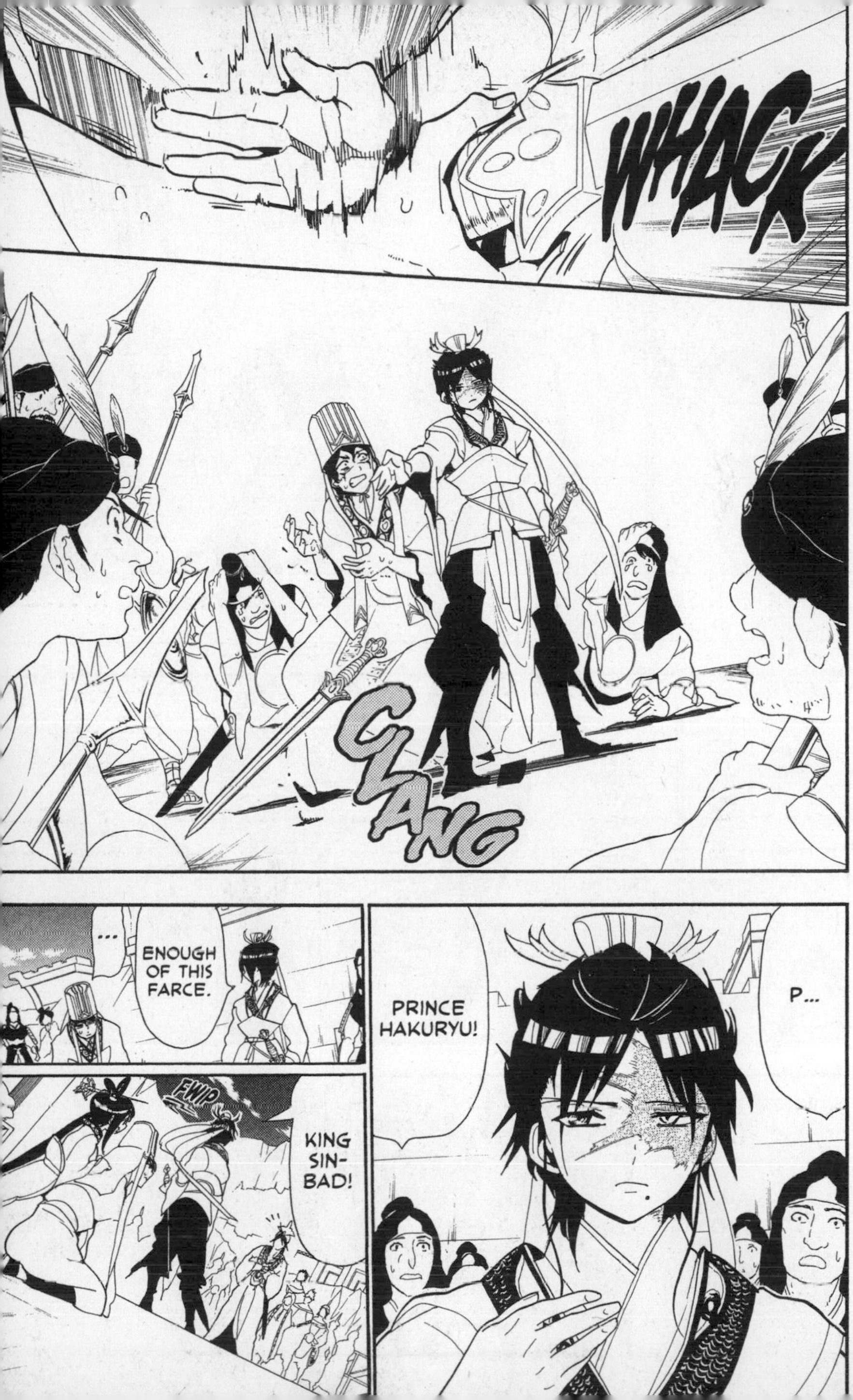
WHACK
CLANG
P...
PRINCE HAKURYU!
...
ENOUGH OF THIS FARCE.
FWIP
KING SIN-BAD!

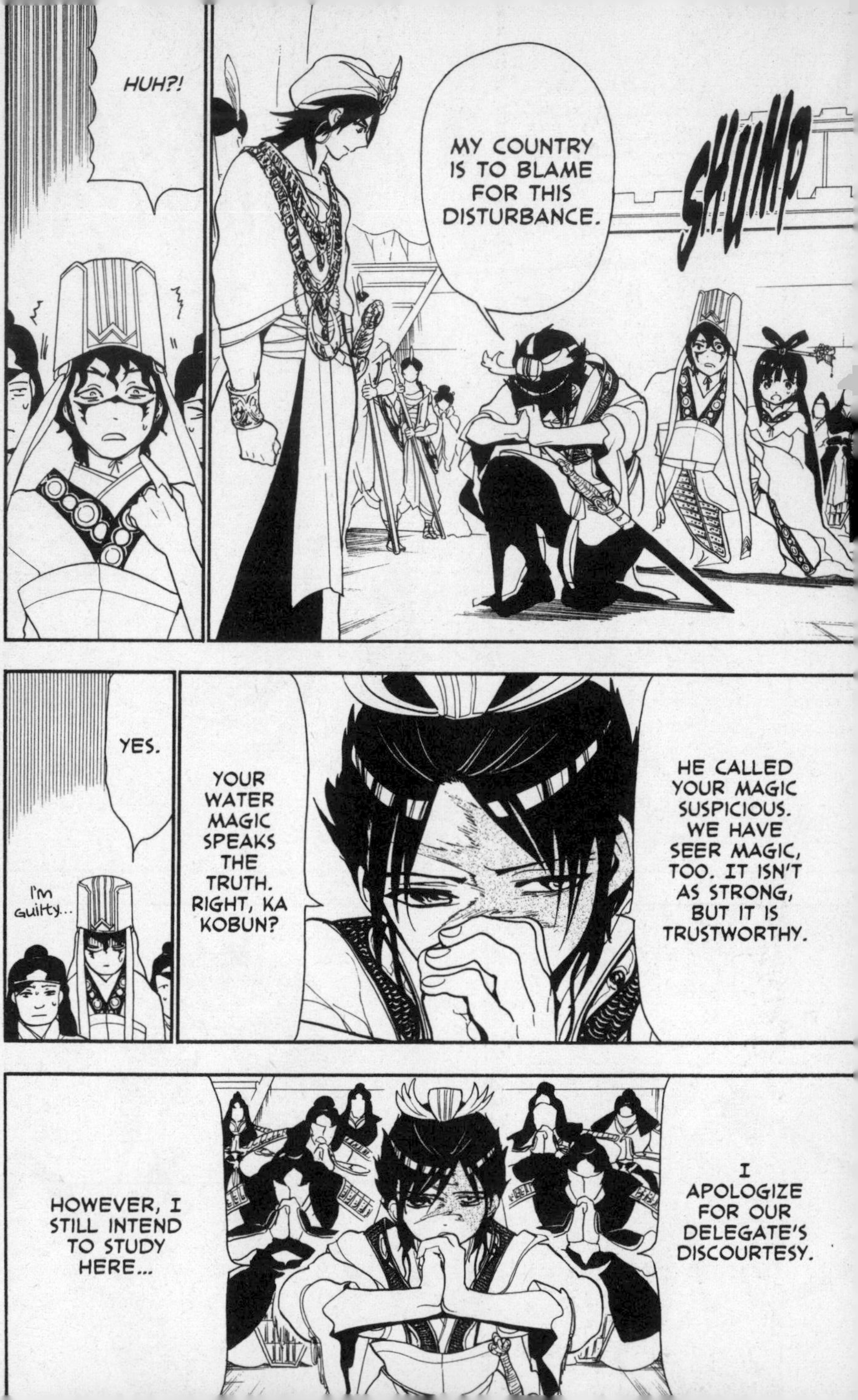
SHUMP
MY COUNTRY IS TO BLAME FOR THIS DISTURBANCE.
HUH?!
HE CALLED YOUR MAGIC SUSPICIOUS. WE HAVE SEER MAGIC, TOO. IT ISN'T AS STRONG, BUT IT IS TRUSTWORTHY.
YOUR WATER MAGIC SPEAKS THE TRUTH. RIGHT, KA KOBUN?
YES.
I'm Guilty...
I APOLOGIZE FOR OUR DELEGATE'S DISCOURTESY.
HOWEVER, I STILL INTEND TO STUDY HERE...

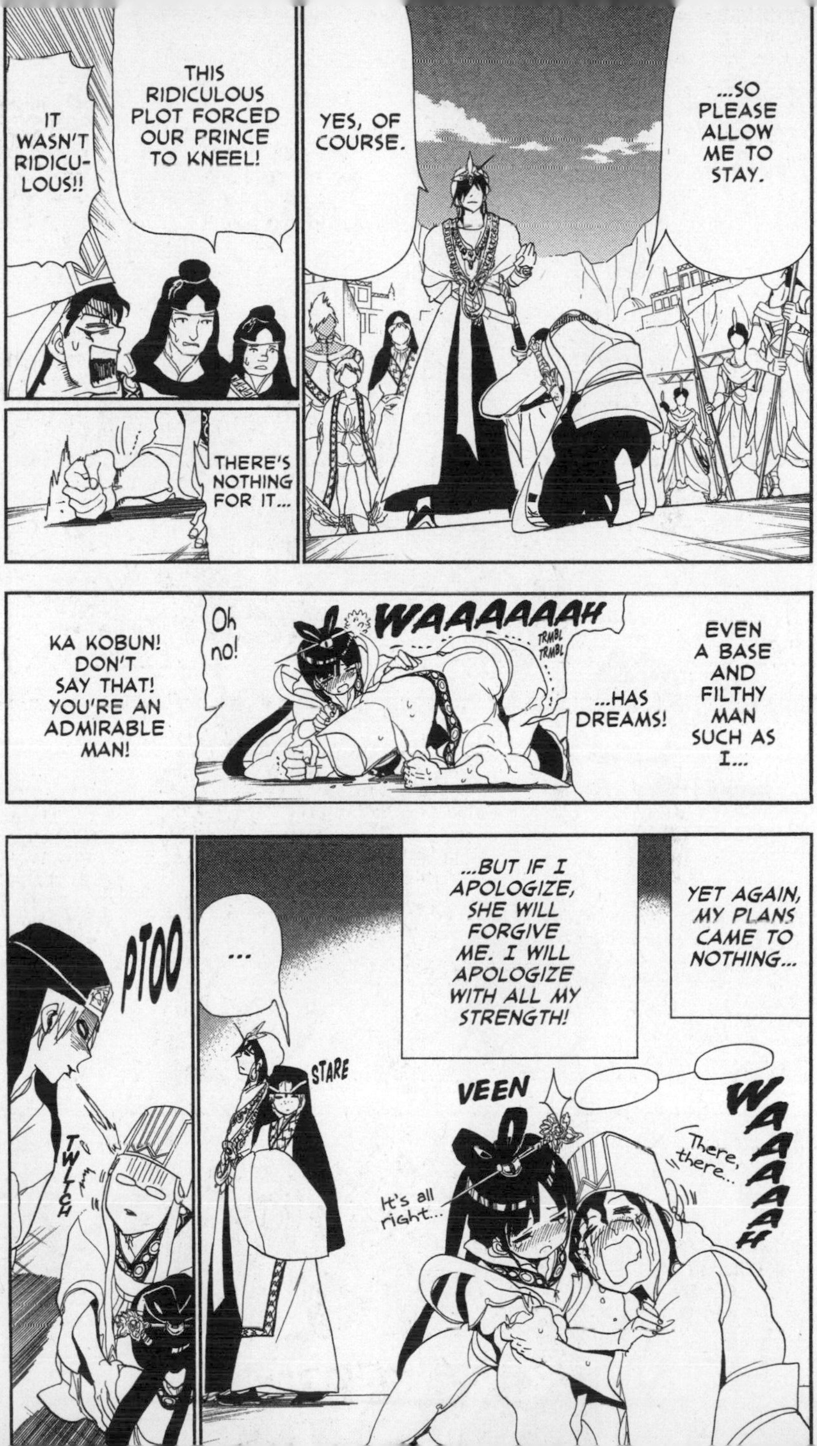
...SO PLEASE ALLOW ME TO STAY.
YES, OF COURSE.
THIS RIDICULOUS PLOT FORCED OUR PRINCE TO KNEEL!
IT WASN'T RIDICU-LOUS!!
THERE'S NOTHING FOR IT...
EVEN A BASE AND FILTHY MAN SUCH AS I...
...HAS DREAMS!
WAAAAAAH
TRMBL TRMBL
Oh no!
KA KOBUN! DON'T SAY THAT! YOU'RE AN ADMIRABLE MAN!
YET AGAIN, MY PLANS CAME TO NOTHING...
...BUT IF I APOLOGIZE, SHE WILL FORGIVE ME. I WILL APOLOGIZE WITH ALL MY STRENGTH!
WAAAAAAH
There, there...
VEEN
It's all right...
...
STARE
PTOO
TWITCH

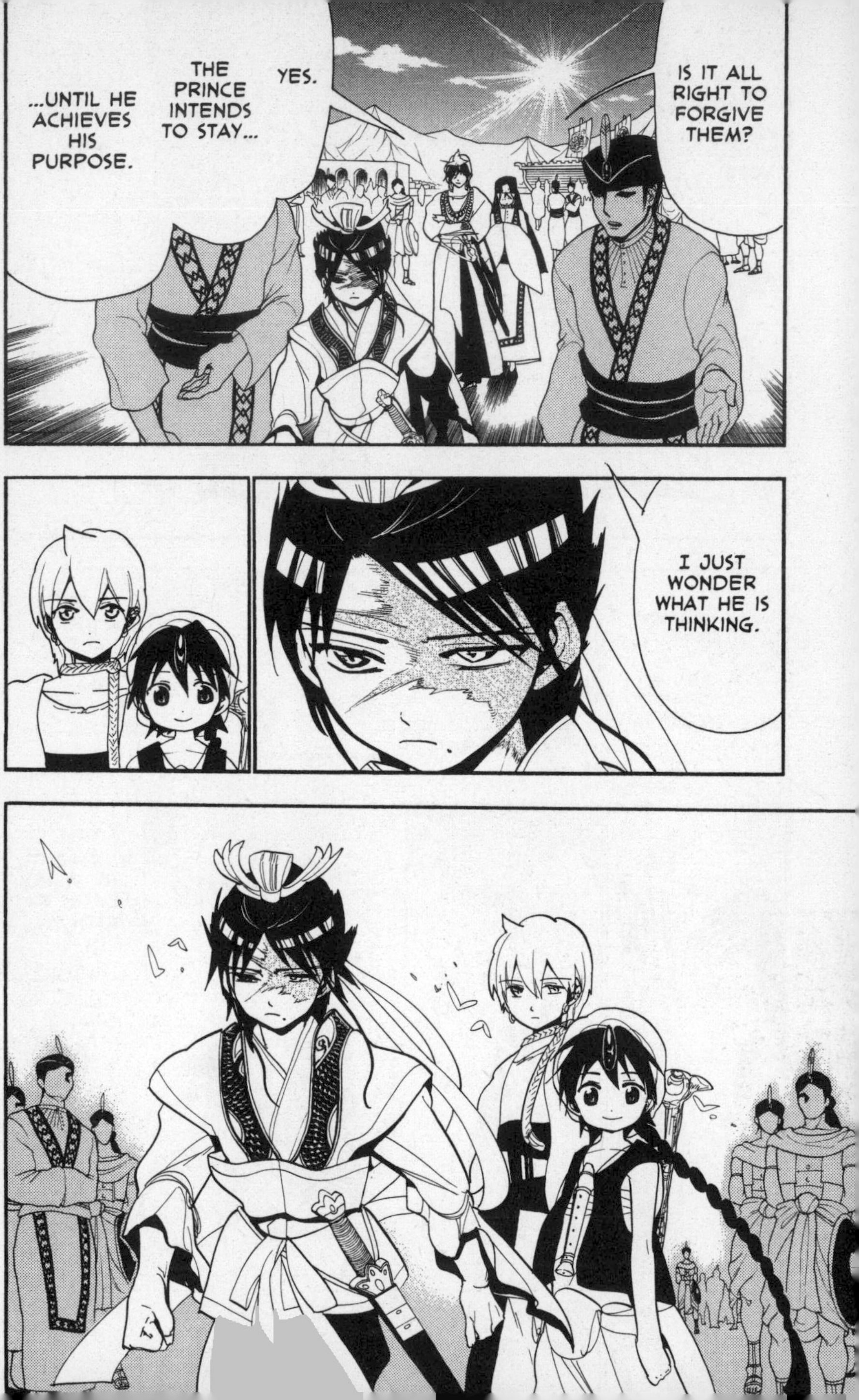
IS IT ALL RIGHT TO FORGIVE THEM?
YES.
THE PRINCE INTENDS TO STAY...
...UNTIL HE ACHIEVES HIS PURPOSE.
I JUST WONDER WHAT HE IS THINKING.

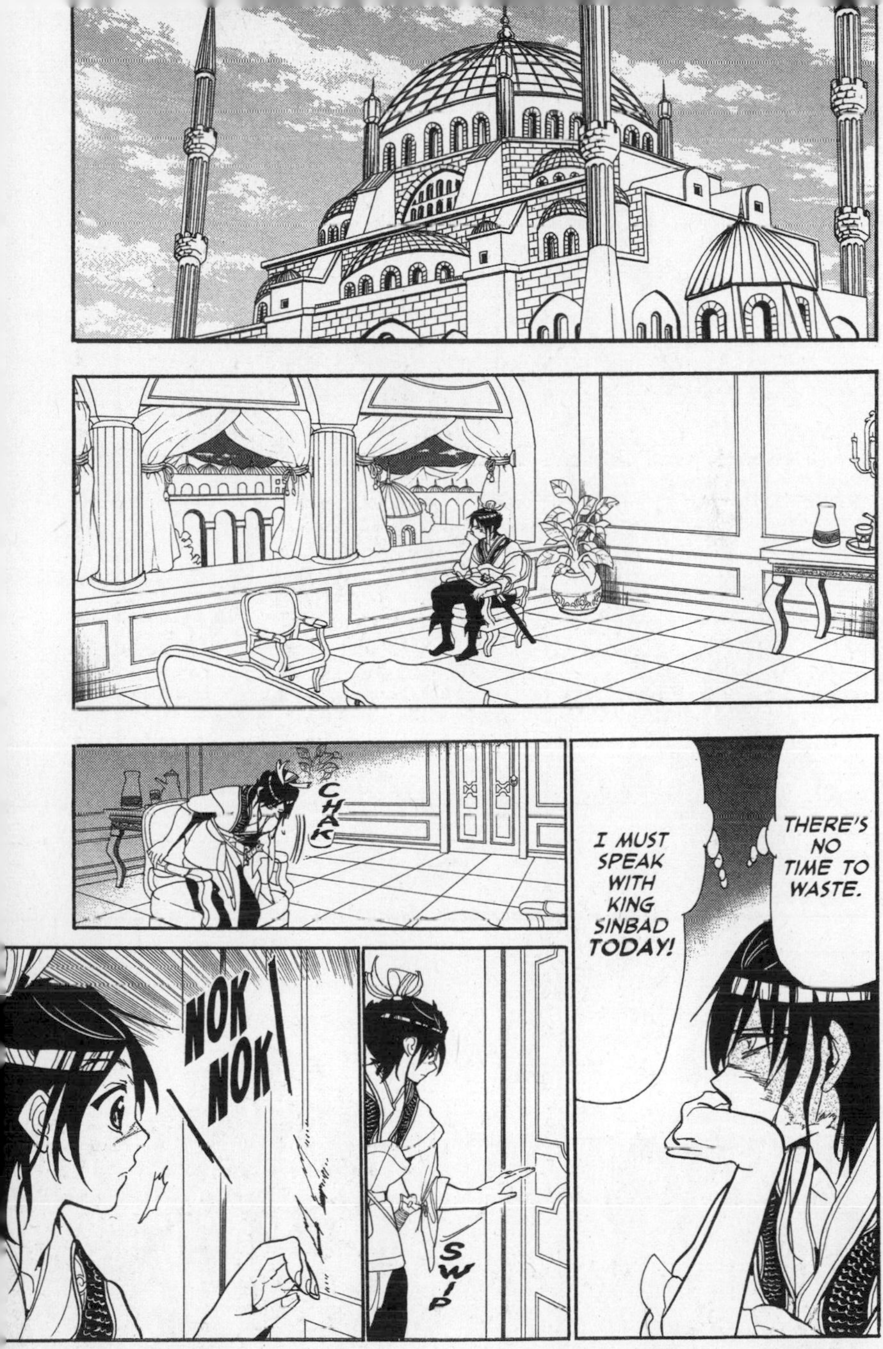
THERE'S NO TIME TO WASTE.
I MUST SPEAK WITH KING SINBAD TODAY!
CHAK
SWIP
NOK NOK

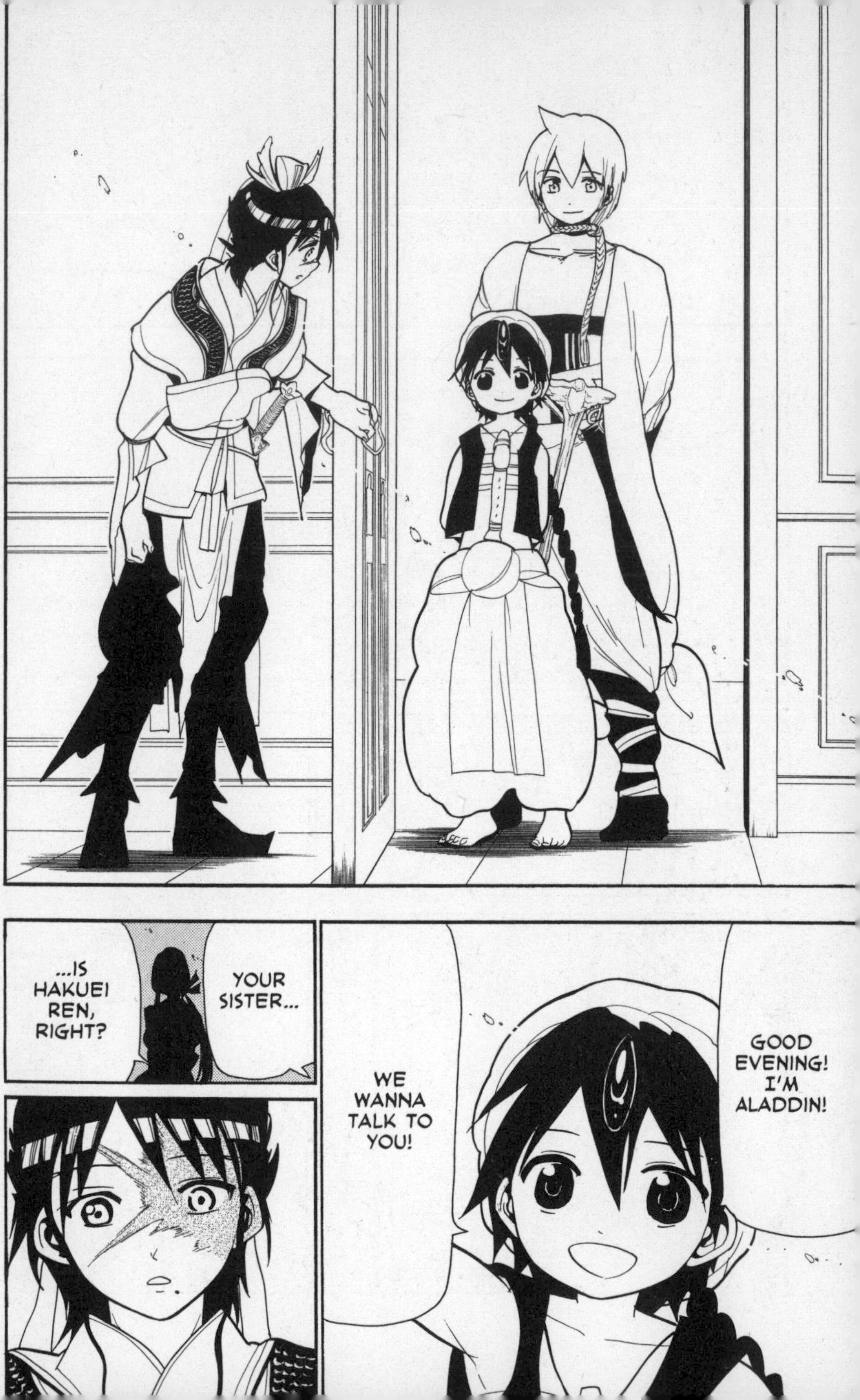
GOOD EVENING! I'M ALADDIN!
WE WANNA TALK TO YOU!
YOUR SISTER...
...IS HAKUEI REN, RIGHT?

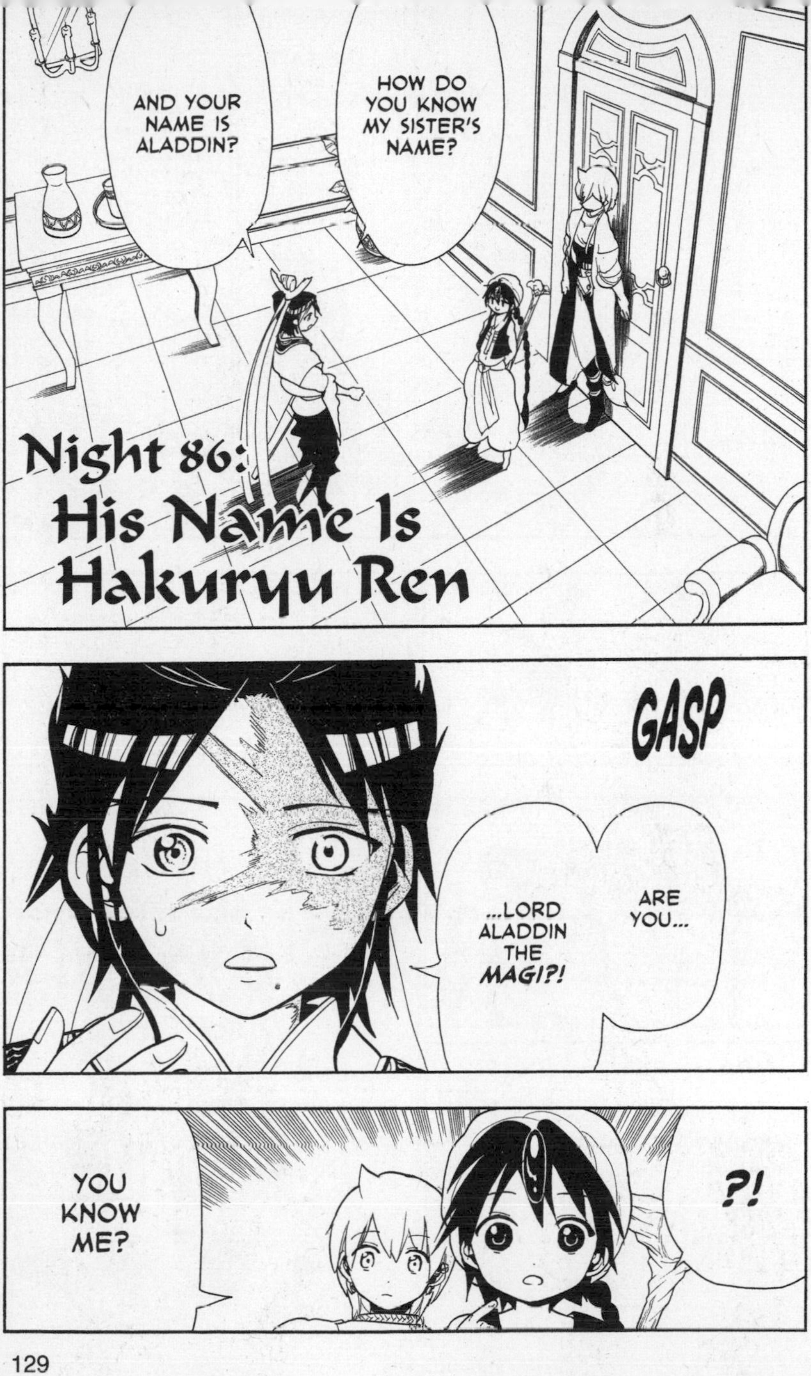
HOW DO YOU KNOW MY SISTER'S NAME?
AND YOUR NAME IS ALADDIN?
Night 86: His Name Is Hakuryu Ren
GASP
ARE YOU... ...LORD ALADDIN THE MAGI?!
?!
YOU KNOW ME?

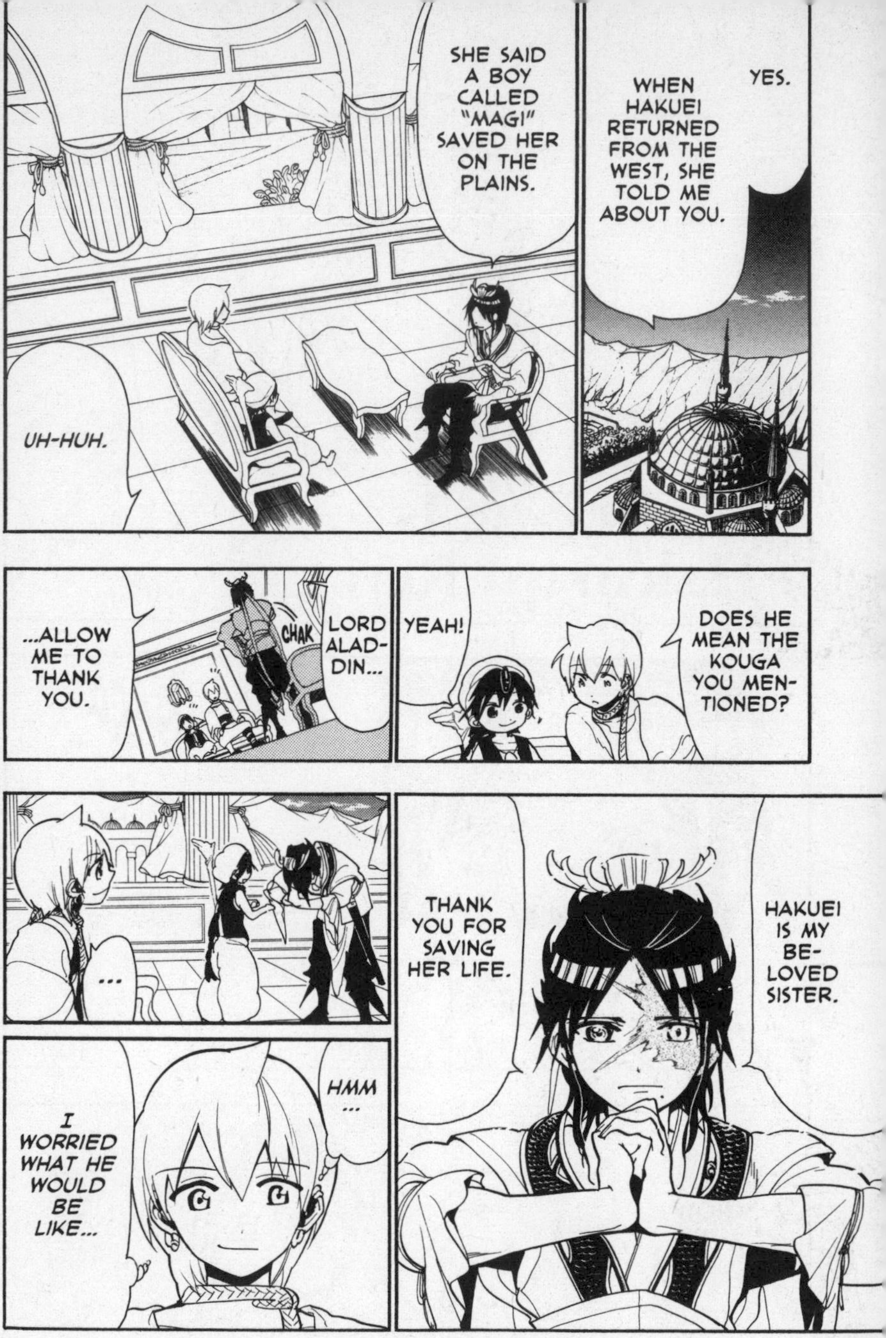
YES.
WHEN HAKUEI RETURNED FROM THE WEST, SHE TOLD ME ABOUT YOU.
SHE SAID A BOY CALLED "MAGI" SAVED HER ON THE PLAINS.
UH-HUH.
DOES HE MEAN THE KOUGA YOU MENTIONED?
YEAH!
LORD ALADDIN...
CHAK
...ALLOW ME TO THANK YOU.
HAKUEI IS MY BELOVED SISTER.
THANK YOU FOR SAVING HER LIFE.
...
HMM...
I WORRIED WHAT HE WOULD BE LIKE...

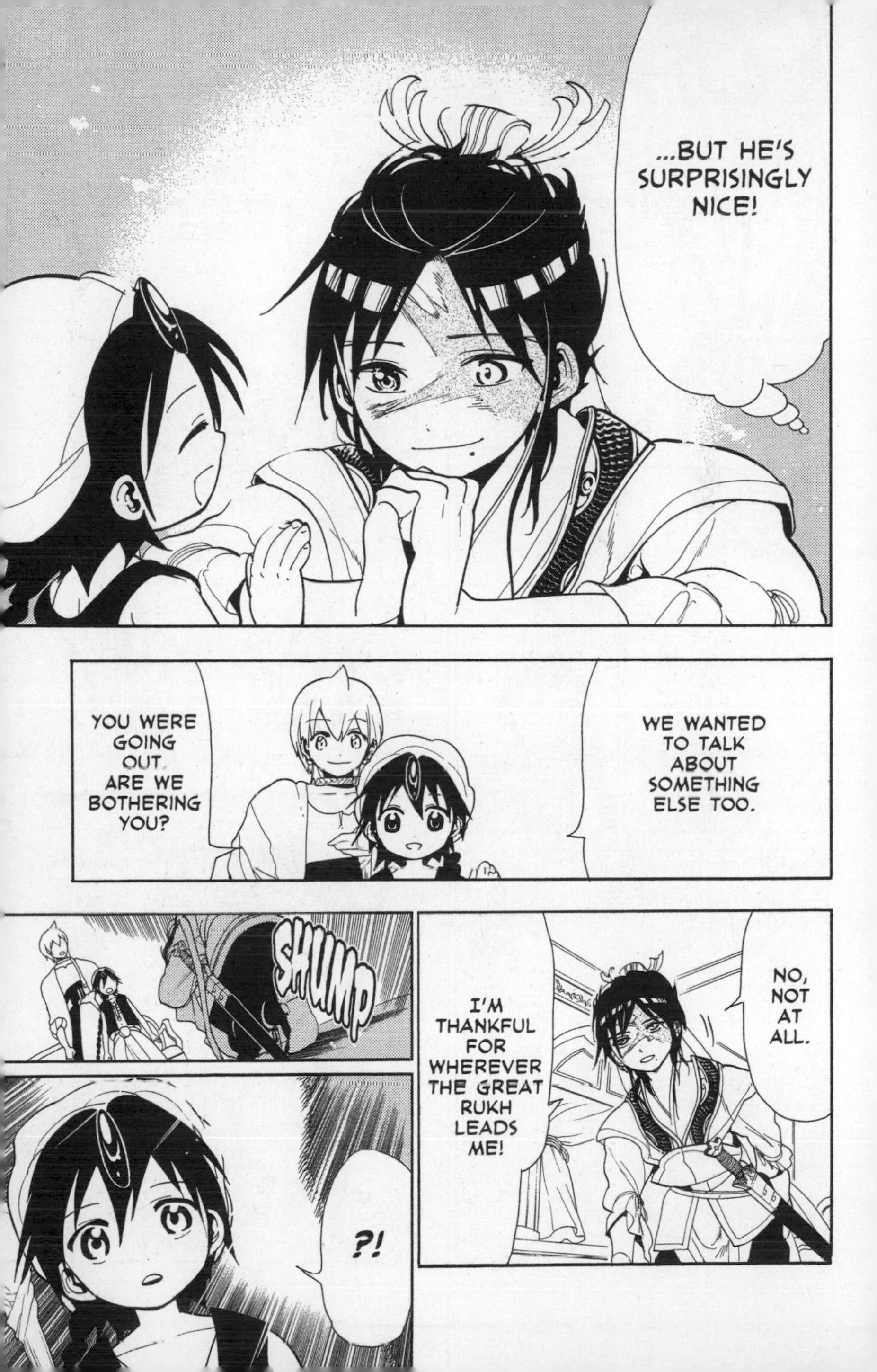
...BUT HE'S SURPRISINGLY NICE!
WE WANTED TO TALK ABOUT SOMETHING ELSE TOO.
YOU WERE GOING OUT. ARE WE BOTHERING YOU?
NO, NOT AT ALL.
I'M THANKFUL FOR WHEREVER THE GREAT RUKH LEADS ME!
SHUMP
?!

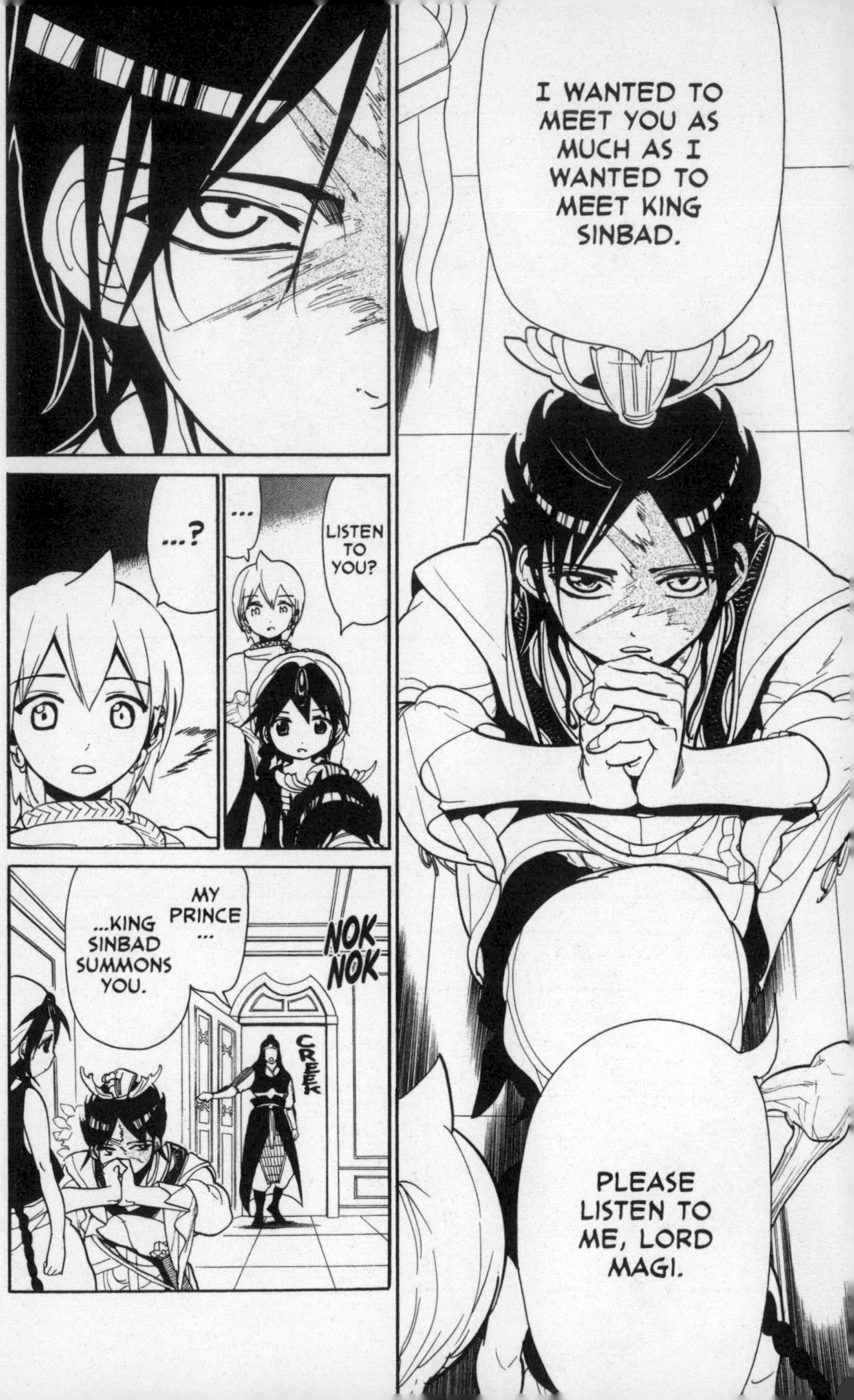
I WANTED TO MEET YOU AS MUCH AS I WANTED TO MEET KING SINBAD.
PLEASE LISTEN TO ME, LORD MAGI.
...
LISTEN TO YOU?
...?
MY PRINCE ...
...KING SINBAD SUMMONS YOU.
NOK NOK
CREEK

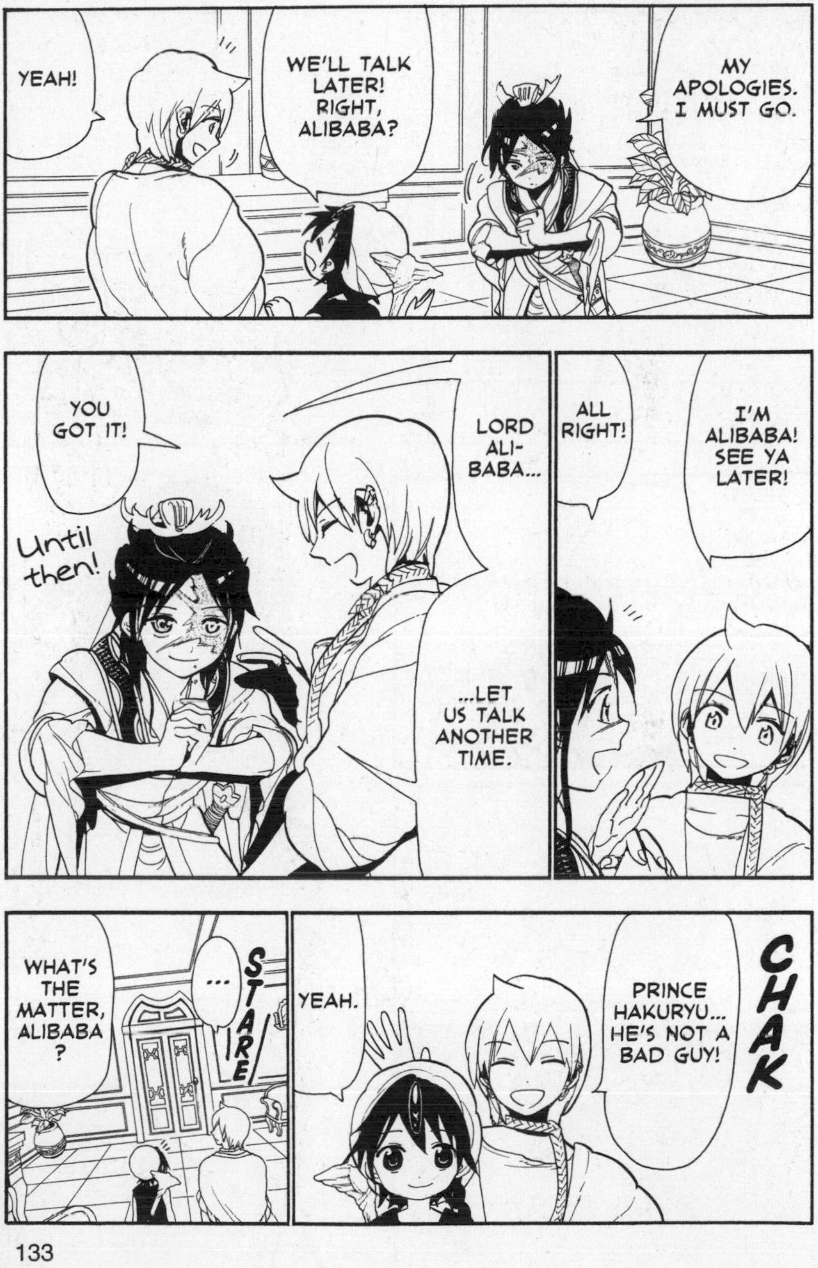
MY APOLOGIES. I MUST GO.
WE'LL TALK LATER! RIGHT, ALIBABA?
YEAH!
I'M ALIBABA! SEE YA LATER!
ALL RIGHT!
LORD ALI-BABA...
...LET US TALK ANOTHER TIME.
YOU GOT IT!
Until then!
CHAK
PRINCE HAKURYU... HE'S NOT A BAD GUY!
YEAH.
STARE
...
WHAT'S THE MATTER, ALIBABA?

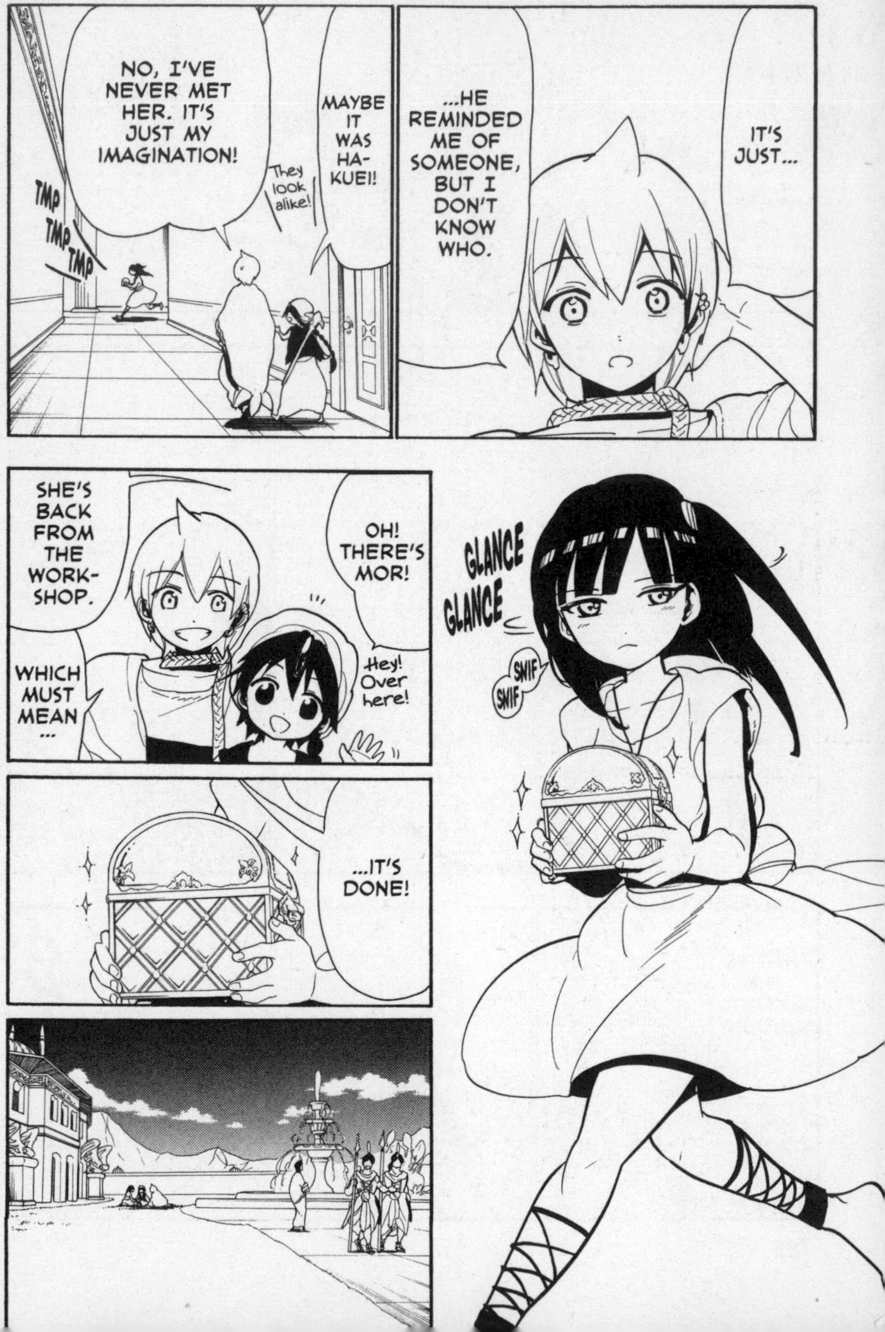
IT'S JUST...
...HE REMINDED ME OF SOMEONE, BUT I DON'T KNOW WHO.
MAYBE IT WAS HA-KUEI!
They look alike!
NO, I'VE NEVER MET HER. IT'S JUST MY IMAGINATION!
TMP TMP TMP
GLANCE GLANCE
SNIF SNIF
OH! THERE'S MOR!
Hey! Over here!
SHE'S BACK FROM THE WORK-SHOP.
WHICH MUST MEAN...
...IT'S DONE!

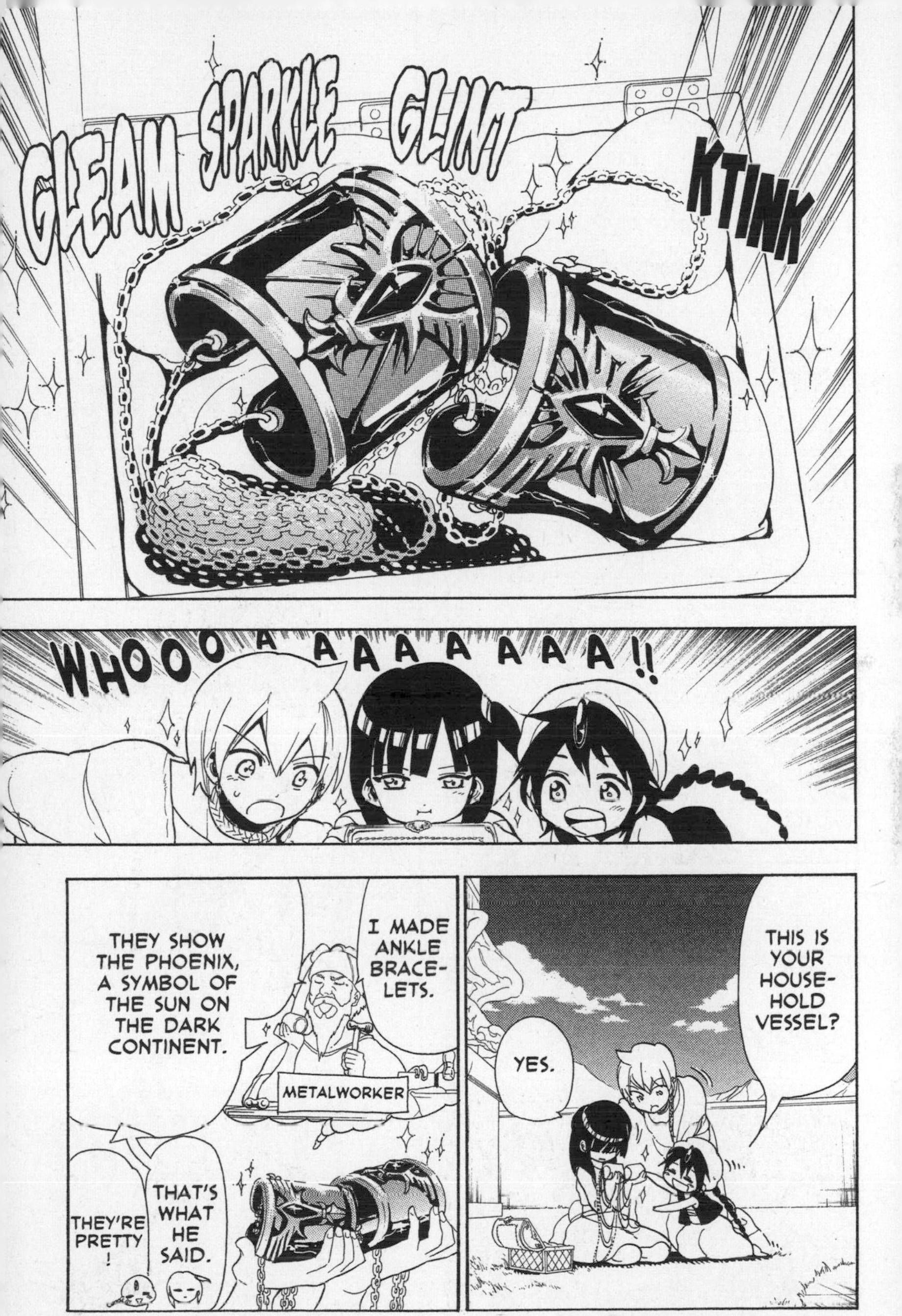
GLEAM SPARKLE GLINT
KTINK
WHOOOAAAAAAAAA!!
THIS IS YOUR HOUSEHOLD VESSEL?
YES.
I MADE ANKLE BRACELETS.
THEY SHOW THE PHOENIX, A SYMBOL OF THE SUN ON THE DARK CONTINENT.
METALWORKER
THAT'S WHAT HE SAID.
THEY'RE PRETTY!

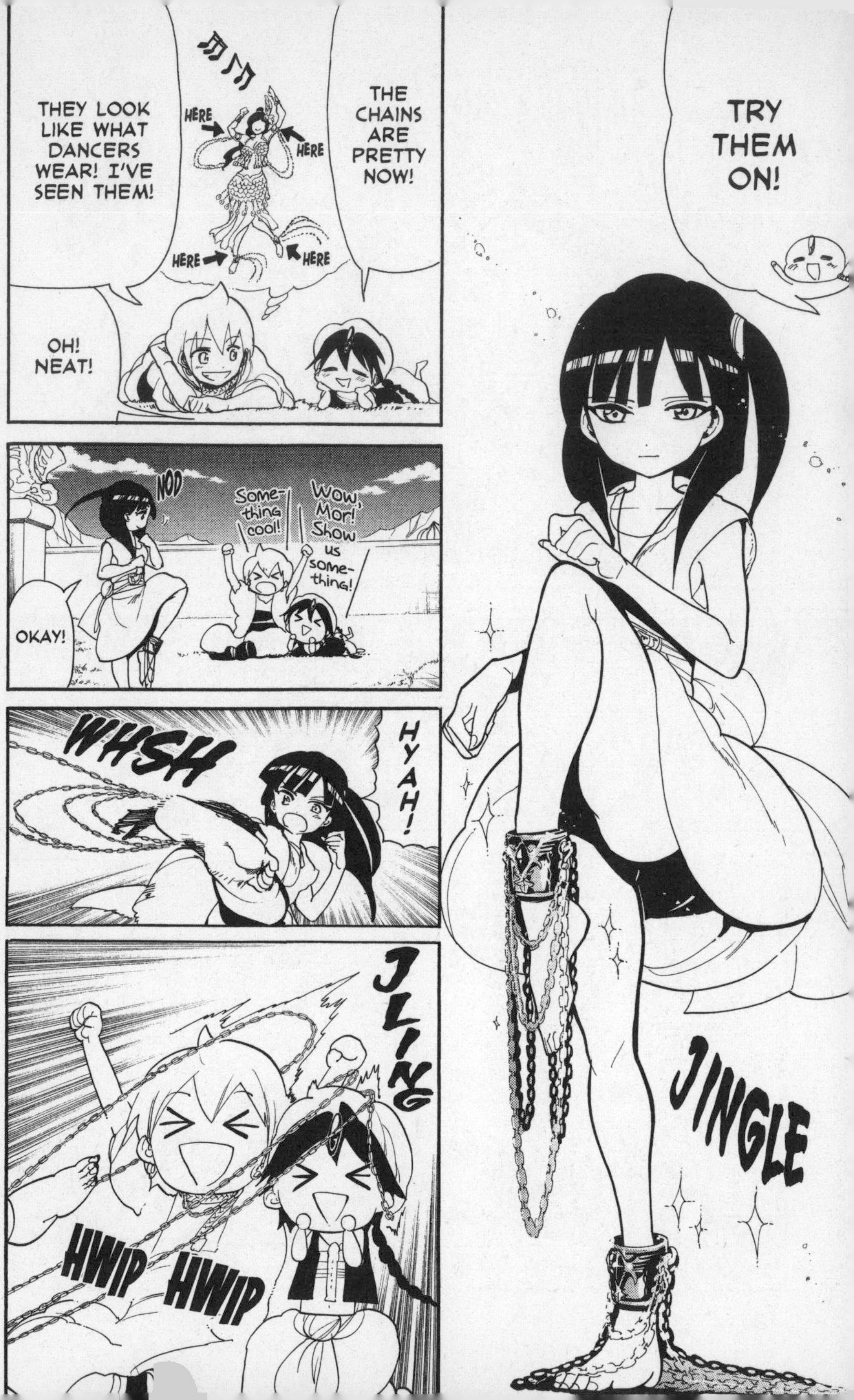
TRY THEM ON!
JINGLE
THE CHAINS ARE PRETTY NOW!
THEY LOOK LIKE WHAT DANCERS WEAR! I'VE SEEN THEM!
HERE
HERE
HERE
HERE
OH! NEAT!
Wow, Mor! Show us some-thing!
Some-thing cool!
NOD
OKAY!
HYAH!
WHSH
JLING
HWIP
HWIP

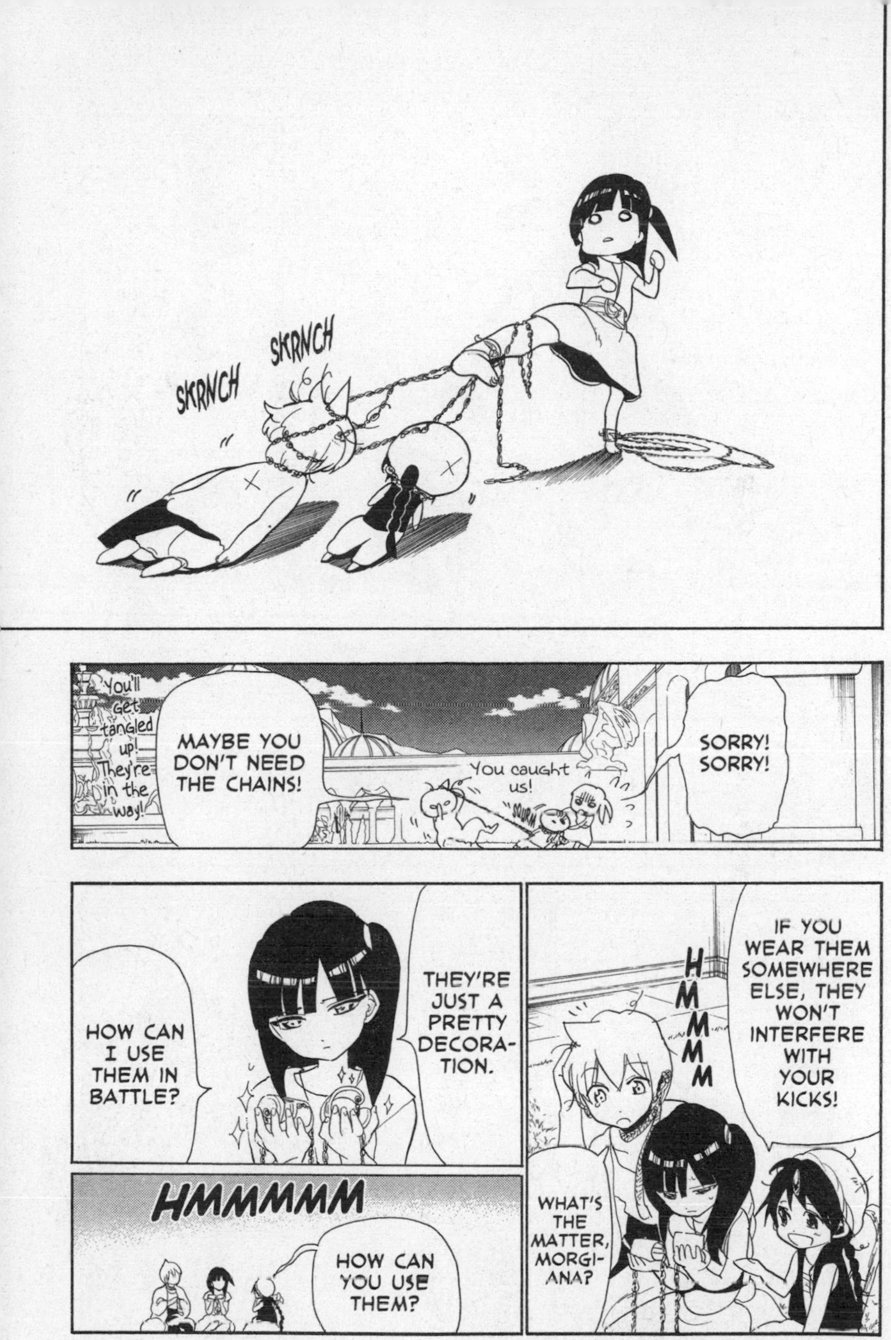
SKRNCH
SKRNCH
SORRY! SORRY!
You caught us!
SQURM
MAYBE YOU DON'T NEED THE CHAINS!
You'll get tangled up! They're in the way!
IF YOU WEAR THEM SOMEWHERE ELSE, THEY WON'T INTERFERE WITH YOUR KICKS!
HMMMM
WHAT'S THE MATTER, MORGIANA?
THEY'RE JUST A PRETTY DECORATION.
HOW CAN I USE THEM IN BATTLE?
HMMMMM
HOW CAN YOU USE THEM?

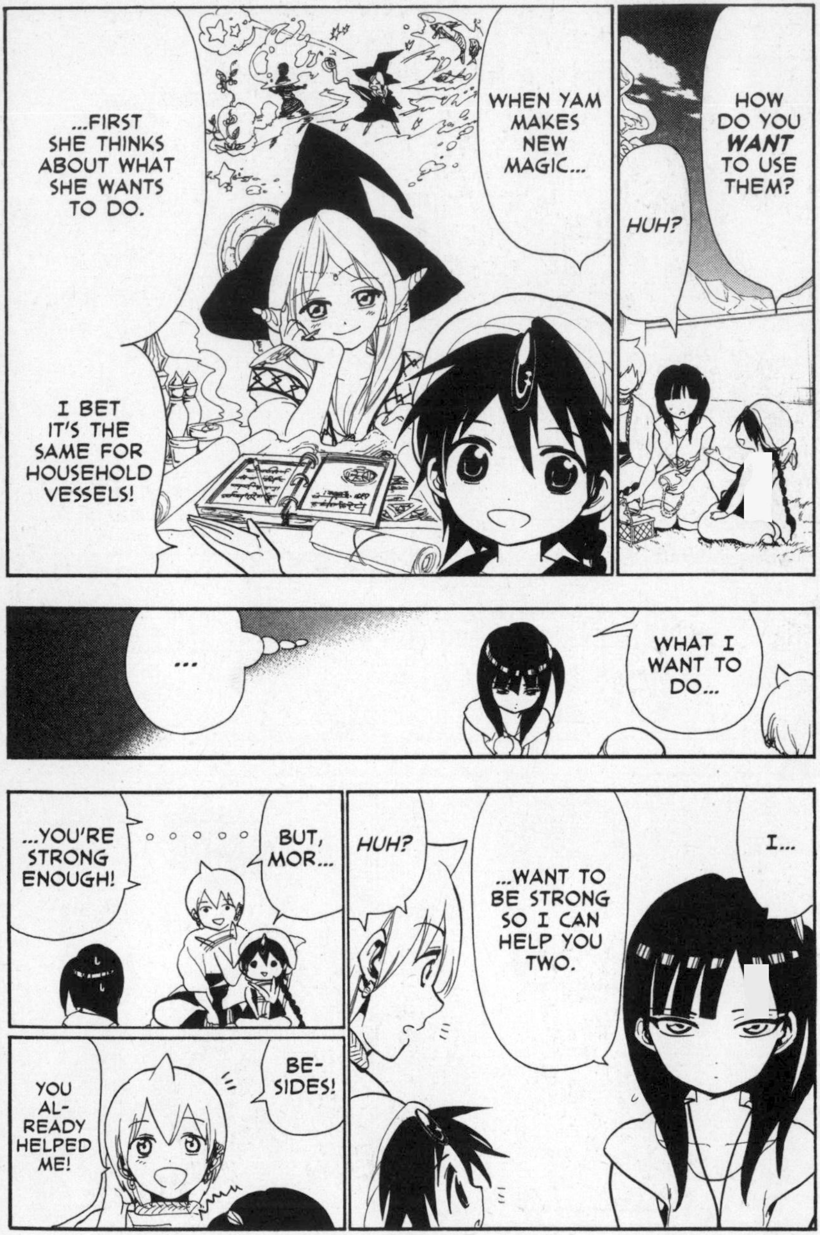
HOW DO YOU *WANT* TO USE THEM?
HUH?
WHEN YAM MAKES NEW MAGIC...
...FIRST SHE THINKS ABOUT WHAT SHE WANTS TO DO.
I BET IT'S THE SAME FOR HOUSEHOLD VESSELS!
WHAT I WANT TO DO...
...
I...
...WANT TO BE STRONG SO I CAN HELP YOU TWO.
HUH?
BUT, MOR...
○ ○ ○ ○ ○
...YOU'RE STRONG ENOUGH!
BE-SIDES!
YOU AL-READY HELPED ME!

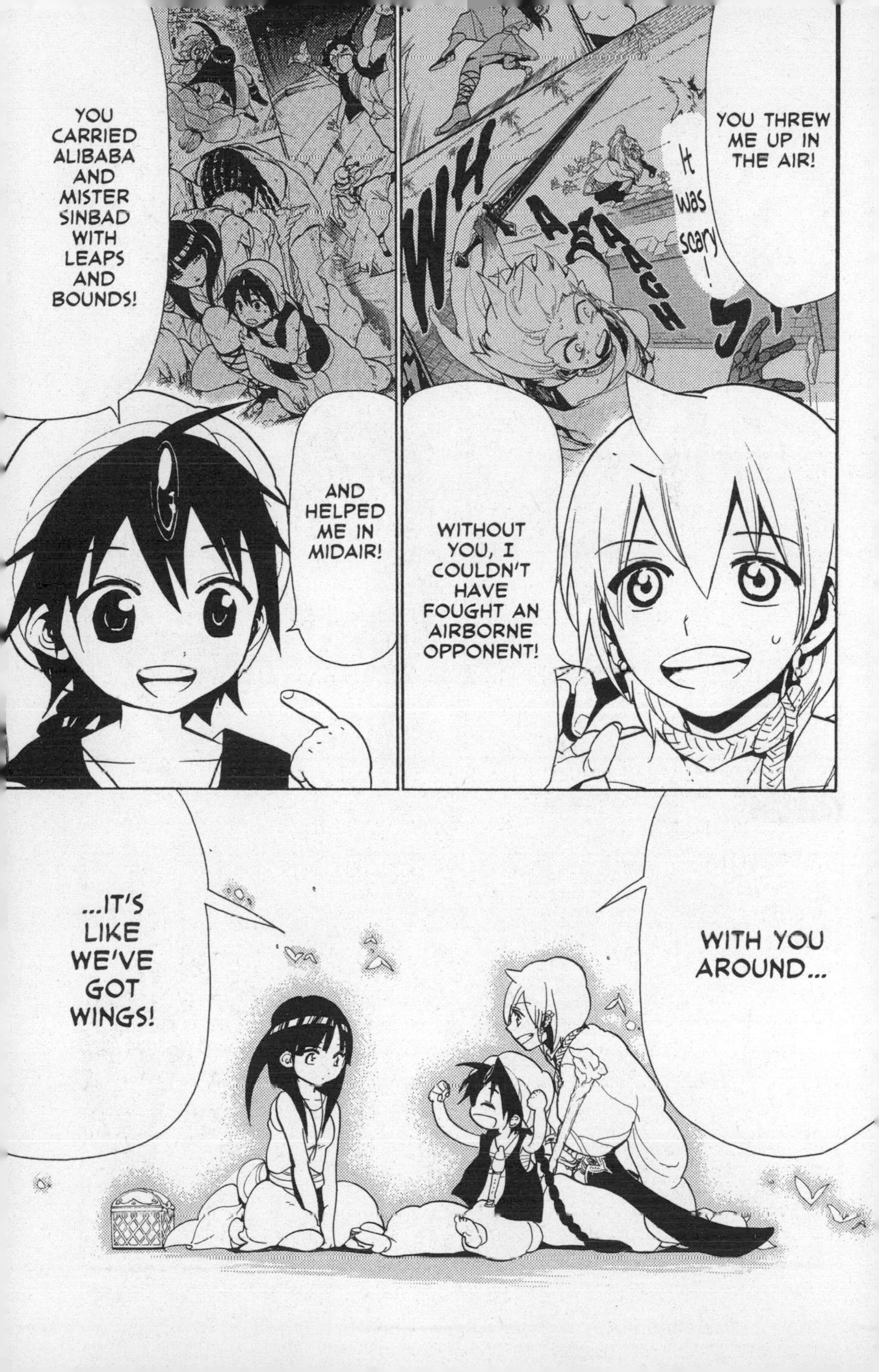
YOU THREW ME UP IN THE AIR!
It was scary!
YOU CARRIED ALIBABA AND MISTER SINBAD WITH LEAPS AND BOUNDS!
WITHOUT YOU, I COULDN'T HAVE FOUGHT AN AIRBORNE OPPONENT!
AND HELPED ME IN MIDAIR!
WITH YOU AROUND...
...IT'S LIKE WE'VE GOT WINGS!

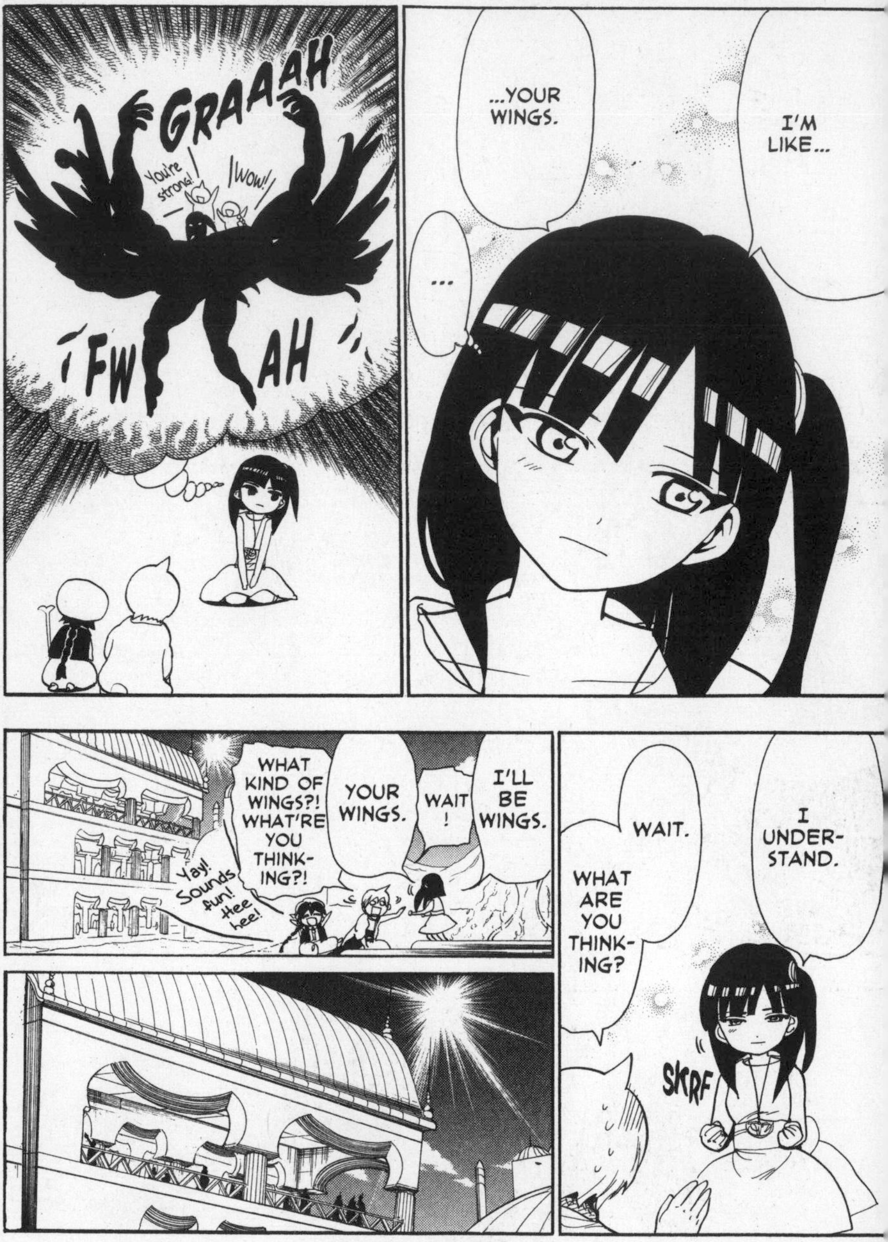
I'M LIKE...
...YOUR WINGS.
...
GRAAAH
You're strong!
WOW!
FW AH
I UNDER-STAND.
WAIT.
WHAT ARE YOU THINKING?
SKRF
I'LL BE WINGS.
WAIT!
YOUR WINGS.
WHAT KIND OF WINGS?! WHAT'RE YOU THINKING?!
Yay! Sounds fun! Hee hee!

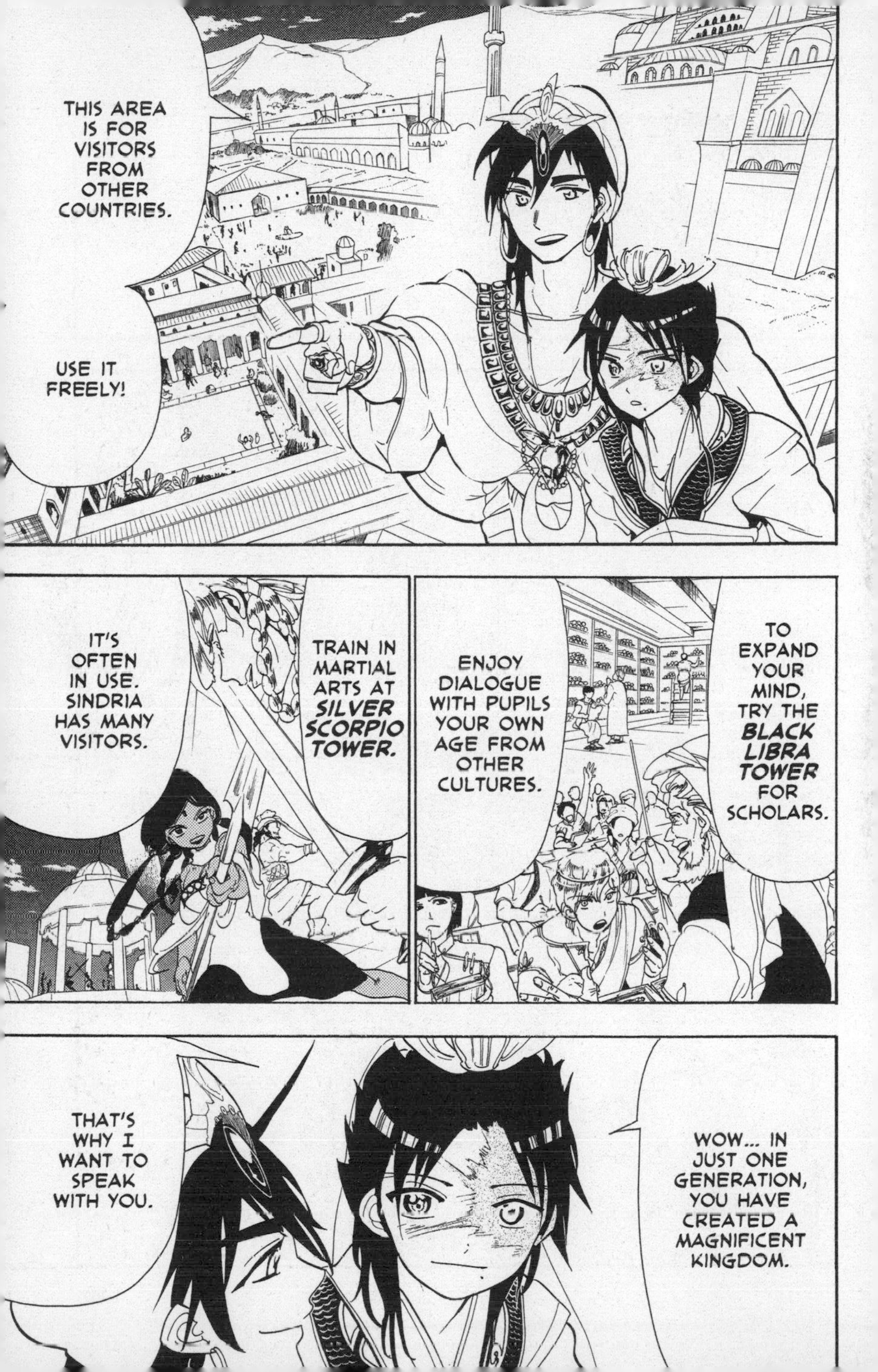
THIS AREA IS FOR VISITORS FROM OTHER COUNTRIES.
USE IT FREELY!
TO EXPAND YOUR MIND, TRY THE ***BLACK LIBRA TOWER*** FOR SCHOLARS.
ENJOY DIALOGUE WITH PUPILS YOUR OWN AGE FROM OTHER CULTURES.
TRAIN IN MARTIAL ARTS AT ***SILVER SCORPIO TOWER.***
IT'S OFTEN IN USE. SINDRIA HAS MANY VISITORS.
WOW... IN JUST ONE GENERATION, YOU HAVE CREATED A MAGNIFICENT KINGDOM.
THAT'S WHY I WANT TO SPEAK WITH YOU.

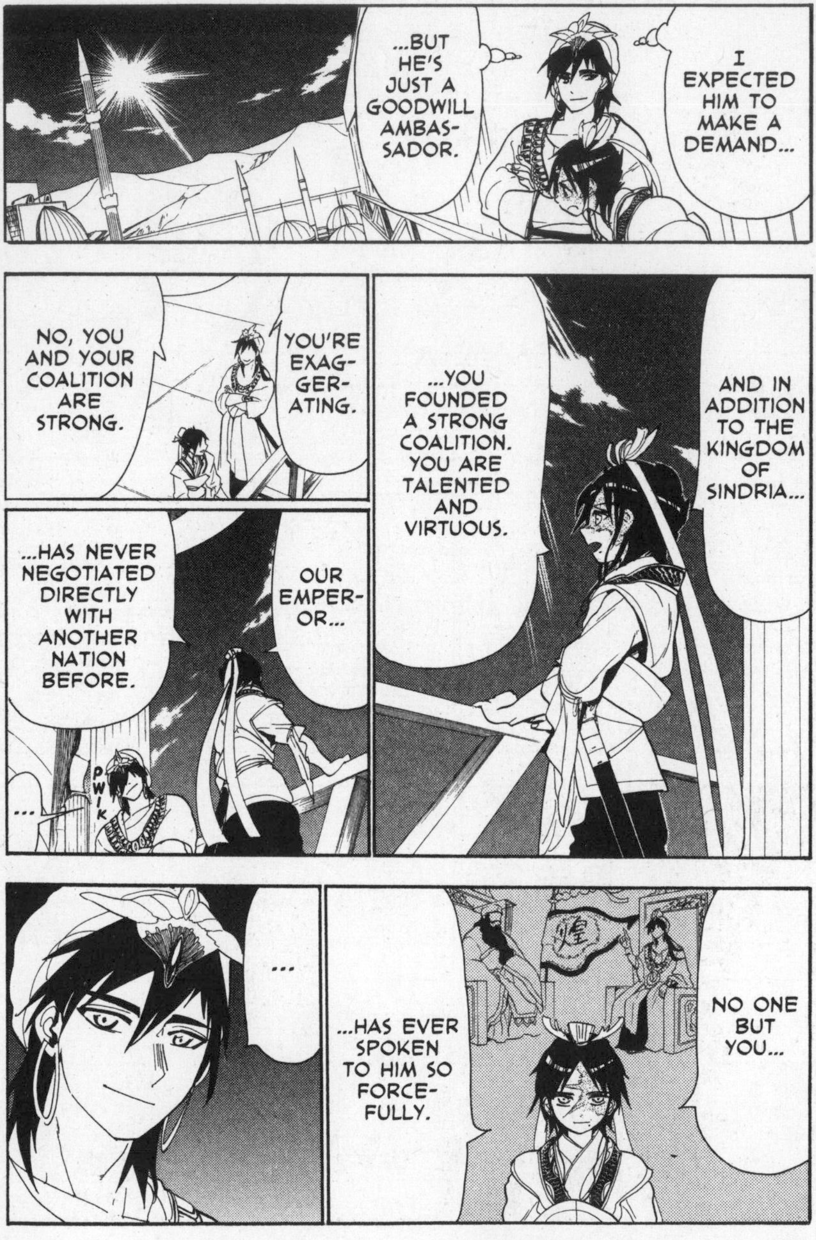
I EXPECTED HIM TO MAKE A DEMAND...
...BUT HE'S JUST A GOODWILL AMBAS-SADOR.
AND IN ADDITION TO THE KINGDOM OF SINDRIA...
...YOU FOUNDED A STRONG COALITION. YOU ARE TALENTED AND VIRTUOUS.
YOU'RE EXAG-GER-ATING.
NO, YOU AND YOUR COALITION ARE STRONG.
OUR EMPER-OR...
...HAS NEVER NEGOTIATED DIRECTLY WITH ANOTHER NATION BEFORE.
PWIK
...
NO ONE BUT YOU...
...HAS EVER SPOKEN TO HIM SO FORCE-FULLY.
...

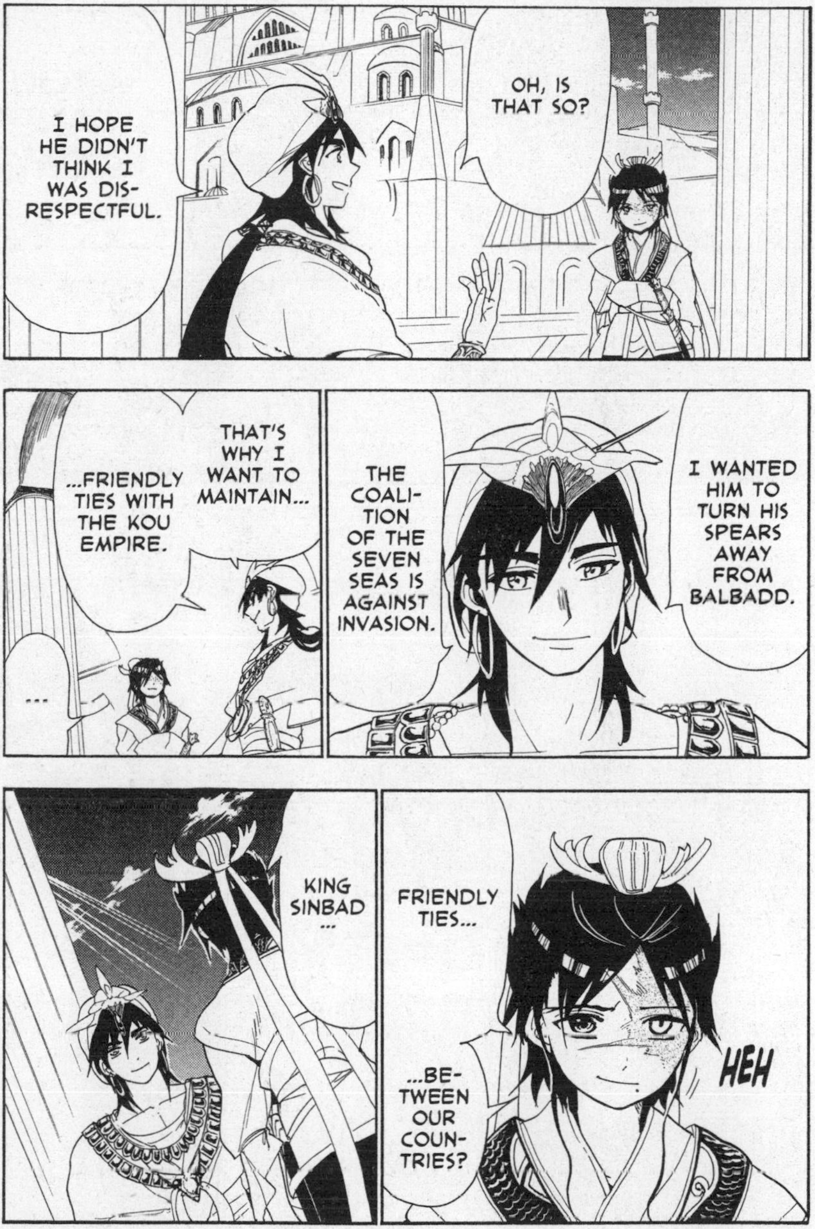
OH, IS THAT SO?
I HOPE HE DIDN'T THINK I WAS DIS-RESPECTFUL.
I WANTED HIM TO TURN HIS SPEARS AWAY FROM BALBADD.
THE COALI-TION OF THE SEVEN SEAS IS AGAINST INVASION.
THAT'S WHY I WANT TO MAINTAIN...
...FRIENDLY TIES WITH THE KOU EMPIRE.
...
FRIENDLY TIES...
...BE-TWEEN OUR COUN-TRIES?
HEH
KING SINBAD...

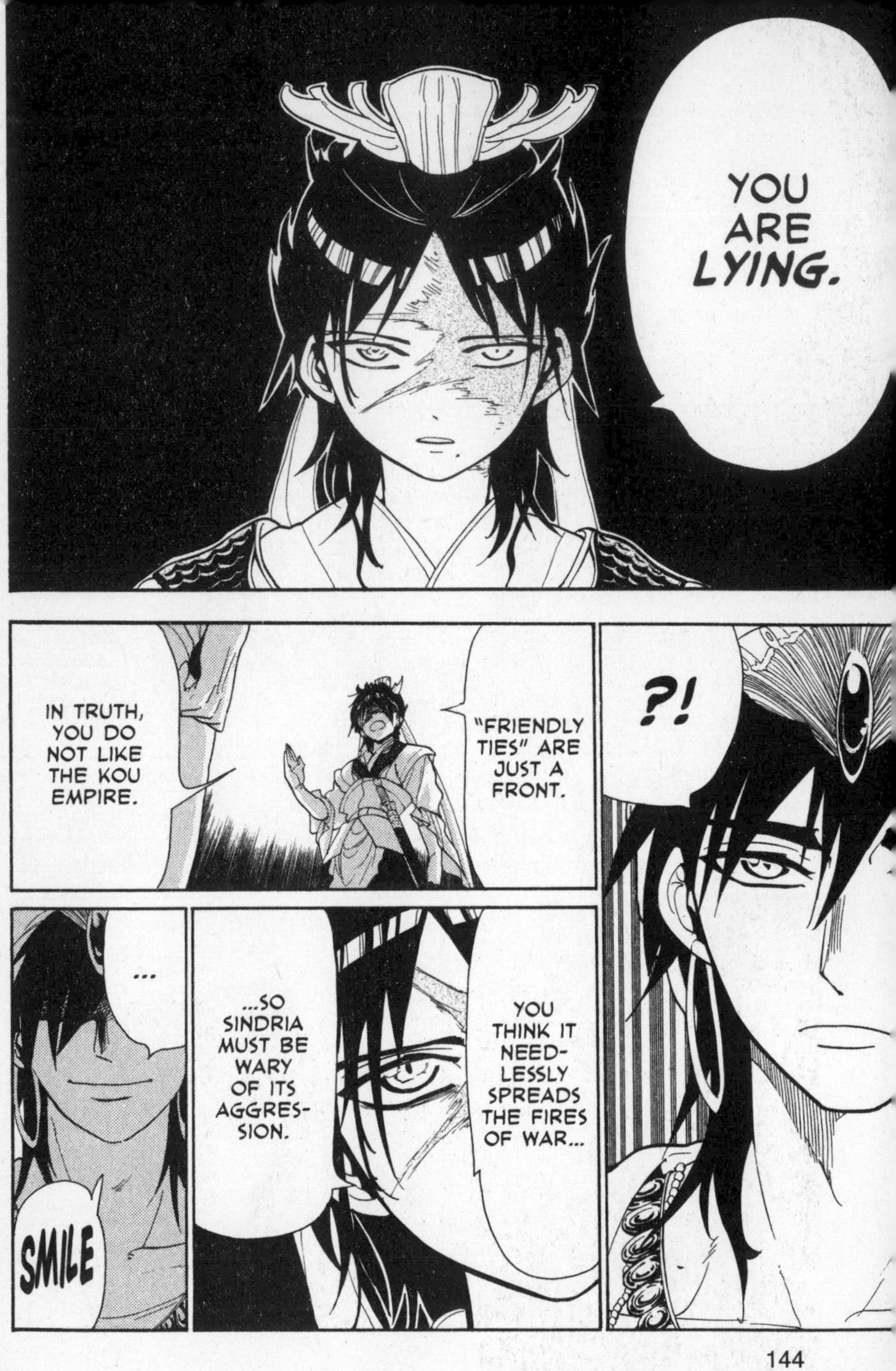
YOU ARE LYING.
?!
"FRIENDLY TIES" ARE JUST A FRONT.
IN TRUTH, YOU DO NOT LIKE THE KOU EMPIRE.
YOU THINK IT NEEDLESSLY SPREADS THE FIRES OF WAR...
...SO SINDRIA MUST BE WARY OF ITS AGGRESSION.
...
SMILE

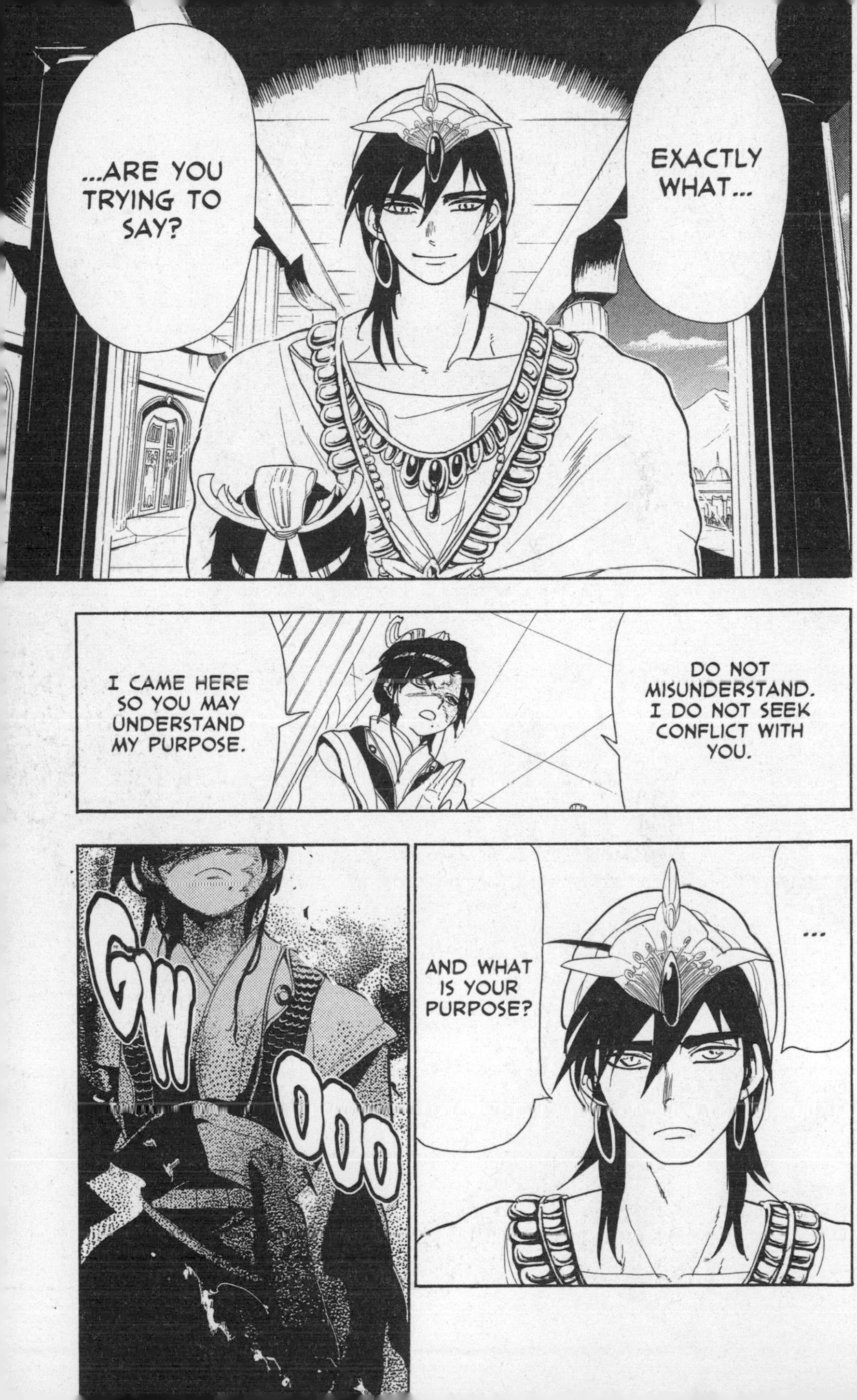
EXACTLY WHAT...
...ARE YOU TRYING TO SAY?
DO NOT MISUNDERSTAND. I DO NOT SEEK CONFLICT WITH YOU.
I CAME HERE SO YOU MAY UNDERSTAND MY PURPOSE.
...
AND WHAT IS YOUR PURPOSE?
GWOOO

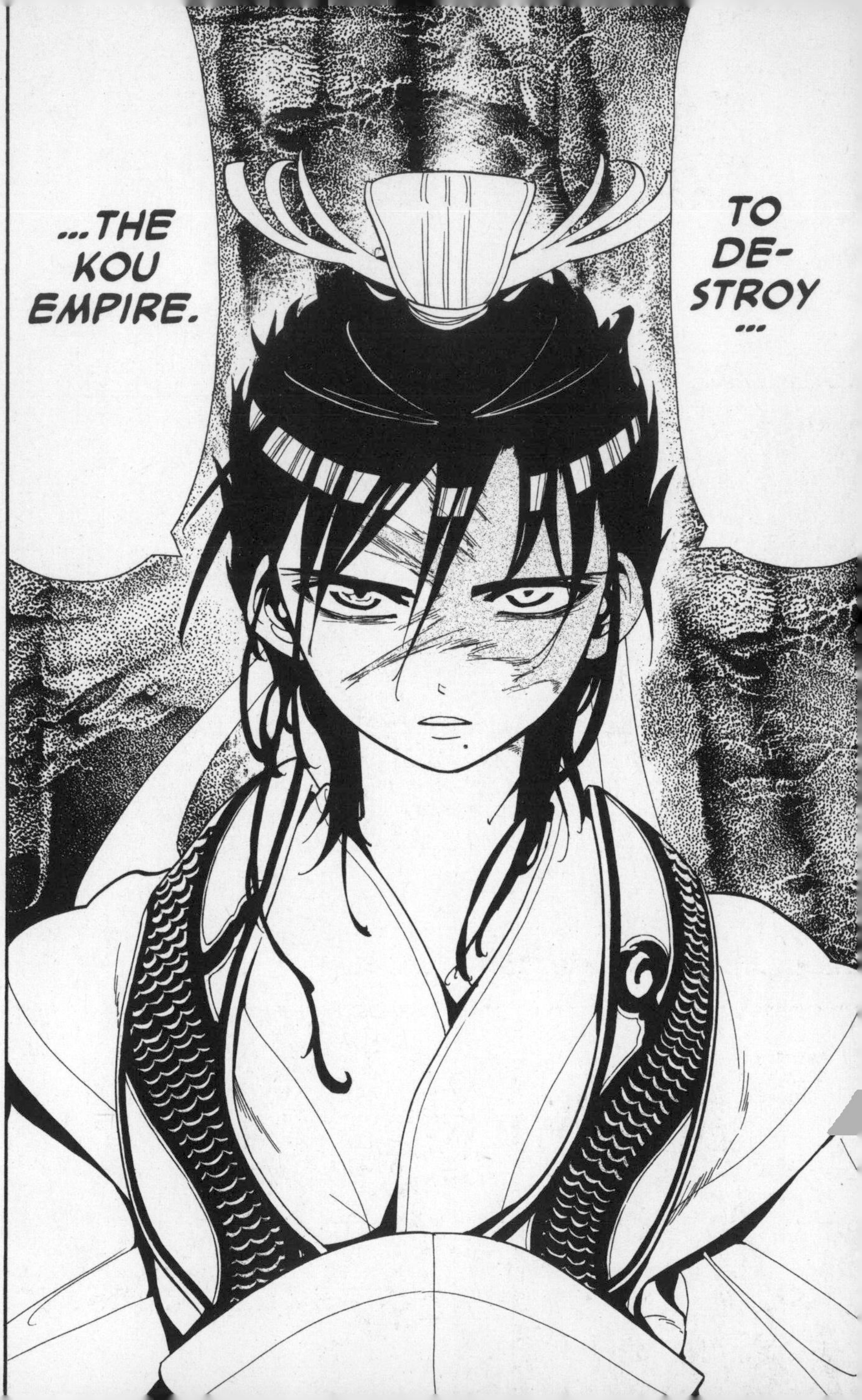
TO DE-STROY ...
...THE KOU EMPIRE.

Night 87: Two Princes

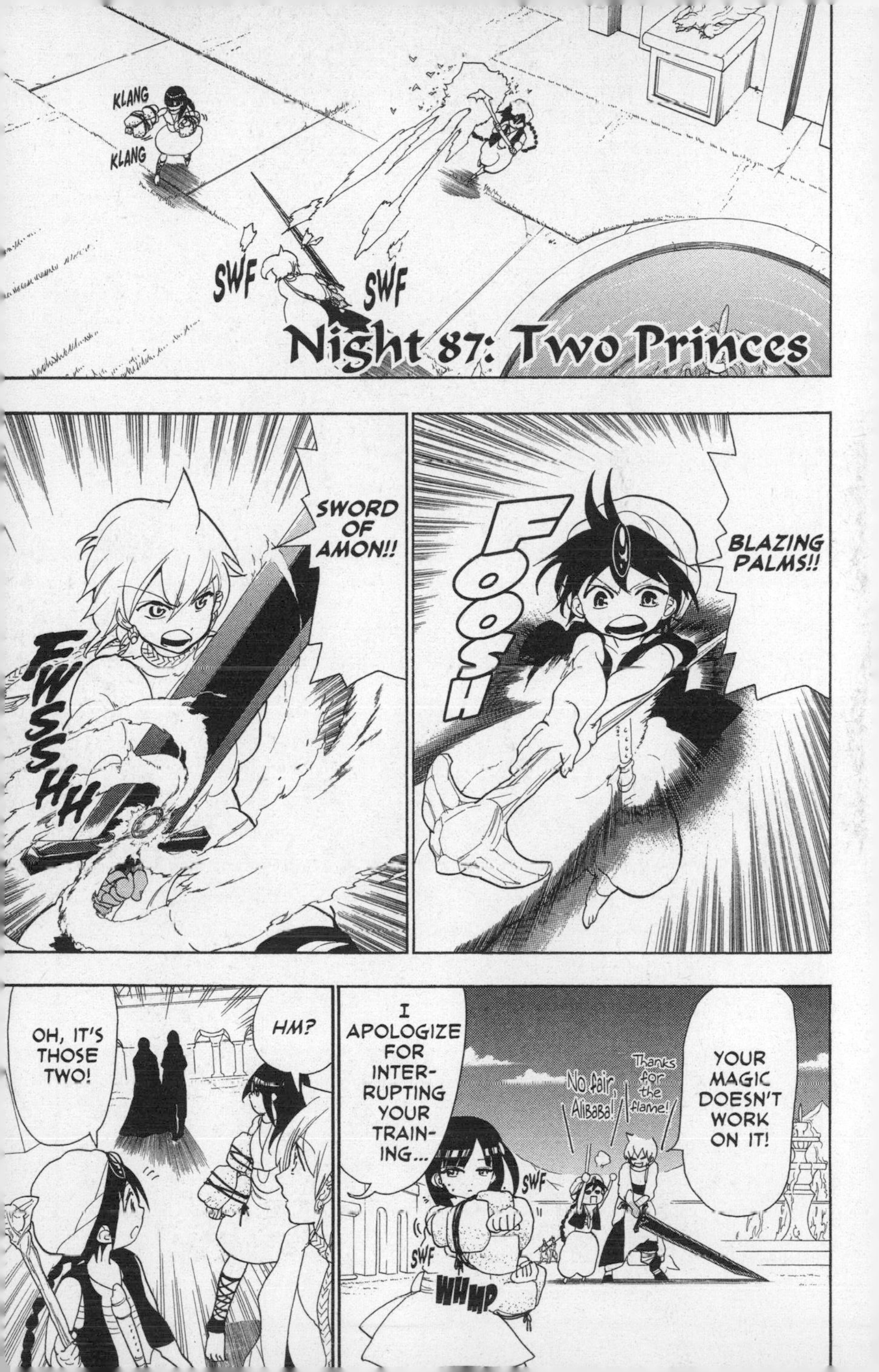
KLANG
KLANG
SWF
SWF
BLAZING PALMS!!
FOOOSH
SWORD OF AMON!!
FWSSHH
YOUR MAGIC DOESN'T WORK ON IT!
Thanks for the flame!
No fair, Alibaba!
SWF
I APOLOGIZE FOR INTER-RUPTING YOUR TRAIN-ING...
SWF
WHMP
HM?
OH, IT'S THOSE TWO!

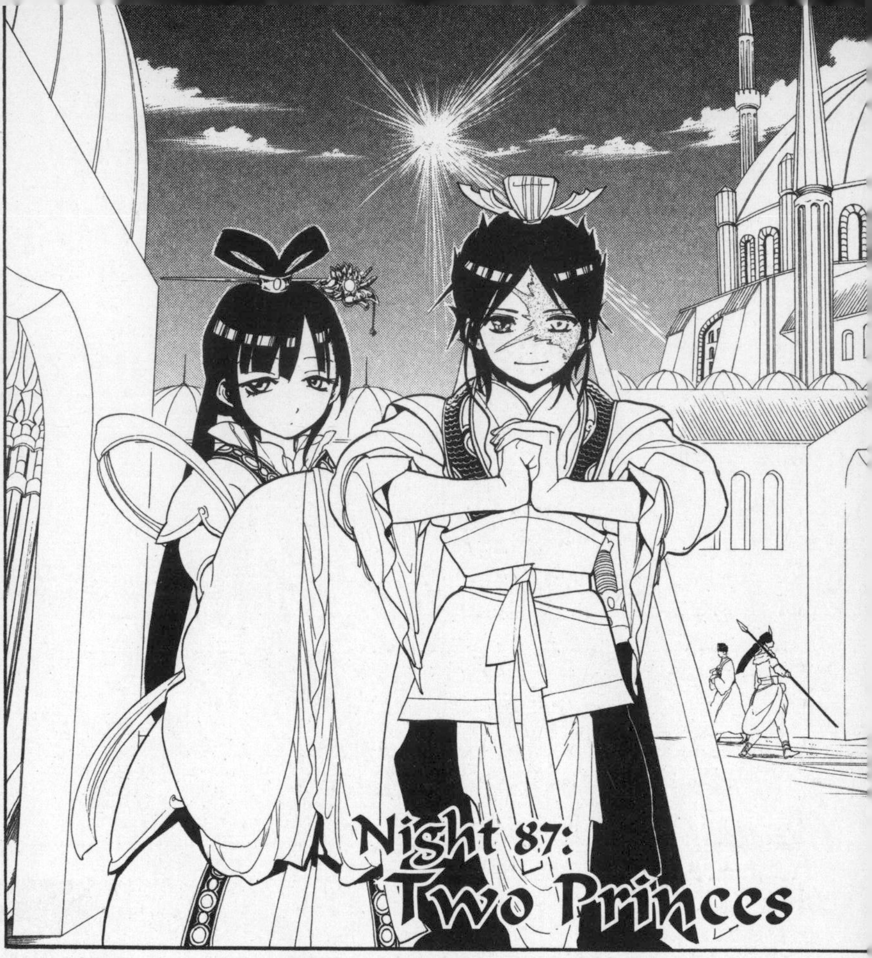
Night 87:
Two Princes

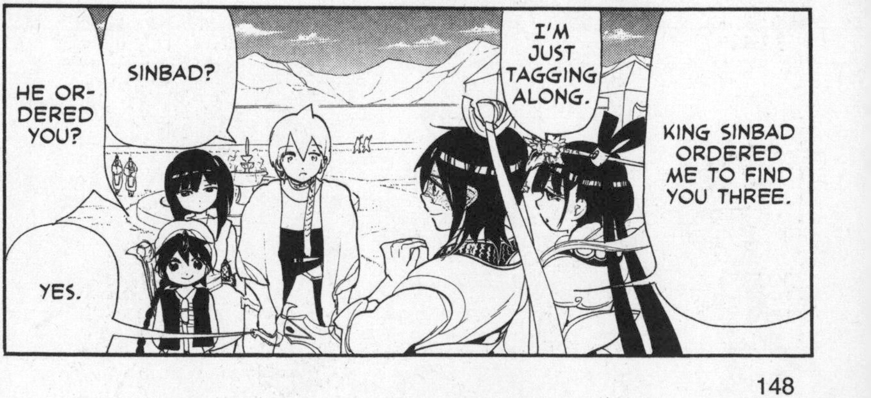
KING SINBAD ORDERED ME TO FIND YOU THREE.
I'M JUST TAGGING ALONG.
SINBAD?
HE ORDERED YOU?
YES.

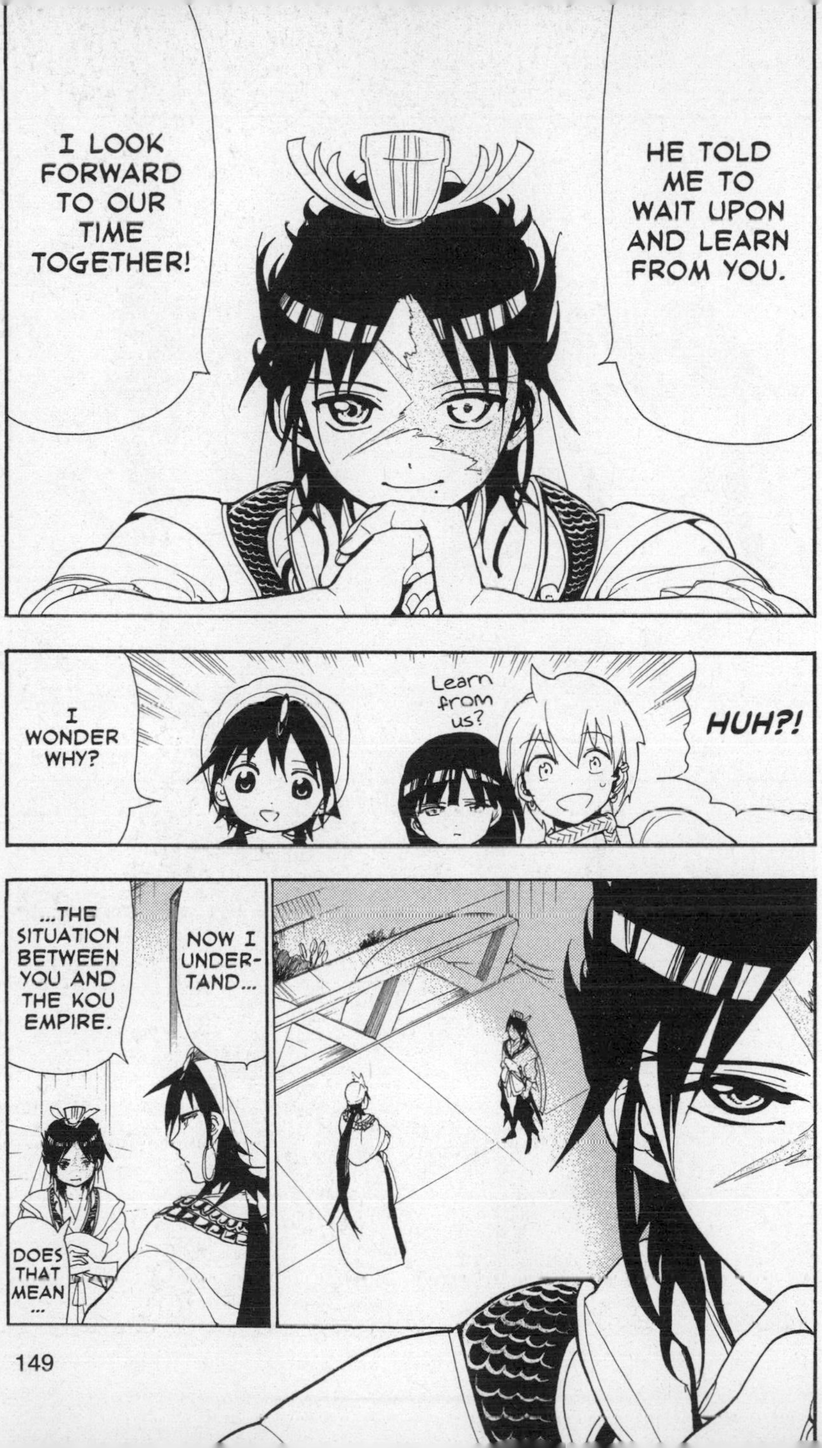
HE TOLD ME TO WAIT UPON AND LEARN FROM YOU.
I LOOK FORWARD TO OUR TIME TOGETHER!
HUH?!
Learn from us?
I WONDER WHY?
NOW I UNDER-TAND...
...THE SITUATION BETWEEN YOU AND THE KOU EMPIRE.
DOES THAT MEAN ...

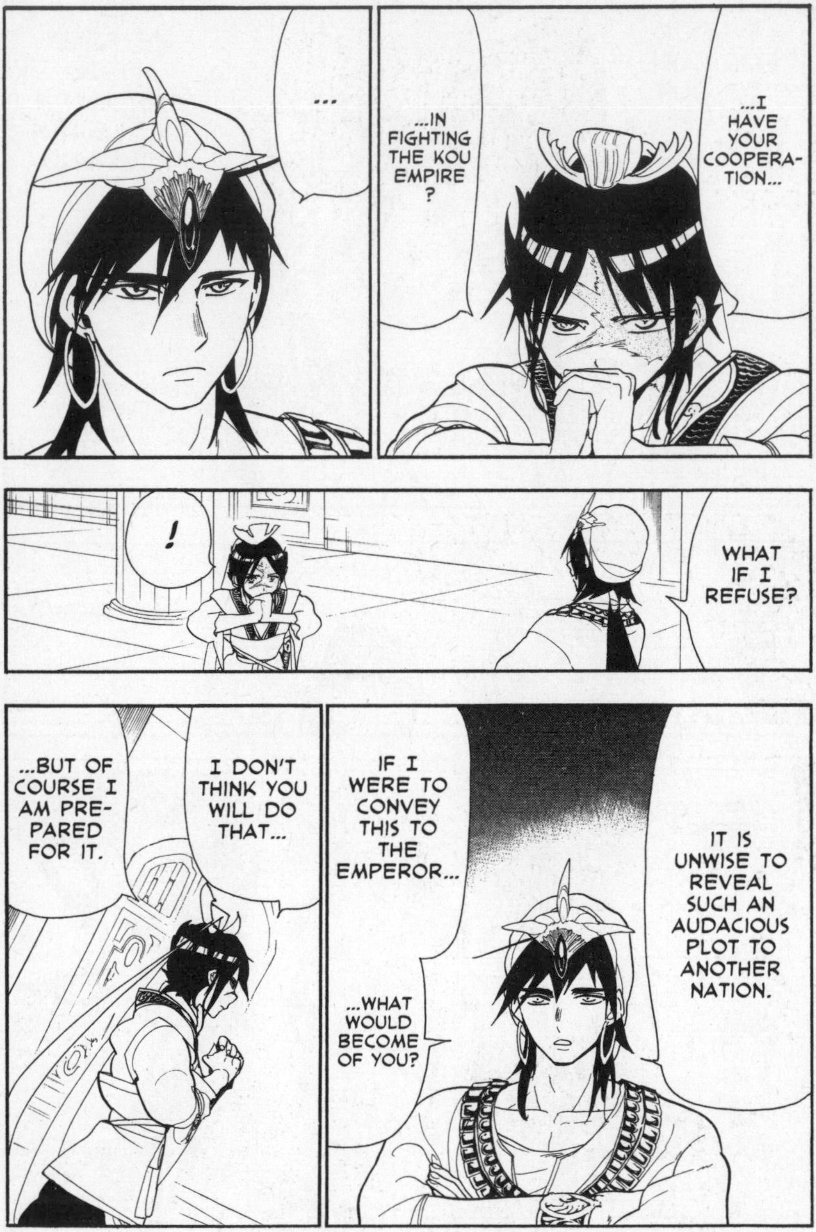
...I HAVE YOUR COOPERATION...
...IN FIGHTING THE KOU EMPIRE?
...
WHAT IF I REFUSE?
!
IT IS UNWISE TO REVEAL SUCH AN AUDACIOUS PLOT TO ANOTHER NATION.
IF I WERE TO CONVEY THIS TO THE EMPEROR...
...WHAT WOULD BECOME OF YOU?
I DON'T THINK YOU WILL DO THAT...
...BUT OF COURSE I AM PREPARED FOR IT.

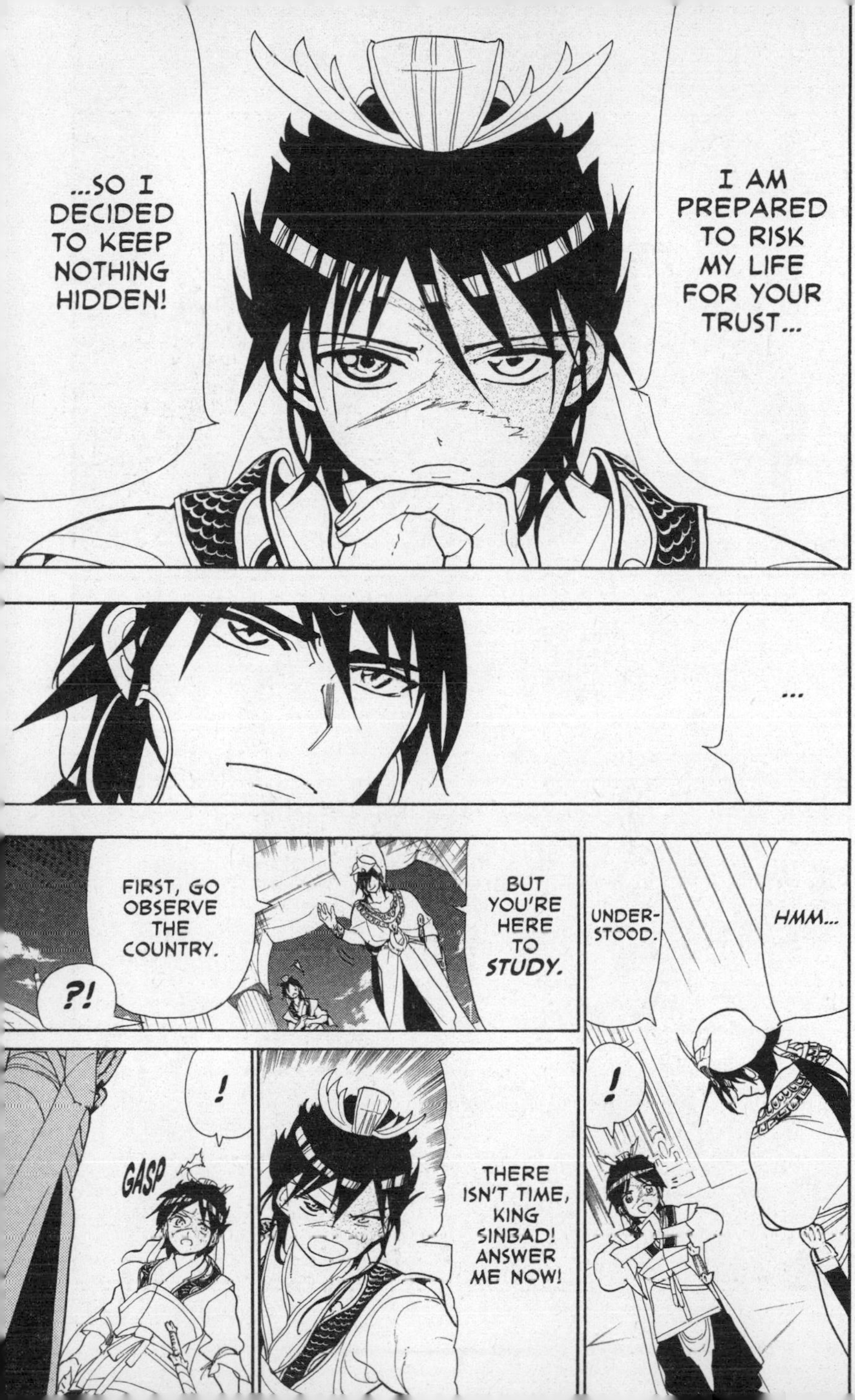
I AM PREPARED TO RISK MY LIFE FOR YOUR TRUST...
...SO I DECIDED TO KEEP NOTHING HIDDEN!
...
HMM...
UNDER-STOOD.
BUT YOU'RE HERE TO STUDY.
FIRST, GO OBSERVE THE COUNTRY.
?!
!
THERE ISN'T TIME, KING SINBAD! ANSWER ME NOW!
!
GASP

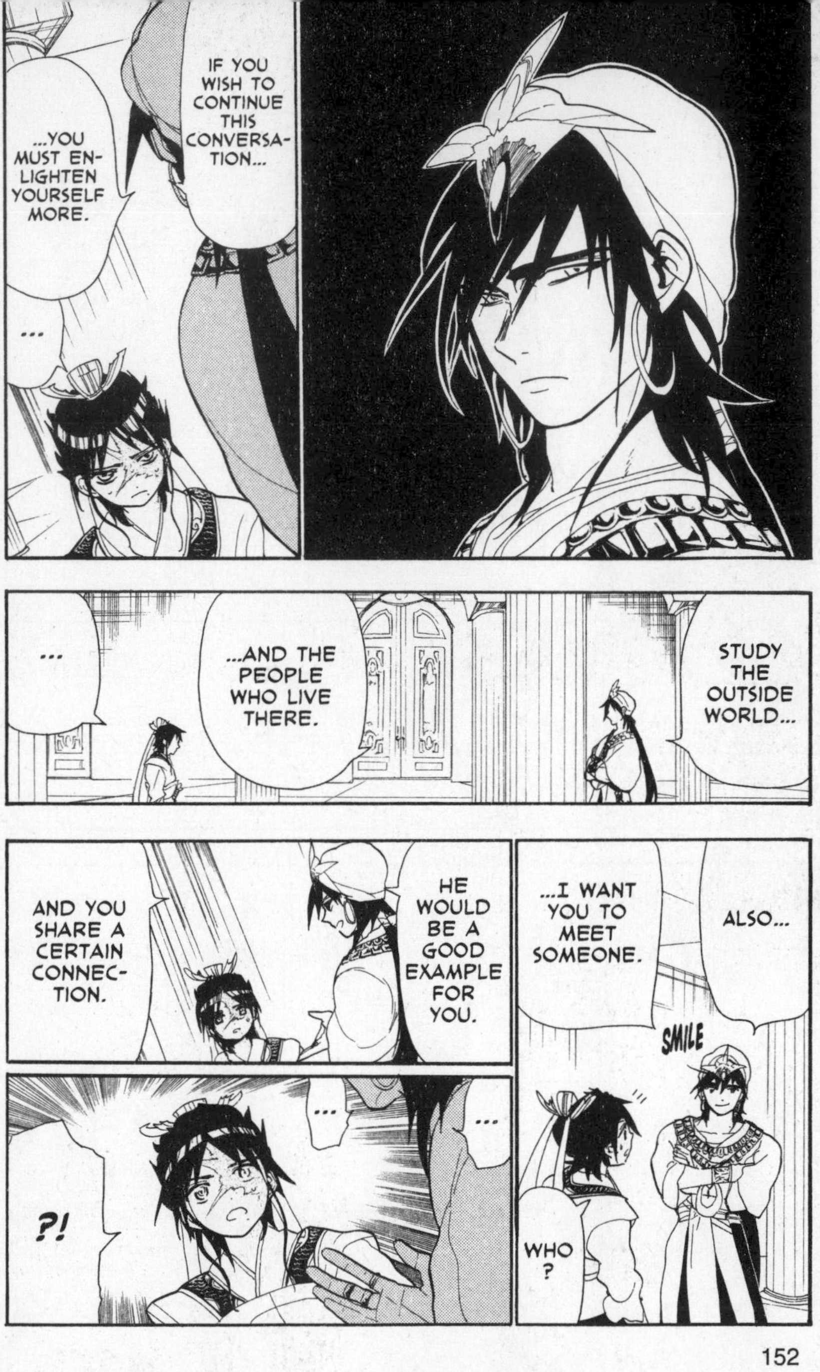
IF YOU WISH TO CONTINUE THIS CONVERSA-TION...
...YOU MUST EN-LIGHTEN YOURSELF MORE.
...
STUDY THE OUTSIDE WORLD...
...AND THE PEOPLE WHO LIVE THERE.
...
ALSO...
...I WANT YOU TO MEET SOMEONE.
SMILE
WHO?
HE WOULD BE A GOOD EXAMPLE FOR YOU.
AND YOU SHARE A CERTAIN CONNEC-TION.
...
...
?!

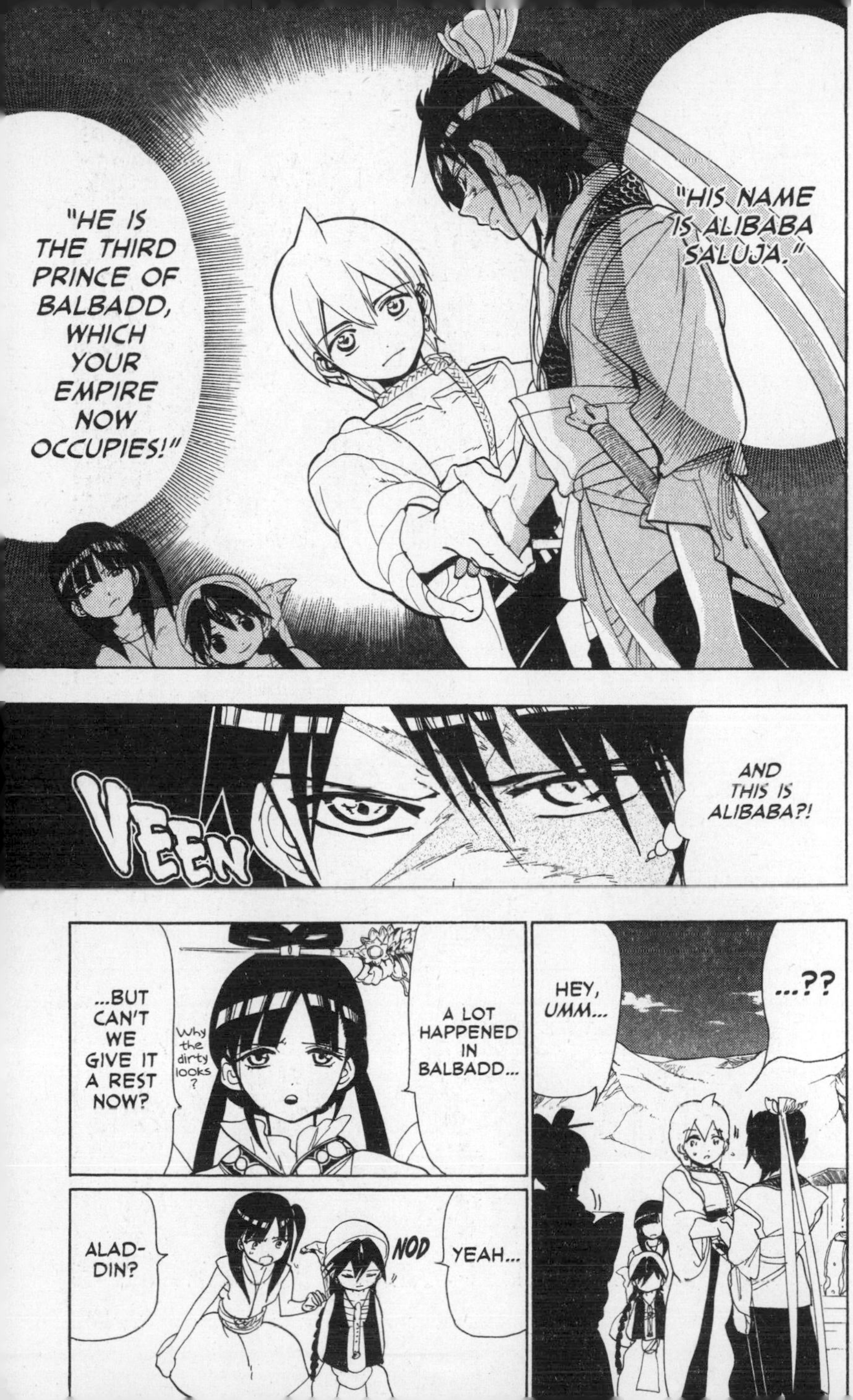
"HIS NAME IS ALIBABA SALUJA."
"HE IS THE THIRD PRINCE OF BALBADD, WHICH YOUR EMPIRE NOW OCCUPIES!"
AND THIS IS ALIBABA?!
VEEN
...??
HEY, UMM...
A LOT HAPPENED IN BALBADD...
Why the dirty looks?
...BUT CAN'T WE GIVE IT A REST NOW?
YEAH...
NOD
ALAD-DIN?

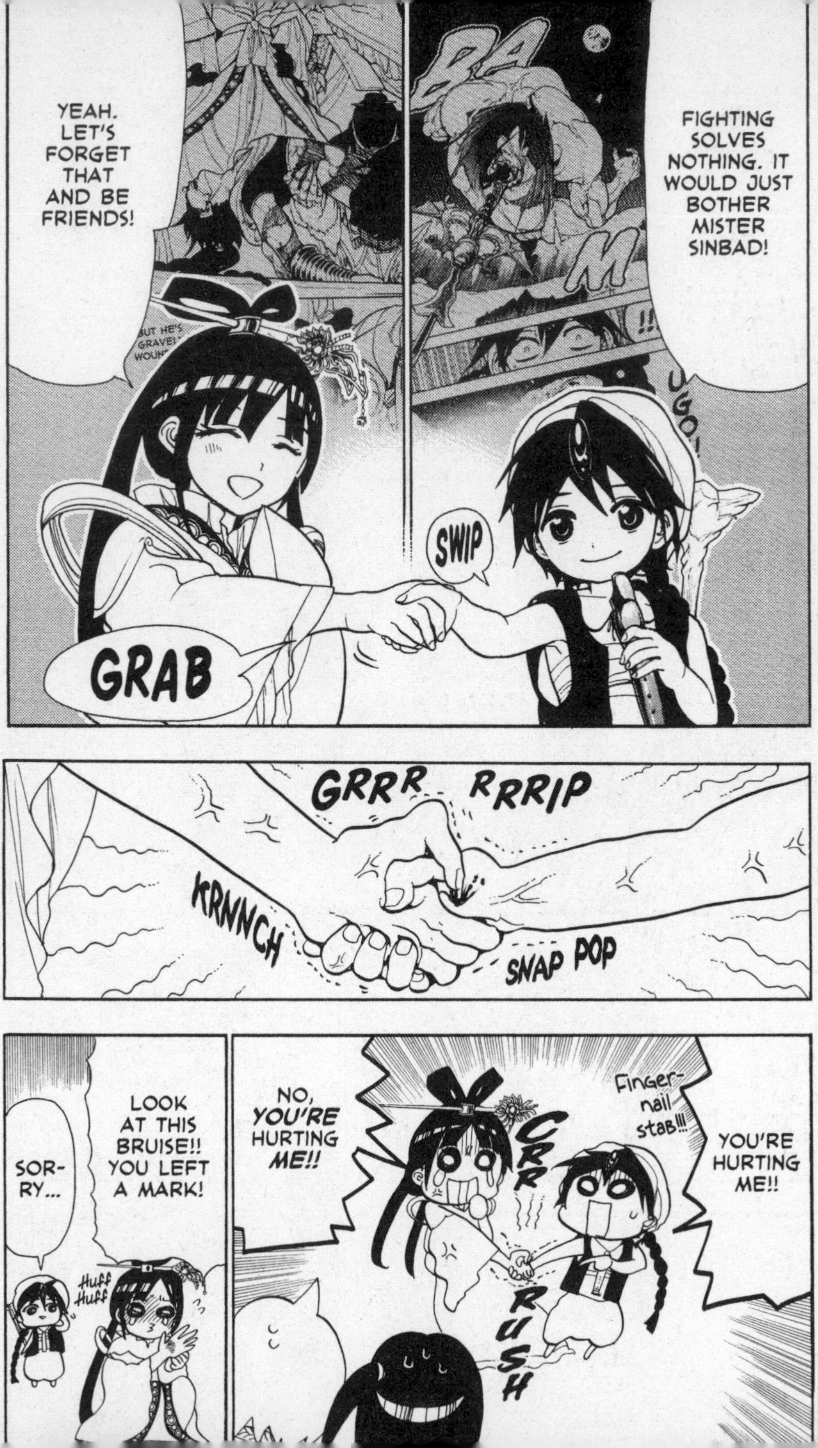
FIGHTING SOLVES NOTHING. IT WOULD JUST BOTHER MISTER SINBAD!
BA
M
!!
YEAH. LET'S FORGET THAT AND BE FRIENDS!
UGO!
SWIP
GRAB
GRRR RRRIP
KRNNCH
SNAP POP
YOU'RE HURTING ME!!
Finger-nail stab!!!
CRR
RUSH
NO, *YOU'RE* HURTING *ME!!*
LOOK AT THIS BRUISE!! YOU LEFT A MARK!
Huff Huff
SOR-RY...

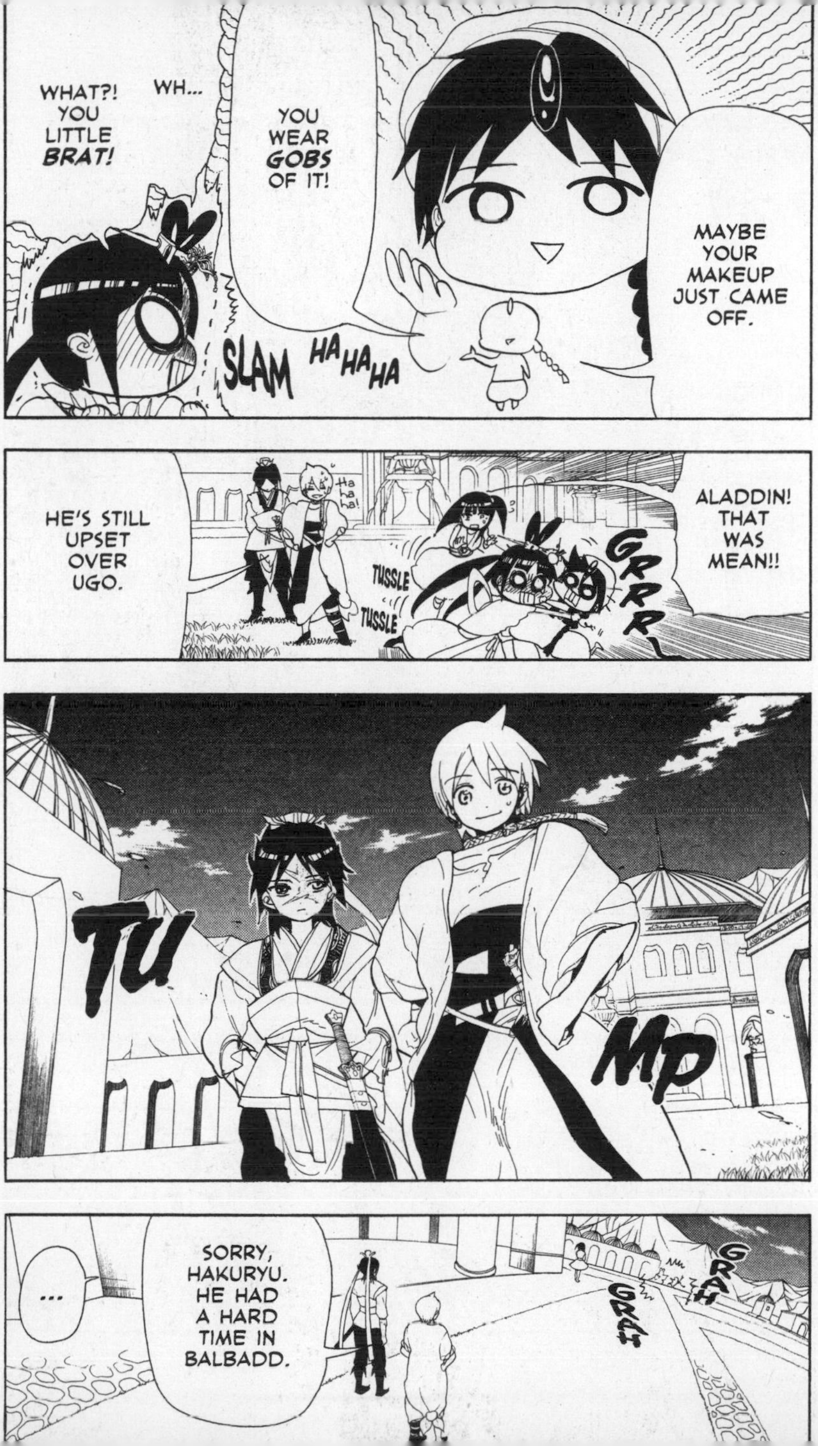
MAYBE YOUR MAKEUP JUST CAME OFF.
YOU WEAR GOBS OF IT!
WH...
WHAT?! YOU LITTLE BRAT!
HA HA HA
SLAM
ALADDIN! THAT WAS MEAN!!
GRRR
TUSSLE TUSSLE
Ha ha ha!
HE'S STILL UPSET OVER UGO.
TU MP
GRAH
GRAH
SORRY, HAKURYU. HE HAD A HARD TIME IN BALBADD.
...

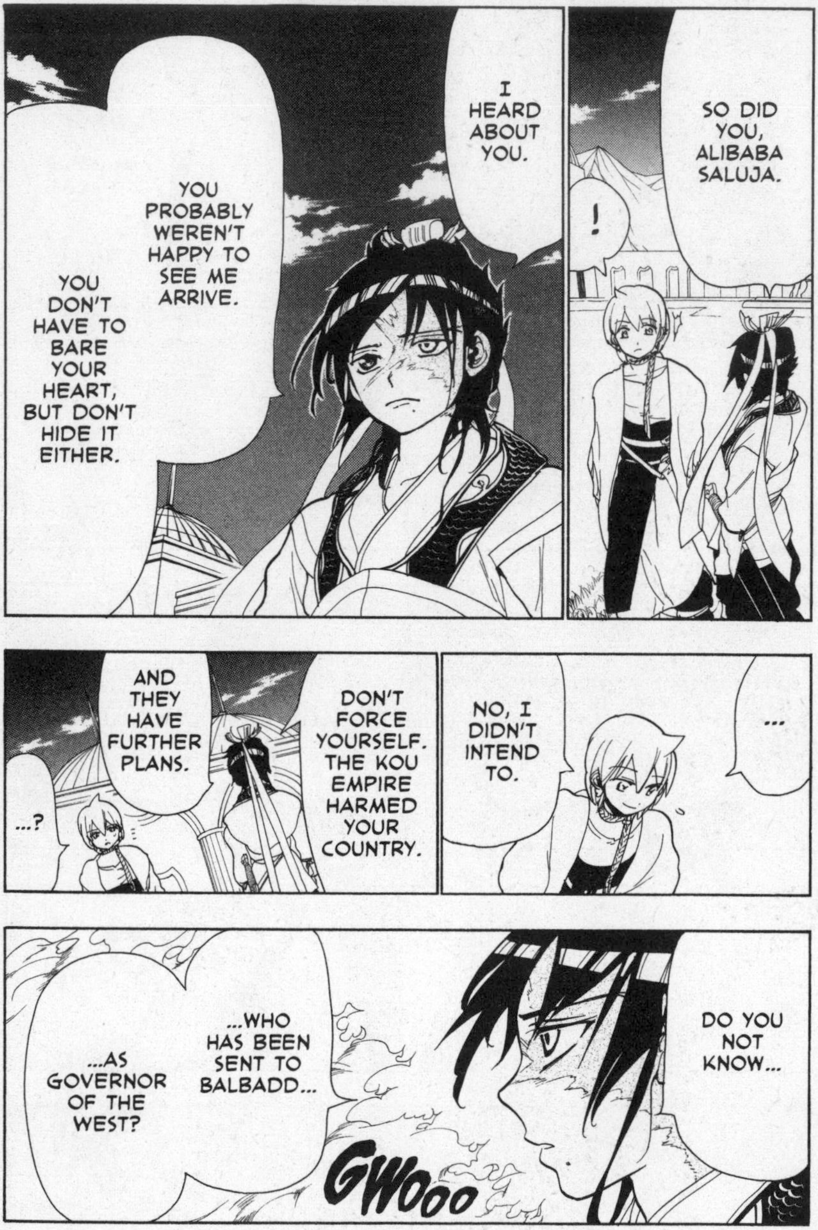
SO DID YOU, ALIBABA SALUJA.
!
I HEARD ABOUT YOU.
YOU PROBABLY WEREN'T HAPPY TO SEE ME ARRIVE.
YOU DON'T HAVE TO BARE YOUR HEART, BUT DON'T HIDE IT EITHER.
...
NO, I DIDN'T INTEND TO.
DON'T FORCE YOURSELF. THE KOU EMPIRE HARMED YOUR COUNTRY.
AND THEY HAVE FURTHER PLANS.
...?
DO YOU NOT KNOW...
...WHO HAS BEEN SENT TO BALBADD...
...AS GOVERNOR OF THE WEST?
GWOOO

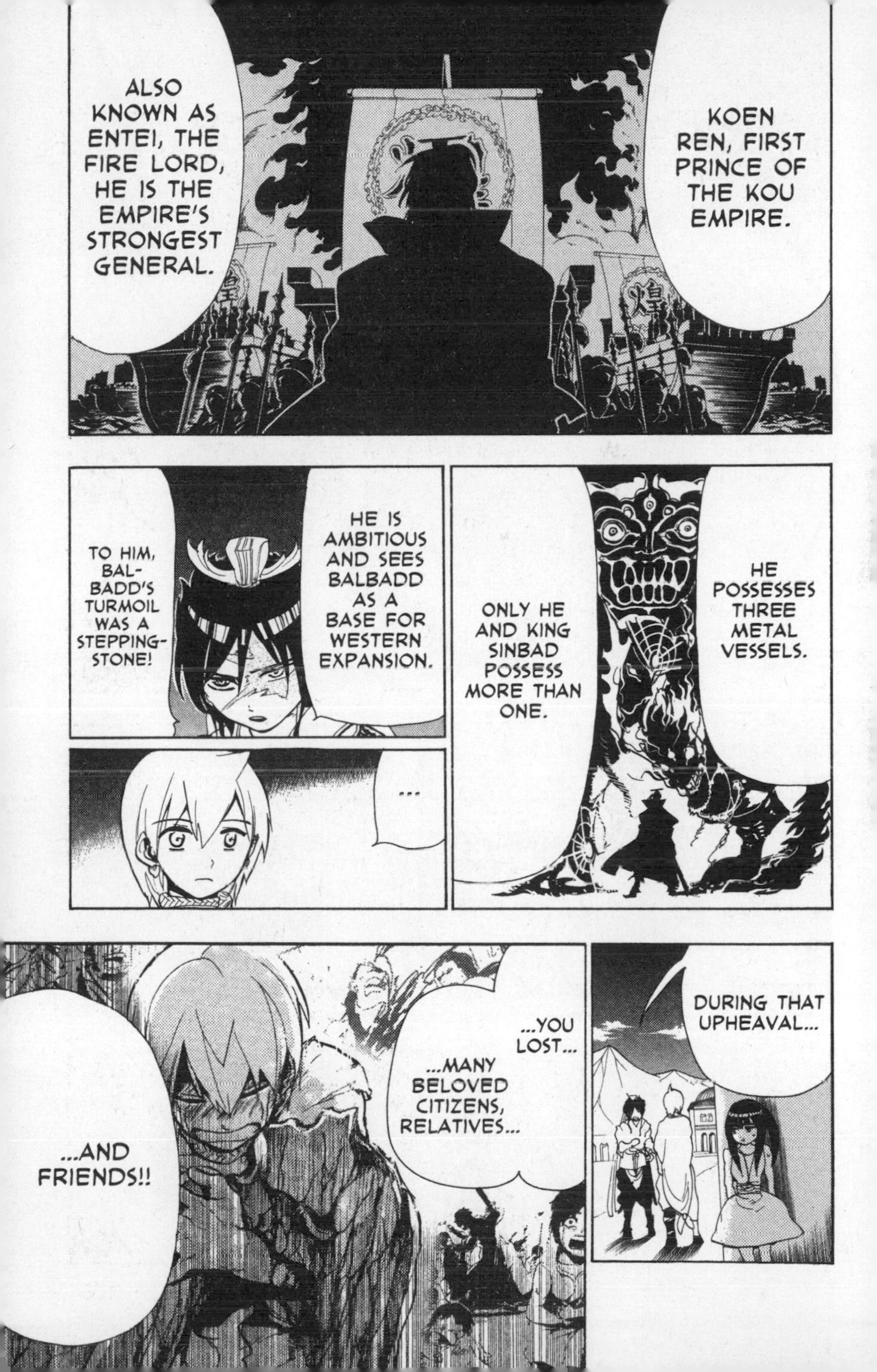
KOEN REN, FIRST PRINCE OF THE KOU EMPIRE.
ALSO KNOWN AS ENTEI, THE FIRE LORD, HE IS THE EMPIRE'S STRONGEST GENERAL.
HE POSSESSES THREE METAL VESSELS.
ONLY HE AND KING SINBAD POSSESS MORE THAN ONE.
HE IS AMBITIOUS AND SEES BALBADD AS A BASE FOR WESTERN EXPANSION.
TO HIM, BAL-BADD'S TURMOIL WAS A STEPPING-STONE!
...
DURING THAT UPHEAVAL...
...YOU LOST...
...MANY BELOVED CITIZENS, RELATIVES...
...AND FRIENDS!!

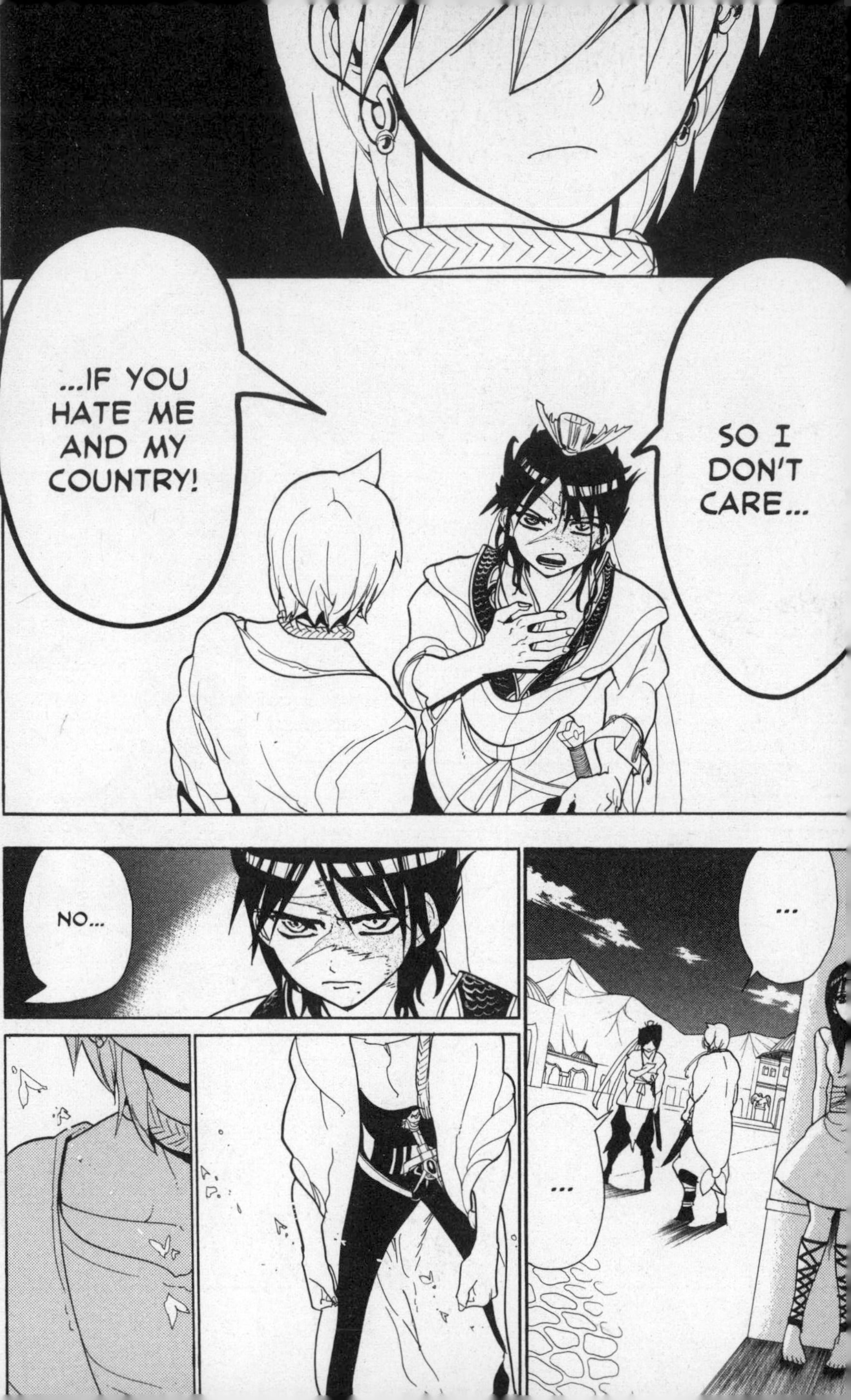
SO I DON'T CARE...
...IF YOU HATE ME AND MY COUNTRY!
...
...
NO...

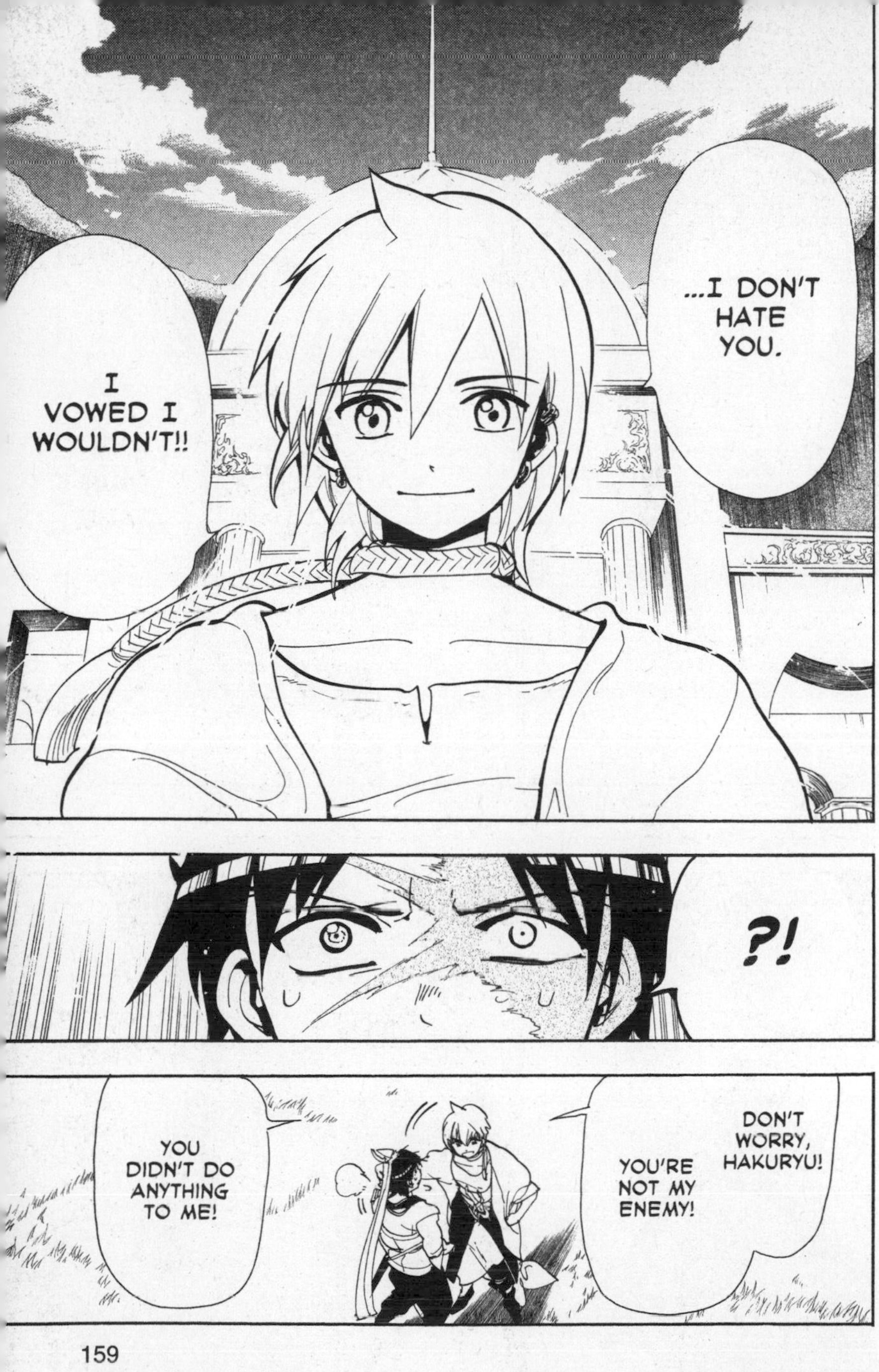
...I DON'T HATE YOU.
I VOWED I WOULDN'T!!
?!
DON'T WORRY, HAKURYU!
YOU'RE NOT MY ENEMY!
YOU DIDN'T DO ANYTHING TO ME!

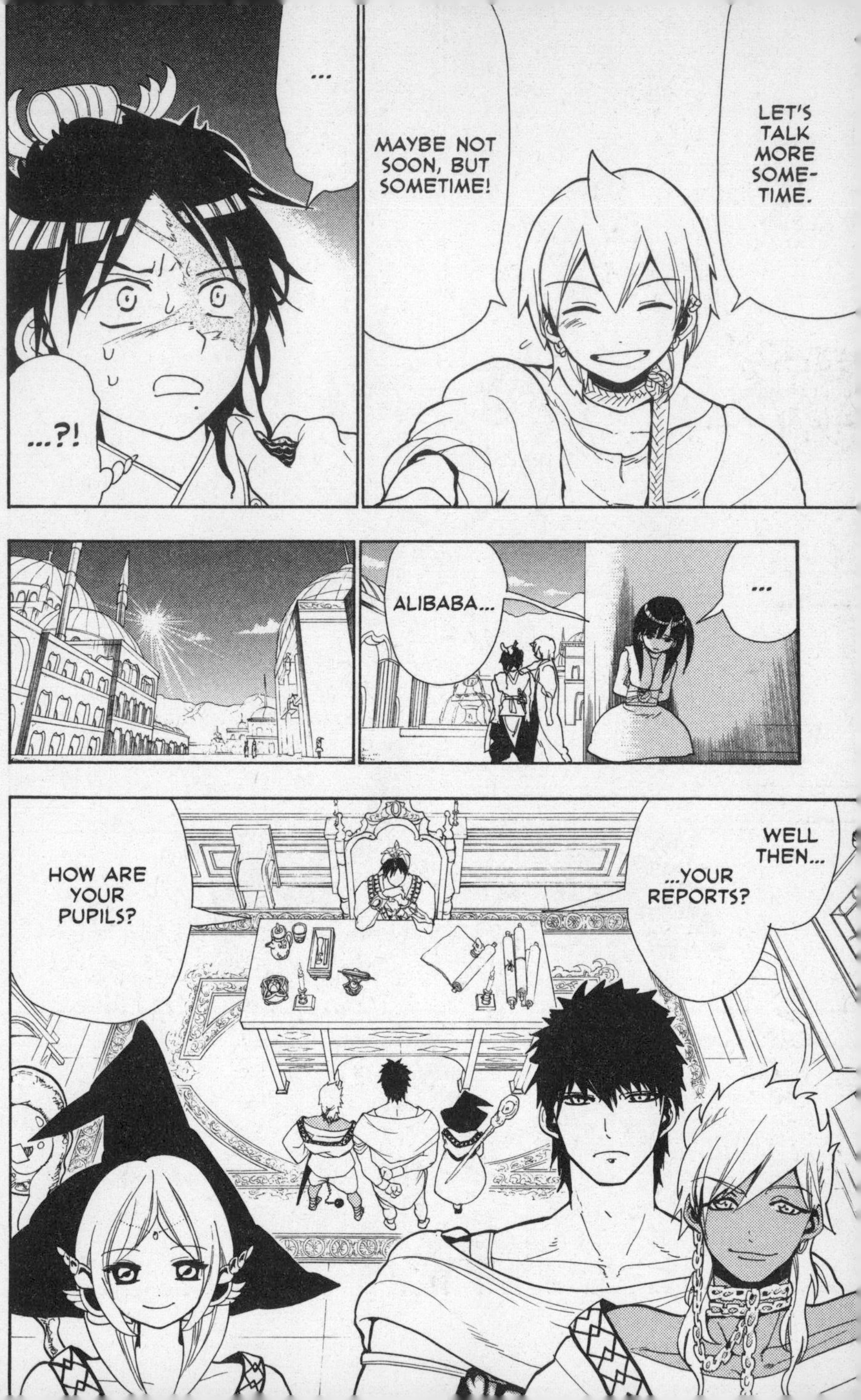
LET'S TALK MORE SOME-TIME.
MAYBE NOT SOON, BUT SOMETIME!
...
...?!
...
ALIBABA...
WELL THEN...
...YOUR REPORTS?
HOW ARE YOUR PUPILS?

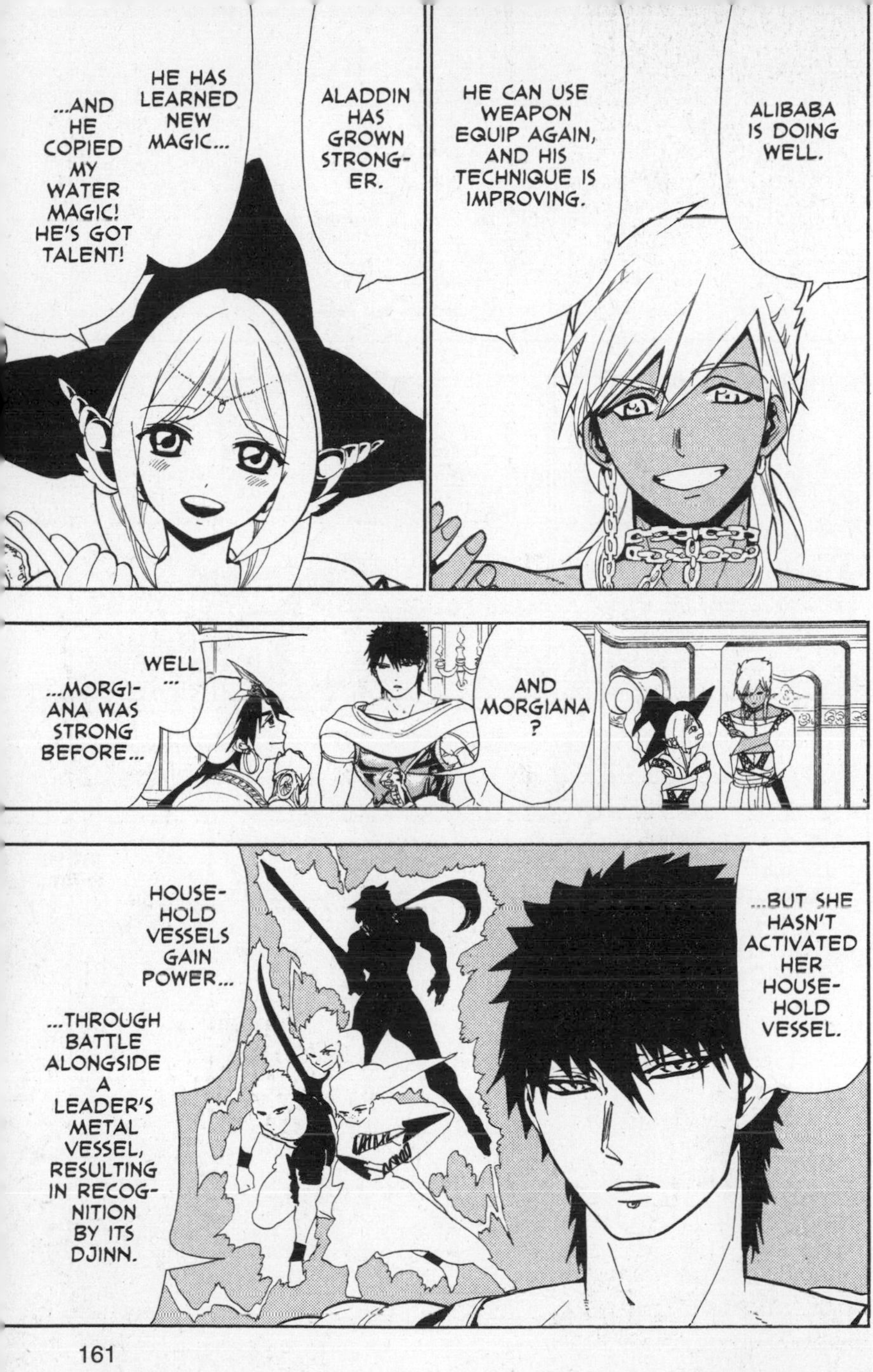

ALIBABA IS DOING WELL.
HE CAN USE WEAPON EQUIP AGAIN, AND HIS TECHNIQUE IS IMPROVING.
ALADDIN HAS GROWN STRONGER.
HE HAS LEARNED NEW MAGIC...
...AND HE COPIED MY WATER MAGIC! HE'S GOT TALENT!
AND MORGIANA?
WELL...
...MORGIANA WAS STRONG BEFORE...
...BUT SHE HASN'T ACTIVATED HER HOUSEHOLD VESSEL.
HOUSEHOLD VESSELS GAIN POWER...
...THROUGH BATTLE ALONGSIDE A LEADER'S METAL VESSEL, RESULTING IN RECOGNITION BY ITS DJINN.

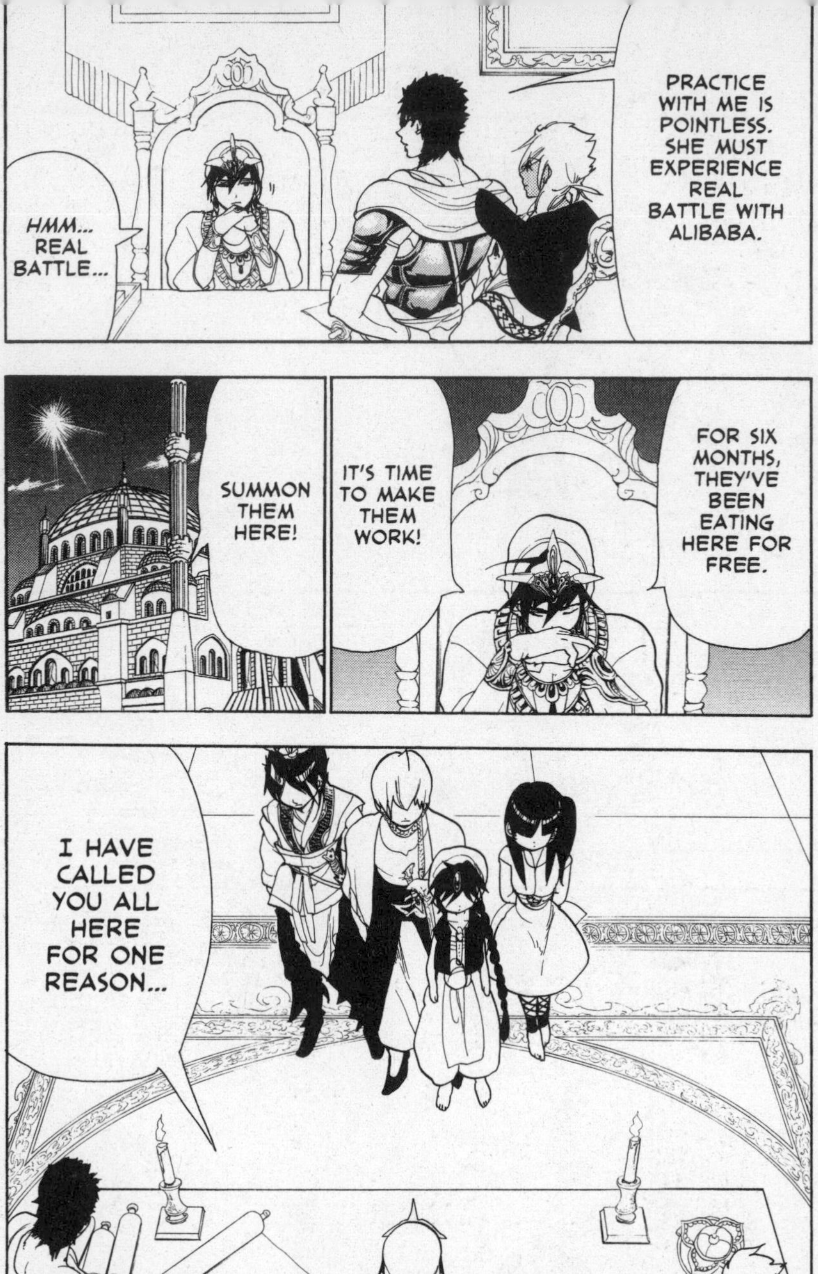
PRACTICE WITH ME IS POINTLESS. SHE MUST EXPERIENCE REAL BATTLE WITH ALIBABA.
HMM... REAL BATTLE...
FOR SIX MONTHS, THEY'VE BEEN EATING HERE FOR FREE.
IT'S TIME TO MAKE THEM WORK!
SUMMON THEM HERE!
I HAVE CALLED YOU ALL HERE FOR ONE REASON...

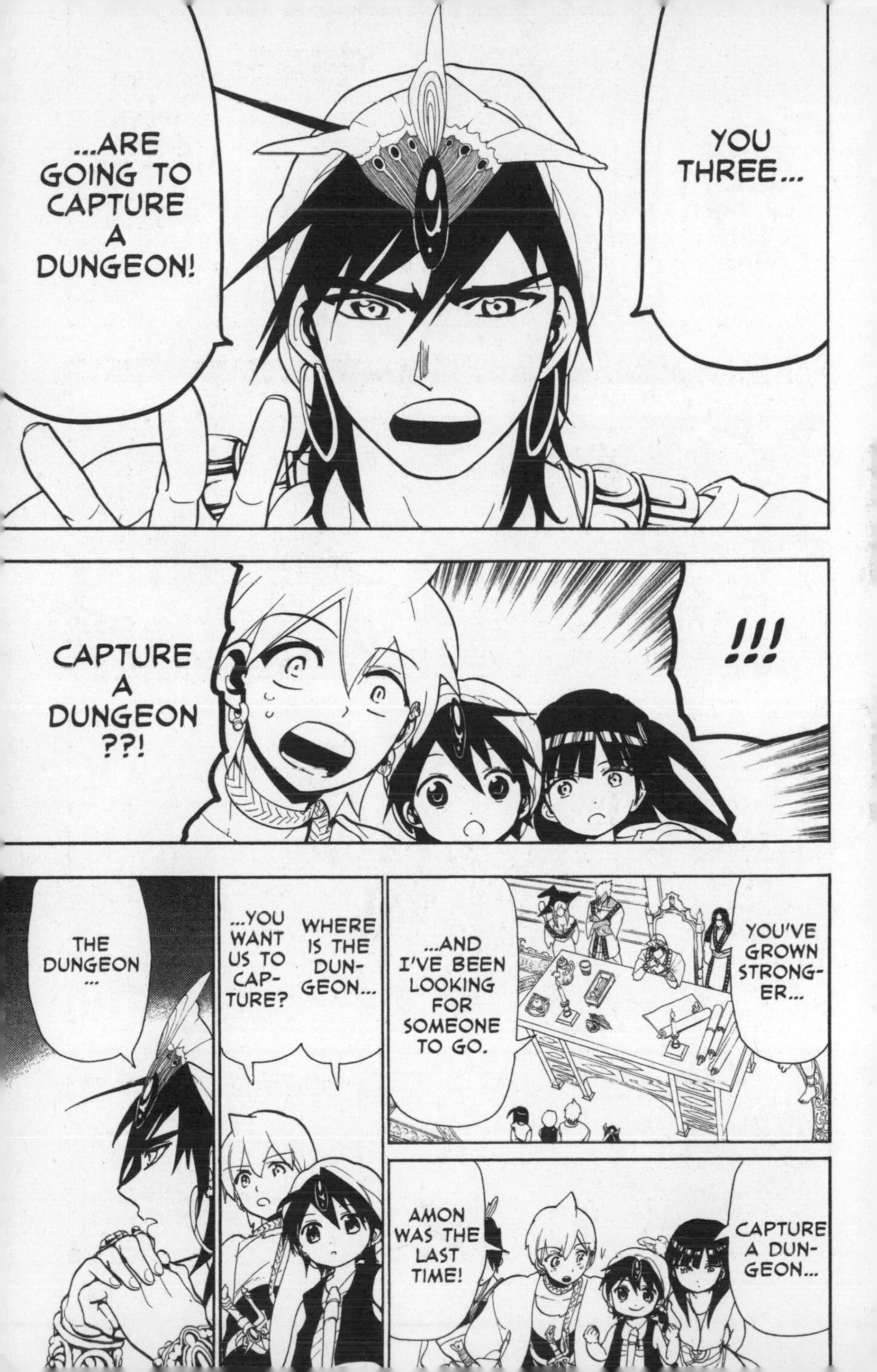
YOU THREE...
...ARE GOING TO CAPTURE A DUNGEON!
!!!
CAPTURE A DUNGEON ??!
YOU'VE GROWN STRONGER...
...AND I'VE BEEN LOOKING FOR SOMEONE TO GO.
CAPTURE A DUNGEON...
AMON WAS THE LAST TIME!
WHERE IS THE DUNGEON...
...YOU WANT US TO CAPTURE?
THE DUNGEON ...

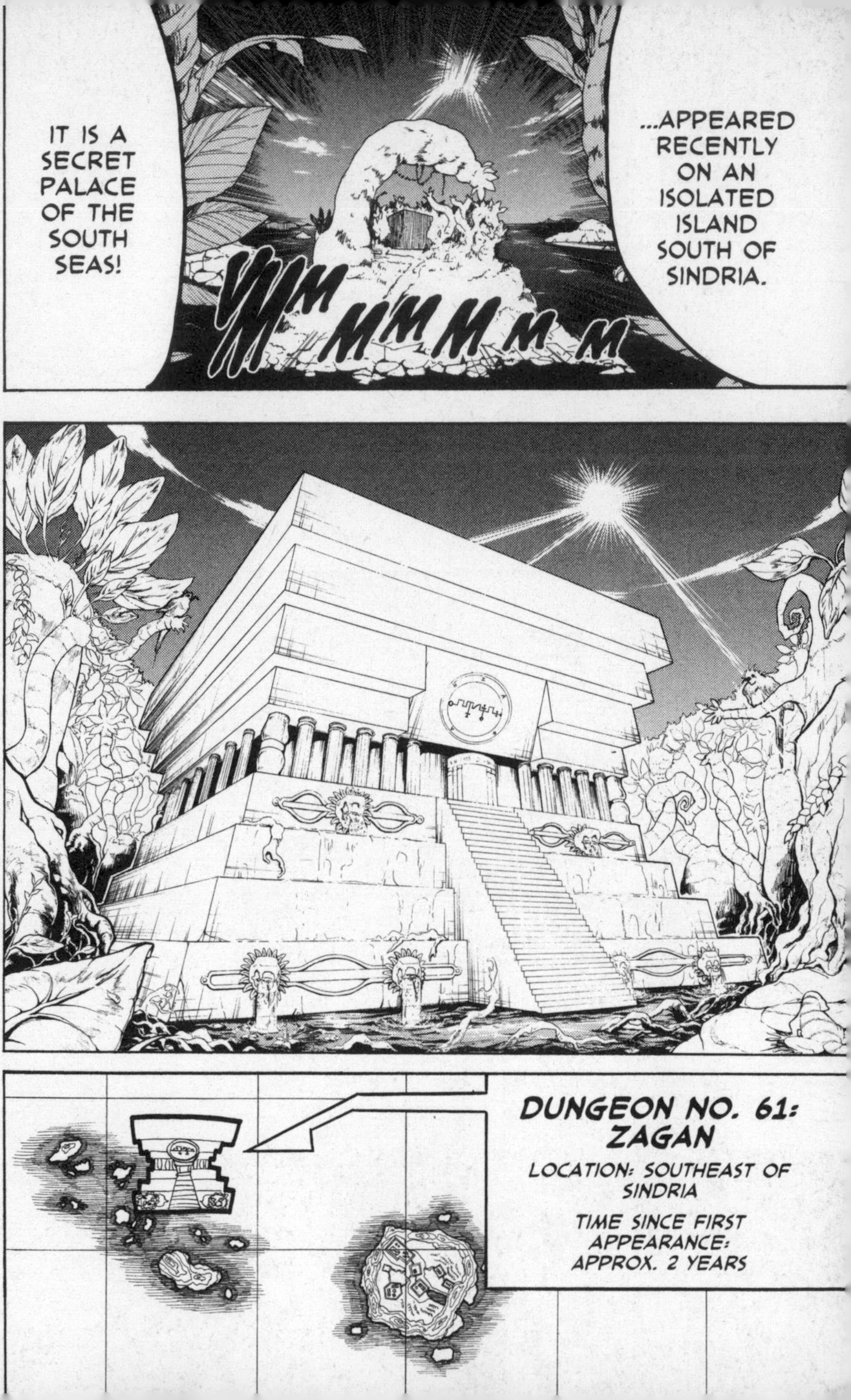
...APPEARED RECENTLY ON AN ISOLATED ISLAND SOUTH OF SINDRIA.
IT IS A SECRET PALACE OF THE SOUTH SEAS!
VVMMMMMMMM
DUNGEON NO. 61: ZAGAN
LOCATION: SOUTHEAST OF SINDRIA
TIME SINCE FIRST APPEARANCE: APPROX. 2 YEARS

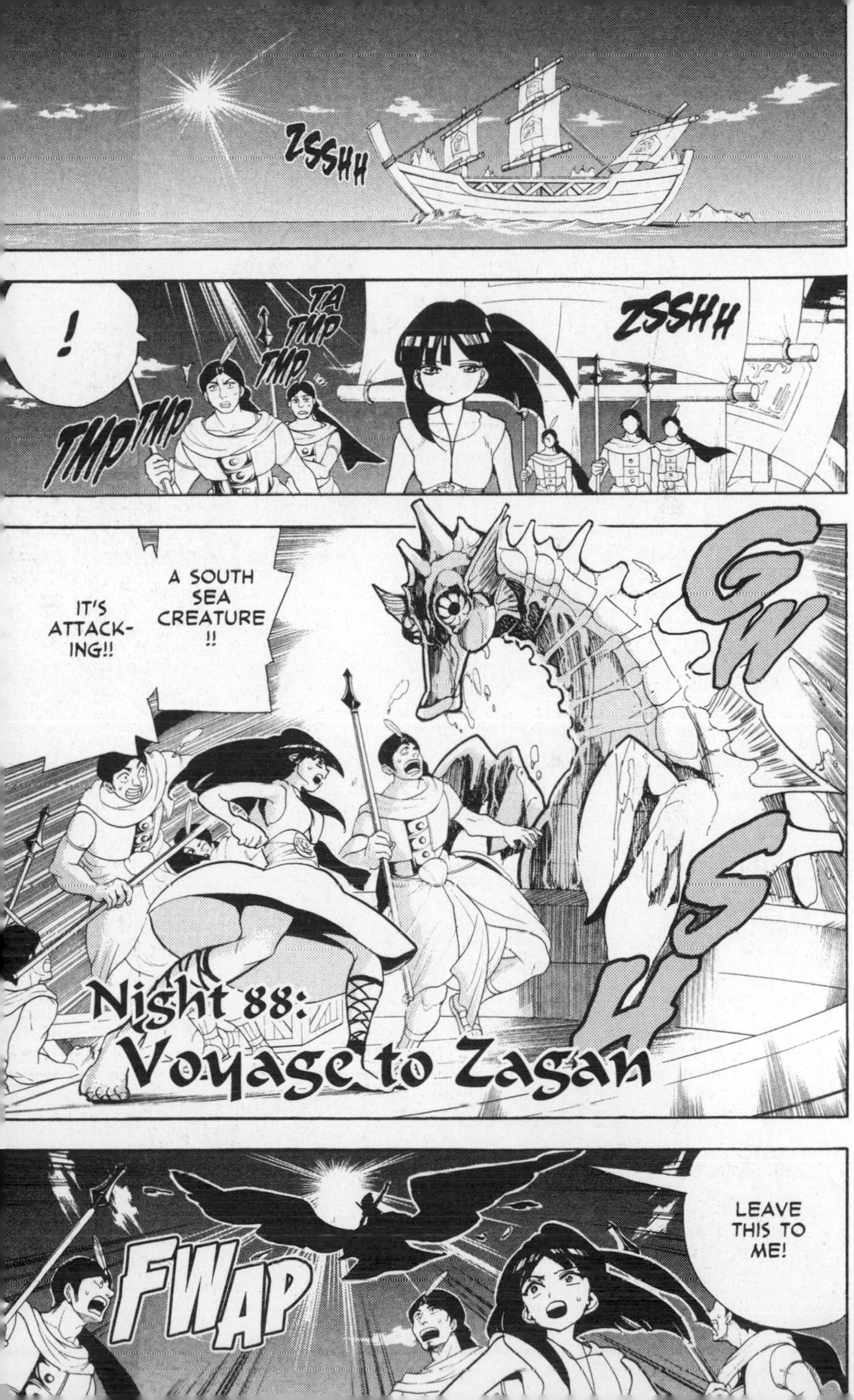
ZSSHH
ZSSHH
TA
TMP
TMP
TMP TMP
!
GWSH
A SOUTH SEA CREATURE !!
IT'S ATTACKING!!
Night 88: Voyage to Zagan
LEAVE THIS TO ME!
FWAP

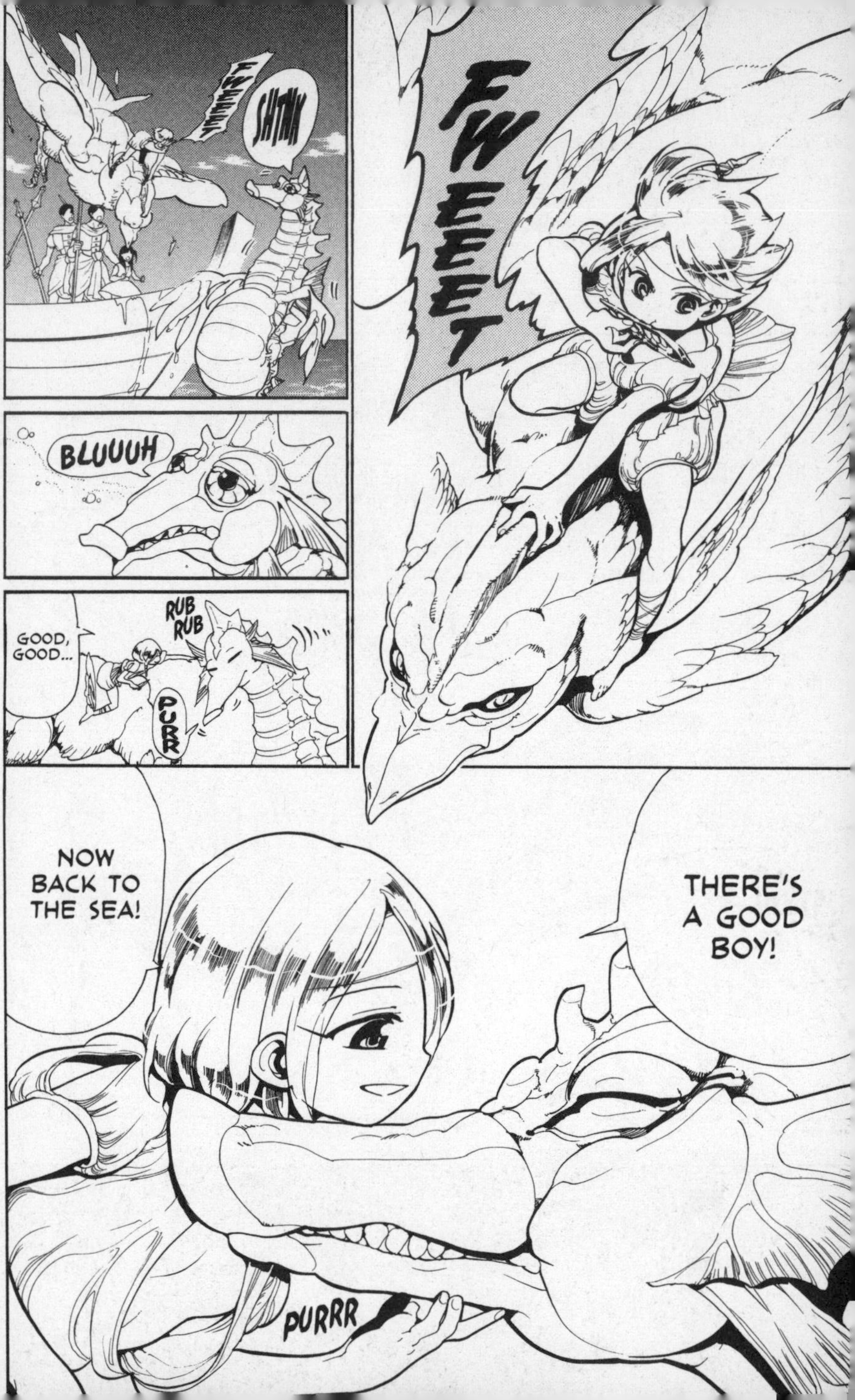
FWEEEET
FWEEEET
SHTNK
BLUUUH
GOOD, GOOD...
RUB RUB
PURR
THERE'S A GOOD BOY!
NOW BACK TO THE SEA!
PURRR

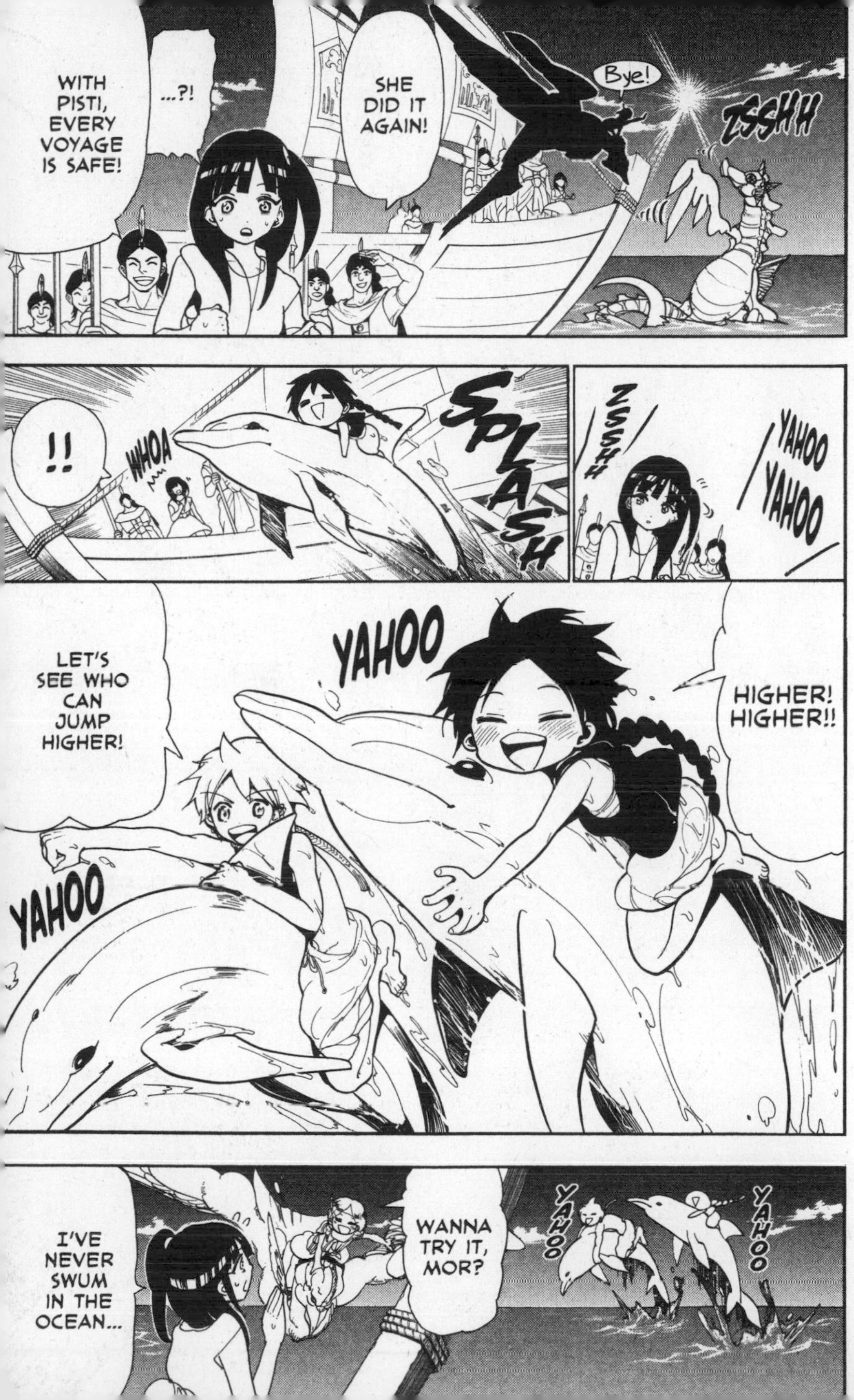
ZSSHH
Bye!
SHE DID IT AGAIN!
...?!
WITH PISTI, EVERY VOYAGE IS SAFE!
YAHOO
YAHOO
ZSSHH
SPLASH
WHOA
!!
HIGHER! HIGHER!!
YAHOO
LET'S SEE WHO CAN JUMP HIGHER!
YAHOO
YAHOO
YAHOO
WANNA TRY IT, MOR?
I'VE NEVER SWUM IN THE OCEAN...

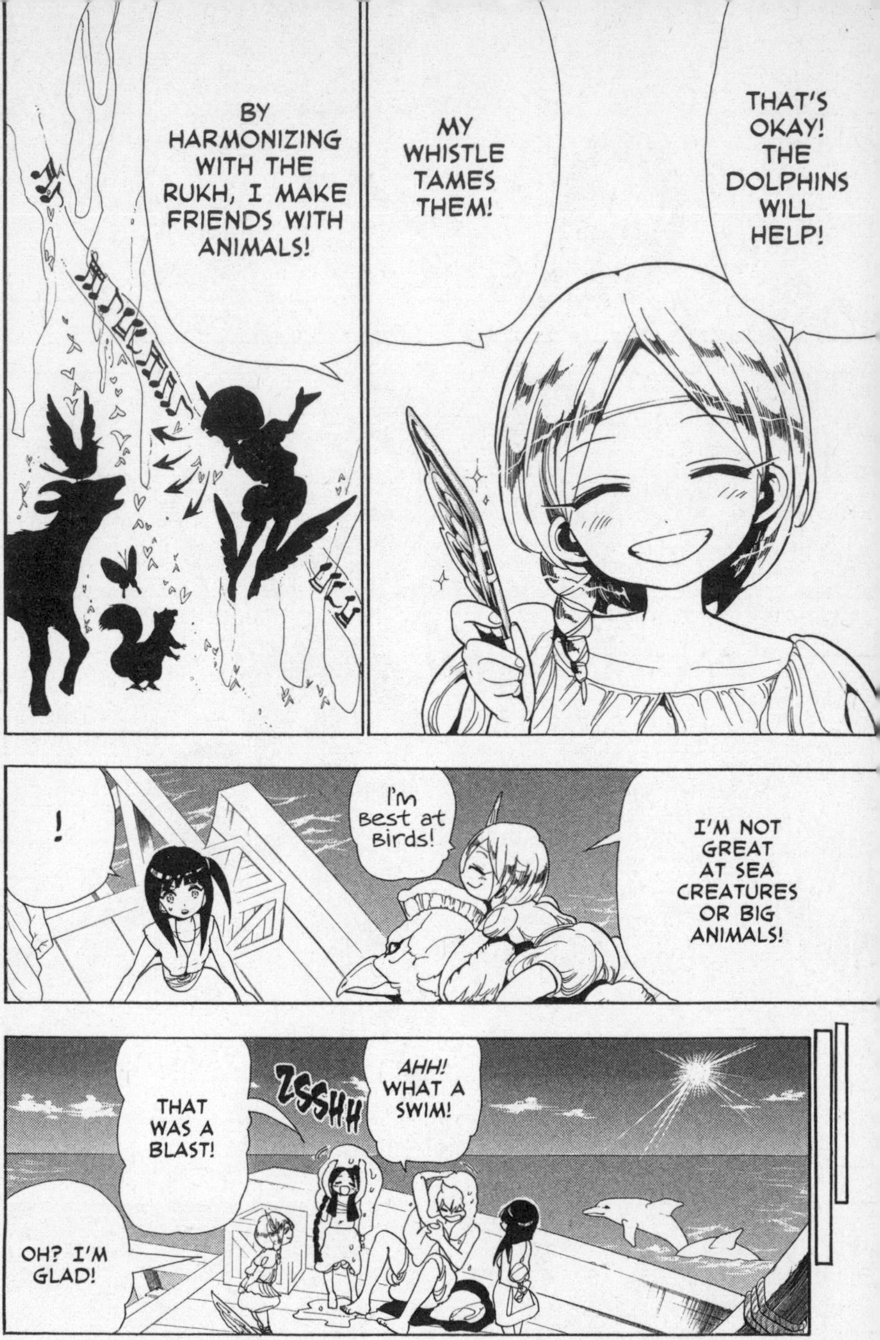
THAT'S OKAY! THE DOLPHINS WILL HELP!
MY WHISTLE TAMES THEM!
BY HARMONIZING WITH THE RUKH, I MAKE FRIENDS WITH ANIMALS!
I'M NOT GREAT AT SEA CREATURES OR BIG ANIMALS!
I'm Best at Birds!
!
AHH! WHAT A SWIM!
ZSSHH
THAT WAS A BLAST!
OH? I'M GLAD!

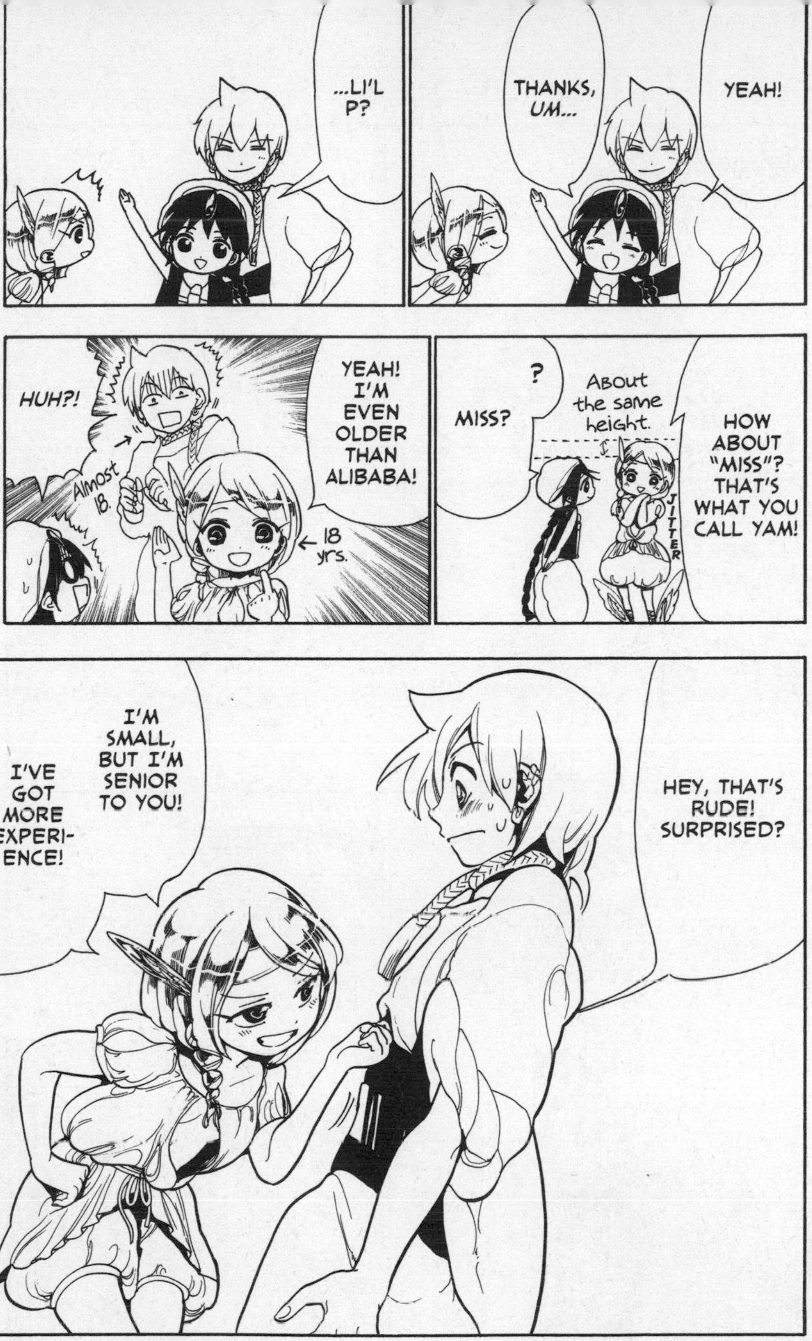
YEAH!
THANKS, UM...
...LI'L P?
HOW ABOUT "MISS"? THAT'S WHAT YOU CALL YAM!
About the same height.
JITTER
?
MISS?
YEAH! I'M EVEN OLDER THAN ALIBABA!
18 yrs.
Almost 18.
HUH?!
HEY, THAT'S RUDE! SURPRISED?
I'M SMALL, BUT I'M SENIOR TO YOU!
I'VE GOT MORE EXPERI-ENCE!

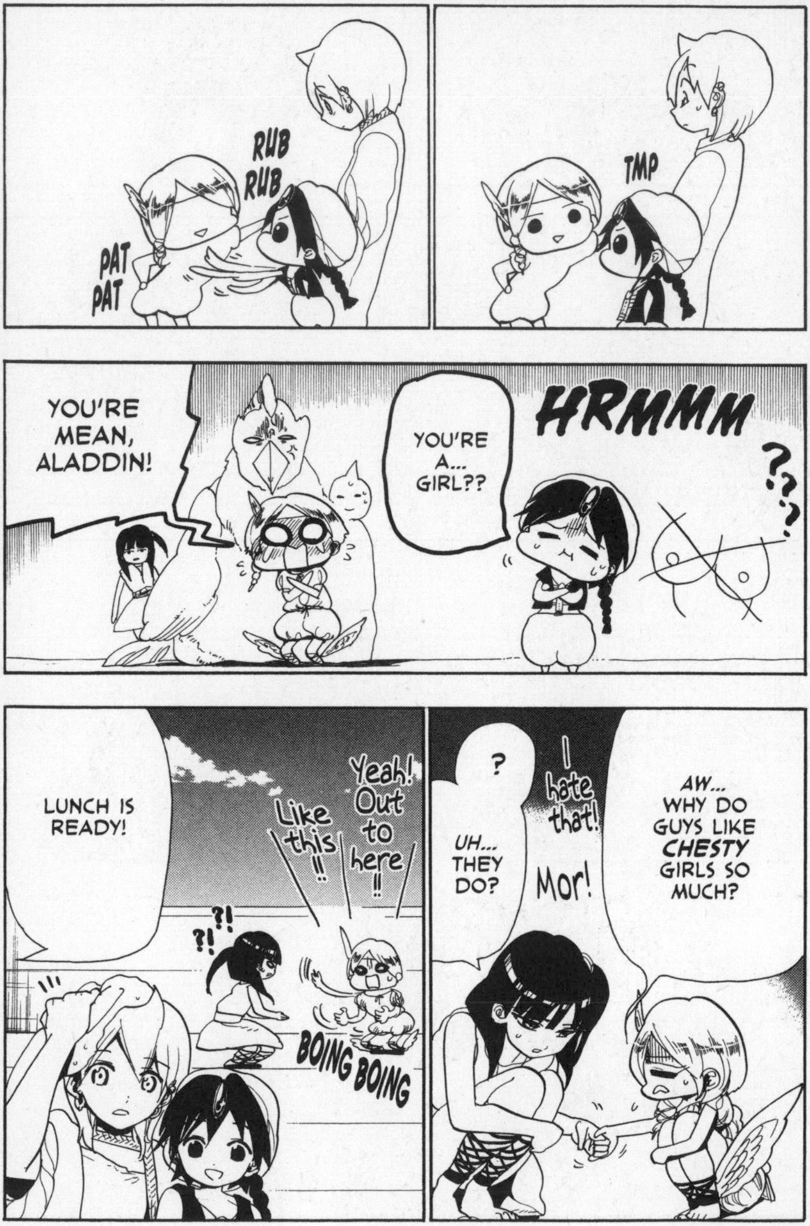
TMP
RUB RUB
PAT PAT
HRMMM
???
YOU'RE A... GIRL??
YOU'RE MEAN, ALADDIN!
AW... WHY DO GUYS LIKE CHESTY GIRLS SO MUCH?
I hate that!
Mor!
?
UH... THEY DO?
Yeah! Out to here!!
Like this!!
?! ?!
BOING BOING
LUNCH IS READY!

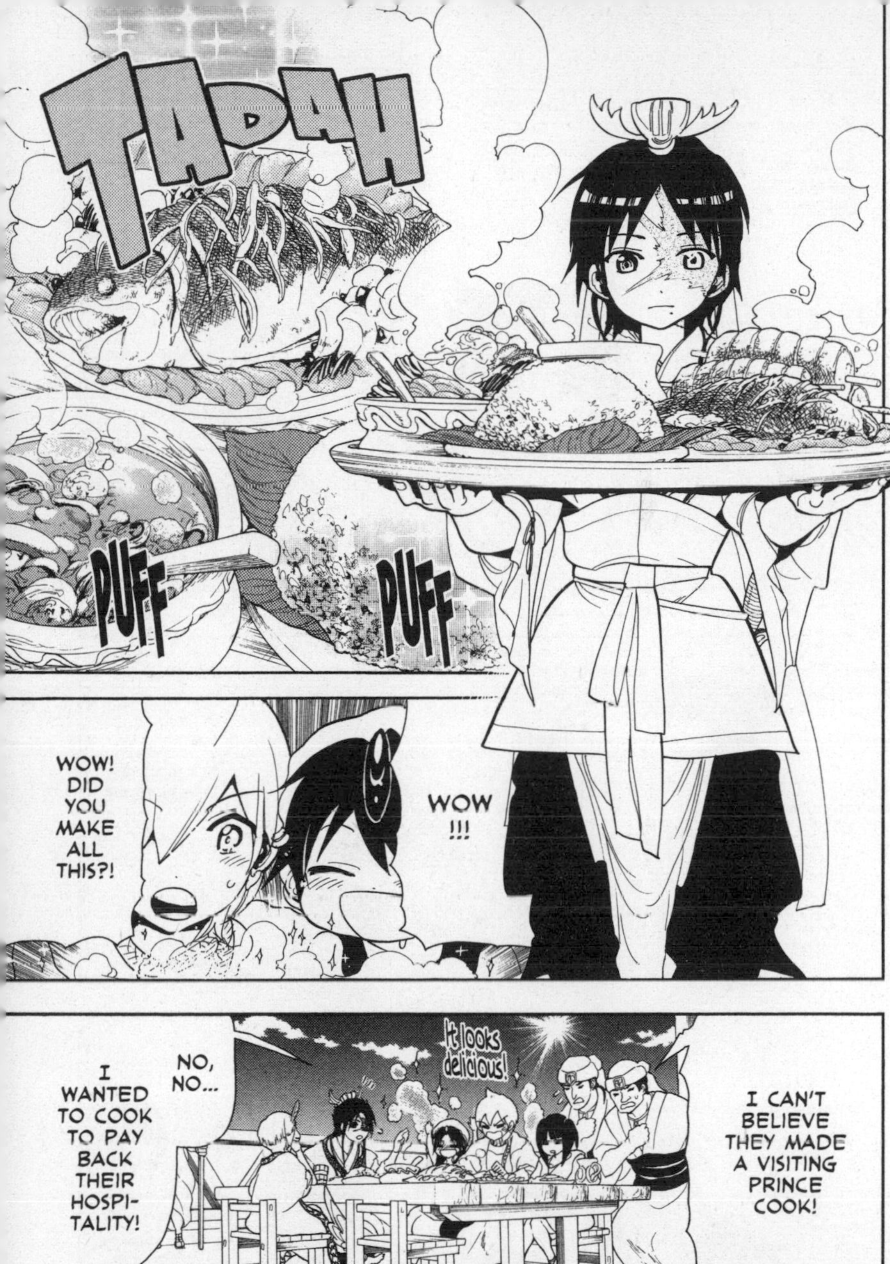
TADAH
PUFF
PUFF
WOW!!!
WOW! DID YOU MAKE ALL THIS?!
I CAN'T BELIEVE THEY MADE A VISITING PRINCE COOK!
It looks delicious!
NO, NO...
I WANTED TO COOK TO PAY BACK THEIR HOSPI-TALITY!

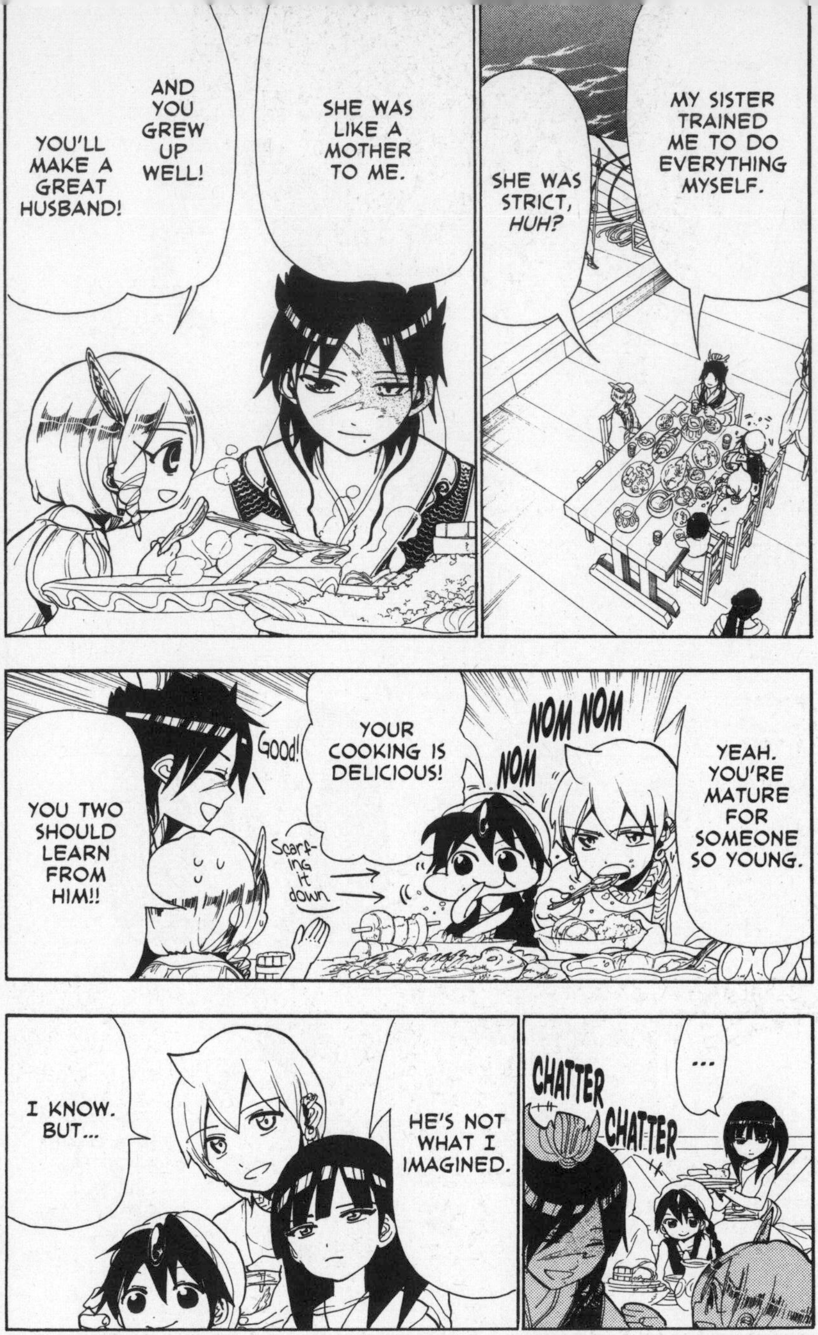
MY SISTER TRAINED ME TO DO EVERYTHING MYSELF.
SHE WAS STRICT, *HUH?*
SHE WAS LIKE A MOTHER TO ME.
AND YOU GREW UP WELL!
YOU'LL MAKE A GREAT HUSBAND!
YEAH. YOU'RE MATURE FOR SOMEONE SO YOUNG.
NOM NOM
NOM
YOUR COOKING IS DELICIOUS!
Scarfing it down
Good!
YOU TWO SHOULD LEARN FROM HIM!!
...
CHATTER
CHATTER
HE'S NOT WHAT I IMAGINED.
I KNOW. BUT...

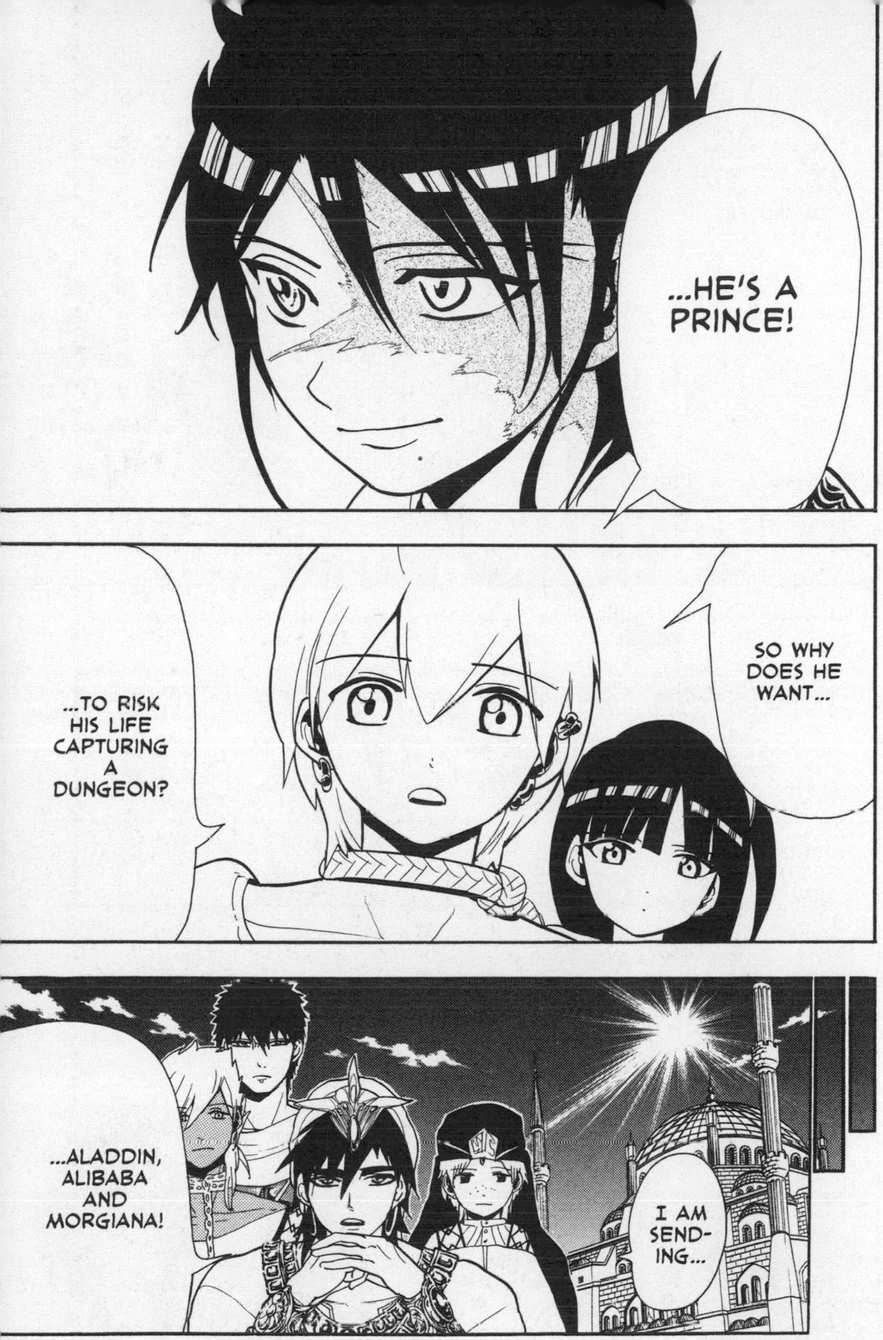
...HE'S A PRINCE!
SO WHY DOES HE WANT...
...TO RISK HIS LIFE CAPTURING A DUNGEON?
I AM SEND-ING...
...ALADDIN, ALIBABA AND MORGIANA!

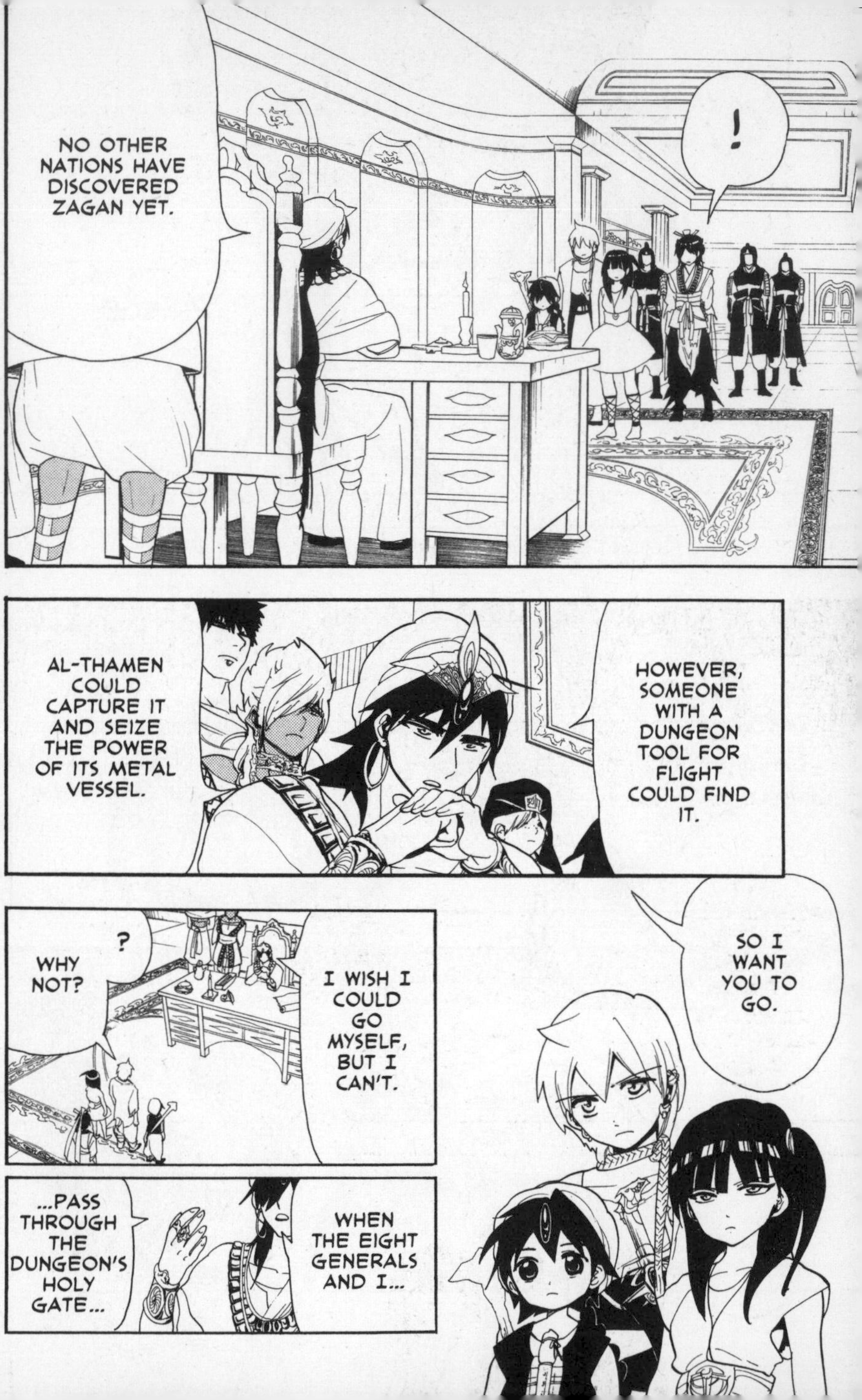
NO OTHER NATIONS HAVE DISCOVERED ZAGAN YET.
!
HOWEVER, SOMEONE WITH A DUNGEON TOOL FOR FLIGHT COULD FIND IT.
AL-THAMEN COULD CAPTURE IT AND SEIZE THE POWER OF ITS METAL VESSEL.
SO I WANT YOU TO GO.
I WISH I COULD GO MYSELF, BUT I CAN'T.
?
WHY NOT?
WHEN THE EIGHT GENERALS AND I...
...PASS THROUGH THE DUNGEON'S HOLY GATE...

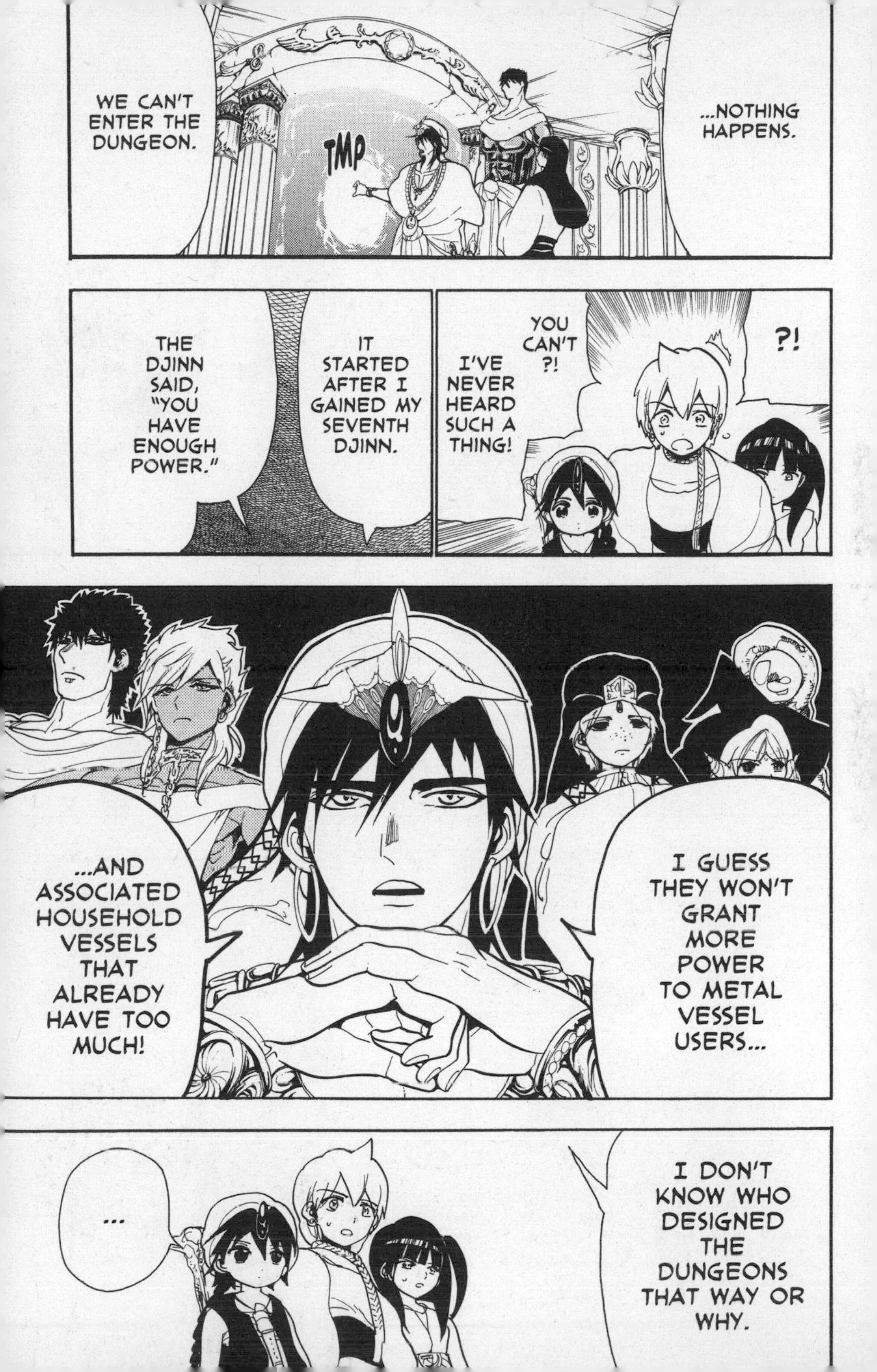
...NOTHING HAPPENS.
WE CAN'T ENTER THE DUNGEON.
TMP
?!
YOU CAN'T ?!
I'VE NEVER HEARD SUCH A THING!
IT STARTED AFTER I GAINED MY SEVENTH DJINN.
THE DJINN SAID, "YOU HAVE ENOUGH POWER."
I GUESS THEY WON'T GRANT MORE POWER TO METAL VESSEL USERS...
...AND ASSOCIATED HOUSEHOLD VESSELS THAT ALREADY HAVE TOO MUCH!
I DON'T KNOW WHO DESIGNED THE DUNGEONS THAT WAY OR WHY.
...

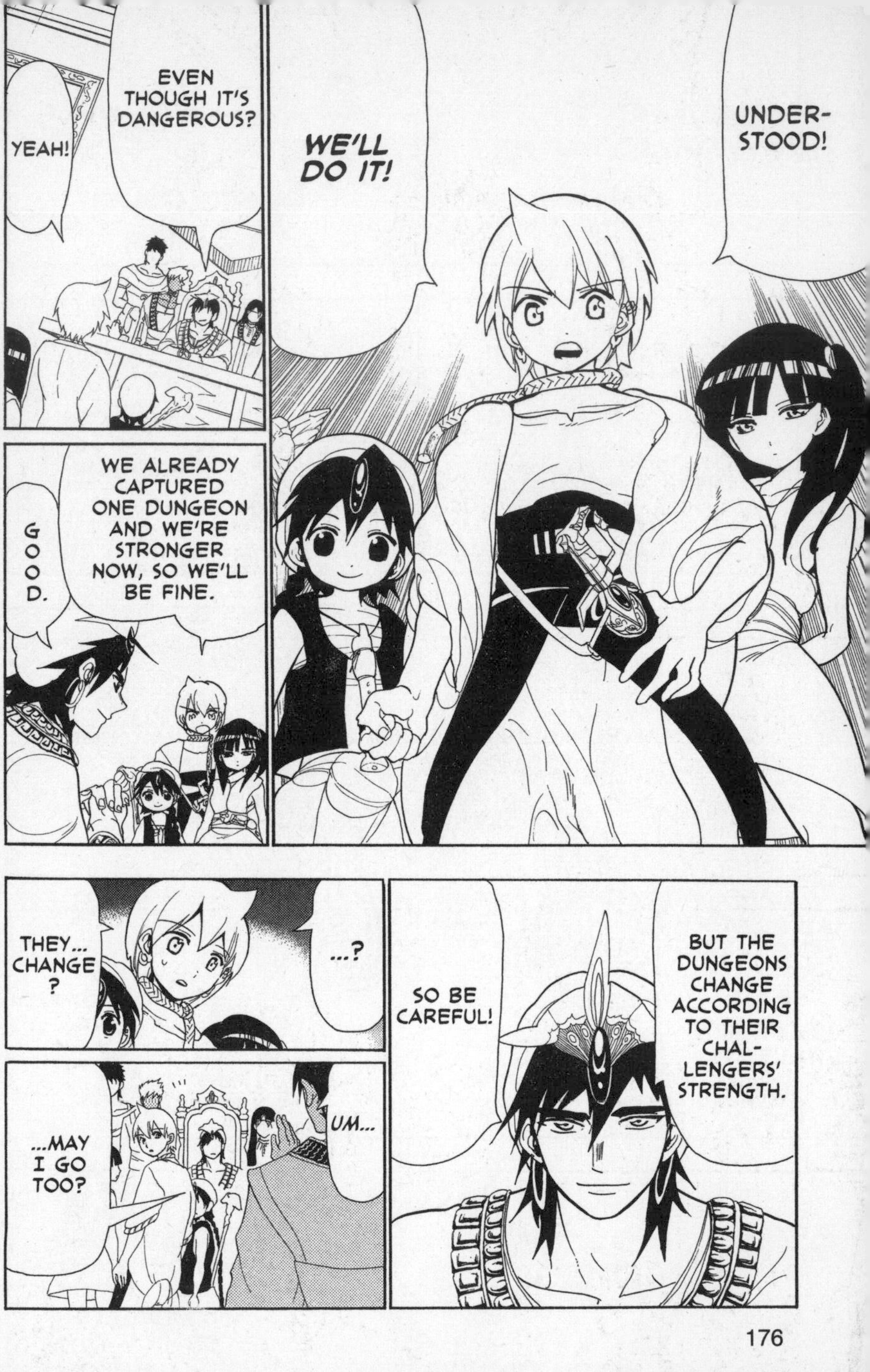
UNDER-STOOD!
WE'LL DO IT!
EVEN THOUGH IT'S DANGEROUS?
YEAH!
WE ALREADY CAPTURED ONE DUNGEON AND WE'RE STRONGER NOW, SO WE'LL BE FINE.
GOOD.
BUT THE DUNGEONS CHANGE ACCORDING TO THEIR CHAL-LENGERS' STRENGTH.
SO BE CAREFUL!
...?
THEY... CHANGE?
UM...
...MAY I GO TOO?

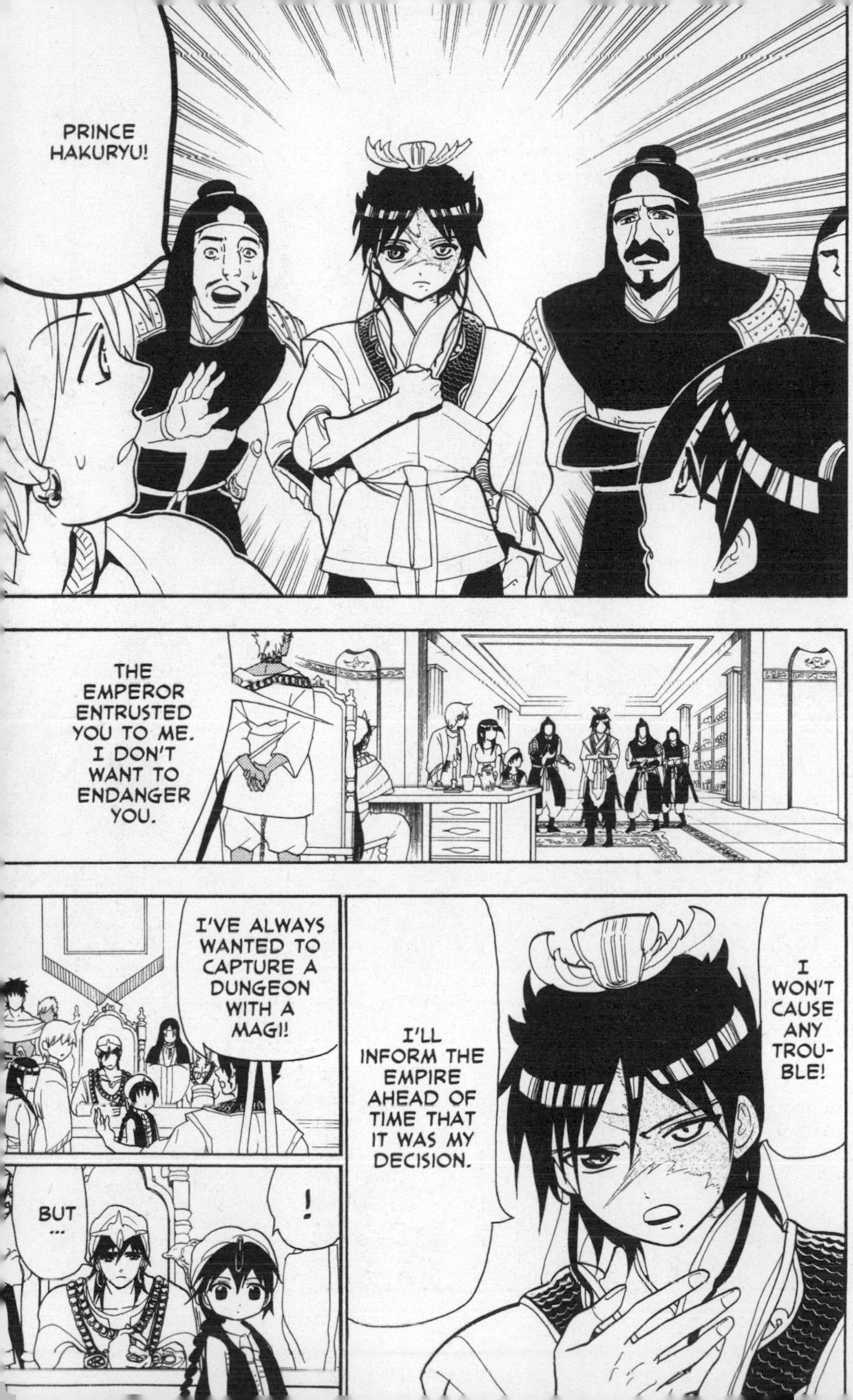
PRINCE HAKURYU!
THE EMPEROR ENTRUSTED YOU TO ME. I DON'T WANT TO ENDANGER YOU.
I WON'T CAUSE ANY TROU-BLE!
I'LL INFORM THE EMPIRE AHEAD OF TIME THAT IT WAS MY DECISION.
I'VE ALWAYS WANTED TO CAPTURE A DUNGEON WITH A MAGI!
!
BUT ...

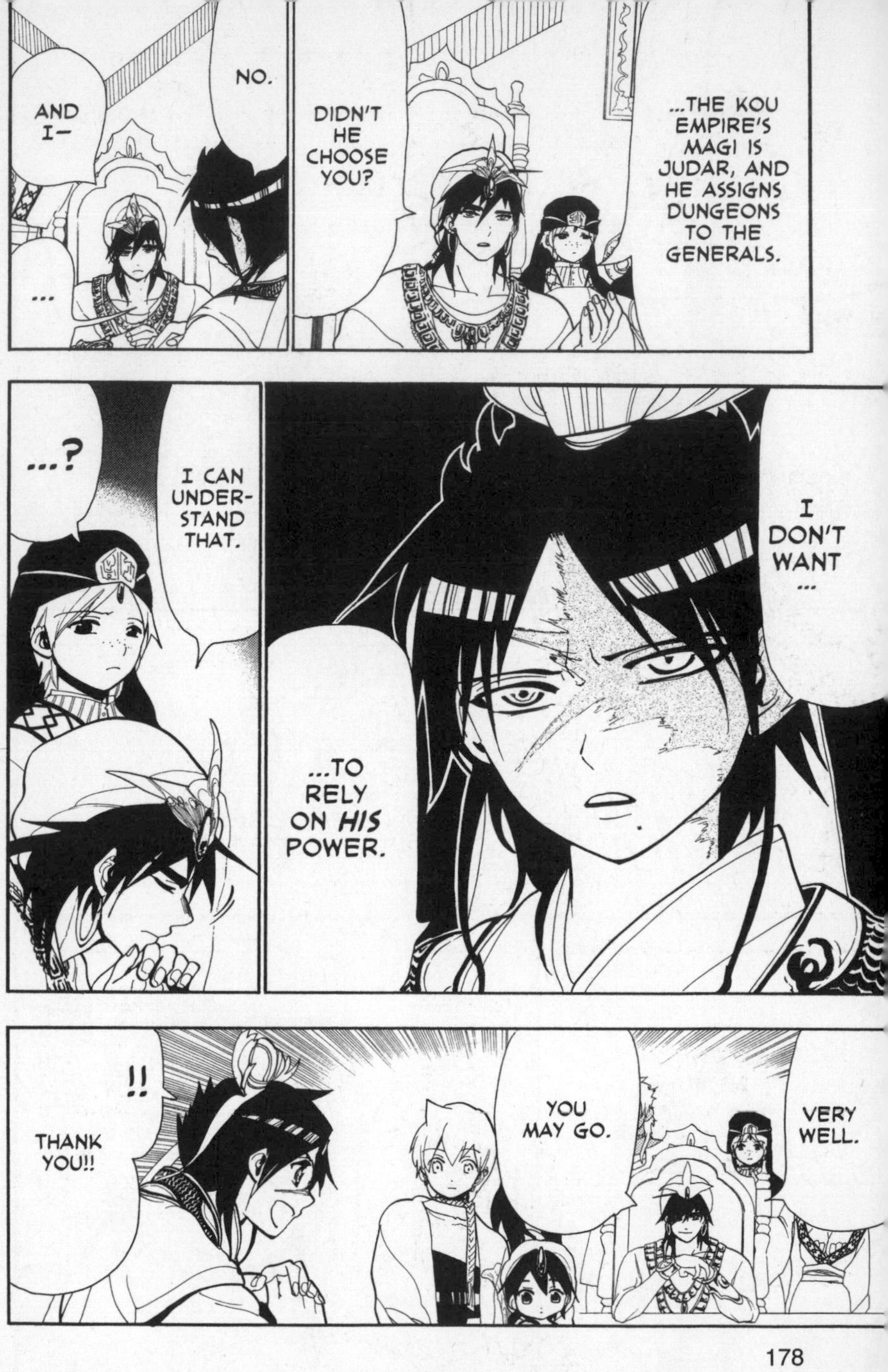
...THE KOU EMPIRE'S MAGI IS JUDAR, AND HE ASSIGNS DUNGEONS TO THE GENERALS.
DIDN'T HE CHOOSE YOU?
NO.
AND I—
...
I DON'T WANT ...
...TO RELY ON *HIS* POWER.
I CAN UNDER-STAND THAT.
...?
VERY WELL.
YOU MAY GO.
!!
THANK YOU!!

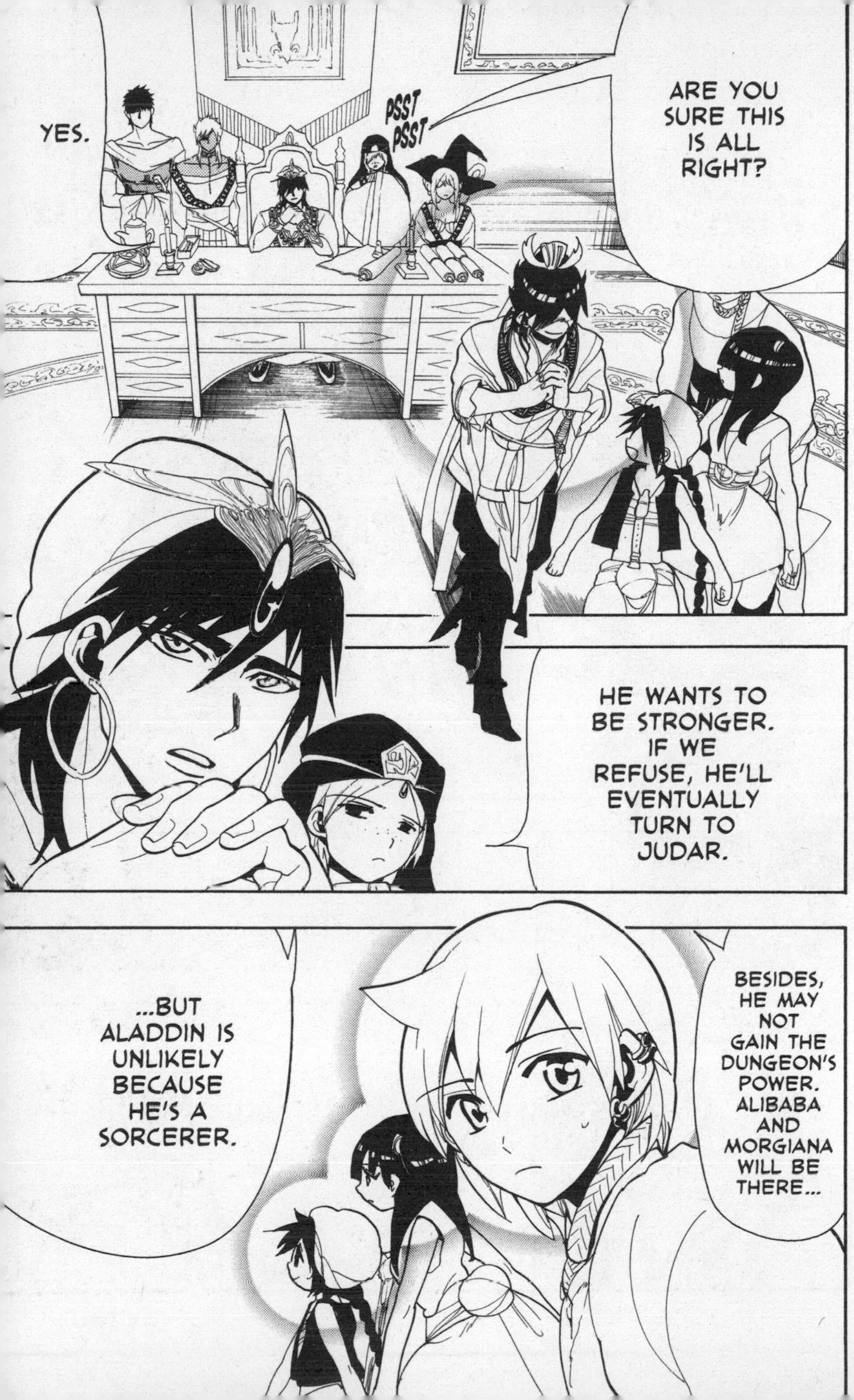
ARE YOU SURE THIS IS ALL RIGHT?
PSST PSST
YES.
HE WANTS TO BE STRONGER. IF WE REFUSE, HE'LL EVENTUALLY TURN TO JUDAR.
BESIDES, HE MAY NOT GAIN THE DUNGEON'S POWER. ALIBABA AND MORGIANA WILL BE THERE...
...BUT ALADDIN IS UNLIKELY BECAUSE HE'S A SORCERER.

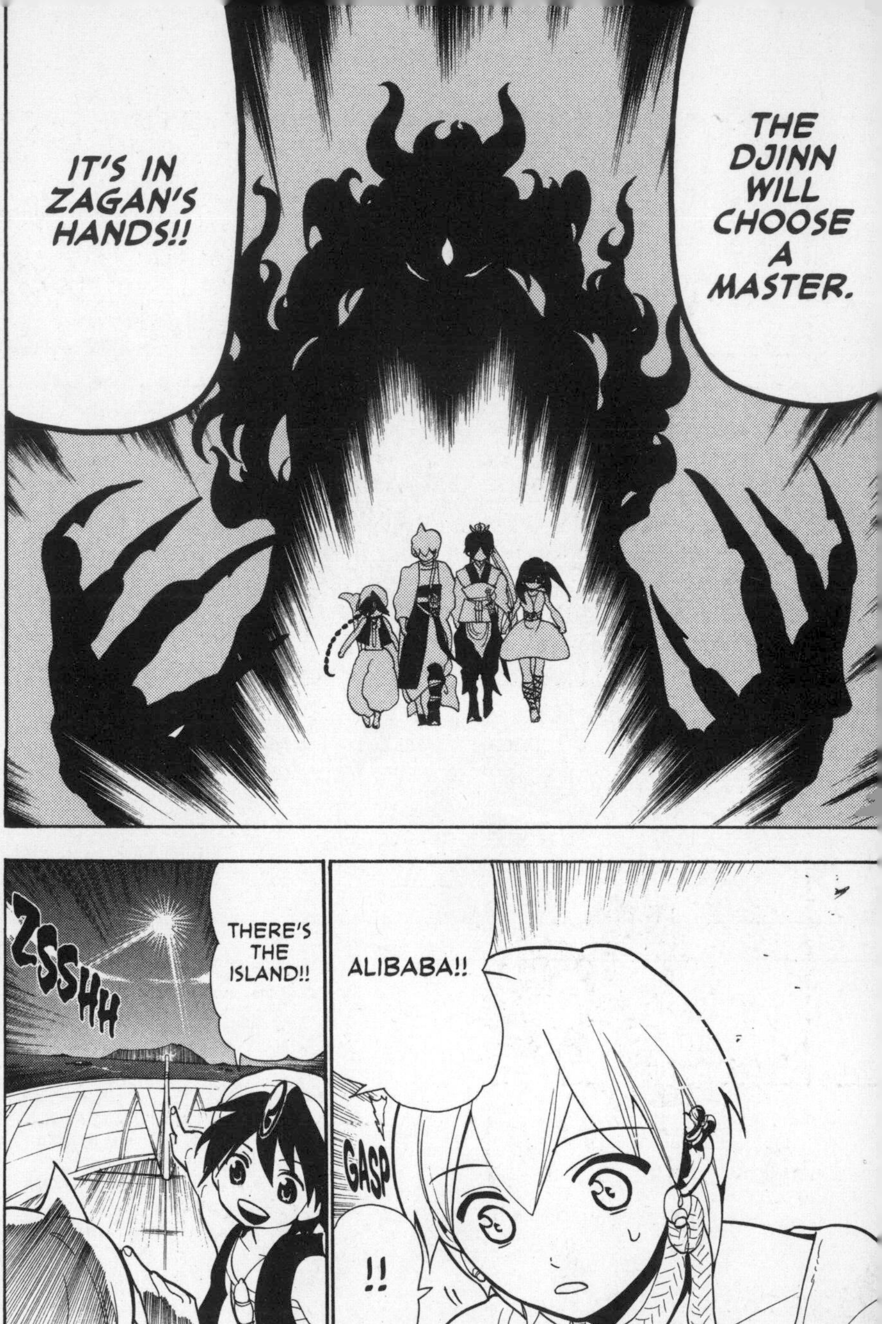
THE DJINN WILL CHOOSE A MASTER.
IT'S IN ZAGAN'S HANDS!!
ALIBABA!!
GASP
!!
ZSSHH
THERE'S THE ISLAND!!

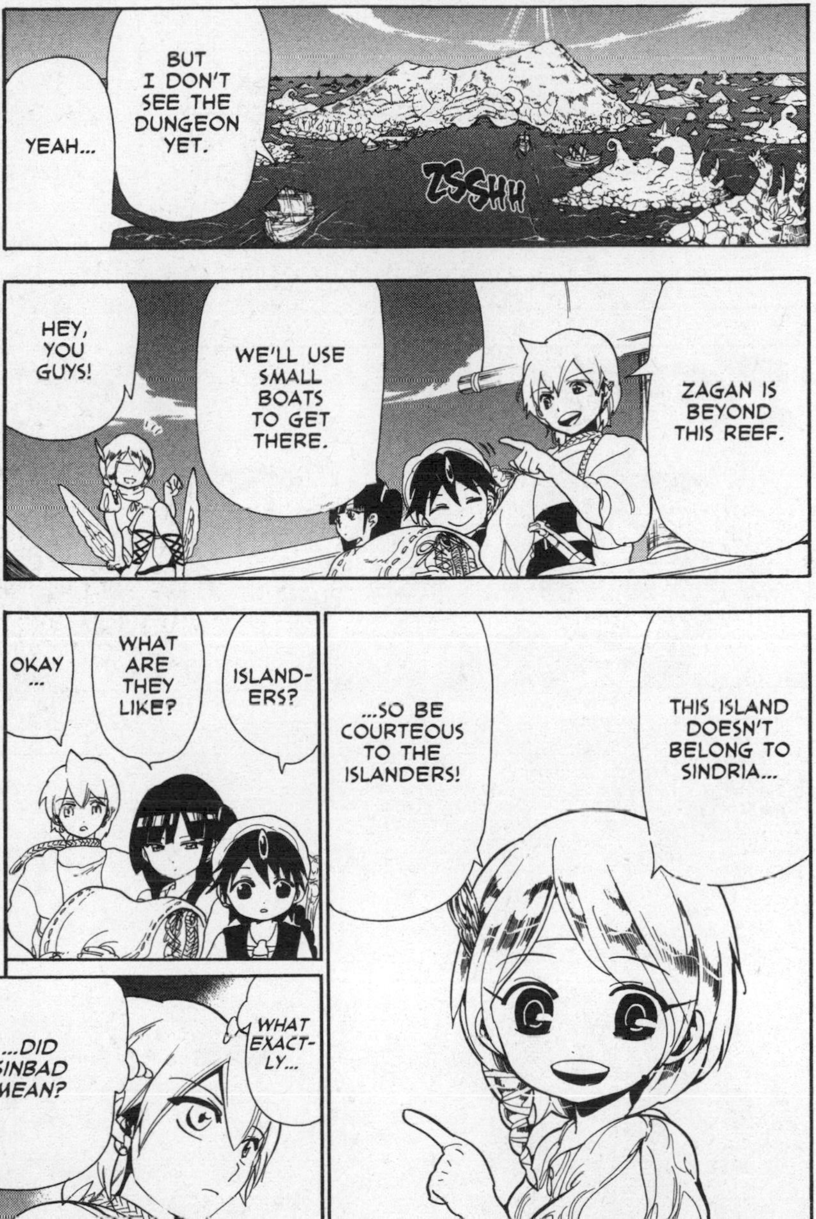
BUT I DON'T SEE THE DUNGEON YET.
YEAH...
ZSSHH
ZAGAN IS BEYOND THIS REEF.
WE'LL USE SMALL BOATS TO GET THERE.
HEY, YOU GUYS!
THIS ISLAND DOESN'T BELONG TO SINDRIA...
...SO BE COURTEOUS TO THE ISLANDERS!
ISLAND-ERS?
WHAT ARE THEY LIKE?
OKAY...
WHAT EXACT-LY...
...DID SINBAD MEAN?

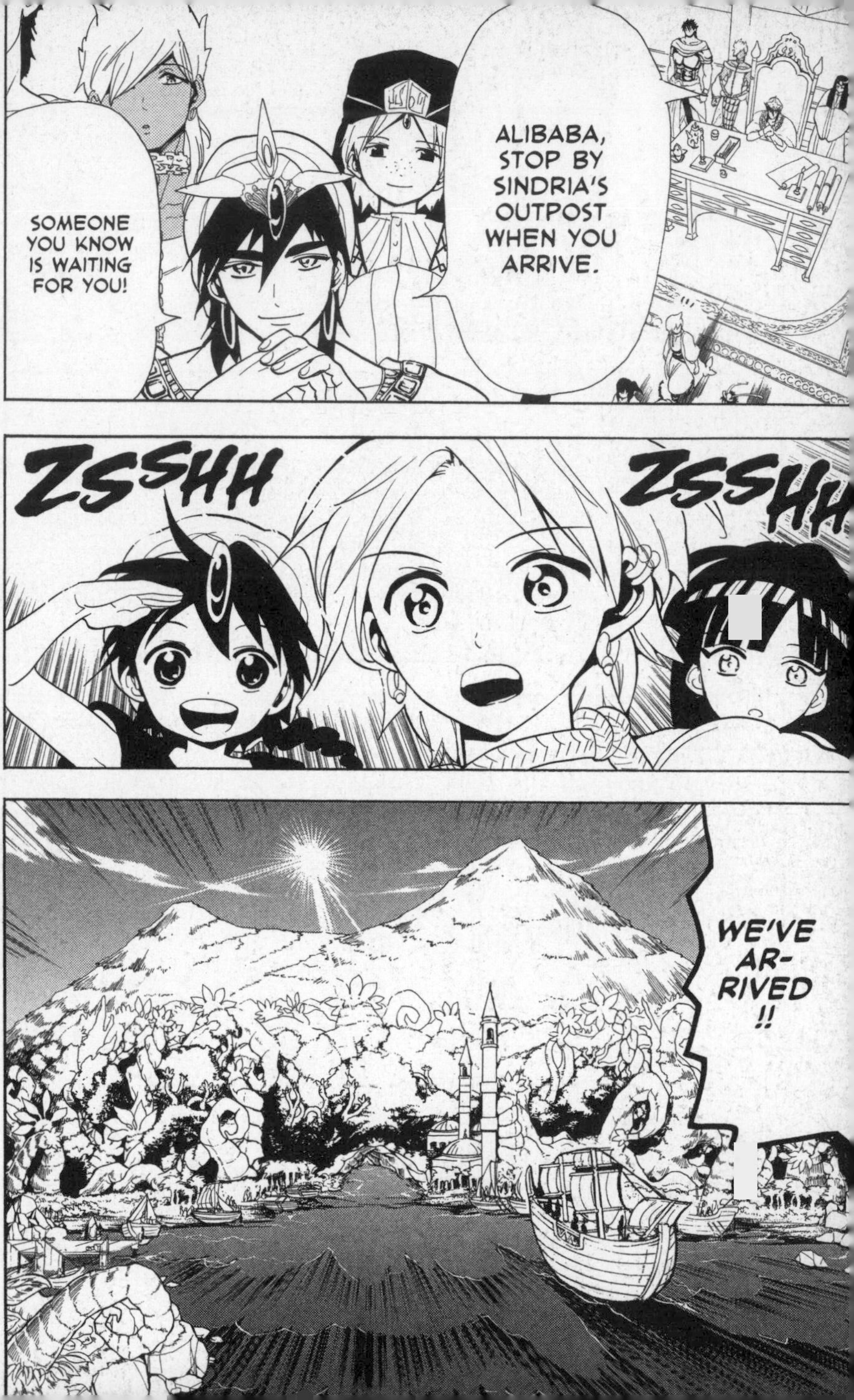
ALIBABA, STOP BY SINDRIA'S OUTPOST WHEN YOU ARRIVE.
SOMEONE YOU KNOW IS WAITING FOR YOU!
ZSSHH
ZSSHH
WE'VE AR-RIVED!!

MAGI

The labyrinth of magic

9

Staff

▩ Story & Art

Shinobu Ohtaka

▩ Regular Assistants

Miho Isshiki

Akira Sugito

Tanimoto

Makoto Akui

Yoshihumi Otera

▩ Editor

Kazuaki Ishibashi

▩ Sales & Promotion

Shinichirou Todaka

Tsunato Imamoto

▩ Designer

Yasuo Shimura + Bay Bridge Studio

THE KINGDOM OF SINDRIA ILLUSTRATED

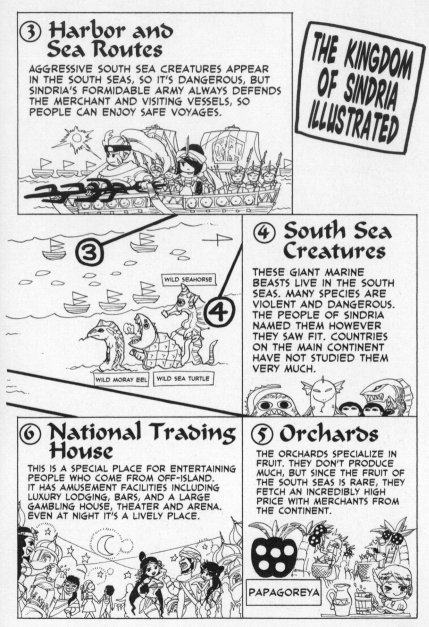

③ Harbor and Sea Routes

AGGRESSIVE SOUTH SEA CREATURES APPEAR IN THE SOUTH SEAS, SO IT'S DANGEROUS, BUT SINDRIA'S FORMIDABLE ARMY ALWAYS DEFENDS THE MERCHANT AND VISITING VESSELS, SO PEOPLE CAN ENJOY SAFE VOYAGES.

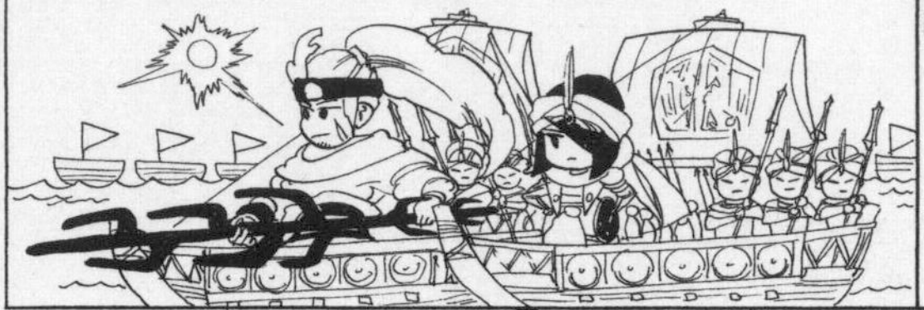

④ South Sea Creatures

THESE GIANT MARINE BEASTS LIVE IN THE SOUTH SEAS. MANY SPECIES ARE VIOLENT AND DANGEROUS. THE PEOPLE OF SINDRIA NAMED THEM HOWEVER THEY SAW FIT. COUNTRIES ON THE MAIN CONTINENT HAVE NOT STUDIED THEM VERY MUCH.

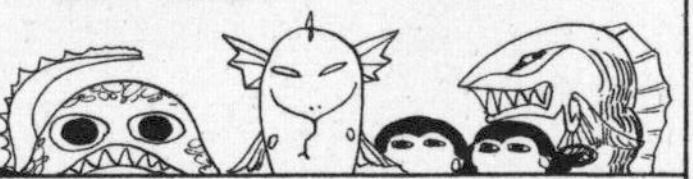

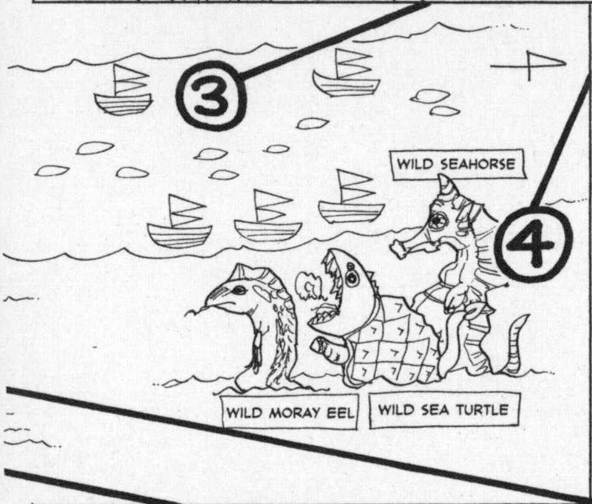
③
WILD SEAHORSE
④
WILD MORAY EEL
WILD SEA TURTLE

⑤ Orchards

THE ORCHARDS SPECIALIZE IN FRUIT. THEY DON'T PRODUCE MUCH, BUT SINCE THE FRUIT OF THE SOUTH SEAS IS RARE, THEY FETCH AN INCREDIBLY HIGH PRICE WITH MERCHANTS FROM THE CONTINENT.

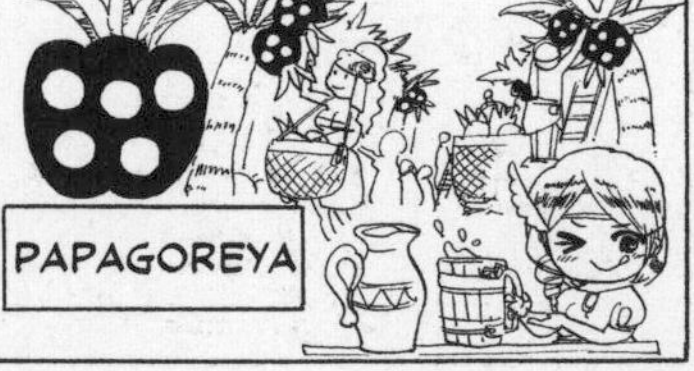
PAPAGOREYA

⑥ National Trading House

THIS IS A SPECIAL PLACE FOR ENTERTAINING PEOPLE WHO COME FROM OFF-ISLAND. IT HAS AMUSEMENT FACILITIES INCLUDING LUXURY LODGING, BARS, AND A LARGE GAMBLING HOUSE, THEATER AND ARENA. EVEN AT NIGHT IT'S A LIVELY PLACE.

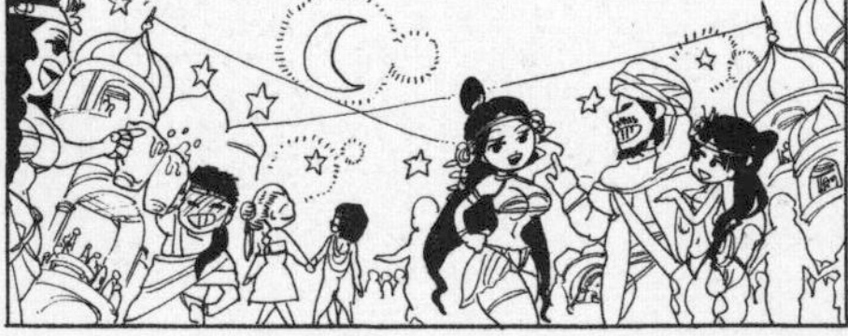

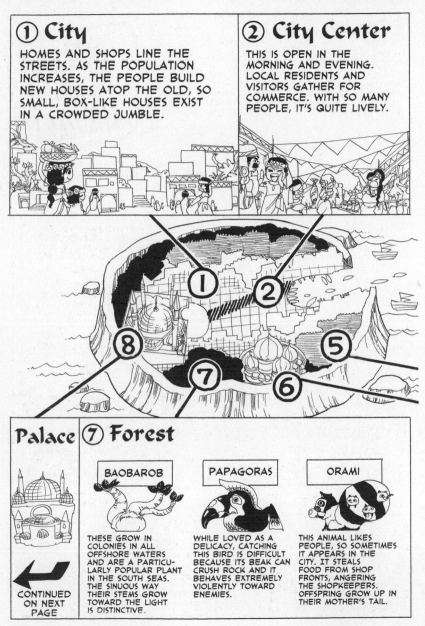

① City

HOMES AND SHOPS LINE THE STREETS. AS THE POPULATION INCREASES, THE PEOPLE BUILD NEW HOUSES ATOP THE OLD, SO SMALL, BOX-LIKE HOUSES EXIST IN A CROWDED JUMBLE.

② City Center

THIS IS OPEN IN THE MORNING AND EVENING. LOCAL RESIDENTS AND VISITORS GATHER FOR COMMERCE. WITH SO MANY PEOPLE, IT'S QUITE LIVELY.

1
2
5
8
7
6

⑦ Forest

BAOBAROB

THESE GROW IN COLONIES IN ALL OFFSHORE WATERS AND ARE A PARTICULARLY POPULAR PLANT IN THE SOUTH SEAS. THE SINUOUS WAY THEIR STEMS GROW TOWARD THE LIGHT IS DISTINCTIVE.

PAPAGORAS

WHILE LOVED AS A DELICACY, CATCHING THIS BIRD IS DIFFICULT BECAUSE ITS BEAK CAN CRUSH ROCK AND IT BEHAVES EXTREMELY VIOLENTLY TOWARD ENEMIES.

ORAMI

THIS ANIMAL LIKES PEOPLE, SO SOMETIMES IT APPEARS IN THE CITY. IT STEALS FOOD FROM SHOP FRONTS, ANGERING THE SHOPKEEPERS. OFFSPRING GROW UP IN THEIR MOTHER'S TAIL.

Palace

CONTINUED ON NEXT PAGE

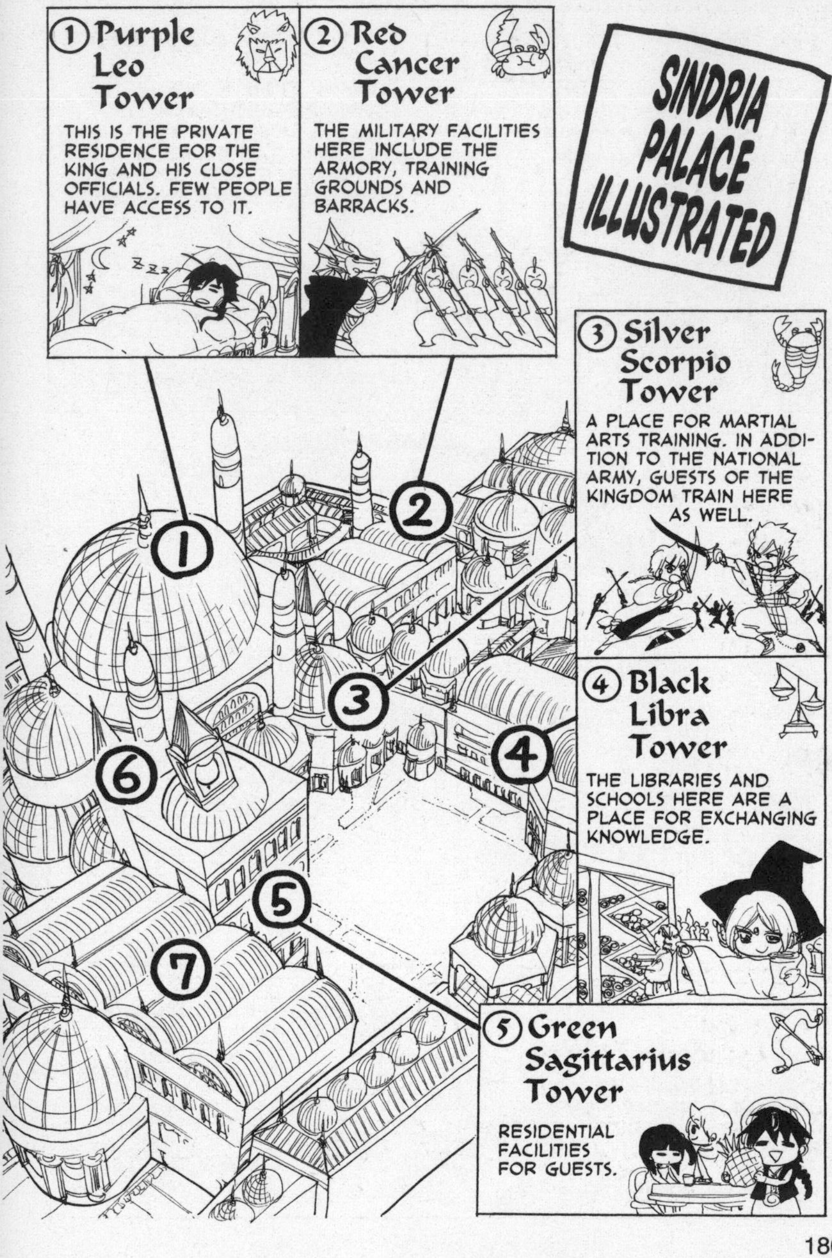
SINDRIA PALACE ILLUSTRATED
1 Purple Leo Tower
THIS IS THE PRIVATE RESIDENCE FOR THE KING AND HIS CLOSE OFFICIALS. FEW PEOPLE HAVE ACCESS TO IT.
ZZZ
2 Red Cancer Tower
THE MILITARY FACILITIES HERE INCLUDE THE ARMORY, TRAINING GROUNDS AND BARRACKS.
3 Silver Scorpio Tower
A PLACE FOR MARTIAL ARTS TRAINING. IN ADDITION TO THE NATIONAL ARMY, GUESTS OF THE KINGDOM TRAIN HERE AS WELL.
4 Black Libra Tower
THE LIBRARIES AND SCHOOLS HERE ARE A PLACE FOR EXCHANGING KNOWLEDGE.
5 Green Sagittarius Tower
RESIDENTIAL FACILITIES FOR GUESTS.
1
2
3
4
5
6
7

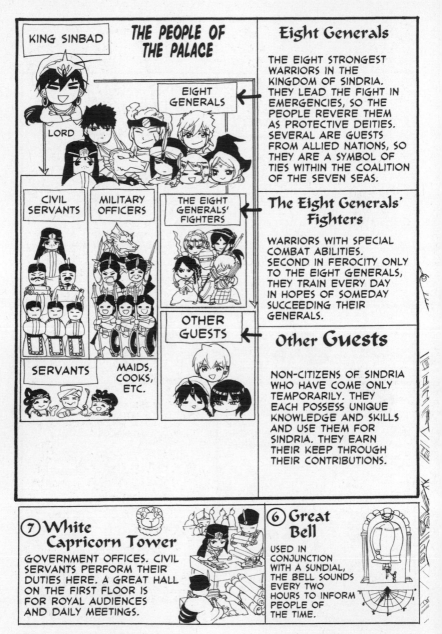

THE PEOPLE OF THE PALACE
KING SINBAD
LORD
EIGHT GENERALS
CIVIL SERVANTS
MILITARY OFFICERS
THE EIGHT GENERALS' FIGHTERS
OTHER GUESTS
SERVANTS
MAIDS, COOKS, ETC.

Eight Generals

THE EIGHT STRONGEST WARRIORS IN THE KINGDOM OF SINDRIA. THEY LEAD THE FIGHT IN EMERGENCIES, SO THE PEOPLE REVERE THEM AS PROTECTIVE DEITIES. SEVERAL ARE GUESTS FROM ALLIED NATIONS, SO THEY ARE A SYMBOL OF TIES WITHIN THE COALITION OF THE SEVEN SEAS.

The Eight Generals' Fighters

WARRIORS WITH SPECIAL COMBAT ABILITIES. SECOND IN FEROCITY ONLY TO THE EIGHT GENERALS, THEY TRAIN EVERY DAY IN HOPES OF SOMEDAY SUCCEEDING THEIR GENERALS.

Other Guests

NON-CITIZENS OF SINDRIA WHO HAVE COME ONLY TEMPORARILY. THEY EACH POSSESS UNIQUE KNOWLEDGE AND SKILLS AND USE THEM FOR SINDRIA. THEY EARN THEIR KEEP THROUGH THEIR CONTRIBUTIONS.

⑥ Great Bell

USED IN CONJUNCTION WITH A SUNDIAL, THE BELL SOUNDS EVERY TWO HOURS TO INFORM PEOPLE OF THE TIME.

⑦ White Capricorn Tower

GOVERNMENT OFFICES. CIVIL SERVANTS PERFORM THEIR DUTIES HERE. A GREAT HALL ON THE FIRST FLOOR IS FOR ROYAL AUDIENCES AND DAILY MEETINGS.

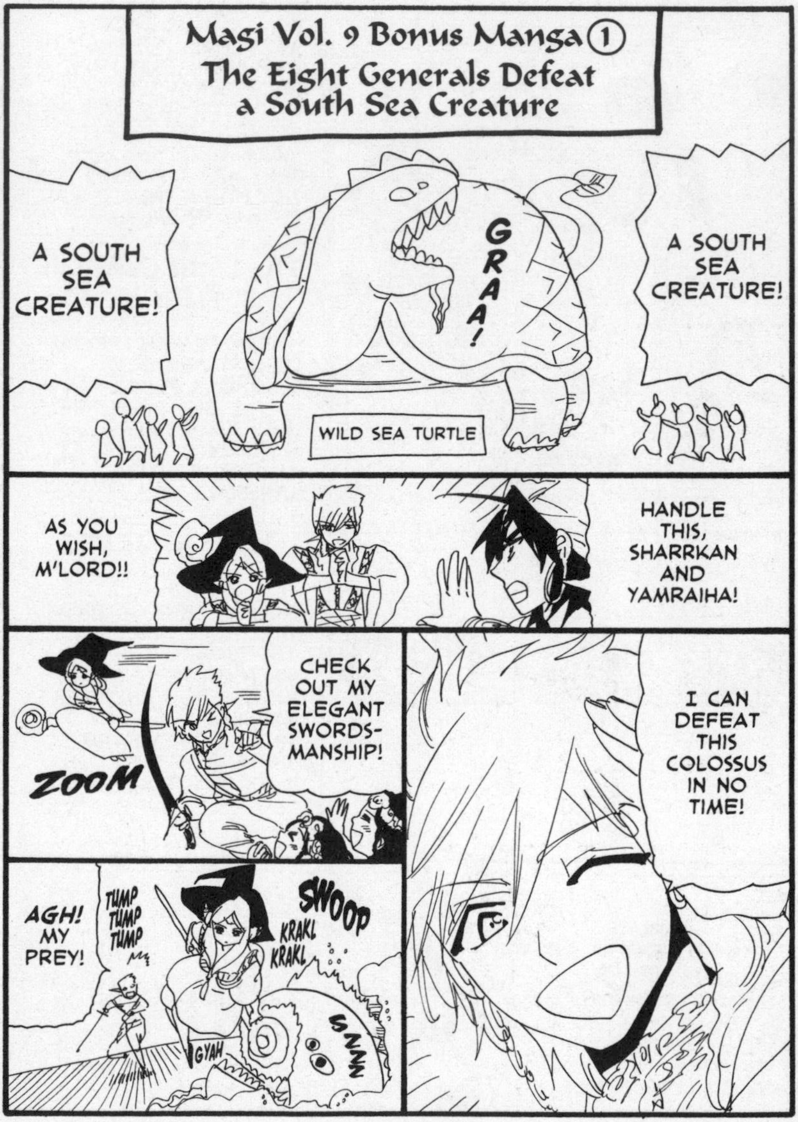
Magi Vol. 9 Bonus Manga ①
The Eight Generals Defeat a South Sea Creature
A SOUTH SEA CREATURE!
GRAA!
A SOUTH SEA CREATURE!
WILD SEA TURTLE
HANDLE THIS, SHARRKAN AND YAMRAIHA!
AS YOU WISH, M'LORD!!
I CAN DEFEAT THIS COLOSSUS IN NO TIME!
CHECK OUT MY ELEGANT SWORDS-MANSHIP!
ZOOM
SWOOP
KRAKL KRAKL
TUMP TUMP TUMP
AGH! MY PREY!
GYAH

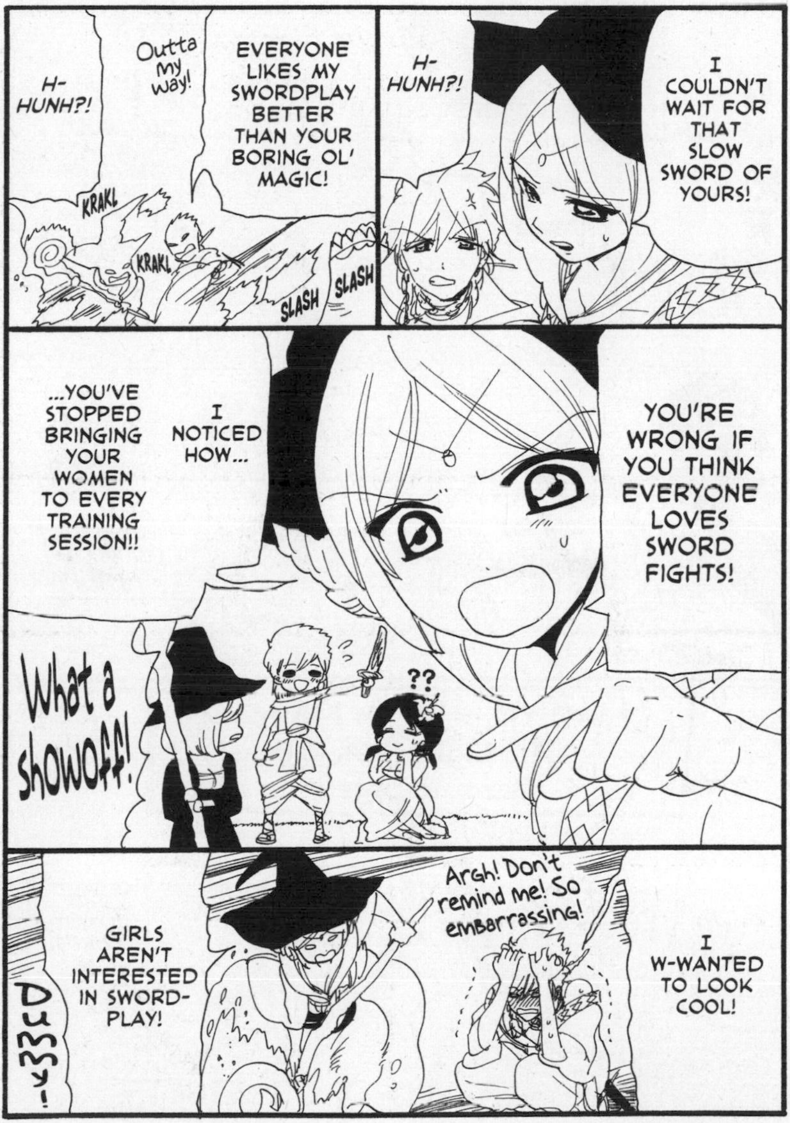
I COULDN'T WAIT FOR THAT SLOW SWORD OF YOURS!
H-HUNH?!
EVERYONE LIKES MY SWORDPLAY BETTER THAN YOUR BORING OL' MAGIC!
Outta my way!
H-HUNH?!
KRAKL
KRAKL
SLASH
SLASH
YOU'RE WRONG IF YOU THINK EVERYONE LOVES SWORD FIGHTS!
I NOTICED HOW...
...YOU'VE STOPPED BRINGING YOUR WOMEN TO EVERY TRAINING SESSION!!
??
What a showoff!
I W-WANTED TO LOOK COOL!
Argh! Don't remind me! So embarrassing!
GIRLS AREN'T INTERESTED IN SWORD-PLAY!
Dummy-!

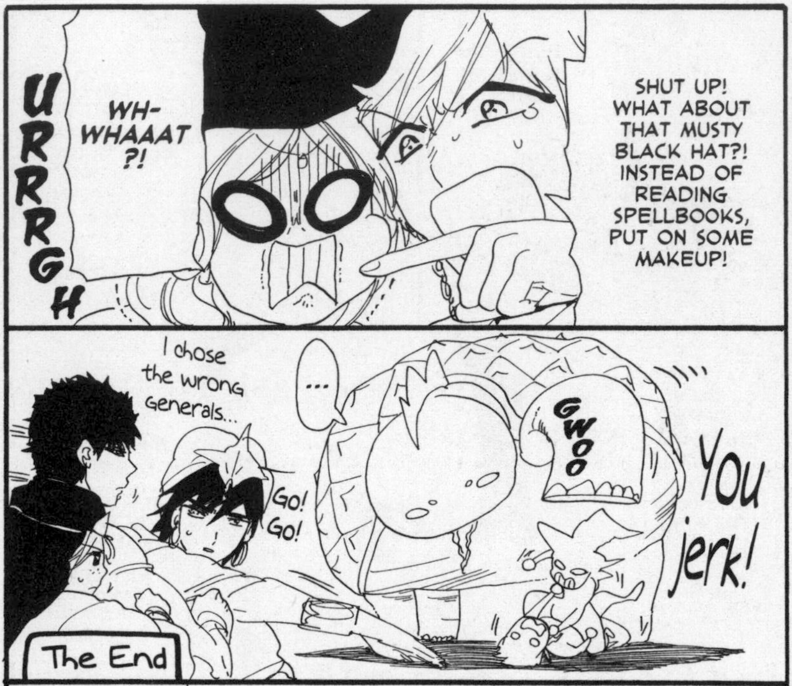
SHUT UP! WHAT ABOUT THAT MUSTY BLACK HAT?! INSTEAD OF READING SPELLBOOKS, PUT ON SOME MAKEUP!
WH-WHAAAT?!
URRRGH
You jerk!
GWOO
...
Go! Go!
I chose the wrong generals...
The End

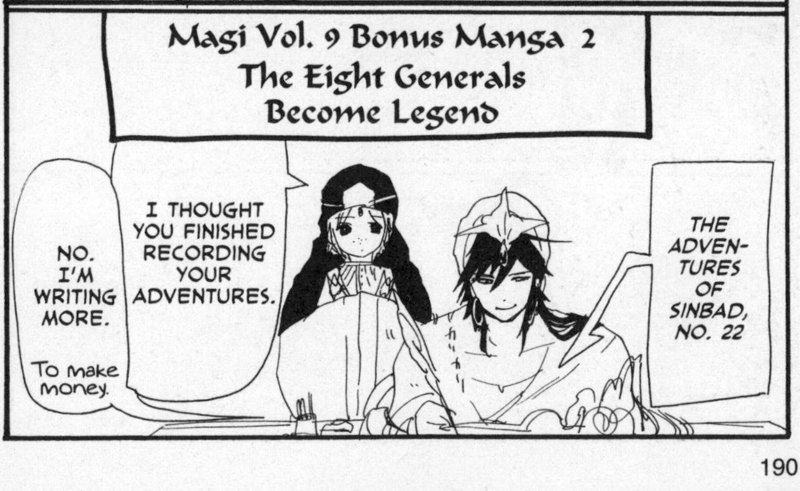
Magi Vol. 9 Bonus Manga 2
The Eight Generals Become Legend
THE ADVENTURES OF SINBAD, NO. 22
I THOUGHT YOU FINISHED RECORDING YOUR ADVENTURES.
NO. I'M WRITING MORE.
To make money.

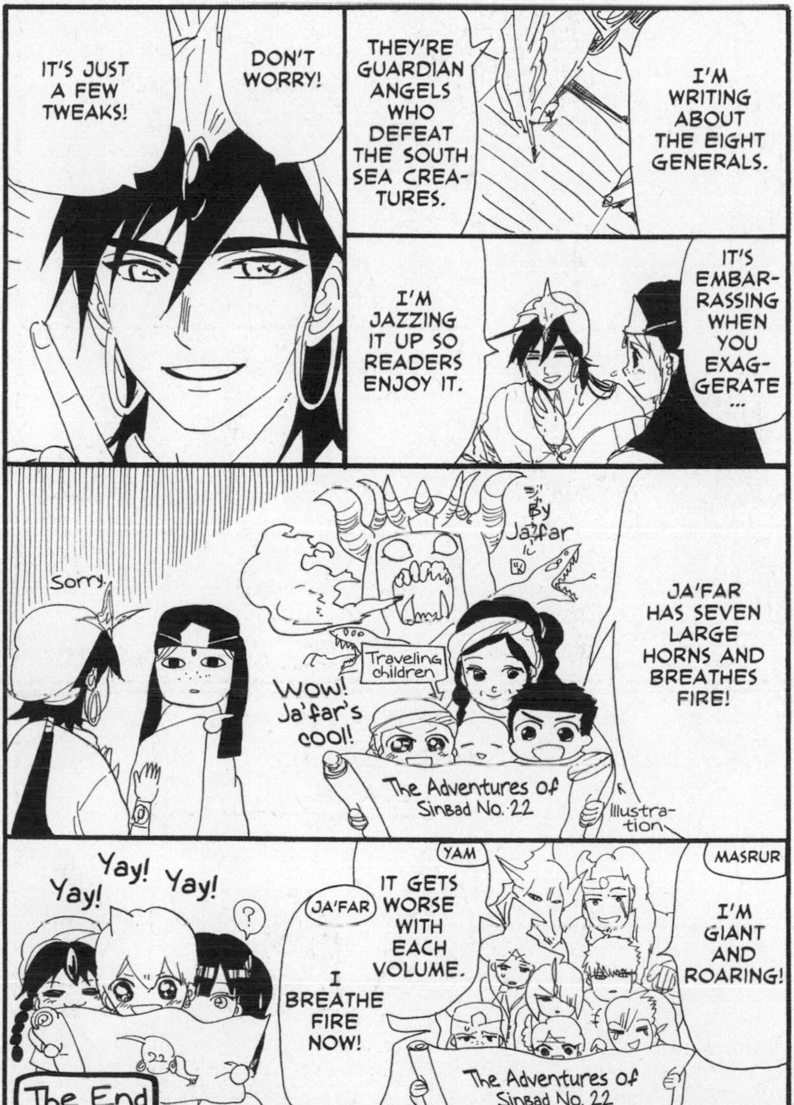
I'M WRITING ABOUT THE EIGHT GENERALS.
THEY'RE GUARDIAN ANGELS WHO DEFEAT THE SOUTH SEA CREA-TURES.
IT'S EMBAR-RASSING WHEN YOU EXAG-GERATE ...
I'M JAZZING IT UP SO READERS ENJOY IT.
DON'T WORRY!
IT'S JUST A FEW TWEAKS!
JA'FAR HAS SEVEN LARGE HORNS AND BREATHES FIRE!
By Ja'far
Illustra-tion
Traveling children
Wow! Ja'far's cool!
The Adventures of Sinbad No. 22
Sorry.
MASRUR
I'M GIANT AND ROARING!
YAM
IT GETS WORSE WITH EACH VOLUME.
JA'FAR
I BREATHE FIRE NOW!
The Adventures of Sinbad No. 22
?
Yay!
Yay!
Yay!
The End

SHINOBU OHTAKA

*It's volume 9,
my lady!*

MAGI

Volume 9

Shonen Sunday Edition

Story and Art by
SHINOBU OHTAKA

MAGI Vol.9
by Shinobu OHTAKA
© 2009 Shinobu OHTAKA
All rights reserved.
Original Japanese edition published by SHOGAKUKAN.
English translation rights in the United States of America, Canada, the United Kingdom,
Ireland, Australia and New Zealand arranged with SHOGAKUKAN.

Translation & English Adaptation ◆ John Werry

Touch-up Art & Lettering ◆ Stephen Dutro

Editor ◆ Mike Montesa

The stories, characters and incidents mentioned in this publication are entirely fictional.

No portion of this book may be reproduced or transmitted in any form or
by any means without written permission from the copyright holders.

Printed in the U.S.A.

Published by VIZ Media, LLC
P.O. Box 77010
San Francisco, CA 94107

10 9 8 7 6 5 4 3 2 1
First printing, December 2014

WWW.SHONENSUNDAY.COM

PARENTAL ADVISORY
MAGI is rated T for Teen.
This volume contains
suggestive themes.
ratings.viz.com

www.viz.com

Ranma ½ Returns!

REMASTERED AND BETTER THAN EVER!

One day, teenaged martial artist Ranma Saotome went on a training mission with his father and ended up taking a dive into some cursed springs at a legendary training ground in China. Now, every time he's splashed with cold water, he changes into a girl. His father, Genma, changes into a panda! What's a half-guy, half-girl to do?

Find out what fueled the worldwide manga boom in beloved creator Rumiko Takahashi's (*Inuyasha*, *Urusei Yatsura*, *RIN-NE*) smash-hit of martial arts mayhem!

Story and Art by Rumiko Takahashi

GET IT ON DVD AND LIMITED EDITION BLU-RAY BOX SETS STARTING SPRING 2014

Watch it for **FREE** on vizanime.com/ranma
Get it on Blu-ray and DVD this Spring.
Packed with tons of extras!
Available at DVD and Blu-ray retailers nationwide.

AND OWN THE MANGA IN THE ORIGINAL RIGHT-TO-LEFT ORIENTATION!

❀ Discover the details with remastered pages!
❀ Now in all new 2-in-1 Editions!

©Rumiko Takahashi / Shogakukan
RANMA1/2 © 1988 Rumiko TAKAHASHI/SHOGAKUKAN

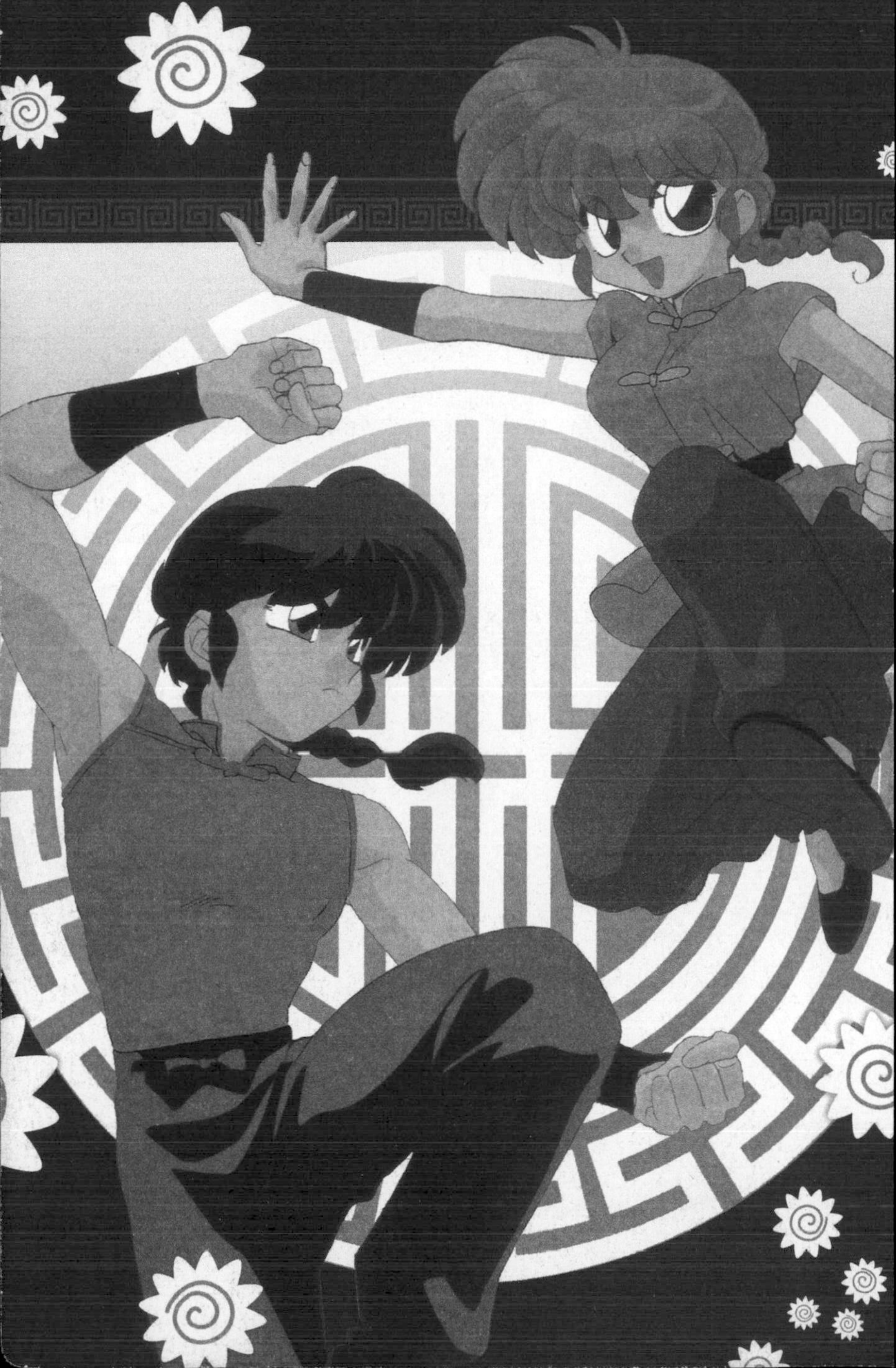

A DETECTIVE IN NEED OF A CLUE

CASE CLOSED™

With an innate talent for observation and intuition, Jimmy can solve mysteries that leave the most seasoned law enforcement officials baffled. But when a strange chemical transforms him from a high school teenager to a grade schooler who no one takes seriously, will this be one mystery this sleuth can't solve?

ONLY $9⁹⁹!

Start your graphic novel collection today!

www.viz.com
store.viz.com

VIZ MEDIA™

©1994 Gosho AOYAMA/Shogakukan Inc.

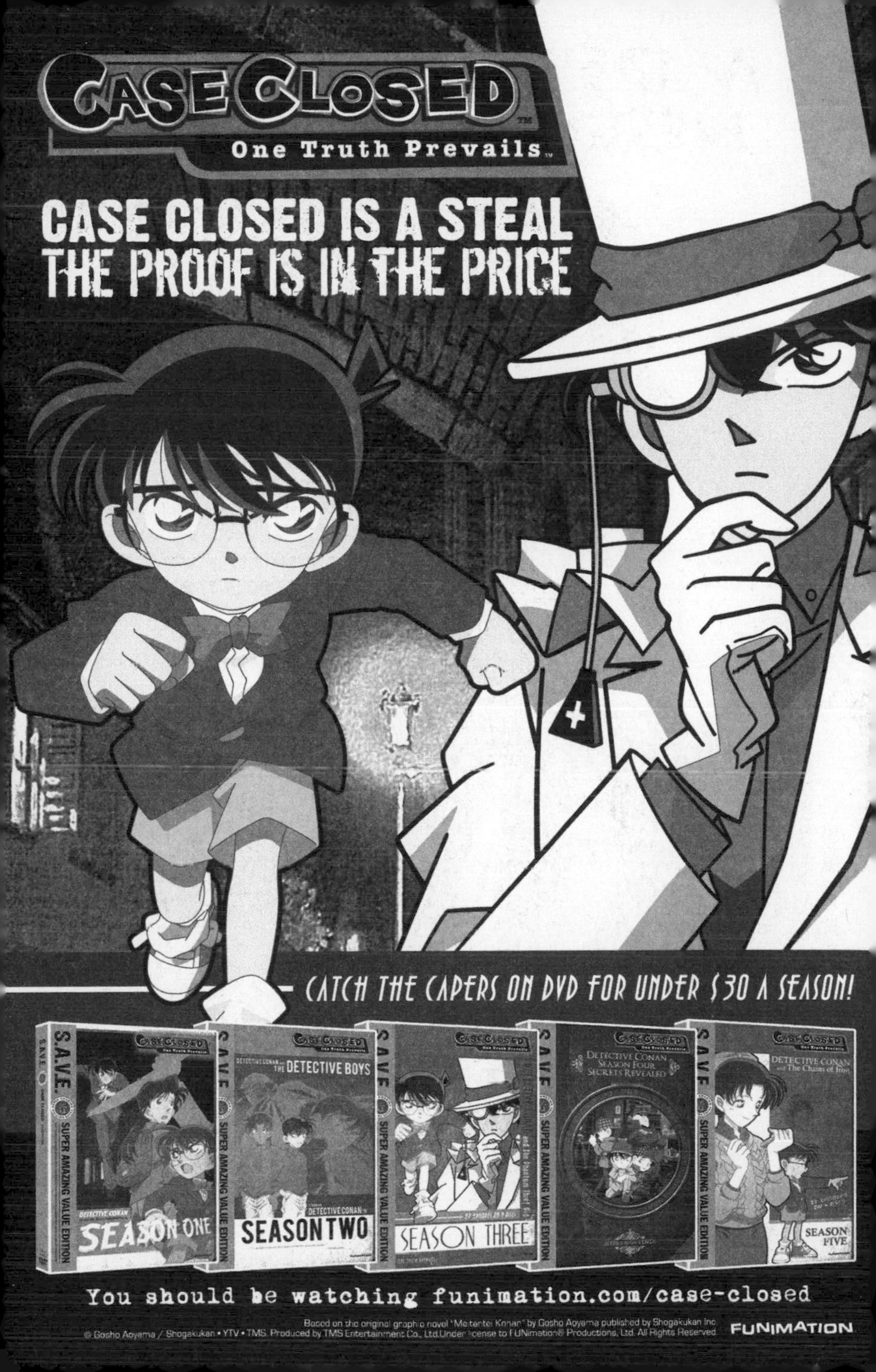

CASE CLOSED IS A STEAL
THE PROOF IS IN THE PRICE

CATCH THE CAPERS ON DVD FOR UNDER $30 A SEASON!

You should be watching funimation.com/case-closed

Based on the original graphic novel "Meitantei Konan" by Gosho Aoyama published by Shogakukan Inc
© Gosho Aoyama / Shogakukan • YTV • TMS. Produced by TMS Entertainment Co., Ltd.Under license to FUNimation® Productions, Ltd. All Rights Reserved   FUNIMATION

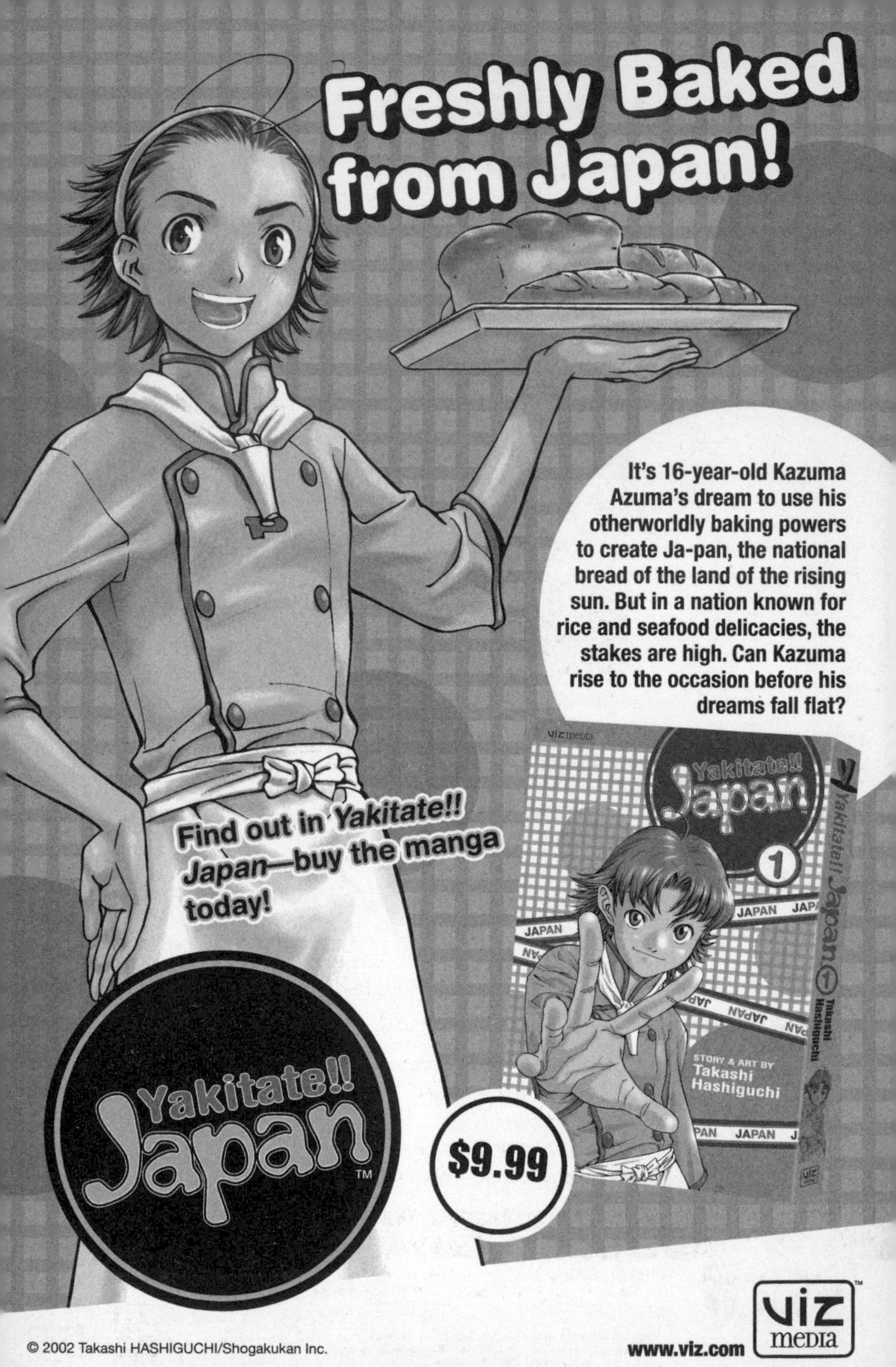
Freshly Baked from Japan!
It's 16-year-old Kazuma Azuma's dream to use his otherworldly baking powers to create Ja-pan, the national bread of the land of the rising sun. But in a nation known for rice and seafood delicacies, the stakes are high. Can Kazuma rise to the occasion before his dreams fall flat?
Find out in Yakitate!! Japan—buy the manga today!
Yakitate!! Japan™
Yakitate!! Japan 1
STORY & ART BY Takashi Hashiguchi
$9.99
www.viz.com
VIZ MEDIA

VIZMANGA
Read manga anytime, anywhere!

From our newest hit series to the classics you know and love, the best manga in the world is now available digitally. Buy a volume* of digital manga for your:

- iOS device (**iPad®**, **iPhone®**, **iPod®** touch) through the **VIZ Manga app**

- Android-powered device (**phone or tablet**) with a browser by visiting VIZManga.com

- **Mac or PC computer** by visiting VIZManga.com

VIZ Digital has loads to offer:

- 500+ ready-to-read volumes
- New volumes each week
- FREE previews
- Access on multiple devices! Create a log-in through the app so you buy a book once, and read it on your device of choice!*

To learn more, visit www.viz.com/apps

* Some series may not be available for multiple devices.
  Check the app on your device to find out what's available.

DEATH NOTE © 2003 by Tsugumi Ohba, Takeshi Obata/SHUEISHA Inc.
NURARIHYON NO MAGO © 2008 by Hiroshi Shiibashi/SHUEISHA Inc.
ONE PIECE © 1997 by Eiichiro Oda/SHUEISHA Inc.

You're reading the
WRONG WAY

MAGI reads from right to left, starting in the upper-right corner. Japanese is read from **right** to **left**, meaning that action, sound effects, and word-balloon order are completely reversed from English order.

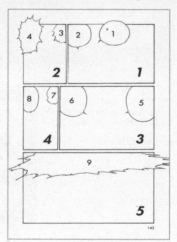